THE
HOME GARDENER'S
GUIDE TO
TREES AND SHRUBS

Other books by John Burton Brimer:

THE HOMEOWNER'S COMPLETE OUTDOOR BUILDING BOOK
CHRISTMAS ALL THROUGH THE HOUSE

Contents

THE
HOME GARDENER'S
GUIDE TO
TREES AND SHRUBS

by John Burton Brimer

With drawings by the author

HAWTHORN BOOKS, INC.
Publishers/NEW YORK

THE
HOME GARDENER'S
GUIDE TO
TREES AND SHRUBS

1

The Garden—
Delight or Dilemma?

As America's population deserts the central city in increasing numbers to take up life in the suburbs, new owners of small houses with large mortgages suddenly awake to gardening—its delights and its dilemmas. The difference between a mere house and a real home often lies in the garden that surrounds it, for a gardening family is in intimate touch with the serenity of nature, the wellsprings of life. However, many have not found this to be true, encountering more of the dilemma than the delight. Possibly this was because they planted with more enthusiasm than forethought, creating problems as they floundered. They learned quickly enough the sobering lesson that Mother Nature teaches, that plants cannot always be bent to man's will; shrubs and trees take foreordained courses and in some spots prodigiously overwhelm the garden while in others they seriously underwhelm it.

There are problems in creating a garden, as there are in building a house. Every garden has its own problems, some serious, some easily solved. Perhaps the main problems for the new gardener are when to purchase and how to go about assembling the plants into a pleasant harmony of communal effort so that none becomes an oversized Frankenstein-monster plant. The purpose of this book, therefore, is to sort out and put into orderly form the components of the garden picture and make this a handy reference guide for their use. The question–answer format is used because the basic questions most gardeners ask are much the same.

Planting a garden has been likened to decorating a living room. Most of us agree that shrubs symbolize the walls, lawns represent the carpet, and overhead arching trees form the ceiling. But if a living room is painted or wallpapered and you decide sooner or later that what was chosen was a mistake, it is not a major disaster. It is relatively inexpensive both in money and do-it-yourself labor to rectify the error. In a garden, however, mistakes may not show up immediately, and when they do, correcting them is costly, for large shrubs and trees need expensive, professional help in shifting them to the proper spot. If you replace them, you lose years of growing time that would have matured the garden picture. Most people end up living with their mistakes and hating them. Good plantings are permanent, easy to maintain, well composed, and therefore eternally satisfying, especially if you are the planner and planter.

HOW TO AVOID MISTAKES

The main cause of gardening trouble is impatience. In a society that offers "instant" antiques, carefully fashioned and finished to look almost like the aged real thing, people are conditioned to expect quick results, even from gardening. Nature, on the other hand, proceeds at the same pace it always has maintained. That is why the one bit of immutable advice that can be given to a gardener is still: Be patient. There are no "instant" gardens. In the end it will pay off to work with nature rather than against it.

If you are rich, it is possible to hire professionals to buy large trees and move in mature shrubs, but even so you must wait a few years until they adapt and grow into some semblance of maturity. Even so, such a garden might have little of the personality of a garden that was loved and worked over for years, achieving its goal more slowly but more surely. Most of us must follow the slow method, and sometimes this proves to be best, for as you live with a garden, you come to know where to improvise and refine the plan. This would be impossible if attempted all at once.

The gardener who plans and tends his plants, working painstakingly year after year toward his goal knows a delight that cannot be bought. Like any creative artist, he finds his own way, and through intimate observation and association he understands the various materials and senses how to work with them. By working closely and observantly with plants, there develops a kinship with all of nature that true gardeners feel, even though they may not boast of it.

BUT GARDENS ARE HARD WORK . . .

Gardening *is* work, there is no gainsaying it. But if you know what you are doing and if you plan properly, it becomes less of a chore. It all depends on your attitude. Surely the millions who garden intensively must enjoy it, never finding it humdrum even though some chores must be repeated from time to time. Perhaps part of the lure is the unpredictability of nature, the gamble you take in planting. Yet Monte Carlo never pays off more handsomely than does a blossoming garden. Even if you lose one season, you still have your capital to gamble again next year and probably be paid off a hundredfold for your labors. At the very least, it is a healthful hobby, and at best it is a fascinating occupation that can last a lifetime.

There are nuances and subtleties in every garden, in every plant. If you have an open mind and an observant eye, these can become part of the rewards. Those who look deeper into the infinite varieties in plants, can appreciate more than just flowers and fruits: the shapes of leaves, the colors of barks, the marvels of engineering that are in the structures, the admirable and complex apparatus of reproduction that is designed to ensure continuity. All these and countless other aspects are there for the amateur to explore and enjoy.

Many of our modern plants were not created in the nursery, those "improved" specimens we often grow today. Sometimes an amateur found something odd and unusual, culled it and fostered its growth, set the characteristic through several generations, and thus made his contribution. It can still be done today, but it takes an observant and keen eye and an inquiring mind to spot that different leaf; that double flower; that unusual habit of growth. If something unusual of this sort occurs in your garden and you can set its characteristics so that it can be reproduced, you will have added your bit to horticulture. The garden is an Eden in miniature, a place of serenity and peace for the gardener and all his family. It is a good place for children to learn about nature and come to know that we must respect and conserve our land.

WHERE YOU GARDEN IS IMPORTANT

One of the first considerations of the new gardener or the one who is moving to a new and different climate is the exact location of the garden. This may be crucial in determining what shrubs and trees you can grow with success.

Old hands at gardening are always amazed and amused when a green-horn is disappointed that, let us say, a palm tree won't grow on the coast of Maine. Outdoors, that is. This extreme example will point up the fallacies that exist in other ways in choosing plants, for many misconceptions are nearly as unthinkable. Still, if someone has never gardened or had contact with nature, it must be quite difficult to know what will grow in the north or the south, in swamps or in deserts.

Even people who have done some gardening often have little perception of soil and the limitation it may impose on choices. There are many kinds of soils, as you will see when you read the sections on soil in Chapters 5 and 7. Either you accept the soil that you have or you adjust it toward a more ideal mixture. This is one of the prime laws of gardening. Some plants grow in acid soils in their native habitat, and some are inclined to grow better in alkaline soils. But most plants do best in a neutral soil, one that is between acid and alkaline. Therefore, in order to be successful, the gardener must know in advance what soil he has or can remake and what the plants he chooses demand or tolerate.

GARDENING IS TOO COMPLICATED

By now some beginners might be getting cold feet. But we shall show them how to warm up those cold feet in the later pages. Gardening is complicated, that is true, but once it is broken down into the various steps and components, it is perfectly logical and even fun. It becomes a kind of fascinating game as the detective work goes on and as one ferrets out what *might* grow, then what *will* grow, and then what is really *best* to grow. Then come the planning and planting, caring for the garden, watching it develop and mature and blossom into a reasonable facsimile of the Eden you pictured when first you thought of gardening.

Because this book attempts to put the various facets of gardening into layman's language, there will doubtless be criticism from some advanced gardeners. But the book is not directed toward them but rather toward easing the way for beginners, with Latin plant names used only where imperative in order to maintain clarity. The various planting and maintenance processes are described so that the reader will easily understand how to proceed.

If a handful of true gardeners emerges from first contact with gardening by planning, selecting, and planting trees and shrubs from the methods described in this book, it will have been worthwhile. And if others who have other interests and will never wish to pursue gardening with the passion of the true gardener find it helpful in putting together a garden that is pleasant, beautiful, and serves their needs, again the book will have fulfilled its function.

WHERE AND HOW TO BUY

If one merely notes the prevalence of garden centers, nurseries, roadside stands, and other outlets across the country, there would seem, at first glance, to be no problem in obtaining shrubs or trees. There are also many mail-order nurseries that ship plants everywhere. But success requires that the gardener be wary about what he buys and selective about where he buys it. By using good common sense and keeping his eyes open, the gardener can soon have a reasonably good yardstick with which to measure the sources. And he can always ask others about their local experience.

As a start toward evaluating plant sources a few points might be made about where not to buy and what not to consider. One to avoid with few if any exceptions is the itinerant salesman who drives about new subdivisions with a truckload of "bargain-priced" shrubs and trees. Remember that there are only two kinds of bargains—good ones and bad ones—and the traveling salesman is probably in the latter category. The plants may have been dug up from the woods some distance away with little attention given to root systems or proper care after digging. Some may even be stolen, for one often hears of "plant hijackings" these days. In either event, drying out on a truck bed in the sun has not improved their chances for survival. Because they do not come from nurseries that are inspected periodically, they may even introduce disease spores and insect pests to your garden. Don't buy plants from any source as unreliable as a traveling salesman. Your bargain may cost you far more than money.

A few mail-order houses are also suspect, although the greater proportion of them are reputable and give good value. The sorts that advertise,

"Enough beautiful shrubs to plant your whole garden," offering a dozen or two dozen plants for an incredibly low inclusive price, are the ones to avoid. Quantity rather than quality is not a reliable approach. Those who make up some glamorous name for a commonplace old species and bill it as the "newest discovery" in order to lure the unknowing should also be avoided. The catchall quantity offer will probably provide third-rate, bare-rooted, commonplace species that are also inferior in other ways. They will be quick growing, in general, which means that they will overgrow and you will have to keep pruning them back or replace them. Such bargains cost money twice over for replacement and labor. The original planting work is the same in any case, but the results with better stock are many times greater. If you consider the time lost in developing good permanent plantings, the cost is prohibitive, whatever the money spent may be.

Garden centers may or may not be good places from which to purchase plants; they have certain advantages, but they also may have drawbacks. Among the advantages offered are that you are able to see what you get, take it home immediately, and plant it the same day if you wish. Nursery garden centers offer this advantage. The "supermarket" kind of garden center offers a large stock, enabling you to select the one that you fancy as you would select fruit from a supermarket bin. A disadvantage, however, is that many of the big centers have no nursery fields attached. Therefore, they must sell their stock quickly or lose money, since they cannot heel in or replant unsold stock as nurseries do, offering it again next season. Hence, they are most likely to stock only those common plants that they are sure they can sell, with few or none of the higher priced, better quality varieties.

Some garden centers do not properly care for their stock. Plants sit in the sun and suffer as a result. Soil balls dry out, and roots are injured, or, in the case of bare-rooted plants, the moisture-proof bags about their roots with moist packing material in them may get hot and steam the interior of the bag. Naturally, growth will be set back in both cases. A good garden center will probably have a lath roof or other shade over its stock, will water root balls every day, fill between root balls with moist peat moss or other mulching material, and keep bare-rooted plants in a cool place indoors. Nurseries with centers may keep their stock in the planting fields with root balls buried until needed to replace displays.

A local nursery may be a good choice for several reasons. If you go early when the nurseryman is not busy, you may be allowed to go in the planting rows and select the plant you want, then have it dug and delivered at the proper time. While most local nurserymen generally no longer propagate their plants and buy young stock from large wholesale propagating nurseries, they are likely to continue growing and shaping at least some of their older, larger sized plants. The wholesale nurseries propagate from cuttings or by other means, grow the shrubs and evergreens until they reach a certain height or age and then sell them. Local nurseries buy such stock and grow it and may also buy large-sized plants already root-balled and burlapped or in containers from other specialists to fill out or augment their own stock.

Very often, large wholesalers are situated in milder climates, where the season is longer and plants grow faster. Also land is cheaper and labor more easily available than in urban centers, so that they can sell for less than it would cost a local nurseryman to grow a comparable plant.

Some mail-order nurserymen are situated in these regions, too, and here the buyer must exercise judgment, because offerings may include many plants that are not hardy in the northern zones. There is also some substantiation to the contention that certain plants that may have a wide natural range of hardiness are less hardy if propagated from seed or cuttings of plants growing in the southern ranges of the zone. There is argument over this among plantsmen, and my own experience of buying from a considerable range of climate zones is not at all conclusive.

It is virtually impossible, of course, to predict whether or not any plant will live, die, or flourish in any given place. So many variables enter into the picture. Hardiness zones are a reasonably good guide for cold-hardiness, but many plants are affected by heat and excessive sun, so that they may not do well in zones to the south of their normal hardiness zone. Plants that are native to far northerly areas may need a rest period, a dormancy time; mild-to-warm climates may cause adverse reactions. But most plants, like most people, are adaptable. If you see certain plants growing in your region, they will very likely do well for you, given proper planting and care. When they mature, they will be a joy and comfort to you in your—and their—older years.

WHAT TO LOOK FOR WHEN BUYING

Let us sum up a few points to follow when you are ordering or buying plants. Keep them in mind as you choose your nursery, go to your garden center, or look at catalogs

Buy good stock. Reputable nurseries or good garden centers and established mail-order houses that offer more than the commonplace plants are good sources. Consult local gardeners for their experiences and sources.

Buy early, plant quickly. Purchasing early means getting fresh stock, often newly dug plants or dormant plants just out of cold storage that have not yet started into active growth. All of these will have a better chance to survive, far better than plants bought late in the season. Mail-order nurseries will fill early orders more quickly, and stock shipped early is less likely to dry out in transit than that which is shipped later on.

Buy container or balled and burlapped (B&B)* plants. Either of these, especially if purchased early in spring, is likely to recover quickly from transplanting, since their compact root systems and the ball of soil containing them (if it has been kept moist) will mean faster growth immediately. Although the prices are higher than for bare-rooted stock, the benefits the garden receives makes it worthwhile.

Look over the displays. If the plants on display are set on hard, hot pavements, with no mulching over and around B&B plants, beware. If there is overhead lath shading to filter the sun's rays or if plants are arranged in the shade of a high structure, you know that the needs of the plants are being met. Check for moisture in soil of container or B&B plants. Bare-rooted plants with moisture-proof bags around them should be well shaded and not bursting into leaf.

Check on prices. In general, you get what you pay for as with any other product. Good plants cost good money, because proper care has been accorded them. If you are willing to wait, you can buy smaller plants, tend them sedulously, and contribute your care rather than money toward the possession of a beautiful garden, though a bit later than if you bought bigger plants right now. Occasionally, you will find a treasure within a job lot at a garden center, superior in size, in structure, or in general shape. Thus you will get a better than ordinary plant for a run-of-the-mill price.

Don't give up easily. All worthwhile works of art take time and pains. Gardens are worth the effort because they can be so personal and so satisfying. Don't settle for less than you feel is right for you and don't feel that anything as long-range as a good garden is not worth your best efforts and attention. Search out unusual plants that give individuality and piquance to the garden composition. If your local nursery does not stock what you

---

* B&B. Plants with a soil ball around the roots, wrapped in burlap.

want, consult your county agent or write to your state agricultural college extension service or query a nearby horticultural society, your regional nurserymen's association, or any other source. Addresses for these sources of information will be found in the Appendix.

LATIN NAMES AND COMMON NAMES

Many beginning gardeners and even some more experienced amateur plantsmen find the use of Latin nomenclature either pretentious or at the very least confusing. They find no reason for using botanical or scientific names or they bypass them with the excuse that they are too hard to spell and difficult to pronounce. Besides, they say, they are unimportant in the general scheme of gardening.

All of this may be true if you relate it to the mere planting and growing of plants. Yet to the individual who wants to be more than just another spade-in-the-ground gardener, a knowledge of specific nomenclature is a necessity, and the common names won't always do.

Why not always use common names?

Because common names are not really common, or they are common only in limited areas. What is the everyday name in one area may be quite another not far away. Certainly in our own country the folk names of plants in the South differ markedly from the ones used in the North or the West. By all means use common names but if you want to get a particular plant that is *exactly* what is needed for that specific spot in your garden, the only safe way is to order it using the botanical name and varietal adjectives.

How on earth do you pronounce some of those mouth-filling names?

Don't worry about it. There is disagreement even among professionals and scholars about pronunciation. Just be sure that you spell it right when you write out an order. It is much more important that you have the correct plant in your garden than whether some superior pipsqueak smiles at your "wrong" pronunciation. In any case, quite a number of common names are the same as the Latin ones—take *Rhododendron*, for instance; or similar, as with *Juniperus* and Juniper.

Are Latin names the same all over the country?

By and large this is true, probably about 99 percent of the plant names are the same. The reason for the exceptions is that scholars are constantly quarreling among themselves about nomenclature, sometimes finding new and better identifying names. In our lists, wherever this is the case (and we know about it), we have inserted the former name in parentheses. For example, the flowering quince is a shrub that was originally called *Pyrus japonica* but was later listed by nurserymen—and some still so designate it—as *Cydonia japonica*. The current name is *Chaenomeles lagenaria*, according to Dr. Donald Wyman of the Arnold Arboretum in Boston, Massachusetts. He points out that this genus hybridizes readily and is easily propagated, thus leading to confusion, especially in former times when there was less exact communication and observation. All you really have to know is that flowering quince is now most likely listed as *Chaenomeles*, but if you see *Cydonia*, you will recognize it as the former name.

If the Latin names are often the same in English, can we depend on this?

This is usually true, but a few exceptions must be pointed out. In the South and some other places the old-fashioned name for mockorange is syringa. However, *Syringa* is the botanical name for the lilac genus, while the Latin name for mock orange is *Philadelphus*! Don't blame the botanists. Let's just attribute this to the universal perversity of human beings and the striving to put a name to something that will describe it.

Do Latin names describe the plants?

Indeed they do. If you are a Latin scholar, you will quickly pick up the definitions contained in the words. As an amateur, you will not be long in recognizing certain characteristic adjectival words—*atropurpurea* will indicate dark, purplish leaves, *japonica* will indicate that the plant probably originated in Japan, and *orientalis* that it came from some place in the Orient. There are many other descriptions that tally as you come to know them, and, even out of season, you will have a pretty good idea of what the plant will look like in leaf and flower.

It seems, then, that Latin names may be necessary and perhaps even fun?

They are not necessary to the "fun gardener," except for ordering plants; but to a person who wants to be a real plantsman or even a serious gardener they are the key, the *open sesame* to the plant world all over our earthly globe. If you visit gardens in France, Sweden, Italy, Germany, Holland, South Africa, Egypt, and just about anywhere else that plants have nameplates you will find on these markers the local-language common name and then the botanical or scientific names. One might term it the *lingua franca* or, more exactly, the *lingua latina* that opens doors and garden gates everywhere. You will be able to note interesting plants, write down the name and check when you get home whether or not it is available and will grow for you, or if there is another species of the genus that will thrive for you.

Will it take a long time to learn this system?

If you take it easy, absorbing as you go along, you will be surprised how soon you begin to find your way, and it will get easier and easier as you progress. In this book the aim has been to keep the nomenclature as simple as is consistent with proper understanding; therefore, common names have been given wherever possible—often two or three—in the interests of clarity and usefulness. Perhaps you will find pleasure in the feeling of accomplishment if your hobby turns in the direction of becoming a fully rounded gardener, one who will someday know a considerable portion of the astounding list of plants. Those in your own area and particularly the ones you make friends with by growing them in your own garden will be the beginning.

How are the Latin names set up?

The first name is the *genus,* and this is always capitalized, while the following words are the descriptions that particularize and give further ways of recognizing the individual plant. Just as humans have a last name (Brown) and a first name (John), so in the plant world we have the scientific names *Hedera* and *helix.* To distinguish one special John Brown from all the other John Browns we may use a further name or two—John Frederick Brown or John Frederick William Brown. Thus, we also have plant names to distinguish, for instance, a special *Hedera helix* from all the other English ivies that stem from the broad genus. *Hedera helix* 'Aureo-variegata' tells us that this English ivy has variegated yellow leaves, or, to put it in literal translation, Ivy, English, yellow, variegated.

The description may indicate that the plant is a dwarf or a giant, that it is narrow growing or spreading, that it has tiny leaves or huge ones, big flowers or multiple ones—all vital characteristics.

What does "cultivar" mean? Or "variety" or "selection"?

These are all terms in use in the nursery trade and botanical circles to designate kinds of the parent genus that are improved and superior in some way. As an example let us take *Rhododendron maximum*, 'Cunningham's White,' a cultivar of the common Rosebay rhododendron. It is a crossbred hybrid named for the plantsman who produced it in 1850. *Variety* is commonly used in the trade for such hybrids, although *cultivar* is the preferred designation today. It need not trouble the amateur. *Selection* is generally accepted as a kind of plant superior to the usual member of the genus that an observant nurseryman, amateur, or botanist has discovered, a natural "sport" that has desirable qualities. It must have been propagated and found to have "set" these characteristics so that the improved plant can be reproduced time and time again. It is not, in other words, a chance sport that nature may abort either by making it sterile or by causing it to revert to the original type.

Are all plants in catalogs listed by Latin names?

Not by any means. However, the best plantsmen will have the Latin name somewhere in the captions of those glowing color pictures, whatever may be the common name by which they are offered. Some less reputable plant sellers (we can hardly call them nurserymen) may dream up some eye-catching name for a perfectly standard plant. If you know your way around, you will not fall for this kind of advertising. More likely than not, you will not find any botanical names in such advertising, for it trades on ignorance. The unwary buyer may end up with an inferior kind of plant or of a size that will not fit into his garden for long. It is best, therefore, for the cautious gardener to proceed more slowly and let enthusiasm grow apace, being careful not to be carried away and later find cause to regret the purchase and the labor of planting. Only doctors bury their mistakes; gardeners bury just the roots and must live with the result.

Once you come to understand the simple structure of the names of plants and know what they mean in terms of your future happiness in the garden you are planting, you will be well on your way to becoming a real plantsman. You will have the solid foundation on which to build a growing knowledge of plants. You will quickly recognize the adjectival words— *alba* or *album* meaning white, *rosea* or *roseum* meaning pink or rose-colored, and *rubra* or *rubrum*, which indicates some shade of red. *Rubri-*

folia means, of course, red-foliaged, for plants that have reddish leaves. The place of origin may also be indicated, as we have previously shown, with *japonica* and *orientalis*; *europaea, chinensis,* and *americana* should require no explanation. Most people find that this actually adds to the enjoyment of gardening, for it affords the intellectual pleasure of acquiring a vocabulary and using it correctly.

2
Trees and Shrubs— What and Where

PLANTS MUST BE HARDY

In order to assure success, trees and shrubs (including evergreens) must be hardy in the area in which your garden is located. This is vital. Even though a plant has been well tended by the gardener and planted properly, if it is not hardy in that climate it may not survive. A cold winter, particularly in the first year or two after planting, can kill a fine plant and leave a hole for some time to come, even if it is replaced. Time is lost in addition to the original cost of the plant and the labor of planting. But plant loss is not invariably caused by low temperatures; high temperatures may be just as harmful, depending on the species. Many a tree or shrub that does well in northern regions will languish and do much less well in the south, particularly in subtropical climates. Nature has decided where the various species will live and eons of time established conditions in which they flourish. Certain genera of plants are surprisingly adaptable, while others are much more conservative and recalcitrant.

This does not mean that you must use only those plants that grow naturally in your area. In this country, as you probably are aware, we have plants in cultivation from all over the world. Plants introduced from Asia, Europe, Africa, Australia, and New Zealand, as well as from tropical and subtropical American areas, are hardy and often do exceptionally well in their new habitat. Through trials and by judicious selection it has been found that certain plants will grow in various other areas, and this work is still going on. Sometimes plants are hybridized, the resulting offspring being hardier than one or the other of the parents in addition to having other desirable qualities. Much research is under way to extend the growth area limits both north and south, and all plantsmen are following this work with great interest.

For the present, the amateur gardener and particularly the beginner has an excellent tool to employ in finding out what plants will serve well in his garden. This is the Plant Hardiness Zone Map, prepared by the United States Department of Agriculture. Divided into zones ranging from north to south, it was compiled after exhaustive studies of records from all over the land. The zones from 1 to 10, are based on the average annual minimum temperatures for each zone. Zone 1 lies in Canada, where temperatures may go below —50 degrees F., while Zone 10 has lowest temperatures of only 30 to 40 degrees F. in winter, often not reaching that nadir. If you will look at the map in these pages, you will very quickly see where your zone lies.

When you come to the lists of trees and shrubs, you will find a column for the zone in which they are known to be hardy. This will immediately narrow down the choices you have; for example, if you live in Zone 5, you will know that it would be risky to plant anything known to be hardy only to Zone 7. Memorize the number of your zone, for you will want to remember it as you cull this book's lists for candidates for your garden. Note also which part of the zone you live in—northern or southern—for this may be important also. The southern half of a zone may sometimes support plants from the upper half of the zone just to the south. This has been covered in our lists, where it was known, by listings such as Zones 5–6, and so on. There are many others, doubtless, that are not listed, for research is far from complete and there are many pockets within zones where conditions are such that small areas are warmer and more favorable to planting.

PLANT HARDINESS ZONES

How have the zones occurred in nature?

You will note that on the edges of both coasts the zones turn northward, sometimes quite sharply. This happens because of the warmth engen-

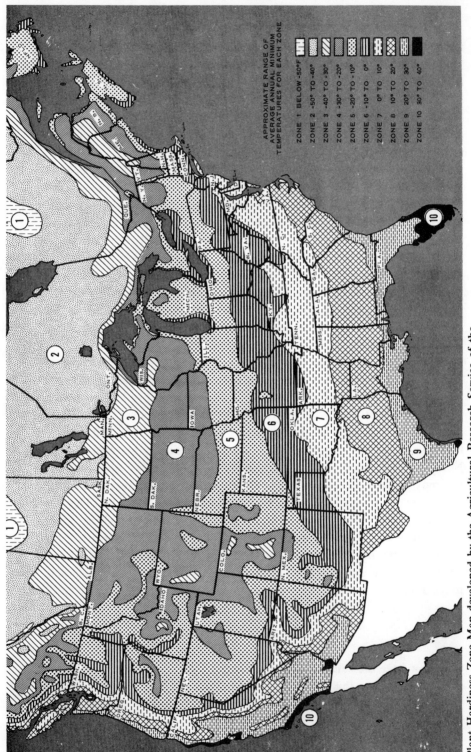

Plant Hardiness Zone Map developed by the Agricultural Research Service of the
U.S. Department of Agriculture.

dered by ocean currents. On the East Coast it is the Gulf Stream and on the West Coast it is the Japan Current. These are warm waters that flow along the coasts, bringing warmed air with them and also more moisture than is found inland. The western coastal areas are narrow because the upthrust of the Rocky Mountains and the Coastal Ranges keeps this warm, moist air confined. In the East, the Appalachians are a factor but are less important because they are not so high, are situated inland, and the coastal plains are much wider.

In our town the temperatures don't seem to match those on the Zonal Map. What is the reason?

Inside each major zone there are many subzones and microclimates. Wherever there is some protection from prevailing cold winds or wherever there is a colder altitude that makes an area colder, you will find either a subzone (if it is widespread) or a microclimate (if it is relatively small). These latter may be only a few square miles or even smaller, while a subzone may be larger. Concerning altitude, the general rule is that a hundred feet of rise is equal to about two hundred miles of northward distance. That is why in the southern Alleghenies you will encounter temperatures usually associated with regions much to the north. In the high Rocky Mountains this may be even more pronounced. If you live in a subzone or microclimate of this sort, you should concentrate on plants that grow in the zones to the north of you. In general, unless your altitude is much higher than that of the rest of your zone, you need not worry too much about this factor.

OTHER FACTORS THAT AFFECT PLANT GROWTH

Are there any other factors associated with hardiness of plants?

Although temperature and altitude are prime factors, there are some other elements we must bear in mind. Plant growth is primarily affected by the soil in which the plants are set. Acidity or alkalinity, if pronounced, may either help or harm plants according to their natural preferences as indicated by their native habitats. Whether the soil is sandy or is heavy clay, rich with organic matter or deficient in humus, moist with rainfall or with ground water from a high water table, or warm from the amount of sun and its intensity—all these are factors governing growth and health of trees and shrubs. Finally, the amount of wind and its general or prevalent direction is another important variable, and this is often unobserved or ignored.

What are the kinds of soil and how do they occur?

Soils vary greatly, often within rather small areas. Even virgin soils are sometimes deficient in the balance that plants require if they are to thrive. Plants are conditioned by eons of living in native habitats, although some have gradually been spread widely enough to have become adapted to varying climates and soils. Acid soils are best for most evergreens and certain broad-leaved evergreens, also a fair number of deciduous shrubs and trees. Alkaline soils are usually less adaptable to plant growth, although semidesert to desert conditions have produced many alkaline-tolerant plants. The bulk of good growing soils are in the neutral range, somewhere between very acid and very alkaline, occuring mostly in broad regions. The areas with much rainfall are likely to have a somewhat acid content, though this is not an invariable rule.

How can you know what kind of soil you have?

The best way is to have the soil tested. You can send soil samples to your state college of agriculture or, for a quick test and one you can do periodically yourself, buy a testing kit at your garden center or from a mail-order seed house. The *p*H test, that is, the acid or alkaline reaction of the soil, will tell you in what range your soil falls naturally. You can then correct it in one direction or the other, should it need adjustment. See the section on soils, pages 311–321, for details.

Can plants grow in sandy or clay soils?

Few plants require either one or the other; in addition, few soils are totally sandy or totally clay. The extremes do exist, of course: seaside dunes are almost pure sand (with the added hazard of excessive sea salt), and certain other places have pure clay, and they are usually mined for pottery and other industrial uses. But many planting soils have a high degree of sandiness and others have so much clay that they can be rated as clay soils. As we shall discuss in the section on soils, adjustments can be made in each condition to bring soil to a more amenable state.

What is "organic matter" and how do soils become "humus rich"?

Organic matter is any sort of vegetable or animal matter that can decompose and become part of the soil. Humus is, in general, fibrous, the decayed animal matter and vegetable wastes that form the black and brown particles in the soil. In other words, the nonmineral content of soil.

What amount of water is needed for plants?

The only answer is "enough" water to fulfill their needs. Some plants need a great deal and will do best in muck soils similar to the swampy or waterside habitat they come from. Others can do with comparatively little or else send searching roots deeply into the subsoil for moisture.

If it rains, should you have to water too?

There is a great range of climates in this country, and the rainfall (this includes snow and sleet) varies considerably. The time of its falling is also of importance to gardeners; in some localities it is spread rather evenly throughout the year, while in other places it may come only in winter. On the high plains, for instance, there is little rainfall during the summer, and such snow as falls in winter usually lasts only a short time, not lying on the top of the soil as in other regions but being absorbed as it melts in the strong winter sun. Underground it replenishes ground water and restores wells, and the runoff refills reservoirs. In the high altitudes of the Rocky Mountains and the highest Allegheny Mountains, winter snow does not melt, but piles up layer by layer. In summer it is gradually released as it melts through the warm months. Some of this is available for farm irrigation as it flows from the mountain streams, but gardens there must depend on well or reservoir water. Hence, in dry areas it must be conserved. As to watering if it rains, the answer, in most places, is probably always yes. Foods in the soil are taken up by the feeding roots only in solution; hence, some moisture around the roots is essential even for plants that need little moisture. Provided there is good drainage, constant weekly watering may be the best plan. Showers are likely to wet only the topmost area of the soil; but feeding roots are always found lower, even for shallow-rooted subjects.

Is sun necessary for plants or can they grow in shade?

Many hardy plants are sun lovers, requiring a good half day of sunlight to flower and/or fruit and put forth their best efforts. Grown in shade, they may survive, but growth will be more spindly and also flowers and fruit will be less in evidence. On the other hand, there are some plants that will do perfectly well in half shade or less than full shade. Lists of plants known to endure these conditions are provided in the shrub chapters.

What does sun do for plants?

The action of the sun on the leaves and general structure of the plants produces cell growth. Hence, some plants that grow moderately well in the more northerly states may flourish for gardeners in southerly areas, where the growing season is longer. Light, even if not direct sun, can be rated along with food and water as a necessity for plants.

Is wind a factor in hardiness?

Most definitely it is. Ordinary prevailing winds are not often recognized to be a problem in maintaining the life of shrubs and trees, particularly the needled evergreens and broad-leaved evergreens. But wind extracts moisture from plant leaves, and in winter, when evergreen needles and leaves of broad-leaved evergreens are exposed to it, the leaves are unable to replace the moisture robbed from them because ground moisture is locked up by frost. They are therefore more vulnerable to the effect of sun as well as continuing winds. Deciduous plantings are less endangered in the nongrowing season, but sudden gusts and high winds often twist and snap branches; weak limbs are broken off; and evergreen tops may also suffer breakage. This latter can sometimes be repaired, as shown in the sketch in the chapter on maintenance, page 288. Deciduous branches and limbs, however, must be pruned back even though this may spoil the symmetry of shape that is desired for most trees and shrubs.

How can a garden be protected from winds?

If it is possible to place the garden in the lee of a house or other building, either on your own property or that of a neighbor, the winds can be broken and lessened. A sturdy, quick-growing hedge will help to protect small and young plants, and if it is composed of plants columnar in habit, it will grow tall and narrow, taking up little room in the small garden. A more comprehensive kind of protection is a fence, either a louvered type that deflects and slows the wind or one that has boards on either side, alternating in placement, so that there is ventilation but not forceful wind coming through. A fence is an "instant" protector and can be used until plants grow sturdy and tall enough to protect themselves, or else be left permanently in place.

Another way to avoid wind damage is to place sensitive plants in the lee of buildings or evergreen tree shelters. Wrapping them in burlap sacking over the winter will also protect them from drying out too much (see the winterizing section in the chapter on maintenance, page 296).

Is deep snow lying around plants good or bad for them?

If the snowfall lies for a long time, it is quite likely to form a sort of mulch that covers the ground and replenishes ground water by melting into it gradually. It will also prevent thawing and refreezing and the resultant heaving that breaks tender young roots. On the other hand, I have known it to protect the low branches of a forsythia so that the blossoms appeared

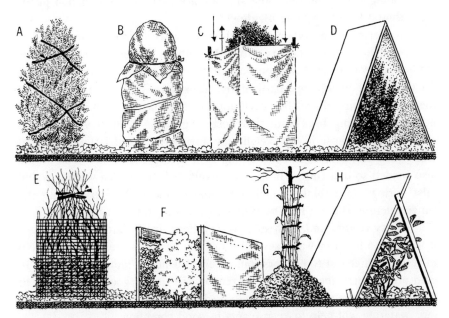

IN WINTER, protection is needed. (*A*) Evergreen lightly tied together to prevent snow from bending out of shape. (*B*) Burlap wrappings and top protect from both sun and wind. (*C*) Burlap fastened to stakes, permits heat to escape and moisture and heat to penetrate to soil. (*D*) A-frame made of plywood protects against snow sliding from roofs. (*E*) Twiggy shrubs, such as shrub roses, are tied together to minimize wind whipping that loosens roots. Wire mesh cylinder staked in place can be filled with straw or leaves to protect root area. (*F*) Burlap on frames, on one or both sides, protects from sun damage to box and tender evergreens and can be filled with leaves or straw if further protection is needed. (*G*) Grafted shrubs or trees need hilling up of soil the first few years in coldest areas. Cornstalks bound around trunk will protect against sun scald. (*H*) A-frame plywood piece held in place by stakes, shields from sun and wind.

in spring below the snow line, while above it the buds had been winter-killed by sun or by having tried to bloom too early and were killed back (I have never been sure). In any case, there is little you can do about it. One caution, however, is that the snow from streets or walks that has been salted to melt the ice and snow should not be thrown around adjacent shrubs and trees. Salt damage is one of the hazards of modern gardening, and this is one reason I do not advocate planting trees or even ground covers on the spaces next to streets where town snowplows pile salty snow.

Sliding snow from roofs and also sun are hazards to foundation plantings. Should I give up these plantings?

In Vermont and other far-north areas where winter snows are frequent and deep, protection is afforded plants in winter by the ingenious method shown in the sketch on page 23: an A-frame open-sided housing for the plants. Evergreens, particularly, are susceptible to damage because they retain their foliage, but deciduous plants may be broken, too, and necessitate cutting back with time lost in growing a shapely plant. Sun shades such as those in the sketch may also be built and installed to protect young plants from the too strong rays of the winter sun. The soil is also shaded so that roots will not be encouraged, by sudden warmings and false springs, into thinking that it is time to move the sap up into the superstructure where it may be trapped by a sudden fall of temperature.

In dry regions and, with some reservations, in all parts of the country it will do no harm to water several times during the winter. This will help to restore water lost to evaporation, much of which is induced by wind. In cold areas where the ground is frozen, it will do no good, of course, to water because the moisture is already locked up. But in open and dry winters, watering will help to keep plants in good condition.

If gardening is so rigorous in so many places, is there any alternative short of not gardening at all?

Gardening is not always as rigorous as the extreme situations above might lead a beginner to believe. There are realities to be faced in all regions, in all situations, and in every garden, but there is no reason to suppose that anyone would have to cope with all of them at once or in any given season, or perhaps at all. If you encounter any one of them, the answers to the various questions here may better enable you to meet the situation and difficulties. The important thing is to take steps to overcome these hazards, wherever possible, but mainly to work within the limits of your climate and the particular site on which you garden. If you are a diligent and observant gardener, satisfying so far as possible the needs of your plants, you will without doubt become a very successful gardener. Best of all is the consolation that whatever the limitations your zone and climate impose on you, probably someone in another zone will be envying you for what you grow. Rejoice in the many blessings that each zone bestows on gardeners; embrace nature and work with it. Then, if there are a few ways in which you want to experiment or to outwit your climate, you can devote time to nursing a few exotic plants and not have to worry about having to minister to a lot of invalids. You can broaden your scope as a gardener, and perhaps, by trying and succeeding with plants not supposed to grow in your region, you can add a bit to the lore of gardening in America.

SECTIONAL TIPS FOR VARIOUS AREAS
WITH HARDINESS ZONE MAPS

A few general observations concerning conditions in the several sections of the country may assist a beginning gardener in getting a head start. Other more experienced gardeners will find that knowledge is sharpened by review. Each zone and section can be discussed only in broad outlines here, because of the many subzones and microclimates within the total areas. But the general and prevailing natural conditions will be covered for each region.

NORTH: Let us divide this large area into two major sections—the Northeast and the North Midwest.

NORTHEAST: This section runs from Maine westward to about the end of Lake Erie and about the middle of Ohio, then directly south to the

northern border of Tennessee, then angling northeastward up the Shenandoah Valley to Maryland's northern border, and going directly east to Delaware Bay, including all of New Jersey. The eastern perimeter will be the coastline north to Maine.

There is generally ample rain in most of this region, more than will be found in the northern areas to the west. In New England and down through the mountainous parts the soil is more or less rocky, sometimes shallow, with glacial soil found in these areas that is probably somewhat acid. Many acid-soil plants will be found native here and others that are acid-tolerant should also thrive, except in the far northern zones where they may not be hardy. A few spots within this area will have soil that is not acid enough to support these plants. If the gardener demands them for his garden, the soil balance must be corrected. In upper New York, Vermont, New Hampshire, and Maine the shorter growing seasons mean that a longer time must be allowed for plants to reach maturity. One compensation is that the moderate daytime temperatures and cool nights allow a longer blooming time for flowering trees and shrubs than in many places to the south. Winter temperatures are often cold, but may fluctuate, especially in the southern part of this area, causing freeze-and-thaw cycles that can cause damage to young wood and to newly planted trees and shrubs. Winter sun may be bright and warm, so that trees should be wrapped to prevent sunscald.

Elsewhere in the westward area of the Northeast, soils will vary, and although cold winds sweep off the lake, the Ohio plain has many fine nurseries with little if any winter danage. Neutral soils, with acid soil here and there, are the general rule. Tests will determine what the local picture is.

NORTH MIDWEST: The other half of NORTH runs from the western border of Northeast, about the middle of Ohio, westward through the Great Lakes region to about the middle of the Dakotas, following the Canadian border, thence southward to the Kansas-Oklahoma border and eastward along it and the Missouri-Arkansas border to join the previously established point on Tennessee's northern border. Where it joins with the Northeast's western line, it goes north to the Great Lakes point in Ohio. This large region is itself divided into two sections—the Upper Midwest and the Lower Midwest.

Upper Midwest: Temperatures in summer are high—90 to 100 degrees F. or more—and they often do not change for days on end. Nights are hot, too, in many parts. Snow and winds are prevalent in winter, very

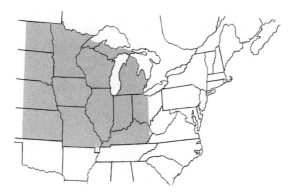

low temperatures are often encountered, with below-zero temperatures sometimes remaining for days. This combination of low temperature and high winds makes growing broad-leaved evergreens a chancy thing, but they are known to survive in spots where they can be protected and cared for. The winter sun may damage them as much as cold and wind can, so they should be protected from excessive exposure to sun. Soil is good, fertile, and deep for the most part and, with the good average rainfall, produces splendidly. It is, on the whole, either neutral or a little on the acid side and therefore conducive to good gardening.

Lower Midwest: Here high temperatures are also found, together with periods of drought in the Kansas-Nebraska and some of the Dakota areas. Torrid temperatures in the daytime linger into the night in summer, low temperatures ranging occasionally to below zero combine with sweeping winds to add to the gardener's problems in this region. In many places it may not be wise to plant roses unless you are willing to give them a great deal of care. Native roses and the tougher species might be the answer for those who love this flower. The soil is somewhat alkaline, making it unwise to plant broad-leaved evergreens and other acid-soil plants, though a soil test might indicate that it is possible in some areas. The same hazards of sun and winter winds as are found in the Upper Midwest obtain here, however, and mean that protection and extra care must be given such plants. It is better, probably, to select those trees and shrubs that will be reliably hardy in the region, give them windbreaks or other wind protection as much as possible, and keep maintenance within reasonable bounds.

SOUTH: Running along the southern perimeter of NORTH, its western borderline continuing directly south from the western border of

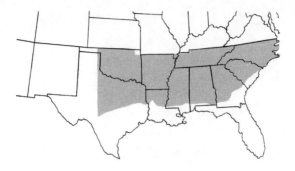

NORTH. This area is also divided into two parts running horizontally from east to west.

UPPER SOUTH: Extending southward from the upper border of the region to the limits of Zone 8 on the Hardiness Zone Map, it follows it westward more or less to the western perimeter of the region. It may be noted that this section embraces widely varying terrain and a correspondingly wide variety of soils. In this section are included the part of Virginia that lies east of the Shenandoah Valley, which has wide valleys and fertile lands; the uplands and hill country of the Carolinas' Appalachians, with its wide valleys and fertile coastal country; Tennessee and western Georgia, Alabama and Mississippi, and the upper part of Texas, which also present much variety in soils and plant life. "Piney" woods and clay soils are found in many sections, but the bottomlands along the rivers and especially the Mississippi valley have very good soils. Louisiana and inland Texas range into prairie land, with Oklahoma also in this category. Semiarid in parts and more or less alkaline in many sections, this soil is less conducive to the wide variety of plants gardeners might wish to choose from. The summers are very hot throughout the region, but winters for the most part are milder than in the NORTH, though snows and winds drift down into the western part of the Upper South from the Midwest and WEST. In the northern to western or prairie parts, water and rains are scarcer than in the eastern regions, where rains from the Gulf of Mexico drift well inland and provide moisture. A little snow may appear in the northeast part in winter, especially in the uplands and hills.

LOWER SOUTH: Running along the northern limits of Zone 9 and embracing all of Florida, the coastal parts of Georgia, South Carolina, and the Gulf States, this is a warm to subtropical region. The soils are

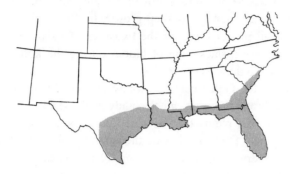

varied, running from extra sandy in much of Florida to muck soils and river-bottom soils elsewhere. Temperatures in winter range from 20 degrees F.+ in northern parts to 30 degrees F.+ on the tip of Florida and a few other far-southern places.

Long hot summers combine with mild winters to dispel any hope of growing plants that need cold and winter dormancy. In Florida the mostly sandy soils need adjustment with compost and other humus, peat moss and other materials, or muck soil from areas that can spare it. Once the gardener adjusts his sights to these conditions and explores the new set of plants available to him, gardening can become a year-round pleasure, for many things grow beautifully in this hot climate. The warm southern subtropical part of Florida indicates exotics from all the hot regions of the world might grow here, and there are many nurseries offering these new delights. A great many evergreen plants are found here, and many that are semi-evergreen or deciduous to the North are hardy and quite reliably evergreen here. Insect and disease problems, unfortunately, are also year-round and may actually increase due to humidity. Water, too, may be a problem, what with brackish and somewhat salty water along the coasts and salts from the sandy soil creating problems, while inland, hose watering may be necessary because water drains so quickly through the soil. However, the average year (nondrought) will bring a good bit of rain in quick and heavy showers. Mulching should be practiced lavishly to keep the soil as cool as possible, and plants that require sun in the North may profit from some protection from it here.

Many plants that are greenhouse or indoor subjects in the North are outdoor plants here, especially the woody ones—shrubs and subshrubs. Hibiscus with its spectacular blooms is one plant that grows beautifully outdoors here. Because of the lush growth, pruning must be practiced more frequently, almost constantly, to keep growth healthy and within bounds. But that is a small price to pay for the treasures of blossom in the cooler season. Summers see a slackening of bloom during the hottest times, but people are less active then, too.

To the west, the Gulf Coast has conditions similar to those of upper Florida, though not always as much sandy soil. Muck soils mean that drainage is poor, and plants that need it should be set at a higher level (see sketch on page 254). In Texas, the inland regions are likely to be influenced by the dry-plains conditions, and watering may be increasingly necessary the more inland the garden is.

WEST: Also divided into northern and southern sections, this is a very large region with many differences in soil and growing conditions. In much of it gardens will need regular watering and irrigation, for in summer rainfall is sparse and even winters are rather dry, and moisture disappears into the soil quickly. Mulching is one way to cope with evaporation and should be widely practiced.

UPPER WEST: The northern perimeter of this section is the Canadian Border; its eastern line is the western border of the NORTH and SOUTH regions; its western limit is roughly that of Zone 7's eastern line, but from west of the southwestern corner of Nevada or thereabouts it keeps a fairly constant line southeast to the Colorado River.

In general this region is one with largely alkaline soil, even into the mountain areas in some places. The soil of the valleys inclines toward neutral and, in a few places, to mildly acid. Through the plains portion and some places beyond there is a need for more humus in soils, and this should be added; in places where alkalinity is a problem, some acidifying may be needed. In the mountain states there is more water available, of course, though most of the annual precipitation will come in the winter. Irrigation by hoses or in some places by small ditches is the rule, and in drier sections water may someday be rationed or become expensive. Hence, dependence on native plants or similar genera is recommended. Hot sun, both summer and winter, but cooler nights than to the east is the rule, and subzero temperatures and freezing are common. Wind, especially on the plains and prairie lands, may be strong and drying. Protection from prevailing wind direction is advisable.

To prevent evaporation and to keep soil cool in summer, mulching is almost mandatory. In winter, sun may cause damage or even kill plants that are hardy in other places where there is more moisture and more humidity. Autumn, winter, and early-spring waterings are therefore needed to keep the roots constantly supplied with water.

LOWER WEST (Southwest): This area is a kind of hodgepodge of many kinds of soils and climate conditions. In general, all that can be said is that it is a dry region—dry ranging from true desert conditions in Arizona and Southern California to pine woods and forests in the moun-

tainous parts of the states, and arid to dry prairie in New Mexico and Texas and parts of other states.

Hardiness here many times is not dependent upon resistance to low temperatures but to resistance to sun and to hot, drying winds. Sometimes it may be both low temperatures and the sun-wind problem. Where water is available somewhat tropical growth is possible, but in many parts the lack of rainfall, even in winter, creates Sahara-like conditions. The soils range from quite acid in a few places to very alkaline in many others. In a good many soils there may be a deficiency of certain trace minerals, so that an analysis not only for acid-alkaline reaction but also for mineral-nutrient content is suggested. In all sections here some watering is needed, and winter-sun protection for many plants may be needed. In general, grow the plants that are indigenous or similar kinds of plants. In desert conditions, follow the guidelines in the sections on desert gardening, pages 248 to 253.

PACIFIC COAST: Although this is a narrow strip running along the coast and inland for a relatively short distance, there are many strips of hardiness zones within it. This is due to the many elevations and mountain ranges that create climate changes. Washed by the Japanese current, the extreme coastal zone is warm, with mild winters and high humidity and rainfall in the northern part. Along the California coast it is drier all year, but lush growth is still found; however, watering becomes more necessary. Inland conditions also vary considerably. There are two, possibly three, divisions of climate.

NORTHWEST COAST: The area extending from Canada to the Oregon-California border, is complex but rewarding. Winters are mild, with fog,

mist, and rain keeping the land moist and the air humid along the coastal areas. Broad-leaved evergreens thrive here and grow spectacularly. Other plants that enjoy cool summers and mild, moist winters also do their best here. Inland there may be increasing need for waterings in summer to keep the soil moist until the rains return. Altitudes may play a part here as elsewhere because there are so many hills and valleys in the varied terrain. Do not plant azaleas, rhododendrons, and other broad-leaved plants near the coastline, where salt spray is whipped inland by ocean winds. Beginning gardeners will do well to go slow, consult gardeners nearby, and seek advice from their county agents or state agricultural college. Observe what sorts of plants thrive in the general area of your garden and make notes. Select accordingly, but be a bit adventurous, selecting according to what zonal regions plants will grow in. Temper judgment with consideration for prevailing wind, average moisture, soil, and other influences in your climate or microclimate.

NORTHERN CALIFORNIA: From a little above Santa Barbara to the northern border of California is the transition area, with many microclimates and conditions that must govern choice of plantings. Around the San Francisco Bay area winters are mild and rainy, with summers cool and relatively dry. Northward it is much the same, while southward summers grow warmer. Inland toward the mountains, the summers are hotter and the winters colder. Hot, semidesert conditions on the southern end merge to good growing conditions around Fresno, and toward the north there are inland forests.

SOUTHERN CALIFORNIA: The range widens here, going from subtropical along the extreme southern coast to desert and semidesert conditions inland away from the coastal moisture. The subtropical areas will be dominated by plants that grow in Zones 7 to 10, according to local microclimates and moisture availability. The dry sections are covered in lists in the section on dry gardening, pages 197–198. Tough native and exotic plants that will survive the rigorous conditions will be the answer to this unique area of American climate.

A note on desert country: Although some sandy wastes occur here, the American Desert region is not like the movie versions of the Sahara Desert. The climate is hot in summer, with blistering temperatures in the daytime, and mild to warm in winter in most areas, but it can be quite cool and even cold in some parts of this large expanse. Ecologists have realized, but the public has still to understand, that even though water may be available from damming up the great rivers or by pumping from deep wells, gardening and even farming cannot be carried on as it was in other sections where immigrating residents lived before. Attempting to grow lawns and produce massive oases can only lead to disaster as more and more water is brought in only to disappear into the hot, sandy soils. The problem of salts and minerals that are present because not enough rains have fallen to leach them out of the upper soils may even be aggravated by watering, which only brings them to the surface to lie there and cause trouble. Heavily alkaline, the soil in true desert country cannot be expected to produce like neutral soil, and it is believed best to leave things pretty much as they are, using the native cacti and other interesting botanical subjects in lieu of the greenery produced elsewhere. There is, after all, a certain exotic beauty in these desert plants.

ZONES ARE USEFUL GUIDES

Now that the broad general picture has been filled in and the overall climate limitations and delights have been indicated, it is time to think about starting the lists of plants one might like to grow. Before that can really be done, however, we must think about what will grow or is most likely to thrive and survive in our own locations. Use your Plant Hardiness Zone as a guide, balance it against other factors that will influence growth and survival—altitude, moisture, wind prevalance, winter and summer sun, and the soil that must be worked with—and you will have straightened and clarified the guidelines still more so that reasonably exact choices involving the least trouble and risk will be possible.

Knowing the plant's needs or preferences is always a good idea, for if we can supply them as nearly as possible, it will simplify gardening and maintenance. In the next chapter these needs will be discussed and evaluated.

3
Using Plants to
Solve Site Problems

Owning a home is the goal of most Americans, and for many, a considerable part of the pride they expect to take in their home will be in the plantings around it. Most homeowners yearn for a beautiful garden but soon come up against hard reality: yearning is not enough; planning, action and work are the only ways to achieve what has been dreamed of. Some take an easy way out and hire a "landscaper" and, depending on his skill and creativity, this may work out well. But far too many results are neither impressive nor individual. This "landscaping by the yard" is banal, and the results that one sees are all too often commonplace. Others decide to do it themselves, and then they must look for guidance. For concrete action to be effective, careful thought and planning must precede it or the dream may dissolve into future trouble as latent problems surface later on.

This is why the beginning is of the utmost importance. We must go slowly in taking the first steps. The wish is parent to the thought, but the thought must be based on knowledge and intelligence if it is to be the progenitor of a successful plan. We must clarify our hazy ideas in the same way that an artist begins with a rough sketch—and maybe you will do just that: make sketches as you pursue the planning. These will become more refined and concrete until at the end an integrated and satisfying composition is achieved. Good gardens are always the result of intelligent forethought, not spur-of-the-moment improvisation. The same principles of composition that are used in all the arts will be present in garden design, too. Unity, balance, harmony, rhythm, and center of interest are the ideals to work for. But most artists find, sooner or later, that some compromise is necessary, and in the garden this is particularly so, for we must combine the practical with the aesthetic.

It would be easier if we could plan the garden and locate the house according to the terrain and our own wishes, but this is not possible in most cases. Gardeners go out to buy a house, find one that meets the family's needs and the limits of purse as nearly as possible, and then they must begin to make a mere house into a real home, pleasant and livable. The garden can do a great deal toward reaching this goal if the homeowner is really interested in gardening. Many people, especially those who have lived all their lives in a city apartment, are unaware of the potential a garden has for enriching the lives of the whole family. For a whole new world can open up once one begins to perceive how wonderfully various and exciting the plant kingdom can be.

Creating a garden is a little like decorating rooms indoors, because we deal with color and line; but it is also like sculpting, for we are working things out in mass and in three dimensions. It is important not to skimp on the preliminaries, the foundation upon which you will build your garden over the years. You can accomplish all sorts of tricks with plantings and solve all kinds of problems if you ask the right questions of yourself at the very beginning.

The reason for failure is usually the speed with which people leap into planting, with little thought and no background preparation. Curiously, these are often the same people who will shop all the car dealers and peruse armloads of specifications before they buy a car. Yet they dash out and recklessly buy a great many plants, and when they bring them home, of course, they have to find a place to put them, so they poke them into inadequate, hastily dug holes wherever they think they might go! Inevitably these prove to be the wrong places. Cars, on the other hand, have a limited lifespan and must be replaced in a few years but a garden is planted, presumably, for the lifetime of the gardener. So you can see why careful forethought will pay off.

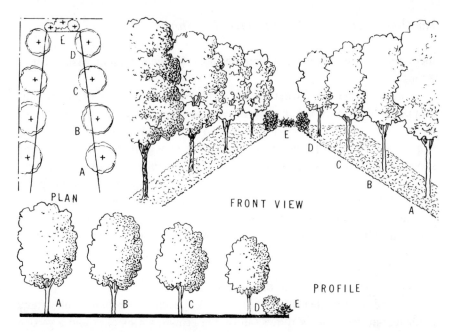

PLAN

FRONT VIEW

PROFILE

A   B   C   D   E

VISUAL ENLARGEMENT. Small areas can be made to look bigger and vistas longer by utilizing the principles of perspective, long known to artists. Use a simple progression of sizes—tallest plants (A) nearest to the point of usual observation (usually the house), the shortest (D) at the most distant point; between, graduated sizes (B,C). The front view (see sketch) seems like a normal perspective but the principle is seen in the profile view. Trees can be planted a year apart, buying according to the budget, if desired. The lines at the edges of the beds are also tapered to converge toward the most distant point (plan) and plantings that end the vista are low-growing evergreens (E). The fences could be tapered, also, to still further force the perspective.

But how can an amateur, a beginner know what to do?

First of all, *really* look at your plot. Evaluate its assets and its drawbacks. Consider it from every angle: look out from the various windows of the house, look at the house from different parts of the property, study the plot from the street as you approach it and from the house looking out toward the street. Look for drawbacks such as utility poles, unpleasant vistas from the windows, neighboring houses too close for privacy, and anything else you can find that might possibly detract from your enjoyment. Then cheer yourself up by looking for the assets. Perhaps there are some existing trees, a fine view from a window, or some other spot that would be worth cherishing. If the builder has put in any plantings, determine whether they are good ones and belong where they are. Plan to move

37

them to a better location if you decide that their present placement is wrong.

Study the terrain—whether it is sloping or flat, whether there are out-croppings of rocks or other features, whether there are any wild plants you may wish to retain, particularly if it is to be a natural garden. If the land slopes, are there any low spots that collect water from rains or melting snow? Are there any spots where showers sluice topsoil away whenever it rains? Write all of these down on a kind of balance sheet and keep the list for reference, because here you see the problems, and once seen, the solution is already begun. Try to get the whole picture into your mind so that you will visualize as you plan, wherever you are and at any hour of the day.

Must I draw a plan for the property?

This is a good idea if it will help you to visualize the final result. Many gardeners prefer to work things out on the ground with stakes and a garden hose or two to outline the beds so that they can then look at them from various angles and see how they shape up, at the same time imagining the trees and shrubs growing. If you are going to make a plan, use graph paper, each square representing one foot. Measure the borders of the property and establish them on the paper. Measure the placement of the house from the borderlines and place it on the plot plan. Measure off and place a circle for any existing trees, and draw the edge of the lawn, if it already exists and does not cover the entire surface of the property. Place the driveway and walks, also. Roughly sketch outside the property the placement of the houses of the neighbors, side and back, and also draw in utility and street-lamp poles. Make a note of where gas and electric meters are placed, also the oil-tank fill pipe and place them on the plan. Now is the time to see, if possible, where sewer lines run and where septic tanks and dispersal fields are located. Draw them in. (If you do not make a plan, do not in any case neglect these latter important service items. You must avoid sewage facilities in planting and you must provide access to the utilities features.)

Now that the survey is made, what is the next step?

This is the moment of truth. You must now ask yourself what it is you want from your garden. Is it to be merely lip-service planting that needs minimal care? Is it to be a really individual planting that garden enthusiasts will praise? Is it to be a hobby garden in which you grow and exhibit the fruits of your labors? Is it to be a kind of outdoor meeting and living place for the whole family? Do you want to have a place to entertain friends for cocktails? for meals? for neighborhood picnics? Do you want to have a food garden plot in some corner where you can raise fresh vegetables and fruit? Are members of the family interested in games, so that shuffleboard or other courts for basketball practice, badminton, etc., should be worked into the plan? All of these and perhaps other considerations will occur as you question yourself and your family, and they are all pertinent to the task of designing in order to get the best and the most from your plot.

When these things have been taken into account, where do we begin?
Start with the breakdown of the property into its three main divisions: the public area, the service area, and the private area(s).

Where is the public area?
The space in front of the house on the street side or alongside it if the house is on a corner plot. This is where all visitors arrive, where service vehicles and service men must enter, and it is usually where the service facilities are located (or adjacent to it)—the electric and gas meters, the fuel tank, the trash and garbage receptacles, and any other facilities. These must all be provided with an easy access. Here, too, is where the sewage pipes, water pipes, and gas lines are located. Sometimes, in suburban areas without sewage lines, the septic tank and dispersal field are located here, if it is the best position for them.

How do we design for the public area?
Keep in mind that this is the face you present to the world, the impression that is made on passersby who will never see the private areas but will form judgments based on this part of the property. Plantings should be designed for easy care and for enhancing the house and its entryways. Alongside driveways, plantings near the street should be kept low, near ground level, so that passing cars can see vehicles backing out of the driveway or emerging in any way and so that drivers can also see oncoming vehicles easily. Note the sketch detailing the views from the driver's seat and you will see how to maintain visibility from the driveway.

The public area may be too public for comfort if picture windows are scenes for passersby to witness rather than for occupants of the house to

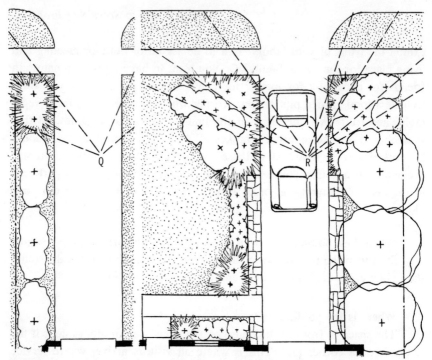

KEEP SIGHT LINES CLEAR. Driveways from which cars must emerge on the street should have little or no plantings toward the end. If plantings are used, keep shrubbery low, putting in prostrate or dwarf types that will never grow tall and block the view. *Left,* dotted lines indicate how sight lines are limited by tall evergreens and treelike shrubs. *Right,* a better arrangement puts prostrate junipers at the ends of paved landing walks; low shrubs behind them will not impede the driver's view, while borderline trees are kept trimmed high to permit visibility toward the sidewalk as well as the street.

look out of. Privacy plantings may be needed here. A pair of flowering trees planted near the front of the property will grow up and spread out, masking the window from view and, when in flower or leaf, providing a pleasing prospect from the house.

Where should shade trees be placed?

Too many beginners, uncertain of where to put shade trees, forget that they are supposed to produce shade for the house, and they therefore place them bisymmetrically on the front lawn of the house. While there is nothing wrong with this (provided the trees do fulfill their function of producing the shade needed to keep the roof cool during the day), a more interesting picture can be obtained by placing the shade tree where it

40

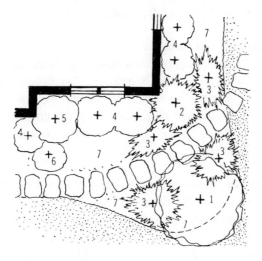

CORNER PLANTING builds out to include a small tree, with stepping stones inside it for foot traffic.

Plants
1. Small flowering tree
2. Evergreen, medium height
3. Evergreen, low
4. Flowering shrubs, medium height
5. Flowering shrubs, tall
6. Shrub, low
7. Ground cover plants, underplanted with spring flowering bulbs

will do its work and then balancing it with a smaller tree, perhaps one that flowers. Often this is integrated with the shrubbery planting near the corner of the house. The illustration shows how this can be done without increasing the chore of lawn cutting. It also shows how to bring into focus the pathway around the side of the house by incorporating stepping stones and ground covers.

How about foundation plantings, and what should they consist of?

There is a new and fresh approach here, too, the old idea of foundation plantings per se being adapted to new conditions or even discarded. Originally, foundation plantings were introduced in order to help tie the house to its site at a time when houses were built above high basements and looked as if they were perched on stilts. Now that houses are lower and more or less hug the ground this need has lessened and even disappeared. Many good landscape designers feel that if the lines of the house are good, there is little need for plantings, but most gardeners seem to feel that some planting softens the severe lines of a house, and they welcome a bit of greenery, some evergreens and flowering shrubs in the public area at least. Traditional houses do not require the foundation plantings one so often sees; in colonial times, in fact, there was no such thing. A lilac bush at the corner, or an evergreen on either side of the doorway or porch was about the extent of the planting, as we see today at many of the houses of Colonial Williamsburg.

How should you approach foundation plantings if you want them?

It is usual to accent the corners of the house with a taller growing shrub or evergreen, not one that will overtop the eaves but one that will be at maturity as tall as is needed for accent. Under windows one would naturally use dwarf shrubs or evergreens that would require little or no pruning to keep them low, while between windows the plantings would rise a bit higher, giving a sort of undulating line. Try also for a variety of color in leafage, for harmony in flower color of those plants blooming simultaneously, and for some variety in the sizes and shapes of leaves so that there is not a monotonous appearance. For year-round effect, evergreens and broad-leaved evergreens are often combined, but the uniform dark green

DIRECTIONS in which plants grow (and their mature heights) should be a prime consideration for planting alongside houses. The dotted lines indicate the directions and suggest choices: horizontal plants under windows; very low growers under big windows; moderate to tall growers at corners (upright growers for constricted spaces); medium-height plants for in between. Corner plants should never top the eaves line.

usually seen may be a little dull. Vary this by using silvery and bluish junipers, by one of the yellow-green needled evergreens, and by use of flowering deciduous shrubs in some places. See the text on design on page 49. This will give you a good start toward assembling a border for this area.

Are service areas planted or how should they be treated?

Since service areas are utilitarian, they might be concentrated into one small area and fenced in to conceal their lack of beauty, but the fence might be planted with a vine that clambers on the outside of it. A bed of shrubs in front of the fence, provided there is room for one, would also be acceptable. However, no plantings should interfere with access, and the gateway should be wide and easily opened for the service personnel.

Be sure to leave room for oil-tank trucks to put their hoses across lawns, not shrubbery, when filling the oil tank. Keep the trash receptacles close to the front of the side yard or wherever it will be most convenient for collectors to reach them. And plant to mask fences, to embellish them or achieve whatever can be done to make these necessary but unlovely areas more acceptable.

What and where are the private areas of the garden?

These are usually in the rear yard, but sometimes a side yard is also wide enough to make a small private area opening off of a living room or bedroom wing. If there is an elderly member of the family living in the house, a small garden that is secluded and for his or her exclusive use might be developed in the side yard.

The main private area would be the back yard and would include the terrace and sitting-out places, the children's supervised play area, the food garden if you have one, and perhaps a hobby garden where roses, herbs, or some other hobby plants could be grown and displayed. Small and narrow yards would, of course, be restricted to whatever the major uses might be. A tool storage shed and potting shelf might be placed at the rear of the garage or it could be set in a corner of the vegetable garden, if access to it were provided so that the lawn mower and any other machines could be taken out easily. A compost pile behind a fence in a corner would be a means of disposing of garden wastes by making compost for use in improving the soil. See pages 316–317.

Privacy for family activities and for entertaining will be the main problem to solve here, unless you do not mind having neighbors' prying eyes observing every move you make.

How can you achieve privacy when neighboring houses are close?

Visual privacy can be obtained immediately by erecting a tall fence beside the terrace. This will also block out noise somewhat, and it can

PLANTING PROBLEMS. *Above,* a front garden shows a large shade tree, placed to shield the house from the sun. Balancing it is a clump of feathery birches, to contrast in texture and silhouette. Moving the clump to the left would help to reduce the street view into the large window. A tall tree behind a row of shrubs masks a utility pole and accents the border. *Right,* privacy may be obtained from a street above a house by means of a fence or a few small trees or tall shrubs. *Below,* various foliages combine to create privacy. Low evergreens and tall, narrow deciduous trees work well. Or, *right,* a single small tree that spreads, is well branched and thickly leaved can do the job alone.

be made more acceptable and less austere if a climbing rose or some other plant can be placed in front of it. This would be a good spot for an espaliered shrub or tree, if there is sufficient sun and light for it. (See section on espaliering in Chapter 6, page 273.) If there is room in front of it, the fence can back up a shrubbery bed, of course, and tall growing plants could be planted there that would later form a living screen so that the fence might eventually be removed.

Overhead privacy can be achieved two ways. Immediate privacy from the upstairs windows of houses alongside the garden and from a sloping plot behind the garden could be obtained by putting up a slatted trellis or pergola and growing vines on it. The slatted trellis alone would give mottled shade, or complete shade as the vine covered it. The other method would be to plant a shade tree, as tall as you could afford at the moment, and make the trellis a temporary one until the tree grew large enough, spreading wide enough to shade the terrace and also conceal it from various angles.

Plantings around the edges of the property, strategically located to block the view of the garden, would also provide privacy, particularly if evergreens were used. Tall columnar types like arborvitae would be good to use as backups for the lower-growing shrubs in front. Narrow-growing deciduous shrubs would also give summer protection, and as the twigs and branches thickened up, some winter protection would be afforded. Note the list of tall-growing hedge plants in the section on hedges, pages 95–102, that fall into this category.

Is there anything else that should be considered in the private area?
Regional climate is a factor. Extra-hot sun and strong winds should be taken into account in the placement of sitting-out spots as well as the plantings that will offer protection to them. Winds are usually prevalent from one direction and can be controlled in various ways. Windbreaks can be planted on large plots, but on small properties other means must be found to break the force of the wind and divert it. If the property is sloping, the terrace may be sunk by digging out the area. If it is level, the best method is to build a fence, latticed or louvered, which will divert the wind's course and at the same time reduce its strength. Tall-growing plants, evergreen or deciduous, can be situated just inside this fence so that they will someday grow up and add their taller protection and wind-diversion qualities. Placing the terrace in the angle formed by an ell on the house, if there is one, will afford some protection, and a fence and plantings extending outward from one side can give further protection. How wind is diminished in force and diverted is shown in the sketch on page 297.

Sun is welcome on the chilly days of spring and autumn, but it may be a trial on the hotter days of summer. If there is a small spot that will catch the morning and noonday sun spring and fall and will also hold a chair or two, this might become a little private place for the family at those times. For summer the main terrace would be placed where it would get shade at mid-day to afternoon from a spreading tree and in spring and autumn might be a place for afternoon outdoor activities early and late in the seasons respectively, when the leaves are off the tree.

Another method of breaking the sun is the trellis, already spoken of, which would give slatted shade, and allow for ventilation on hot days, but the best recommendation for hot-weather country is to put in immediately as big a shade tree as you can afford, placing it where it will shade the terrace and soon will also shade the roof of the house to keep it cool. A tree taller than one of the middle height might be in order here, as well as a faster-growing type, as shown on the Ten-Year Growth Chart on pages 164–165. For light shade in summer and open growth and more sun in the house in winter in cold areas, the thornless honey locust would be a good choice. It is reasonably quick growing, a handsome tree that gives light shade because of its open structure.

How can a tall utility pole visible from the house be screened?

Utility poles, even when not on your property, are problems. The best solution is to plant a medium to small tree to block the view, a columnar one if the space is constricted, positioning it where it will best screen out the pole from most points of view. However, do not plant any trees that will at maturity grow high enough to interfere with the wires.

Can other "ugliness" be blocked out by plantings?

Shrubbery borders and trees can be used to obscure or conceal most ugly views, but it may take a little while for the plantings to grow up sufficiently. Nevertheless, this aspect of planning should be very much a part of the original laying out and selection of materials to plant. The sooner plantings are put in, the sooner the problem will be solved.

What comes next in planning?

Refer now to your Plant Hardiness Zone, which will govern your choice of plants. Also study your soil and make sure it is of the quality it should be, for it can be adjusted to make it more amenable. See page 317. Consider, too, the exposure of your plot. If it is on a northern slope, the air may be more moist and cool than if it is on a southern slope. Northern slopes get less sun, especially if steep; therefore, they are less likely to dry out and will be cooler, while southern slopes that get more sun are more likely to be drier and warmer. Eastern and western slopes vary less, but eastern ones are likely to be a little cooler in general. These factors will also affect your choice of material.

If there are outcroppings of rock or boulders, what can you do?

Now that hillsides are being utilized more for building, stones and outcroppings in the mountainous and rockier areas have become more of an element to be reckoned with. If these do not interfere with the garden activities or outdoor-living plans, where such outcroppings or big boulders naturally occur and look right, it may be best to leave them and plant around them, making a natural garden. It is less and less necessary to clear the land and make a lawn—the cliché of suburban gardening—and more and more ecology-minded people are turning to natural or wild gardens.

If a stone interferes with plans for a terrace, it can be cut out or blasted out, professional help being recommended for any extensive digging and certainly for blasting if such is needed. If boulders are the problem, they may be bulldozed and moved out of the way, or small ones can be shifted to a place where they can be assembled and combined with several others for a natural look. Plant low-growing plants, arching small flowering shrubs and dwarf needled evergreens with them to give a natural look.

How do you go about laying out beds?

Here is where we encounter composition. Beds next to a house or a fence have a back line that must be straight, following the lines of the structure. It is perfectly acceptable to have square-edged beds and a formal look to the garden, especially if it complements a formal kind of architecture. This is the easiest way to lay out beds. If you want curving edges, lines that go best with informal gardening, the problem is to make these curves look natural and not contrived. One of the main troubles with most beginners' beds is that the curving edge is kinky rather than flowing. Here is where your garden hose will come in handy. Lay it out on the bare ground and adjust the curves in an undulating, flowing line. Step back and look at it from various angles—front, sides, from the house. Are the curves so equal that they look almost like scallops? Are they too abrupt every time the line changes direction? A good bed has an assortment of curves, assuming it is long enough to admit them, and may include big, medium-sized, and small undulations, all connected and rhythmic. This is one of the places where the compositional element of rhythm is most important. Like musical rhythm, there is not a 1, 2, 3, 1, 2, 3 repetition but a 1, 3, 2, 3, 1, 2 kind of repetition, for instance, the numbers standing for small, medium, and large.

When you have outlined the bed to your satisfaction, put in stakes or spade the bed so that the outline is retained. Corrugated metal lawn edging, widely available at garden centers, can be inserted at the edge to keep the lawn from encroaching on the bed and to give a crisp outline.

Is there any way to adjust proportions of a garden by planting?

Small gardens can be made to look larger by the use of perspective principles, adding visual feet to a vista, subtracting length from a too long, too narrow plot. The trick is to use tapering lines to make a shallow area look longer, as demonstrated in the sketches. And by utilizing perspective in size of leaf and careful choice of color, the apparent length can be

ADVANCE RECEDE

COMPOSING WITH LEAF SIZES AND COLORS. Use visual tools of perspective and color to help small areas to look larger, narrow spaces to seem wider. *Left,* large-leaved plants nearby, tiny-leaved ones at far end, and diminishing sizes in between will add visual length to a border. *Right,* light-colored foliage in the foreground on tiny-leaved plants, with leaf size gradually increasing as the border curves toward the big-leaved, deep-colored plant at the end, makes a too long space advance and seem shorter, visually widening a narrow plot.

shortened or lengthened. Big-leaved plants and bold structure in the fore-ground, small-leaved plants and refined habit far away will make vistas seem longer. Visually light and bright colors advance, dark and duller colors recede. Hence, using light colored and bright foliage in the fore-ground—silvery, bluish, yellowish—and the deeper tones—purples and dark greens—in the background will give an illusion of space. These are principles painters utilize in doing landscapes to create in two dimensions the illusion of three-dimensional perspective.

What other compositional elements should be used?

Balance is achieved in a large border by using repetitions of the same plants and textures. For instance, in a border beside a house, repeating the same texture and color at each corner—yew, let us say—introduces an element of good balance. Or the balance may be one of size and weight of color if some other genus is used.

Harmony is achieved by the use of plants to prevent any jarring note in the general interrelationship. This means that with flowering plants that bloom simultaneously no discordant colors of flowers should be placed next to each other. For instance, bright orange and bright magenta set up a violent vibration. Warm pinks go better with scarlet and hot reds, while cool pinks and rose pinks harmonize with crimson. Yellows, oranges, and warm reds are attractive together, especially when some are pastel in tone. Rose pinks and crimsons blend with flowers of bluish or purplish tones. The background is also important in considering colors of flowers. Magentas and pastel orchid pinks do not harmonize with red brick or painted wood walls of yellow-orange or orange or warm reds. It is better with such backgrounds to stick to the warm side of the color chart.

Are there other principles to remember in designing?

Scale is a most important principle, especially in the smaller garden. As shall be discussed at greater length in Chapter 5, tall trees make small, one-story houses look insignificant. Similarly, a preponderance of large-leaved plants can make a border and the house seem smaller. Keep in mind the mature heights expected and chose plants in scale with each other and with the area to be filled. Good borders step up from procumbent or lowest-growing plants to ones of medium height and finally to tall growers at the back. (See sketch, page 60.) Lest this be too rigid, a variety of medium and tall growers are introduced to give an undulating, up and down, in and out effect. And of course there is a need for accent.

Where should accents be placed?

Accents can be strong or they can be modulated, according to the need felt by the creator of the design. An excellent place for an accent is at the center of interest or focal point, which is usually placed at the greatest distance from the observation point. This may be some outstanding specimen plant or it can be something of year-round interest; for instance, a piece of sculpture or an interestingly convoluted piece of driftwood. This is enhanced by plants around it that give contrast in depth of color as well as in the color itself, if the accent is a living plant.

Minor accents would be placed at the corners of the house and at one or more places in the border. Placement might also be determined on the basis of where a masking plant is needed to blot out a utility pole or other ugliness. Another place for accent might be beside a door that is placed in the central area of a façade, to make that door important but not so important an accent (tall) as the corner plants.

If the terrace is used mostly at night, is there any way of making the garden show up?

Garden lighting is one of the frills of gardening that appeals to many, and indeed, lighting brings out new facets everywhere. To light the terrace, keep lights as high as possible so that insects will not be attracted too close to the people on the terrace. The major companies that make lighting appliances have spotlights and diffused-lighting fixtures, which can be placed here and there in the garden, as shown in the illustrations here, to bring out the structure of the various plants and to give a kind of fairy-tale atmosphere to the garden at night. Local dealers in appliances may have such weatherproof-type fixtures for sale, or they can most likely be ordered.

What is an ideal soil for shrub beds and trees that will give trees and shrubs the best start when they are planted?

Ideal soil—one that is right for average plants that do not demand a special soil—would be one that is composed of a variety of elements: humus, sand, clay, and possibly some particles of gravel. Too much clay holds water on the surface where it cannot drain down to root level, and the soil may bake hard in hot summer sun. Too much sand retains little or no water, drains too fast, and does not afford good anchorage for roots. Humus is necessary to lighten the soil, to provide a spongelike quality that

NIGHT IN THE GARDEN need not blot out the beauty of trees and shrubs. It may, in fact, add new dimensions of loveliness as new facets are picked out by night-lighting and new viewpoints discovered. Lit from below, the structure of branches and tree trunks and masses of foliage may be even more striking than in daylight. Shrubbery lit from behind makes dark patterns against a house wall, while textures are often enhanced. (*Westinghouse*)

will retain moisture for sometime yet is open enough so that moisture can drain through when there is an excess. Adding and mixing in well what the natural soil lacks, replenishing it later on if necessary, will adjust soil toward the ideal. Good soil, however, should provide some of its own elements originally and later when compost is added to the top and cultivated in lightly from time to time. The sketches on pages 313 and 315 show how the soil is adjusted according to need.

What is compost?

Compost is usually a mixture of many things: vegetable matter (garden wastes, such as leaves and healthful but dead plants, trimmings from hedges, weeds, and other materials) and occasionally animal matter and manure, all of which have been piled together and have decomposed into a humusy, nutrition-rich dark matter. This usually takes a year or more and is the natural way of returning nutrients and elements to the soil. Roots dredge up and send along minerals and other building elements to make leaves and woody growth. When these are removed or discarded by the plant in nature, they fall to the ground and are eventually incorporated again as they decompose, allowing their elements to be reused by the plants. Leaf mold, of course, is a prime example of natural composting. In our gardens these wastes are removed in order to keep the garden neat and are often burned or sent off with the trash-disposal collection. Valuable nutrients are thereby lost. As fertilizers become more expensive, it is good economy as well as good ecology to compost rich garden wastes and reuse them. The compost when ready will be a deep, dark color, pleasant as a background, and open enough for moisture to penetrate through it. Within a short time even a two-inch depth will have become fertile soil and will be found to be offering up its treasures.

Are there any special instructions for the placement of shrubs and trees?

The best plan is to place them far enough apart to give good space for mature development, but not so far that each will eventually stand alone. A border should be a mass, broken down into submasses of unequal area. Thus, planting two of this and five of that, four of something else and seven of another thing is good thinking. Then, considering how the plants vary in size and in spread, we have to realize that perhaps three of this may equal in mass five of something else, so we must adjust one or the other to get unequal sizes. Or such plantings can be used in other places in the border to balance each other, with some larger or smaller mass between.

For small gardens where a variety of plants is desired, upright-growing medium-sized plants rather than too many sprawlers and spreaders would be a good thought to pursue, varying the picture with a few of other habit. A greater number of upright plants, of course, can be fitted into a border than can the spreading ones.

GROWTH HABIT OF SHRUBS, seen in the upper panel, also demonstrates what a hodgepodge a border might become if all types were planted together. *Upright* has all or most growth ascending. *Spreading* may arch or be horizontal branching, high or low growing. *Angular branching* is often open in habit. *Conical* or *Pyramidal* is most usually found among evergreens, while *Ball, Columnar, Horizontal Oval,* and *Procumbent* or *Prostrate* may be seen in both deciduous and evergreen types. *Picturesque* or *Irregular* will be encountered most often among tall, treelike shrubs. *Vase* shape, with leafage and flowering confined more or less to the top above tall canes or trunks, is also more common among the larger shrubs.

VARIOUS TEXTURES OF SHRUBS are shown in the lower panel. Not all types should ever be combined in one bed, of course. Stiff needles of spruce create a fuzzy, distinctive texture quite different from that of the arborvitae, whose scale leaves are grouped in vertical clusters. Big leathery evergreen leaves of rhododendron contrast sharply with tiny fine ones of a semi-evergreen prostrate cotoneaster. Opposite-leaved arching branches on many shrubs have a more formal aspect than the upswept branches of feathery, low-growing junipers. Irregular-trunked, picturesque tall shrubs such as nannyberry contrast with well-clothed pines, whose limbs may conceal trunk. Needles may vary from short, stiff one-inch kinds to those of plumey long-leaved pine, well over a foot long.

What should the beginner avoid when choosing shrubs?

The most common mistake is to choose one of this and one of that, making the border into a veritable plum pudding of variety. The sketch on page 53 shows how distracting such an effect can be, although it also graphically shows the various elements of a border—habit of growth and leaf types and textures. If the area is small or if it is too narrow for much chance for varietal difference, it is a good plan to use the same plants all the way through.

What suggestions for procedure would you give a beginner?

If you are truly interested in becoming a gardener, start immediately to get to know plants. Visit arboretums and botanical gardens where plants are marked, and note names, approximate habit of growth, and any other information you can assemble. This will train your eye to know what to look for and give you a good idea of the kind of questions to ask when visiting nurseries to select plants or when reading catalogs.

Do not try to plant the entire plot at once but take one section and develop it, say the front garden or as much of it as can be done at one time. Invest your biggest outlays in the slow-growing plants—shade trees, large-sized ones with a good ball of earth around the roots; slow-growing dwarf evergreens that may take some years to develop; privacy plantings, so that they can start to grow immediately and soon deliver the privacy for which they were chosen; wind breaks and wind-stopping plantings, so that they can get established and perform their function as soon as possible. But perhaps first of all, get your soil into condition for the first plantings as soon as possible. Then work on the next area to be planted and improve that soil, then the next, and so on. Set up some sort of schedule of priorities and follow it year by year so that the garden progresses in orderly fashion toward the goal.

There is no satisfaction equal to that of the gardener who has had intimate contact with his plantings over the years, working with them and nurturing them, shaping them, training them, most of all coming to love them. While scientists go on arguing the merits or lack of merit in the theory that plants respond to love, there is no equestion but that the person who cares for his garden and tries to put himself in tune with nature, not expecting too much from plants but working with nature in all ways, will be the one who gets the best results and, incidentally, the most fun out of his garden.

4

Shrubs and How to Select Them

In the past, shrubs were often taken for granted when gardens were being planned, or ignored in favor of the showy effects and floral fireworks of annual and perennial flowers. Gardeners were often oblivious to the natural law that makes both perennials and annuals transient and impermanent. This is not to say that the latter do not have a secure place in the garden but merely that shrubs, because of their permanence, should also take a prominent place in planning floral effects. Their attributes need little emphasis to the true gardener, however, for in America there has been a growing awareness of the useful contributions shrubs make to the garden and, best of all, of how little work it takes to get a bonanza of blossoms year after year. There is still, however, a general lack of understanding of this fact, particularly among beginning gardeners. This may account for the unimaginative, dull, and uninteresting plantings one sees, repetitious and banal in their combinations and often in the choices of material.

A treasure house of shrubs is there waiting to be tapped, a wealth of choices and a myriad of combinations for imaginative gardeners to explore and develop. The trend today is toward using hardy, native material that allows gardeners to enjoy it without slaving to keep it alive. Nurserymen, too, have been augmenting such staple plants with more unusual genera and varieties and with improved flowers, more refined forms, and clearer colors in the blossoms. However, our feeling is that the staples need not be ignored or scorned. Often they are stocked because they have proved to be hardy, their reliability is time tested, and they will grow as easily in the home garden as they have in nursery rows. Producing blossoms dependably, sometimes with dividends of fruit or interesting foliage, they are an asset to the do-it-yourself gardener. The staple shrubs when mixed in with more unusual types will probably complement and enhance them.

Too often the rarity of plants from foreign parts is the standard judgment by which certain gardeners evaluate plants. Familiarity may breed contempt for native genera as well as for the widely available staple shrubs. Yet if nobody had yet discovered, let us say, slender deutzia (*Deutzia grandiflora*) or the widely planted bridalwreath spirea (*Spiraea prunifolia*) they might prove to be the find of the century and gardeners would flock to buy them. That is why I feel we should look at the plant, not its wide availability in choosing shrubs.

Native shrubs are another aid to the aspiring gardener who has little time to spend on his garden. With the wide interest today in native plant

HILLS OF SNOW hydrangea, a small shrub that blooms from early July on, is often so covered with its snowball-like flowers that it resembles a snowdrift. (*Paul E. Genereux*)

gardens, shrubs from your region might be utilized for a natural woodsy effect. Augment them judiciously with some of the hardy plants that may have improved flowering qualities—size, color—habit of growth that will mean less training and pruning or some other bred-in quality that improves on the species. You will be guided by the Hardiness Zone Map (page 18) and the zonal preferences in the shrub lists.

SELECTING SHRUBS

At first glance, the problem of choosing shrubs may appear to be a staggering one. Even from our pared-down lists you will appreciate the richness of what riches there are to choose from. Do not be intimidated; it is not really complex. It can become a fascinating game as you go along, sorting out possibilities and evaluating them, then cutting down the list bit by bit. It becomes easier as you get into the spirit and as you work out the final compositions from your choices.

The first thing to do is to decide what you would *like* to grow. Then check this list against what can grow in your climate and soil and general conditions. It might further help if we first make sure that we know what we are looking for.

DEFINING AND CATEGORIZING SHRUBS

What, exactly, is a shrub?

Although it is hard to say "exactly" what a shrub is, a general definition is that they are perennial woody plants of various sizes, shapes, and habits, usually developing multiple stems rather than a single trunk. Another distinction is that, while trees (some evergreens are exceptions) discard their lower branches as they grow, most shrubs are likely to retain theirs. It is difficult to define shrubs by height, since many shrubs grow as tall as small trees; others are low growing and of tender growth so that they fall into the category called "woody perennials"—that is, plants that persist from year to year, growing new wood to replace dead or spent wood. As you can see, this embraces a great deal of plant territory, particularly if you include all the shrubs of the world.

Basic sizes, shapes, and branching habits of shrubs.

How can we narrow down such a tremendous list?

We do this, first of all, by pinpointing the location of the garden in which the shrubs are to be planted. Consult the Plant Hardiness Zone Map, page 18, to see in what major zone your garden lies. Then run through the list of shrubs and check all those that are listed for that zone. Immediately the list shrinks a great deal, even if you include as pertinent the fact that most shrubs will grow considerably to the south of the zone listed. If your garden is exposed to wind or if it lies in a low spot to which frost and cold air drains and stays, it may be well to consider plants a little hardier than your location would indicate; in other words, the zone to the north of yours—unless of course, you know that the plants you want are growing successfully in similar conditions nearby. If there is a great deal of wind, it might be possible to plant the particular plants you want in a protected place, or to erect wind-deflecting fences or other protection to prevent the drying and bending caused by winds. Evergreens and broad-leaved evergreens are particularly vulnerable to drying winds.

What are broad-leaved evergreens? Are they shrubs?

Many are shrubs, although some small trees and a few large ones fall into this category. Broadly speaking, there are only two kinds of evergreens: the ones with narrow leaves, such as pine and spruce, and those with broad leaves that may be tiny, as on some hollies of dwarf habit, or large leathery ones found on certain rhododendrons. For convenience, the lists in succeeding chapters will group all narrow-leaved evergreens as "needled" evergreens. This will include the scale-leaved sorts such as arborvitae, juniper, white cedar and a few others.

Broad-leaved evergreens is equally inclusive as a category. Some gardeners feel that only the acid-soil plants should be included. While rhododendrons, certain azaleas, hollies and others are certainly acid-soil plants—and appear on our lists—there are many others that retain their leaves all year and should be included. Some broad-leaved plants are rather tender, dependably hardy only in a mild to warm climate. Others are quite hardy even in the northern states, although somewhat demanding in the soil requirements for certain genera. Acid-soil plants thrive naturally in a humusy, adequately moist soil with good drainage. Soils can be adjusted to supply needed acid, if it is not present. See page 321. Probably a good many plants can be eliminated from your list on the grounds of hardiness, or soil requirements, if you do not have soil that meets their needs.

Are all needled evergreens hardy?

Many, perhaps even most, evergreens that bear needles or scale needles are hardy, a number of them growing quite far north into Canada and high in mountain altitudes, as you will note from the hardiness-zone numerals on our list. Others are rather finicky and insist on warmer climates, while a few are desert subjects or dry-soil plants that will do well only in their particular milieu. Narrow the list further by eliminating any that do not meet your zone and soil requirements.

BORDERS

What is the next step in narrowing down the list?

The next step is to begin to consider the remaining plants from other angles, to see how they may best be utilized. Creating a shrub border is a

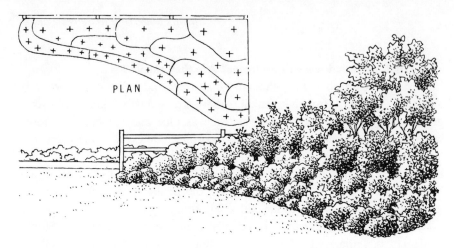

INTEGRATING SHRUBS. Putting a border together is more than merely digging holes and planting bushes. To get the most out of it, plan in advance and know how many of each you will need. First choose the tallest, placed for height at the back and in corners. Next select the front-border shrubs closest to the spectator. Then choose the in-between heights and kinds. Some should be upright, some spreading, while the front ones may be prostrate. All may be blossoming if you wish, and consider a few needled or broad-leaved evergreens. Plant several of one kind together rather than one or two only—this latter makes a spotty and unimpressive border. Uneven quantities are also desirable so that uniformity is not rigid or exactly the same in numbers. Try to select shrubs that bloom at different times so that there is continuous bloom so far as possible. *Sketch*: Plan indicates quantities and sizes of diameter. A low planting at the end lures the visitor to explore behind it.

little like putting together a jigsaw puzzle. Shrubs must be fitted together with a little overlapping or overhang here, a little extra space allowed there for development, both horizontally and vertically. The diagram here shows a border in profile and in plan, giving the general effect to strive for. The front-border plants dress up the edge, then step up and up to the point where the back-border plants complete the composition. One or two really tall shrubs or small trees may be added to give height (page 52) at corners and where it would be most effective in the back row. Note in the plan here that the circles indicate *mature* diameter expected. All borders should be analyzed this way and a general pattern of low to high plantings followed.

What do you mean by "mature diameter"?

Borders are planted with young shrubs that may be only a fifth or even less of the eventual height and spread of the mature, older plant. In order to provide optimum conditions for the shrubs, with proper room

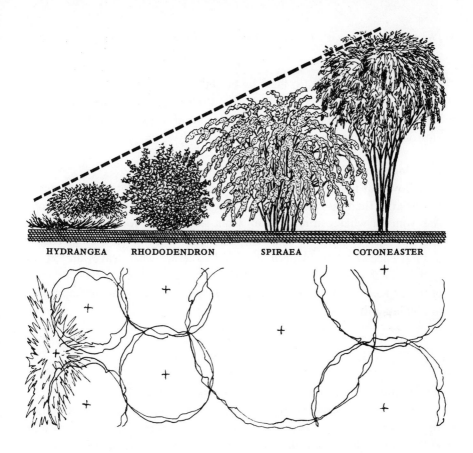

HYDRANGEA   RHODODENDRON   SPIRAEA   COTONEASTER

to develop and display their beauty of structure, adequate spacing between plants should be worked out. Wherever reliable spacing information was available, it has been incorporated in our lists. Tiny shrubs look lost when first planted and cut back, but within a surprisingly short period of time they will fill out the space provided for them.

Should all borders be planted with rows of plants stepping up?

Only in the general sense. To give variety and spice to the composition, the "rows" may be varied by plantings of slightly higher or lower shrubs, varied in quantity—five, seven, eleven—thus giving a kind of undulating or three-dimensional effect from various viewpoints, avoiding the monotony of rigid height regulation.

Suppose the border is a kind of projecting peninsula extending outward, so it is seen from both sides?

It should be planted with the taller shrubs in the center and then taper down on both sides.

61

Should we list shrubs, then, by height?

Yes, selecting them from the list at the end of the chapter and checking for hardiness will give you a quick checklist. Note also the time of blossoming, if they are flowering plants.

Once we have shrubs categorized, what is next?

Now that the limitations are beginning to be apparent, the next step is to work out the best combinations of the shrubs you have to choose from. Ask yourself what you really want from shrubs: Do you want all-year or seasonal effects? What do you want most—flowers, fruit, leaf color and/or textural effects? winter pattern and good structure when leaves are off the plant? winter color from twigs and shoots? combinations of two or more of these? Knowing the right answers to your questions is the best approach to obtaining the best results.

FLOWERING SHRUBS

Suppose what is wanted most are flowers, what then?

This can be the most creative as well as the most crucial point of designing a border. A good border has a blooming sequence that overlaps in time so that in spring, at least, there is never a time when it is out of bloom; an ideal border pushes the growing, blooming season as far as possible in both directions, early and late. Now there are two areas of consideration—height and blooming period. Colors come next, so you must work for harmony. Some gardeners keep to a single color range—all white, all pink, all red, all orange, and so on—or to a related color range—such as yellow, orange, and orange-red, with pastel shades of these colors varying the brighter, deeper shades. It is a good plan to keep colors related in other ways, too. Warm reds go best with oranges, yellow-oranges, and yellows; the scarlets and vermillions and the pastels of coral pink and flesh pink also relate to these warm shades. The cool reds—magenta, crimson, bluish pinks—are better with white, lavender, blues, and purples. The background against which the flowers will be seen should also be considered.

Orange-red brick walls are not a suitable background for magenta and cool reds, orchid and bright purplish flowers. Similarly, placing, let us say, an orange-flowered azalea beside a vivid magenta-red azalea (something one sees too often) or an egg-yellow forsythia beside an early orchid-

FLOWERING ALMOND puts on a dashing display in spring, every branch and twig studded with double pink blooms. Give it room to spread and develop. (*Paul E. Genereux*)

tone Korean rhododendron (*R. mucronulatum*) sets up unpleasant visual vibrations in the perceptive observer. White and ivory do much to pull together and knit color compositions into either exciting or serene effects.

What other considerations of color should we take into account?

Dark or deep colors tend to recede into the background of darkish foliage, though viewed close they are often quite beautiful. But for garden effect, particularly at some distance from the point of observation, brighter and lighter colors will give a gayer air to the border. Blues and purples— though not their pastel shades—are also receding colors and are best used close to and against light walls. For shady areas or against evergreens and other dark leafy backgrounds the lighter-toned flowers are more effective. Against white or pale-colored walls and in full sunshine, brilliant and even darkish flowers can be effective.

63

Are there shrubs aside from roses that are fragrant?

Indeed, there are many, and the list is long and exciting. In the South the gardenia or Cape-jasmine and the common white jasmine—this latter a subshrub that is semiclimbing—are the most fragrant. Elsewhere, many of the azaleas, especially the native swamp azalea, lilacs, sweet mock-orange, star magnolia, the honeysuckles, abelia, daphne, deutzia, Korean spice or fragrant viburnum, Burkwood viburnum, and other viburnums, as well as a number of other shrubs are fragrant in varying degrees. In the flowering shrub list (page 102) you will find fragrant flowering shrubs specially designated.

FRUITING SHRUBS

Do all flowering plants also produce fruit?

Most produce fruit in the sense that they have seed pods, if not the bright-colored berries one usually means when referring to fruiting shrubs. And not all shrubs that are attractive or spectacular when fruit is present have conspicuous flowers as well. However, many fruiting shrubs do also have interesting and attractive foliage and make a good textural foil for other more spectacular flowering shrubs. Certain shrubs—hollies, for instance—will fruit only if male and female plants are present so that fertilizing can take place. Some such plants may have a male branch grafted to the female plant and this is usually effective in producing the desired berries or fruit. Some quite spectacular flowering shrubs produce no visible fruit, or at least garden-effective fruit, and among the needled evergreens, yews, with their bright red drupes, and junipers, with small silvery-to-blue berries, are interesting close up, but from a distance their fruit is not as impressive as that of other plants. A few plants are grown mainly for foliage color or effects of texture and give a good account of themselves in the border composition. See the lists of fruiting shrubs (those requiring both sexes are marked) at the end of this chapter.

Should all fruiting shrubs be planted together in the border?

Not necessarily, unless you have a particular reason for doing so. Perhaps you have a border visible from a particular window from which you might watch the birds feasting off the berries; if so, fruiting shrubs would logically be planted together there. But in general the berried or fruiting shrubs should be planted where they belong, first by height, then by color of blossom or foliage, and time of bloom.

Are shrub fruits edible?

Some are but many are not, except by birds, and even they eschew a few kinds. Some are either poisonous or should be avoided for other reasons, the red drupes of yew for instance, which are attractive to birds but must be avoided by humankind. Some, such as beach plum and Manchu cherry, are edible and make excellent jams and jellies. Make sure that you know the fruit is edible before you essay its ingestion.

LEAF TEXTURES

What are leaf textures? How do they affect borders?

Any good composition—painting, music, embroidery, or garden border—should have variety, subtle or bold, just as in working with colors we want variety but also harmony. So it is with leaf textures. Leaf sizes, shapes, surfaces, the way they grow on the twig or branch—all these have an effect that is textural in the overall composition. Small, big, medium sized; pointed, rounded, single or multiple; wide or narrow; coarse or refined—all of these contribute to texture. Fine leaves give a feathery, fragile appearance that contrasts interestingly with sturdier and heavier leaves. Sparse leaves give a different appearance than close-set ones.

In addition, there is leaf color, which is important both in summer and in autumn. Using leaves alone, you can make a fascinating color composition, and for part of the growing season that is what you will have, for not all shrubs and not in all locations will flower throughout the entire season. Choose from yellowish leaves, yellow-green, green-green, blue-green, bluish (especially in evergreens), reddish or purplish, even very dark foliage toning toward black. There is also the question of surface. Some leaves are dull-surfaced while others are glossy, and some are in between, with only a moderate gloss. Silvery leaves are another important factor in composing with shrubs: some are silvery all over, many are some shade of green above but slightly silvery to bright silver or whitish on the

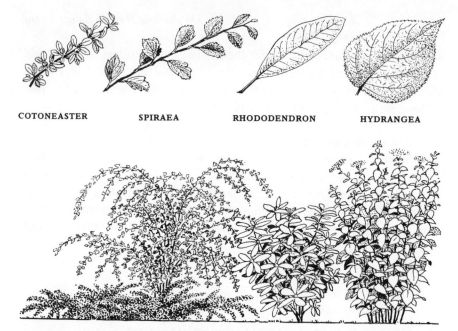

COTONEASTER   SPIRAEA   RHODODENDRON   HYDRANGEA

COMPOSING WITH LEAF SIZES. Varying sizes and textures as well as leaf colors make a simple border enchanting, even when not in flower. The cotoneaster has tiny dark-green glossy leaves; Vanhoutte spiraea, pale green leaves, larger but more fragile in appearance. Rhododendrons have long medium-green leaves, rather leathery, in a spokelike arrangement about the blossom bud. All hydrangeas have rather large leaves, in colors ranging from deep, glossy green on the blue and pink kinds to dull textured yellowish green on the lacecap and hills-of-snow sorts. The four illustrated here demonstrate how vital the leaf size is in planning a border, using size, color, and texture to achieve variety, even when the shrub is not in flower.

underside. Many leaves are different shades of color on the upper and undersides, the underside being always lighter. This makes for a certain excitement, a kind of staccato note when a breeze stirs the leafy twigs, flickering the silvery undersides and sparkling the green of the border with additional interest. While color is not strictly texture, it falls within that general area because of these qualities.

SHADE

If there are old trees already in the garden, can you plant shrubs near them and would shade be a problem?

Shade does restrict choices, for there are a great many shrubs that require sun or at least sun for a good part of the day. However, many more

66

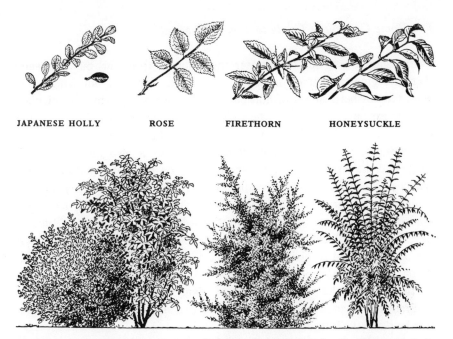

JAPANESE HOLLY   ROSE   FIRETHORN   HONEYSUCKLE

TEXTURAL AND COLOR VARIETY are desirable if not too obviously displayed. *Left,* small dark green glossy leaves such as those on Japanese holly are a good foil for dull, light green, or green foliage like the alternate leaves on roses. Sometimes leaves have a wrinkled texture, as found on rugosa roses. Firethorn has myriads of smallish, discreetly shiny leaves alternately arranged on branches that terminate in many sharply tapering new shoots. Pointed and wide-spaced opposite leaves, shown here on a honeysuckle, give still another accent to texture. Note how shrub silhouettes are affected by the way leaves are arranged, by the way they are held on the stem, and imagine how their glossiness or dullness and different colors spice up a shrubbery border.

shrubs than one might think are tolerant of part shade, and quite a number will grow under high shade and in dappled light. Those that in their natural habitat grew in similar locations would be the first choices.

In a garden where there is already some shade, what shrubs would be able to cope with this problem?

Many shrubs do not require shady conditions, but quite a number will tolerate it in varying degrees. Only a few shrubs can endure deep shade. In general, the greater the shade the less flowering and fruiting will occur; as light increases, shrubs will correspondingly produce more bloom and fruit. All plants require light, though it need not always be direct sunlight. Plants will grow on the north side of a house, provided there are no

67

overhanging trees, but the greater the distance from the building (and therefore greater light on all sides), the better they will flourish. In the wild, the northern slopes of hillsides usually have a different kind of plant from those on the sunny southern slopes. This has to do with a number of factors, one of which is the drying effect of the sun's rays on the soil, northern slopes being generally more moist, but it also has to do with shade and the lessening of light—particularly on steep slopes. Let us take our cue from this. In open woodlands with high shade and only dappled sunlight many shrubs will do rather well. Tree limbs are high, making a kind of umbrella, and the sun filters through or perhaps at some time of day full sun will actually reach the plant. Protection from the hottest sun at midday but receiving it in the morning and late afternoon is a condition that many shrubs will enjoy. Shaded shrubs may tend to grow more spindly and tall than the same sort of plant in the open unless they are naturally shade-adapted plants. If they are in a shaded bed, they may therefore be planted a little closer.

Many broad-leaved evergreen shrubs, such as box, barberries, hollies, rhododendrons, and azaleas, will profit from having their leaves protected in winter from direct sunlight. They all need some sun, of course, but can do with merely strong light. At the end of the chapter is a list of shade-tolerant shrubs, some more tolerant than others.

For a hillside garden that is to be kept natural, native plants would be desirable to reduce care and make hardiness more certain. Where can such plants be obtained?

First try local nurseries, or ask your county agent for recommendations about a possible place to purchase them. Many nurseries, particularly in the West and Far West are now meeting this need, offering indigenous deciduous and evergreen shrubs. If there is no establishment in your own region, then perhaps you can arrange with a landowning friend or a farmer who has a tract where such plants grow naturally to let you dig up a few plants. The township road office is also a good place to go to ask about projected roads where you might get in ahead of the bulldozers and "liberate" or rescue some natives. Do not attempt to go in without permission, for the least offense you might be committing would be trespassing, and others might be charged against you.

Do not try to dig up big plants, thinking you will save years of development. In nurseries, plants are root-pruned year after year to keep

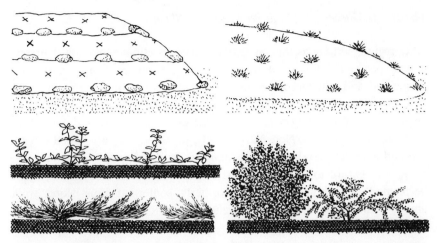

HOLDING SOIL ON HILLSIDES. Ground cover plants cannot hold soil on steep bare-soil slopes until they become established and roots spread. *Left:* Burlap or plastic strips held in place with stones and stakes protect against washouts. The plants are set in the x-cuts in the covering. *Right:* On gentle slopes, plant ground covers and space them; keep heavily mulched as plants grow and cover the soil and mulch. *Below:* Some plants spread by rooting runners that make new plants as they touch the soil. Others are merely prostrate, not often rooting, but with good cover potentials. *Right:* Not all ground cover plants are prostrate; some grow 18 to 24 inches tall, some are low arching sorts, interlacing in undulating mounds to give dimensional interest.

roots short and bushy. In nature, roots straggle everywhere in search of nutrients; the tap root (the main feeding root) is often big, and cutting off a tap root will reduce drastically any chance of survival so that all your work and time will have been spent in vain. Digging in rocky soil is also difficult and tricky when tracing roots. Therefore, the answer is to choose a small plant, dig it carefully with as many roots as possible and as long as possible. Be sure the main or tap root is virtually intact, and if you cannot get a ball of soil, have a bucket of water for immersing the root system, or a piece of wet sacking to wrap up the roots. Put a piece of plastic sheeting around the sacking to reduce the danger of roots drying out. Once home heel in or plant the shrub immediately, and don't forget to cut tops back to compensate for loss of feeding roots. See Chapter 7, where planting procedures are detailed.

Should all plants in a native garden be authentic and indigenous?

Unless your purpose is to create a completely native botanical garden, you may fill in with any nursery-grown specimens or shrubs from any other region, so long as they are suitable to your climate and soil. Nursery-grown specimens of both native plants and "immigrants" are more likely to succeed and will recover more quickly than those dug up in the wild. And many plants that are not true natives may give a greater display of flowers and/or fruits because they have been developed and hybridized for these very qualities. Non-native plants, provided they are suited to your soil and climate, may be the very thing to provide extra interest and give color and texture to your plantings. Mountain laurel, for instance, might be planted under high shade on a northerly, somewhat moist slope, while any of a number of the junipers might be used for a sunny and somewhat dry southern slope.

Should shrubs be traditional kinds to go with traditional houses?

This will depend largely on the taste of the owners and whether or not they wish to follow traditional dicta for plants and plantings. In defense of changing and revitalizing the plantings so usual in the past, it might be pointed out that in colonial times, for instance, there were no "foundation plantings" of the sort that have been installed around repro-ductions of houses of that period. Gardens were formal and usually bisym-metrical, and for the person interested in authenticity, re-creating an Early American garden will be a most worthwhile pastime. But it need not restrict others who wish to improvise and create something of the aura of the period without slavishly following in the paths of the past. On the other hand, it would be quite exciting to see someone with a totally modern house create a garden that is not in the present cliché of the Oriental style as visualized by people who often overload a "Japanese" garden with more plants and genera than a Japanese would ever dream of using. A daring gardener might boldly design a modern garden and use, let us say, old roses. However, they would not be set in the formal and well-worn patterns of the past but would be integrated into a design compatible with the freshness of the modern house.

Should shrubs be planted first and trees later?

This is not often recommended, because trees usually take longer to reach maturity, and if a large tree is purchased, the price is likely to be costly enough for the average budget that shrub planting will have to be delayed for a year or so. A shrub, on the other hand, being smaller and less costly, can be replaced if a wrong choice is made or if, within a short time, it is decided that moving it to another location would be desirable.

Because of the smaller root spread, controlling the composition of the soil is easier for shrubs, too, than it is for wide-spreading trees.

FOLIAGE

What shrubs produce good autumn color and also have good summer foliage?

Autumn color is somewhat dependent upon the location of the garden, just as it is for trees. High-altitude areas in many places and most of the lower lands in the Northeast are the areas for brilliant, sometimes spectacular, foliage displays. Southward the gardens become less brilliant, even though leaves do undergo a change before falling. But in the higher reaches of the southern Appalachians there is a good bit of autumn color wherever there is deciduous material and where it is likely to be chilly. In the West, there are many spots where the native shrubs as well as introduced material will color quite vividly. This would be east of the coastal ranges in the Northwest and along the eastern slopes of the Rocky Mountains, particularly in the northerly regions. Here quite brilliant color is to be seen frequently. The list at the end of this chapter, therefore, cannot be applied equally over the entire country. It must be considered regionally. A good guide is to observe and note autumn color. Local queries also should elicit information regarding autumn coloration in your area.

Do variegated-leaved shrubs make the border more interesting?

Most landscape designers would agree, but with strong reservations. Leaf variegation occurs because of some upset in the plant's chlorophyll system, the imbalance of components making leaves spotted, sometimes outlined with a color that differs from the basic natural color of the leaf. When this becomes set in the propagated plants, it can be a novel and often beautiful attribute. But like all bizarre elements, a sparing use is indicated, and as accents, they can often be quite telling. Too many variegated plants in a border, however, gives a restless, exciting effect that will destroy the essential serenity associated with nature. On the other hand, variegations or white- or yellow-edged leaves will contribute zest to an all-green leafy border if placed where this accent will strike the right note. A shady border, beds against a dark house, or somber evergreen backgrounds will be lightened and lent interest by using a shrub or two of variegated

71

foliage. Similarly, shrubs with light green or yellow-green foliage, silvery or pale bluish green leaves will also heighten interest in a shady spot.

What other colors of foliage are there?

Myriads of shades are found in shrub leaves. Some have brighter green leaves than others, some have a distinctly yellowish or yellow-green cast, some are reddish, purplish or bronzy in color. Shiny-leaved plants will give a subtle lift to leafage that is dull or nonglossy. Judicious employment of these in the border composition bring a subdued excitement to a border so that even when it is not in flower it is likely to attract the eye pleasantly. A few shrubs may sport brightly colored foliage in spring, as leaves emerge. Later this color will change into the more sober hues of the summer color. Some have colors other than green all summer and give the gardener a rich palette to work with. A few of these leap to mind immediately: the smaller Japanese maples—reds, yellow-greens, plum colored; the red-leaved barberries; and some of the weigelas and a couple of honeysuckles have a purplish cast to their leaves that is telling in the summer border. Purple smoke-bush with purplish leaves is worthy of noting here. Some evergreens take on a different hue in winter: Some junipers, greenish silver or bluish silver in summer, may have tones in winter ranging from pinkish to purplish, adding gaiety to the winter landscape. Not all junipers change, of course, but according to variety this can be a most welcome change when winter comes and spring seems far behind.

All-season yellow makes the vicary golden privet stand out, while the yellow-leaved sweet mockorange will darken only a little during the summer. The use of silver, as well as gold, can make a treasure out of a border. Silvery leaved plants range from light, feathery types to quite substantial leaves. Also don't forget the leaves that are green to dark green above but quite silvery below or perhaps a lighter, brighter green.

When the shrubs are bare of leaves in winter, are there any that are still interesting?

Winter is when the true habit of growth shows, of course, when the skeleton is exposed. Some are quite interesting, either from a distance or when closely examined. The corkscrew willow, actually a small tree that can be kept to large-shrub proportions, has contorted and twisted twigs and branch structure that is at its most interesting in winter. Likewise, the corky growth on the twigs of the winged euonymus and its dwarf variety *Euonymus alta* 'Compacta' are most unusual and most apparent after the beautiful rose-colored autumn leaves have fallen. Other shrubs are memorable in winter because of their twig color. The red-twigged Tatarian dogwood and the even more brilliant Siberian dogwood are well known for winter interest. Our native red osier dogwood also is red twigged on the younger twigs and shoots, brighter sometimes than others according to the moisture and the season. Many of the species of rose native to America are also red barked and when bare in winter shine out in the drab landscape, sporting their red seed pods called hips.

Shrubs with yellowish to really yellow bark include the yellowtwigged dogwood and several willows. Other shrubs may have green or dull greenish bark. Kerria and broom are examples of green-barked shrubs. But most shrubs are grayish to brownish, though some grays are quite light and shine in the winter sun, while the brownish ones may be toned toward orange, as is the case with spiraea 'Anthony Waterer' and certain others. If you select your shrubs in late winter or earliest spring when they are dormant, you can tell pretty well what their winter color will be. Evergreen shrubs occasionally have colored bark, but it may be obscured by the foliage so that it matters less than with deciduous ones. The listing at the end of the chapter indicates some of the good shrubs for bark color.

SEVERE ENVIRONMENTAL CONDITIONS

Are there shrubs that will endure polluted air and other city conditions?

Few plants grow really well where these conditions are severe, and the best hope is for survival and slow development. But with ecologists and the general public awakened and agitating for relief, the future is somewhat brighter than it was some years ago. Already some cities are less polluted, and more, it is hoped, will follow suit. Meantime, city gardeners are finding some shrubs that will survive the rigors of town life and the hurdles of the city environment that must be surmounted—sour soil, too little water, sometimes almost no ground water, smoke and polluting fumes from industry, poor light or at times no sun at all for a good part of the day due to shading by buildings.

Evergreens are not always recommended unless the pollution is light. Needled and broad-leaved are both poor candidates for survival, for they retain their leaves together with the soot and dust that collect on them. Deciduous shrubs that discard old leaves once a year rid themselves of these encrustations and next season grow new leaves. Frequently washing off the leaves with a hose during the summer will help to free the leaf openings that absorb air and exude oxygen, but it may be impossible to wash off all the fallout. Some commercial firms set evergreens in tubs or planters and as often as need be—twice a year, usually—replace them with new plants. This is expensive, of course, but most of us feel it is better than employing the tawdry plastic plants that soon are dirty and drab and never give any semblance of a natural look.

The list at the end of the chapter is comprised of plants found by many gardeners to have city survival potential. Check your hardiness zone.

What are some good shrubs for soil that is rather dry and sandy?

If the soil is naturally dry and not totally sand (as at the seashore or in a desert), there are a number of shrubs that might grow reasonably well with a bit of watering and some encouragement. The soil will prove better for them if it is improved with humus, compost, or peat moss in order to hold moisture a bit longer than it now does. If this is done, and as the soil is improved more and more, the list can be far longer than the one we append at the end of this chapter, limited to shrubs that can be expected to adapt to dry conditions better than others. The list must not be considered infallible, though, for it cannot meet all conditions and needs everywhere. Desert conditions, for instance, demand their own peculiar kinds of plants. See desert gardening, page 248.

Are there shrubs that will endure moist and even wet soils?

Many shrubs grow naturally in such conditions, and quite a number of others will adapt to or be tolerant of moist soils. The method of planting shown on page 254 in the sketch will often work where soils are too moist due to a high water table or poor drainage. Then there are the plants that naturally like or even need moisture. Certain of the shrubby dogwoods live in places where moist soil is the rule, even though they may live about as well on average and drier soils. Many broad-leaved evergreens are moisture lovers, though they do not want constantly wet soils. Rhododendrons and azaleas are rather shallow-rooted plants, which fact enables them to live in soils with conditions other plants might resent. The native American spice bush is hardy even in Zone 4 and occurs usually in moist and boggy conditions, although usually in summer the moisture abates somewhat. One of the native shrubs called swamp azalea, grows in moist

AZALEAS, wherever conditions are suited to them, make most spectacular spring displays, huge masses of blooms in brilliant colors or pale pastel shades. (*Paul E. Genereux*)

to wet soil but has flourished on a rather dry north-sloping bank on my own property. But the list of moisture-tolerant shrubs is too long to cover here, so it will be found at the end of this chapter.

Are there shrubs that will grow in acid soil?

A number of shrubs will grow best in soil that is moderately acid to acid. Some require it if they are to flourish at all. Planted in neutral or near-neutral soil many will grow well if the soil is given periodic treatments to increase the acidity. See pages 320–321.

Seashore conditions are hard on plants. What will grow there?

Try plants that grow naturally along seashores. A good many others, particularly cultivated plants, will endure the conditions if certain requirements are met. Sandy soil, increasingly sandy nearer the shore, should be adjusted by adding more humus and topsoil. If necessary, deep beds should be created that will retain moisture longer. One of the most trying conditions is salt spray, which is whipped inland by the wind. Many of the plants on the list at the end of this chapter will endure salt spray as well as other conditions. They adapt to seashore life.

If the area available is very narrow but with a high wall behind it, can shrubs be planted to make this wall interesting?

Any number of shrubs, many of them reasonably tall, will fill the bill here. The trick is to train them against the wall, either espaliering them so that they make a definite pattern or merely keeping their outgrowing branches and twigs trimmed back so that they are flattened against the wall. See page 273. Pyracanthas, the flowering and fruiting firethorns, take very well to this treatment and any of the taller hedge plants might be used this way. Or, for patterned espaliering, consider Hicks yew, some of the junipers, forsythia, Japanese quince, camellia, and any other shrubs suitable to your region. This will take extra work, of course, because keeping such plants in trim is more demanding than planting shrubs in the open and allowing them to develop as they naturally would. For a wider bed, another solution would be to choose columnar-growing shrubs or evergreens and plant them in the area, keeping them from encroaching on the walk or driveway or other boundary by occasional pruning back of straggling branches.

Some people say that shrubs flower for only a little while so they are not important to grow in the garden. Is this true?

This is about as true as the statement that great literature should be digested and the story given to save people the trouble of reading the whole books. Certainly it is true that most shrubs and flowering trees blossom for only a few weeks, more or less, depending on the climate and the particular season. We do not expect Fourth of July fireworks to go on all year; wouldn't it be tiresome if they did? But half the fun of gardening is watching the season advance and enjoying the seasonal overlapping of the flowers and fruits that many shrubs produce. And then, of course, there is the textural display and the color of the leaves to enjoy, not to mention their autumn colorings. To think of flowers only in terms of "investment returns" is to shortchange yourself. Insensitive people do not make good gardeners, for one must be capable of recognizing subtleties and not just the obvious and the commonplace.

What makes gardeners go on gardening is the developing sensitivity within themselves of which they may not have been at first aware. Then, one fine day, it is as if a door had opened and the light streamed forth. They wonder why they did not see this revelation before; and the revelations never cease. Some people garden because they love it, some because they must since it is expected of anyone having a house and a plot of ground, and many who may start out reluctantly get caught up in the delights of gardening and become passionate gardeners when they find themselves in tune with the world at last.

BROAD-LEAVED EVERGREEN SHRUBS

Broad-leaved evergreens will grow in our region. Which are the best?

"The best" is often a matter of opinion and in any case covers a great deal of territory. Don't forget that it will also depend on your hardiness zone and in many cases on the amount of moisture present or applied to the soil. However, the following short list may be useful. Check locally to see if conditions can be met.

Zone 7: Camellias, common and sasanqua; Dahoon; thorny eleagnus; also many shrubs from the northerly lists.

Zone 6 and south: Hollies (English, Chinese, Yaupon and Japanese); leatherleaf mahonia; holly osmanthus; pyracantha, scarlet firethorn; and others from the northern lists.

Zone 5 and south: Barberries, wintergreen and threespine; box, common and littleleaf, especially *koreana* variety of the latter, which is very hardy; American holly; Oregon hollygrape (mahonia); Japanese pieris; many species and hybrids of rhododendron and azaleas; and others from Zone 4.

Zone 4 and south: Daphne (garland flower); heathers and heaths; inkberry; mountain laurel; drooping leucothoe; mountain pieris; native and other broadleaved evergreens and azaleas from here are known to be hardy; Catawba rhododendron and hybrids; sweetshell rhododendron; Keisk rhododendron, in protected places; rosebay rhododendron; Smirnow rhododendron; and a number of hybrids, some of which may need protection in winter but grow hardier southward in this zone.

There are, of course, many others that might be added and even some of these may have soil, exposure, or other preferences. There are, in addition, many broad-leaved evergreens hardy in the North except that they lose their leaves. These are called semi-evergreen. When planted in milder areas southward they are likely to become evergreen.

Are broad-leaved evergreens ever sheared when used for hedges?

Yes, if a formal hedge is wanted, although flowering may be restricted or be less conspicuous and beautiful. Hollies, for instance—whether native, such as Yaupon and American, or from elsewhere, such as Japanese holly, which has smallish leaves and some cultivars leaves that are very small and rounded—are often sheared and make very neat hedges. For informal hedges, only occasional heading back—and once in a while a severe cutting back—is needed, to maintain a more or less natural form. Upright-growing types, if available in the species, are good choices for natural hedges because they will require less maintenance and keep their form more naturally.

CHECKLIST FOR SELECTION

Let us sum up the discussion by reviewing briefly the major points to be considered in the selection of shrubs for a final, more intelligent choice. The following list may be used as a guide:

- Climate and hardiness restrictions
- Mature height (probable)
- Rate of growth (probable)
- Habit of growth—form or shape
- Soil preferences—acid, neutral, alkaline
- Moisture preferences—wet, moist, dry
- Sun or shade tolerance, preference
- Flowering—time, color, fragrance, repeat bloom
- Fruiting—time, color, edibility, lasting on shrub
- Leaves—size and shape, color, glossiness or not glossy
- Autumn-winter aspect—leaf coloring, bark color, structure
- Garden style—formal, informal-formal, natural
- Evergreens—kind of leaf or needle, color, and many of the above points
- Location in city—pollution factors.

SHRUB LISTS

SMALL SHRUBS (TO THREE FEET)

Comprised of low-growing shrubs and subshrubs, this is a very important category for gardeners, for they are useful in many ways. Small shrubs dress up the front of shrubbery borders; prostrate ones and some of the subshrubs can be used as ground cover plants. Some of the species are naturally limited in height while others are diminutive natural varieties of species that usually grow much taller, proving that not all of these dwarf types are man made. In the plant world (as among humans and animals) an occasional type will appear in which growth is retarded. An alert plantsman may note this, separate and nurture this plant, growing it till it is apparent that the dwarf quality is fixed and not ephemeral. Other small plants have been produced by man. Cross-breeding produces many results, among which may be a plant distinctly shorter than its fellows, and either one or both parents. If observation proves that the dwarf is of good quality, the plant may be reproduced, named and enter the trade.

Whether selected from naturally occurring dwarfs or cross-bred ones, these named varieties are called cultivars, but to be valid, the name must be registered with the International Registration Authority. This means that, since January, 1959, no new cultivated variety is permitted to have a Latin name or a Latin ending, as was formerly the case. Latin names in valid use before that date are continued. Cultivars may be recognized in these lists by being enclosed in single quotation marks and the first letter is capitalized, thus: x*Forsythia* 'Arnold Dwarf' or *Hibiscus syriacus* 'Blue Bird', among others. (The "x" denotes that it is a hybrid.) Named varieties are different from the species in some respect, usually superior in color, in habit of growth or flowering.

Some shrubs have been omitted from these lists for, although they qualify in height, they may spread by suckering or are otherwise not suited to the average small garden. On the other hand, there are some that have been included that are natives of some special region and because we advocate and stress the use of native plant material, especially for natural and informal gardens. Where climate may make it imperative to use naturally-hardy plants rather than trying to adapt material unsuited to that climate, native shrubs may be the answer. Some of them are not widely available outside the immediate native area, although some are offered by good nurseries. This growing trend is to be encouraged everywhere.

COMMON NAME	SCIENTIFIC NAME	HEIGHT	HARDI-NESS ZONE
Arborvitae,* Globe American (E)	*Thuja occidentalis* 'Globosa'	3'+	2–3
Dwarf cultivars:	'Tom Thumb'	2'+	3
	'Little Gem'	1'–2'	2
Ardisia, Coral (E)	*Ardesia crispa*	to 12"	9
Aucuba, Dwarf Japanese (BLE)	*Aucuba japonica* 'Nana'	to 3'	7–8
Azalea, Coast	*Rhododendron atlanticum* (native, East Coast)	1½'	6
Hiryu* (SE)	*Rhododendro obtusum* 'Hinodegiri' and cultivars	3'+	5–6
	'Kaempferi' and cultivars	3'+	5–6
	'Kurume'	to 3'+	5–6
Barberry, Dainty (SE)	*Berberis concinna*	to 3'	6
Dwarf Magellan (BLE)	*Berberis buxifolia* 'Nana'	12"–15"	5
Dwarf Red-leaved	*Berberis thunbergii* 'Atropurpurea Nana'	1'–3'	5
Cultivar:	*Berberis thunbergii* 'Crimson Pygmy'	12"–15"	5
Golden	*Berberis thunbergii* 'Aurea'	1½'–2'	5
Paleleaf (BLE)	*Berberis candidula*	15"–24"	5
Warty (BLE)	*Berberis verruculosa*	to 3'	5
Beach-wormwood (Dusty Miller)	*Artemisia stelleriana* (native Northeast)	2½'	2
Bluebeard (Blue Spirea)	*Caryopteris incana* 'Nana'	3'	5–6
Cultivar:	x*Caryopteris* 'Heavenly Blue'	1½'–2½'	5–6
Box, Edging (BLE)	*Buxus sempervirens* 'Suffruticosa'	2'–3'	5
Korean Littleleaf (BLE)	*Buxus microphylla* 'Koreana'	to 1'	5
Kingsville Dwarf (BLE)	*Buxus microphylla* 'Compacta'	to 1'	5

Key:
E = Needled evergreen
BLE = Broadleaved evergreen
pros = prostrate
SE = Semi-evergreen (may lose leaves in Northern area of hardiness)
var. = varies
x = hybrid variety
+ = may need pruning to stay low

Note: Some very dwarf types are to be found in rock garden plant nurseries.

* Shrubs used as groundcovers as well as small shrubs.

COMMON NAME	SCIENTIFIC NAME	HEIGHT	HARDI-NESS ZONE
Bog-rosemary (BLE)	*Andromeda polifolia* (native, wet acid soil)	1'–2'	2
Box-huckleberry (BLE)	*Gaylussachia brachycera* (native, acid soil)	15"–18"	5
Broom, Bean's	*Cytissus beanii*	1'–1½'	5
Butchers-, *see Butchers-Broom*			
Gorse, Dwarf Spanish	*Genista hispanica* 'Compacta'	8"–10"	6
Ground	*Cytissus procumbens*	1'	5–6
Kew	*Cytissus kewensis*	6"–12"	6
Portuguese	*Cytissus albus*	to 12"	5
Prostrate	*Cytissus decumbens*	pros.	5–6
Purple	*Cytissus purpureus*	1½'–2'	5
Spanish Gorse	*Genista hispanica*	1'	6
Butchers-broom	*Ruscus aculeatus*	1½'–3'	7
Caryopteris, *see Bluebeard*			
Ceanothus, *see New Jersey Tea*			
Checkerberry, *see Wintergreen*			
Chokeberry, Black	*Aronia melanocarpa*	1½'–3'	4
Cinquefoil, Bush (Potentilla)	*Potentilla fruticosa* and cultivars	to 3'	2–4
Cultivars:			
	'Gold Drop ('Farrerii')	2'–3'	3–4
	'Jackman's Variety' (upright)	to 3+	2
	'Katherine Dykes'	2½'–3'	2
	'Parvifolia'	to 3'	2
	'Sutter's Gold'	1½'–2½'	2
	'Tangerine'	to 2½'	2
Manchurian	*Potentilla mandshurica*	1'–2'	3–4
Coontie	*Zamia integrifolia* (palm relative)	1½'	9
Coralberry, Chenault	x*Symphoricarpos chenaultii*	3'	5
Indian-currant	*Symphoricarpos orbiculatus*	3+	2
Cotoneaster, Bearberry (BLE)	*Cotoneaster dammeri*	12"	4–5
Box-leaved (Roundleaved) (BLE)	*Cotoneaster buxifolia*	2'–3'	6–7
Cranberry (SE)	*Cotoneaster apiculata*	1½'–2½'	5
Creeping (BLE)	*Cotoneaster adpressa*	to 2'	5
Dwarf Rockspray (SE)	*Cotoneaster horizontalis* 'Minor'	1'–2'	4
Dwarf Small-leaved (BLE)	*Cotoneaster microphylla* 'Minor'	1½'–2'	5–6
Rock spray (SE)	*Cotoneaster horizontalis*	to 3'	4–5
Small-leaved (BLE)	*Cotoneaster microphylla*	2'–3'	5–6
Willowleaf cultivar	*Cotoneaster salicifolia* 'Autumn Fire'	6"–12"	5–6

COMMON NAME	SCIENTIFIC NAME	HEIGHT	HARDI-NESS ZONE
Cranberry-bush, Dwarf	*Viburnum opulus* 'Nana'	to 2′	3
Crowberry (BLE)	*Empetrum nigrum* (native, N.E. to N.W. USA; acid soil)	10″	3–4
Cryptomeria, Common, Dwarf (E)	*Cryptomeria japonica* 'Nana'	to 3+	6
Vilmorin (E)	*Cryptomeria japonica* 'Vil-moriniana'	to 3+	6
Cydonia, *see Quince, Dwarf Japanese*			
Daphne, Rose	*Daphne cneorum*	6″–15″	4
Giraldi	*Daphne giraldii*	2′	3
Dusty Miller, *see Beach-wormwood*			
Dyers-greenweed (Woadwaxen)	*Genista tinctoria* (upright)	to 3′	2
Erica, *see Heath*			
Euonymus, Dwarf	*Euonymus nanus*	to 3′	2
False cypress, Dwarf Hinoki (E)	*Chamaecyparis obtusa*		
Cultivars: (E)	'Pygmaea'	to 2′	3–4
Dwarf Sawara (E)	*Chamaecyparis pisifera*		
	'Filifera Nana'	to 3′	3–4
	'Lycopodioides'	to 3	3–4
	'Nana'	1′	3–4
	'Squarrosa Dumosa'	to 3′+	3–4
	'Squarrosa Pygmaea'	to 2′	3–4
Fir, Dwarf silver (E)	*Abies alba* 'Compacta'	to 3′+	5–6
Forsythia	x*Forsythia* 'Arnold Dwarf' (sparse bloom)	to 2′	5
Fothergilla, Dwarf	*Fothergilla gardenii*	3	5
Fuchsia, Magellan	*Fuchsia magellanica* and cultivars 'Scarlet Beauty' 'Senorita'	3′	6
Garland-flower, *see Daphne*			
Genista, *see Broom and Woadwaxen*			
Germander, Chamaedrys (E)	*Teucrium chamaedrys*	10″–12″	5
Bush	*Teucrium fruticans* (shady)	2½′–3′	6–7
Gorse, *see Broom, Spanish*			
Heath, Erica (E)	x*Erica darleyensis* (quick grower)	to 2′+	7–8
	x*Erica williamsii*	to 2′	7–8
Spring (E)	*Erica carnea*	1′–2½′	5–6
Spring cultivars:	'Praecox Rubra' 'Snow Queen' 'Springwood Pink' 'Winter Beauty'		

COMMON NAME	SCIENTIFIC NAME	HEIGHT	HARDI-NESS ZONE
Heath, Common (E)	*Calluna vulgaris*	8″–18″	4
Cultivars:	'Alba'		
	'Alportii'		
	'Aurea' (golden leaves)		
	'Cuprea' (golden leaves)		
	'Decumbens' (somewhat prostrate)		
	'H. E. Beale'		
	'J. K. Hamilton'		
	'Mair's White'		
	'Nana Compacta'		
	'Searlei Aurea' (Golden leaves)		
Heath, Irish	*Daboecia cantabrica* (acid soil)	1½′	5
Hemlock, Dwarf common (E)	*Tsuga canadensis* 'Nana'	to 3+	4
Holly, Japanese (BLE)	*Ilex crenata*, dwarf	var.	5–6
Dwarf cultivars:	'Globosa'		
	'Green Lustre'		
	'Hellerii'		
	'Kingsville'		
	'Stokes'		
Hollygrape, Oregon (BLE)	*Mahonia aquifolium* (native of W.)	to 3+	5
Creeping Oregon (BLE)	*Mahonia repens* (native of W.)	1′	5
Longleaf (BLE)	*Mahonia nervosa* (native of W.)	1½′	6
Honeysuckle, Privet (BLE)	*Lonicera pileata*	to 3′+	5–6
Hydrangea, Hills-of-Snow	*Hydrangea arborescens* 'Grandiflora'	3′–4′	4
Cultivar:	*Hydrangea* 'Annabelle'	4	4
Hypericum, *see St. Johnswort*			
Jersey tea, *see New Jersey tea*			
Indian-currant, *see Coralberry, Indian-currant*			
Indigo, Potanin	*Indigofera potanini*	3	5
Juneberry, Dwarf (Service-berry)	*Amelanchier stolonifera* (Northeast to Midwest native)	to 3′	3–5
Juniper, Creeping (E)	*Juniperus horizontalis*	to 15″	2
Cultivars:	'Procumbens'	5″–10″	2
	'Bar Harbor'	8″–12″	2
	'Blue Rug'	8″–12″	2
	'Wiltonii'	8″–12″	2
	'Waukegan' ('Douglasii')	pros.	2
Sargent (E)	*Juniperus chinensis* 'Sargentii'	pros.	4
Shore (E)	*Juniperus conferta* (seaside)	1′	5

83

COMMON NAME	SCIENTIFIC NAME	HEIGHT	HARDI-NESS ZONE
Labrador-tea (BLE)	*Ledum groenlandicum* (bog plant)	3'	2
Laurel, Alexandria (BLE)	*Danae racemosa* (bamboo-like)	3'	7
Lavender-cotton (E to SE)	*Santolina chamaecyparissus*	1½'	6–7
Hoary (E to SE)	*Santolina incana*	1'–1½'	6–7
Lavender, True	*Lavandula officinalis*	1'–3'	5–6
Mescal-bean	*Sophora secundiflora* (arid, dry soil)	3'+	7
New Jersey tea	*Ceanothus americanus*	3'	4
Inland	*Ceanothus ovatus*	3'	4
Pachistima, Canby	*Pachistima canbyi*	10"–12"	5
Myrtle	*Pachistima myrsinites* (western USA native)	1½'–3'	6–7
Pea-tree, Dwarf	*Caragana pygmaea* (Canada prairie use) (also sold as *C. aurantiaca*)	to 3'	2–3
Pernettya, Chilean (BLE)	*Pernettya mucronata*	1'–1½'	6–7
Pine, Dwarf Mugo (E)	*Pinus mugo* 'Pumila'	to 2'	2
Quince, Dwarf Japanese (SE)	*Chaenomeles japonica* (*Cydonia*)	to 3'	4
Dwarf cultivars: (SE)	'Alpina'	1'	4
	'Knaphill' (taller in favorable locations)	1½'–2'	4–5
Rhododendron, Mayflower (BLE)	*Rhododendron racemosum*	2'–4+	5
Rhododendron, Cultivar (BLE)	'Ramapo'	2'	5
Wilson	*Rhododendron wilsonii*	to 3+'	5
Rhodora	*Rhododendron canadense*	3'	3
Rock spray, *see Cotoneaster, Rock Spray*			
Rose-acacia	*Robinia hispida*	3'	5
Rose, *see also pages 123–141 and Rose Lists, 141–148*			
Rose, Alpine	*Rosa pendulina*	to 3'	4
Carolina (Swamp)	*Rosa carolina* (native to eastern half of USA)	3'	4
Fairy	*Rosa chinensis* 'Minima' and cultivars	10"–12"	6–7
Glossy Virginia	*Rosa virginiana* 'Lampaophylla' (New England and Canada)	3'	3
Memorial rose	*Rosa wichuriana* and cultivars	pros.	5
Scotch	*Rosa spinosissima* and cultivars	3'	4
Other locally native roses			

COMMON NAME	SCIENTIFIC NAME	HEIGHT	HARDI-NESS ZONE
Rosemary, Bog, *see* Bog-rosemary			
Sagebrush, Fringed (Fringed wormwood)	*Artemisia frigida* (native species, western plains and in Canada, Rocky Mountains)	1½'–3'	2–3
Sarcococca, Small Himalayan (BLE)	*Sarcococca hookeriana* 'Humilis'	2'–4'	5
Serviceberry, Dwarf, *see* Juneberry			
Serviceberry, Low	*Amelanchier humilis* (native Northeast to Northwest and Canada)	3'+	5–6
Sheep-laurel (BLE)	*Kalmia angustifolia* (acid soil native, northeast USA)	3'	2
Skimmia, Reeves (BLE)	*Skimmia reevesiana*	1½'	7
Snowball, Dwarf, *see* Cranberry-bush, Dwarf			
Snow-wreath	*Neviusia alabamensis* (native southeast USA)	3'+	5
Spike-heath (E)	*Bruckenthalia spiculifolia*	10"–12"	5
Spirea, Blue, *see Bluebeard*			
Spirea, Boxwood cultivar	*Spiraea nipponica* 'Snow-mound'	to 3'+	4–5
Bumalda	*Spiraea bumalda*	2'	5
Bumalda cultivars:	'Anthony Waterer'	2'	5
	'Crispa'	to 2'	5
	'Froebelii'	3'	5
	'Wallufii'	2'–3'	5
Daphne (Dwarf Japanese)	*Spiraea japonica* 'Alpina'	10"–12"	5
Dropmore	*Spiraea albiflora* 'Menziesii Dropmore' (available in Canada)	2'	2
Hardhack	*Spiraea tomentosa* (native eastern USA)	3'	4
Japanese white	*Spiraea albiflora*	1'–2'	4
Reeves	*Spiraea cantoniensis*	3'	6
Sanssouci	x*Spiraea sanssouciana*	to 3'+	5
Cultivars:	x'Rosabelle' (available in Canada)	18"	3
	x'Summersnow' (available in Canada)	2'	3
Spruce, Dwarf Norway	*Picea abies* 'Procumbens'	to 3'	2
St. Johnswort (Hypericum)			
Aaronsbeard	*Hypericum calycinum*	12"–18"	5–6
Cultivars:	'Sun Goddess'	2'–3'+	6–7
	'Sungold'	1½'–2'	6–7
Goldflower	*Hypericum moserianum*	2'	7

85

COMMON NAME	SCIENTIFIC NAME	HEIGHT	HARDI-NESS ZONE
St. Johnswort (*cont.*)			
Henry	*Hypericum patulum* 'Henryi'	to 3'	6
Hidcote	*Hypericum hookerianum* 'Hidcote'	2'–3'+	6–7
Kalm	*Hypericum kalmianum*	2'–3'	4
Tea, Labrador, *see* Labrador-tea			
Tea, New Jersey, *see* New Jersey tea			
Viburnum, David (BLE)	*Vibrunum davidii*	3'	7
Willow, Arctic (Dwarf Purple Osier)	*Salix purpurea* 'Nana' (shear to 8"–10")	8"–10" to 3'	2–3
Bearberry	*Salix uva-ursi* (Canada native, to northeast USA)	pros.	2
Creeping	*Salix repens*	to 3'	4
Dwarf gray	*Salix tristis* (native eastern half of USA and Canada. Do not confuse with weeping willow tree cultivar: *Salix* 'Tristis')	1½'	2
Wintergreen, Miquel* (BLE)	*Gaultheria miqueliana*	to 1'	5
Veitch (BLE)	*Gaultheria veitchiana*	3'	7
Teaberry,* Checkerberry (BLE)	*Gaultheria procumbens* (acid soil subshrub)	3"–4"	3
Withe-rod, Dwarf	*Viburnum cassinoides* 'Nanum'	3'	3
Woadwaxen, Ashy	*Genista cinerea*	2½'	7
Silky-leaf*	*Genista pilosa*	1'	5
Woadwaxen, *see also Dyers-greenweed*			
Wormwood, *see Sagebrush*			
Wormwood, Beach, *see* Beach-wormwood			
Yellow-root*	*Xanthoriza simplicissima*	2'	4
Yew, Canada (E)	*Taxus canadensis*	3'+	2
English (E)	*Taxus baccata* 'Repandens'	to 3'+	6
Dense Japanese (E)	*Taxus cuspidata* 'Densa'	to 3'+	4–5
Dwarf Japanese (E)	*Taxus cuspidata* 'Minima'	12"–15"	4–5

MEDIUM-HEIGHT SHRUBS, 4 TO 7 FEET

COMMON NAME	SCIENTIFIC NAME AND COMMENTS	HEIGHT (IN FEET)	HARDI-NESS ZONE
Abelia, Glossy (SE)	*Abelia grandiflora*	3–5	7
Hybrid (SE)	*Abelia* 'Edward Goucher'	5–7	7
Mexican (BLE)	*Abelia floribunda*	6	8
Schuman (SE)	*Abelia schumanii*	5	7
Abelia-leaf (White forsythia)	*Abeliophyllum distichum*	5	5
Almond, Dwarf flowering	*Prunus glandulosa*	4–5	5
Dwarf Russian	*Prunus tenella* 'Alba'	4½	2
Andromeda, Japanese (BLE)	*Pieris japonica*	to 7+	5
Mountain (BLE)	*Pieris floribunda*	6	4–5
Apache plume	*Fallugia paradoxa* (native Utah, Nev.)	5	5
Arborvitae, American	*Thuja occidentalis* 'Ericoides'	to 5 (?)	2
Dwarf globe	*Thuja occidentalis* 'Globosa'	to 6–7	2
Arborvitae, Oriental dwarf	*Thuja orientalis* 'Decussata'	to 6–7	6
Siebold	*Thuja orientalis* 'Sieboldii'	to 7	6
Dwarf globe	*Thuja orientalis* 'Globosa'	to 6–7	6
Azalea, Exbury	*Rhododendron* 'Exbury Hybrids'	4–7+	5
Gable	*Rhododendron* 'Gable' cultivars	5–6	5–6
Ghent	*Rhododendron gandavense*	5–7+	4–5
Glen Dale Hybrids	*Rhododendron* 'Glen Dale' cultivars	5	5–6
Indian	*Rhododendron indicum*	6	5–6
Knaphill Hybrids	*Rhododendron* 'Knaphill'	4–8	5
Korean	*Rhododendron mucronulatum*	6	4
Kurume	*Rhododendron obtusum* 'Kurume' cultivars	4–6	5–6
Mollis Hybrids	x*Rhododendron kosterianum* and cultivars	5–6	5
Pinkshell	*Rhododendron vaseyi* (native North Carolina)	6–8	4

Key:
   E = Needled evergreens
  BLE = Broad-leaved evergreen
   SE = Semi-evergreen, may loose leaves in northern part of hardiness zone
  var. = varies
    x = hybrid or cultivar

Note: Some shrubs, particularly dwarf evergreens, may eventually grow beyond the size noted in favorable conditions. Pruning will keep them within bounds.

COMMON NAME	SCIENTIFIC NAME AND COMMENTS	HEIGHT (IN FEET)	HARDI-NESS ZONE
Pinxterbloom	*Rhododendron nudiflorum* (native Massachusetts to North Carolina)	6	3
Pontic	*Rhododendron ponticum (luteum)*	to 7+	6–7
Snow	*Rhodendron vuykiana* 'Palestrina'	to 7	5–6
Sweet	*Rhododendron arborescens*	to 7+	4
Yodogawa	*Rhododendron yedoense*	5	5
Compact Yodogawa	*Rhododendron yedoense* 'Poukhanense'	5+	5
Barberry, Black (BLE)	*Berberis gagnepainii*	6	5
Darwin (BLE)	*Berberis darwinii*	4–7+	7
Japanese	*Berberis thunbergii*	7	5
Korean	*Berberis koreana*	to 6	5
Mentor (SE)	x*Berberis mentorensis*	to 7	5
Rosemary (BLE)	*Berberis stenophylla*	to 7+	5
Threespine (BLE)	*Berberis triacanthophora*	4	5
Warty (BLE)	*Berberis verruculosa*	4	5
Wintergreen (BLE)	*Berberis julianae*	6	5
Bayberry (Sweet gale)	*Myrica gale* (native wetsoil or sandy soil plant)	4+	2
Bayberry	*Myrica pensylvanica* (native sandy soil, seashore plant)	to 7+	2
Beach plum	*Prunus maritima*	6	4
Beauty-berry, Japanese	*Callicarpa japonica*	4½	2
Black alder, Winterberry	*Ilex verticillata* (in the North to 5')	to 8	3
Bluebeard	x*Caryopteris clandonensis* and cultivars 'Blue Mist' 'Heavenly Blue'	4	5–6
Blueberry, Box, *see Box-blueberry*			
Box-blueberry (BLE)	*Vaccinium ovatum* (West Coast native, USA and Canada)	to 8	7
Box, Littleleaf (BLE)	*Buxus microphylla*	4	5
Myrtleleaf	*Buxus sempervirens* 'Myrtifolia'	4–5	5
Rosemary	*Buxus sempervirens* 'Rosmarinifolia'	4–7	4
Bridal wreath, *see Spirea*			
Broom, Warminster	x*Cytisus praecox*	6	5
Dallimore	x*Cytisus dallimorei*	6	6
Scotch	*Cytisus scoparius* and cultivars	6	5
Spike	*Cytisus nigricans*	4–6	3–4
Hybrid varieties	x*Cytisus*, named cultivars	var.	var.

COMMON NAME	SCIENTIFIC NAME AND COMMENTS	HEIGHT (IN FEET)	HARDI-NESS ZONE
Buffalo-berry, Russet	*Shepherdia canadensis* (native to central USA, Canada)	to 7+	2
Bush-cherry, Chinese	*Prunus japonica* 'Nakai'	4½	2
Bush-honeysuckle, Southern	*Diervilla sessilifolia*	4–5	4
Butterfly-bush	*Buddleia davidii* (may grow taller in favorable conditions)	5–8	5–6
Cape-jasmine (Gardenia) (BLE)	*Gardenia jasminoides*	4–6	8–9
Caragana, Shrubby	*Caragana frutex* (Canada)	6–8	4–5
Ceanothus, Delisle (BLE)	*Ceanothus delilianus* and cult. 'Autumnal Blue' 'Gloire de Versailles' 'Henry Defosse'	6+	7
Cinquefoil (Potentilla) Cultivar:	*Potentilla fruticosa* and cults. 'Mount Everest'	to 4	2
Coralberry, Indian Currant	*Symphoricarpos orbiculatus* (native to southeast and southcentral USA)	to 6	2
Cotoneaster, European	*Cotoneaster integerrima*	to 6	2
Harrow (SE)	*Cotoneaster harroviana*	6	7
Peking	*Cotoneaster acutifolia*	4–10	2
Showy	*Cotoneaster multiflora*	to 7	5–6
Spreading	*Cotoneaster divaricata*	6	5
Vilmorin	*Cotoneaster bullata* 'Floribunda'	6	5
Cryptomeria, Compact	*Cryptomeria japonica* 'Jindai-sugi'	7	7
Currant, Alpine	*Ribes alpinum*	to 7	2
Clove (Buffalo)	*Ribes odoratum* (native east of Rocky Mountains in USA)	6	4
Golden	*Ribes aureum* (native Pacific Coast, west of Rocky Mountains)	6	2
Winter	*Ribes sanguineum* (native northwest USA and Pacific Coast)	to 7+	7
Currant, Indian, *see* Coralberry			
Cydonia, *see Quince, Flowering*			
Cytisus, *see Broom*			
Daphne, Winter	*Daphne odora*	4–6	7–8
Deutzia, Lemoine	*Deutzia lemoinei*	to 7	4
Dwarf Lemoine	*Deutzia lemoinei* 'Compacta'	4–5	4
Rose, Cultivars	x*Deutzia rosea* 'Carminea' 'Eximia'	6	5

COMMON NAME	SCIENTIFIC NAME AND COMMENTS	HEIGHT (IN FEET)	HARDI-NESS ZONE
Deutzia, Lemoine (*cont.*)			
Pride of Rochester	*Deutzia scabra*	to 7	5
Slender	*Deutzia gracilis*	5–6	4–5
Dogwood, Greentwig	*Cornus stolonifera* 'Nitida'	to 7	3
Red osier (Redtwig)	*Cornus stolonifera* (native, moist soil)	7	3
Yellowtwig	*Cornus stolonifera* 'Flaviramea'	7	2
Dogwood, Tatarian	*Cornus alba* and cultivars	to 8	2
	'Coral Beauty'	4–7	2
	'Sibirica'	6–7	2
Elscholtzia, Staunton	*Elscholtzia stauntonii*	5	4–5
Euonymus, Dwarf winged	*Euonymus alata* 'Compacta'	4–5	3
Sarcoxie	*Euonymus fortunei* 'Sarcoxie'	4+	5
Fatshedera (BLE)	*Fatshedera lizei*	6	8
False-cypress, Hinoki (E)	*Chamaecyparis obtusa* cultivars 'Filicoides' 'Compacta' 'Gracilis'	var.	3–4
False-cypress, Sarawa (E)	*Chamaecyparis pisifera* (dwarf cultivars may need pruning to stay low)	var.	3–4
	'Filifera Aurea'	6–8	3–4
Firethorn, Scarlet (SE)	*Pyracantha coccinea* and cultivars (cutting back may be needed to keep within height area) 'Kasan' 'Lalandii' 'Orange Glow'	6–10	6
Firethorn (SE)	x*Pyracantha*	to 10+	6–7
	'Mojave'		6–7
	'Oxford'		7
	'Rosedale' (Canadian)		8
Forsythia cultivars:	x*Forsythia* 'Beatrix Farrand'	6–8	5
	'Karl Sax'	to 7+	5–6
	'Lynwood Gold'	5–7+	5–6
Forsythia, Siebold	*Forsythia suspensa* 'Sieboldii'	4–9	5
Fothergilla, Alabama	*Fothergilla monticola* (native North Carolina to Alabama)	6	5
Hawthorn, Yeddo, *see Yeddo-hawthorn*			
Heath, Mediterranean (E)	*Erica mediterranea*	5+	7
Hebe, Boxleaf (BLE)	*Hebe buxifolia*	4	7–8

COMMON NAME	SCIENTIFIC NAME AND COMMENTS	HEIGHT (IN FEET)	HARDI-NESS ZONE
Holly, Chinese (BLE)	*Ilex cornuta*	to 7+	7
Dwarf Burford (BLE)	*Ilex cornuta* 'Burfordii Globosa'	6–7	7
Inkberry (BLE)	*Ilex glabra* (native Northeast USA and Canada) (may grow less tall in the North or in poor soil)	4–15+	3
Japanese (BLE)	*Ilex crenata* 'Convexa'	4–7	6
Holly-grape, Oregon (BLE)	*Mahonia aquifolia*	to 6	5
Honeysuckle, Belle	*Lonicera bella* and cultivars 'Atrorosea' 'Candida' 'Rosea'	6	3–4
Albert Thorn	*Lonicera spinosa* 'Albartii'	4	3
Morrow	*Lonicera morrowii*	6	4
Privet (BLE)	*Lonicera pileata*	4–5	5–6
Saccata	*Lonicera saccata*	4½	5
Tibet	*Lonicera thibetica*	6	5–6
Hydrangea, Oakleaved	*Hydrangea quercifolia*	6	5–6
Winter	*Lonicera fragrantissima*	6	5–6
Indian-currant, *see Coralberry*			
Indigo, Pink	*Indigofera amblyantha*	6	5
Jetbead	*Rhodotypos scandens* (kerriodes)	6+	5
Juniper, Meyer's (E)	*Juniperus squamata* 'Meyeri'	6	4
Juniper, Red-Cedar, *see Red-cedar*			
Kerria	*Kerria japonica*	4–7	4
Double	*Kerria japonica* 'Plena'	4–7	4
Lead-plant	*Amorpha canescens*	4	2
Leadwort, Wilmott Blue	*Ceratostigma willmottianum*	4	8
Lilac, Cutleaf	*Syringa laciniata*	6	5
Littleleaf	*Syringa microphylla* 'Superba'	5–6	5–6
Persian	x*Syringa persica*	6	4–5
Pink Pearl	x*Syringa swegiflexa*	6–7	5
Lilac, Hybrid varieties	x*Syringa* cultivars 'James MacFarlane' 'Miss Kim'	var.	var.
	x*Syringa* Preston cultivars (Canada) 'Coral' 'Donald Wyman' 'Hiawatha' 'Isabella' 'Jessica'	to 9	2
Locust, Kelsey	*Robinia kelseyi*	9	5

91

COMMON NAME	SCIENTIFIC NAME AND COMMENTS	HEIGHT (IN FEET)	HARDI-NESS ZONE
Manzanita, Hairy (BLE)	*Arctostaphylos columbiana*	to 8	7–8
Stanford (BLE)	*Arctostaphylos stanfordiana* (native California)	6	7
Mescal-bean (BLE)	*Sophora secundiflora* (native dry soil Texas and New Mexico)	to 8	7
Mockorange, Canadian hybrids	x*Philadelphus,* Dropmore cultivars (for the prairies)		
	'Galahad'	4	3
	'Patricia'	4	3
	'Silvia' (double)	4	3–4
Mockorange, Cymosus	x*Philadelphus cymosus* and cultivars	5–8	4–5
	'Atlas'		
	'Conquete'		
	'Norma'		
Mockorange, Lemoine	*Philadelphus lemoinei* and cultivars	4–8	5
	'Avalanche'	4	
	'Belle Etoile'	6	
	'Boule d'Argent' (double)	5	
	'Girandole' (double)	4	
	'Innocence'	to 8	
	'Mont Blanc' (extra hardy)	4	
Mockorange, Named hybrids	x*Philadelphus* 'Bouquet Blanc'	5	4
	'Enchantment'	6	4
	'Minnesota Snowflake'	to 7	5
	'Silver Rain' ('Silver Showers')	3–4	5
Mockorange, Virginal	*Philadelphus virginalis* and cultivars	5–8+	4–5
	'Albatre' (double)	5	4
	'Argentine' (double)	to 5	4–5
	'Glacier' (double)	to 5	
	'Virginal' (double)	to 8	4
Ninebark, Eastern	*Physocarpus opulifolius*	5–8	3
Twin-pod	*Physocarpus bracteatus*	6	5
Pea-shrub, *see Pea-tree and Caragana*			
Pea-tree, Chinese	*Caragana sinica* (available in Canada)	4	4
Maximowicz	*Caragana maximowicziana*	4½	2
Shortleaved	*Caragana brevifolia*	4	2
Shrubby	*Caragana frutex* (available in Canada)	6–8	2

COMMON NAME	SCIENTIFIC NAME AND COMMENTS	HEIGHT (IN FEET)	HARDI-NESS ZONE
Pine, Mugo (E)	*Pinus mugo* 'Mughus'	to 7+	2
Privet, Regel	*Ligustrum obtusifolium* 'Regelianum'	9	3
Quince, Flowering Cultivars:	*Chaenomeles lagenaria* 'Cameo' 'Coral Sea' 'Crimson and Gold' 'Hollandia' 'Knaphill' 'Nivalis' 'Phyllis Moore' 'Pink Lady' 'Rubra' 'Spitfire'	to 6	4–5
Rabbitbrush, Greenplume	*Chrysothamnus graveolens* (native dry soil, Montana to New Mexico)	5	3
Raspberry, Boulder	*Rubus deliciosus* (native, Colorado and western North America)	7+	3–4
Flowering	*Rubus odoratus* (native Nova Scotia to Georgia, and Michigan)	7+	3
Red-cedar, Fountain (E)	*Juniperus virginiana* 'Tripartita'	5	2
Rhododendron, Carolina (BLE)	*Rhododendron carolinianum* and cultivars	6	4
Mayflower (BLE)	*Rhododendron racemosum*	to 6	6
Rock-rose (E)	*Cistus* species and cultivars	to 6–7	7
Laurel (E)	*Cistus laurifolius*	6–7	7–8
Rose, Arnold	x*Rosa arnoldiana*	5	4
French	*Rosa gallica*	4	5
Kamchatka	*Rosa amblyotis* (native of Kamchatka)	5	2
Redleaf	*Rosa rubrifolia*	6	2
Roxburgh	*Rosa roxburghii*	to 7	4
Scotch	*Rosa spinosissima*	3–4	4
Swamp	*Rosa palustris* (native eastern USA)	6	4
Virginia	*Rosa virginiana* (native eastern and northern USA)	6	2
Sallon (Salal) (BLE)	*Gaultheria shallon* (native Alaska to Southern California)	5	5

COMMON NAME	SCIENTIFIC NAME AND COMMENTS	HEIGHT (IN FEET)	HARDI-NESS ZONE
Salt-bush	*Atriplex* species (dry soil, seashore)	4+	5–7
Salt-tree	*Halimodendron halodendron* (good for dry soil, prairie, seashore)	6	2
Sarcococca, Fragrant (BLE)	*Sarcococca ruscifolia*	to 6	7
Silk-tassel, Wright	*Garrya wrightii* (native Arizona to Texas)	6	6
Skimmia, Japanese (BLE)	*Skimmia japonica*	4	6
Snowberry	*Symphoricarpos albus* 'Laevigatus' (Native southeast and south central USA)	6	2
Snow-wreath	*Neviusia alabamensis* (native Alabama)	to 6	5
Southernwood	*Artemisia abrotanum*	4	5
Spirea, Garland	x*Spiraea arguta*	5–6+	4
Big Nippon	*Spiraea nipponica* 'Rotundi-folia'	7	4
Billiard	*Spiraea billiardii*	6	4
Margarita	*Spiraea margaritae*	4	4
Mikado	*Spiraea japonica* 'Atrosan-guinea'	4	5
Thunberg	*Spiraea thunbergii*	5–6	4
Vanhoutte	*Spiraea vanhouttei*	to 6+	4
Willowleaf	*Spiraea salicifolia*	4	4
Stephanandra, Cutleaf	*Stephanandra incisa*	6–7	4–5
Sweetspire	*Itea virginica*	4	6
Tamarix, Odessa	*Tamarix odessana*	6	4
Tree peony	*Paeonia suffruticosa*	4–6	5
Viburnum, Burkwood	*Viburnum burkwoodii*	6	5–6
Fragrant (Korean spice)	*Viburnum carlesii*	5–6	4
Fragrant Snowball	*Viburnum carlecephalum*	5–7	5–6
Japanese	*Viburnum japonicum*	6	7
Judd	*Viburnum juddii*	6–7+	5
Mapleleaf (Arrow-wood)	*Viburnum acerifolium* (native Canada and eastern half USA)	4–6	
Sandankwa	*Viburnum suspensum*	6	9
Withe-rod	*Viburnum cassinoides*	6	3
Wright	*Viburnum wrightii*	5–7+	6

COMMON NAME	SCIENTIFIC NAME AND COMMENTS	HEIGHT (IN FEET)	HARDI-NESS ZONE
Weigela, Early	*Weigela praecox*	6	5
Flowering	*Weigela florida* and cultivars	5	4–5
Cultivars:	'Bristol Ruby'		
	'Bristol Snowflake'		
	'Dame Blanche'		
	'Dropmore Pink' (Man-churian Pink)		
	'Eva Rathke'		
	'Variegata'		
Maximowicz	*Weigela maximowiczii*	4	5
Wormwood	*Artemisia absinthinum*	4	5
Yeddo-hawthorn	*Raphiolepis umbellata*	6	7
Yew, Canadian	*Taxus canadensis*	3–6	2
English	*Taxus baccata* 'Expansa'	5–6	6
	'Repandens'	4+	6
Hatfield	*Taxus media* 'Hatfieldii'	5–7+	4
Hicks	*Taxus media* 'Hicksii'	5–7+	4
Japanese, cultivars:	*Taxus cuspidata* 'Densa'	to 4+	4
Upright Canadian	*Taxus canadensis* 'Stricta'	3–6	2
	'Thayerae'	to 8+	4
Zenobia, Dusty	*Zenobia pulverulenta*	6	5

TALL SHRUBS, TREELIKE SHRUBS, 10 FEET OR MORE

At best, the boundary between tall shrubs and small trees is a tenuous one. It is further complicated by climates and soils, for in some places a small tree may behave like a shrub, growing shorter than its normal height and it may be lower branched and quite shrubby. Conversely, shrubs that may have a bushy habit of growth in their native habitat may become distinctly treelike, or at any rate grow much taller than is usually believed possible.

For the amateur gardener—and many professional plantsmen—this is confusing and quite perplexing. For most of us who plant small gardens, however, the question is moot, for a great many of the treelike shrubs will not fit into the space we have to deal with. Where they are employed, they may best be considered as small trees. You will, in fact, find some overlapping of Tall Shrubs on this list with Small Trees (especially Flowering

Trees) in the Tree chapter. Note also that the heights given here are the maximum known, usually under the most favorable conditions, and may not necessarily be the height in your Zone. Your nurseryman may be able to advise you on this question. Where information is available or examples are known, an asterisk has been used to indicate that shrubs in most areas will grow less tall.

Gardeners with larger plots and those who are building natural gardens will find that the shrubs listed as natives will thrive best and probably perform better in their native habitat area or in similar conditions.

COMMON NAME	SCIENTIFIC NAME	HEIGHT (IN FEET)	HARDI-NESS ZONE
Acanthopanax	*Acanthopanax sessiliflorus* (for prairie)	9–12	2–8
Alder	*Alnus species* (suited only to wet soil)		
American green	*Alnus crispa* (native Canada to North Carolina)	10	3
Hazel	*Alnus rugosa* (native eastern Canada to Florida)	to 25	3
Italian	*Alnus cordata* (will grow in dry soil)	to 45	5
Mountain	*Alnus tenuifolia* (native British Columbia to California)	to 30	7–8
—	*Alnus sinuata* (native Alaska to northern California)	to 50	5
Red	*Alnus rubra* (native West Coast, Canada to California)	to 50	5–6
Speckled	*Alnus incana* and cultivars	to 60	2
Almond, Flowering	*Purnus triloba* 'Multiplex'	15	5
Angelica tree, Japanese	*Aralia elata* (thorny, not for small gardens)	10–35	4–5
Arborvitae (E)	*Thuja orientalis* 'Bonita' (West Coast)	20+	6
Cultivar:	'Texana Glauca' (West Coast)	20+	6
Arrow-wood	*Viburnum dentatum*	12–15	3

Key:
  E = Needled evergreen
 BLE = Broad-leaved evergreen
  SE = Semi-evergreen (may lose leaves in northern reaches of hardiness zone)
  var. = varies
   x = hybrid or cultivar
   * = May grow less tall, especially in northern or less favorable conditions.

COMMON NAME	SCIENTIFIC NAME	HEIGHT (IN FEET)	HARDI- NESS ZONE
Aucuba, Japanese	*Aucuba japonica*	to 15	7
Autumn-olive	*Eleagnus umbellata* (spreading)	to 12	5
Azalea, Flame (E)	*Rhododendron calendulacea* (native northern half USA)	rarely to 15	4–5
Royal (E)	*Rhododendron schlippenbachii*	to 15	4
Swamp (E)	*Rhododendron viscosum* (Maine to South Carolina)	rarely to 15	3
Bayberry, California	*Myrica californica* (native Washington to California)	to 35	7
Black haw	*Viburnum prunifolium* (native eastern USA)	to 15	3
Southern	*Viburnum rufidulum* (native southeastern USA)	to 30	5
Bladder-senna	*Colutea arborescens*	to 12	5
Blueberry, Highbush	*Vaccinium corymbosum* (acid soil)	to 12	3
Blueblossom (BLE)	*Ceanothus thyrsiflorus* (native Oregon to California)	to 30	8
Bottlebrush, Lemon	*Callistemon lanceolatus*	to 30	8
Box, Common	*Buxus sempervirens* and cultivars 'Angustifolia' 'Arborescens' 'Pendula'	to 20	5
Buckeye, Flame	*Aesculus splendens* (native Alabama to Mississippi)	12+	6
Buckthorn, Dahurian	*Rhamnus davurica*	to 30	2
Alder	*Rhamnus frangula*	to 18	2
Buttonbush	*Cephalanthus occidentalis* (moist soil only)	15	4
Butterfly-bush*	*Buddleia davidii*	to 15	5
Camellia, Common (BLE)	*Camellia japonica*, species and cultivars	to 40+	7
Sasanqua (BLE)	*Camellia sasanqua*, species and cultivars	to 20+	6–7
Chaste-tree, Cutleaved	*Vitex negundo* 'Incisa'	12–15	5
Cherry-laurel (BLE)	*Prunus laurocerasus*	18	6–7
Shipka	*Prunus laurocerasus* 'Schipkaensis'	to 18	5–6
Clethra, Cinnamon	*Clethra acuminata*	15–18	5
Cornelian-cherry	*Cornus mas*	10–25	4
Cotoneaster, Henry (SE)	*Cotoneaster henryana* (spreading)	12	7
Himalayan (SE)	*Cotoneaster frigida* (West Coast, mainly)	to 25	7

COMMON NAME	SCIENTIFIC NAME	HEIGHT (IN FEET)	HARDI- NESS ZONE
Cotoneaster, Henry (*cont.*)			
Willowleaf (SE)	*Cotoneaster salicifolia* 'Floccosa'	to 15	5
Chokeberry, Purple	*Aronia prunifolia*	to 12	7–8
Cranberry-bush, American	*Viburnum trilobum*	12	2
European High	*Viburnum opulus*	12	3
Crape-myrtle	*Lagerstroemia indica*	to 20	7
Currant, Winter	*Ribes sanguineum*	rarely 12	5
Dahoon (BLE)	*Ilex cassine* (native south- eastern USA)	to 36	7
Dogwood, Gray	*Cornus racemosa* (native eastern USA)	to 15	4
Siberian	*Cornus alba* 'Sibirica'	to 10	2
Silky	*Cornus ammomum* (native eastern Canada to Florida)	9–10	4
Tatarian	*Cornus alba* and cultivars	to 10	2
Elder, American	*Sambucus canadensis* and cultivars	to 10	3
Blueberry	*Sambucus caerulea* (native West Coast)	25–45	5
European red	*Sambucus racemosa*	12	4
Scarlet	*Sambucus pubens* (native eastern USA)	12–25	4
Eleagnus, *see also Russian Olive*			
Eleagnus, Thorny (BLE)	*Eleagnus pungens*	12	7
Enkianthus, Redvein*	*Enkianthus campanulatus*	10–30	4
Euonymus, Broadleaf	*Euonymus latifolia*	20	5
Burning-bush (Wahoo)*	*Euonymus atropurpurea* (native Ontario to Florida	10–20	4
Evergreen (BLE)	*Euonymus japonica*	to 15	8
Redleaf	*Euonymus sanguinea*	20	5
Yeddo	*Euonymus yedoensis*	to 15	4
Farkleberry (BLE)	*Vaccinium arboreum* (native southeastern USA)	25–30	7
Fig*	*Ficus carica*	12–30	6
Filbert	*Corylus avellana*	15	4
Great	*Corylus maxima*	to 30	4
Firethorn (Pyracantha)	*Pyracantha* species and cultivars	var.	6
Gibbs* (SE)	*Pyracantha atlantoides*	15–20	6
Laland Scarlet*	*Pyracantha coccinea* 'Lalandii'	to 20	6
Fringe-tree	*Chionanthus virginicus*	to 30	4
Glory-bower	*Clerodendron trichotomum*	to 20	6
Hardy-orange*	*Poncirus trifoliata* (thorny)	to 30+	5–6
Hazel, American	*Corylus americana* (native eastern Canada, USA)	10+	4

COMMON NAME	SCIENTIFIC NAME	HEIGHT (IN FEET)	HARDI-NESS ZONE
Hibiscus, Chinese*	*Hibiscus rosa-sinensis* and cultivars	to 30	9
Hobblebush*	*Viburnum alnifolium* (native northeastern USA)	12	3–4
Holly, Japanese* (BLE)	*Ilex crenata*	rarely 20	6
Long-stalk* (BLE)	*Ilex pedunculosa*	to 30	5
Perny* (BLE)	*Ilex pernyi*	to 30	6
Hydrangea, House*	*Hydrangea macrophylla* 'Hortensia'	rarely 12	5–6
Peegee*	*Hydrangea paniculata* 'Grandiflora'	to 25	4
Inkberry*	*Ilex glabra* (native eastern Canada and USA)	to 20	3
Judas tree, Chinese*	*Cercis chinensis* (shrubby in North)	to 30	6
Juniper, Pfitzer's (E)	*Juniperus chinensis* 'Pfitzeriana'	to 10	4
Pyramidal Chinese (E)	*Juniperus chinensis* 'Pyramidalis'	15+	4
Laurel, Cherry-, *see Cherry-laurel*			
Laurel, Portugal-, *see Portugal-laurel*			
Laurel (Sweet bay)	*Laurus nobilis*	rarely to 30	6
Leatherwood, Southern	*Cyrilla racemiflora* (native Virginia south)	to 25	6
Laurestinus	*Viburnum tinus*	10–20	7–8
Lilac, Chinese	x*Syringa chinensis*	to 15	5
Common	*Syringa vulgaris* and cultivars	12–18	3
"French" hybrids Cultivars	*Syringa vulgaris* cultivars SINGLE: 'Cavour' 'Lucie Baltet' 'Ludwig Spaeth' 'Marechal Foch' 'Maude Notcutt' 'Mont Blanc' 'Moonglow' 'President Lincoln' DOUBLE: 'Alice Eastwood' 'A. M. Brand' 'Edith Cavell' 'Interlude' 'Katherine Havemeyer' 'Mrs. Edward Harding' 'President Grevy' (semi-double) 'Victor Lemoine'	15–18	3–4

99

COMMON NAME	SCIENTIFIC NAME	HEIGHT (IN FEET)	HARDI-NESS ZONE
Lilac, (*cont.*)			
Hungarian	*Syringa josikaea*	12	2
Japanese tree	*Syringa amurensis* 'Japonica'	to 30	4
Magnolia, Star	*Magnolia stellata*	to 20	5
Sweet bay (SE)	*Magnolia virginiana* (shrubby in North)	to 20–30	5
Mahonia, Leatherleaf (BLE)	*Mahonia bealii*	to 12	6
Maple, Amur	*Acer ginnala*	to 20	2
Japanese	*Acer palmatum* and cultivars (small trees)	20	2
Mountain	*Acer spicatum*	to 25	2
Vine	*Acer circinatum* (Florida)	20	5–7
Mockorange, Purple-cup	*Philadelphus purpurascens*	12	5
Mountain-laurel	*Kalmia latifolia*	to 30	4
Nannyberry	*Viburnum lentago*	10–25	2
Natal-plum	*Carissa grandiflora*	18	9
Ocean-spray	*Holodiscus discolor* 'Ariae-folius'	12	5
Oleander	*Nerium oleander*	to 20	7–8
Olive, Russian	*Eleagnus angustifolia*	20+	2
Osmanthus, Fortune's (BLE)	*Osmanthus fortunei*	12	7–8
Holly	*Osmanthus ilicifolius*	18	6
Pearl-bush, Wilson	*Exochorda giraldii* 'Wilsonii'	15	4–5
Pea-tree, Siberian	*Caragana arborescens* (for prairies)	15–18	2
Photinia, Oriental	*Photinia villosa*	15	4
Portugal-laurel* (BLE)	*Prunus lusitanica*	to 60	7
Possum haw	*Ilex decidua*	to 30	5
Privet, Amur	*Ligustrum amurense*	to 15	3
California	*Ligustrum ovalifolium*	to 15	5–6
Chinese	*Ligustrum sinense*	to 12	5
Common	*Ligustrum vulgare*	15	4
Glossy	*Ligustrum lucidum*	to 30	7
Henry	*Ligustrum henryi*	12	7
Ibolium	*Ligustrum ibolium*	12	4
Japanese	*Ligustrum japonicum*	to 18	7
Vicary Golden	*Ligustrum vicaryi*	12	5
Pyracantha, *see Firethorn*			
Rhododendron	*Rhododendron*, species and cultivars	var.	4–6
Catawba* (BLE)	*Rhododendron catawbiense* and cultivars	rarely to 18	4
Rosebay* (BLE)	*Rhododendron maximum* (native eastern USA)	12–35	3
Smirnow* (BLE)	*Rhododendron smirnowii*	to 18	4
Sweetshell (BLE)	*Rhododendron decorum*	to 18	4

COMMON NAME	SCIENTIFIC NAME	HEIGHT (IN FEET)	HARDI-NESS ZONE
Rose of Sharon, *see* Shrub-althea			
Sea-buckthorn*	*Hippophae rhamnoides*	to 30	5
Serviceberry, Apple	x*Amelanchier grandiflora*	25	4
Allegheny (Sarvistree)	*Amelanchier laevis*	20–30	3
Shadblow*	*Amelanchier canadensis*	25–50	4
Shrub-althea* (Rose of Sharon)	*Hibiscus syriacus*	to 15	5
Silkworm tree	*Cudrania tricuspidata*	25	7
Smoke-bush	*Cotinus coggygria*	to 15	5
Smoke-tree	*Cotinus americanus*	to 30	5
Snowball, Chinese	*Viburnum macrocephalum* 'Sterile'	to 12	5–6
Snowbell, Japanese	*Styrax japonica*	to 30	5
Spice-bush	*Lindera benzoin* (native eastern USA)	15	5
Spindletree, Aldenham	*Euonymus europaeuus* 'Aldenhamensis'	20	3
Stewartia, Showy	*Stewartia ovata* 'Grandiflora'	15	5
Japanese*	*Stewartia pseudo-camellia*	to 30	5
Strawberry-tree*	*Arbutus unedo*	10–30	8
Sumac, Shining*	*Rhus copallina*	to 30	3
Smooth*	*Rhus glabra*	15–25	2
Staghorn*	*Rhus typhina*	to 30	3
Summersweet	*Clethra alnifolia*	9	3
Sweetleaf, Asiatic*	*Symplocos paniculata*	10–35	5
Tamarix, Five-stamen (Amur)	*Tamarix pentandra*	15	2–3
Small-flowered	*Tamarix parviflora*	15	4
Viburnum, Leatherleaf (SE)	*Viburnum rhytidophyllum*	8–15	5–6
Orange-fruited tea	*Viburnum setigerum* 'Auranticum'	to 12	5
Sargent Yellow Cranberry-bush	*Viburnum sargentii* 'Flavum'	12	4
Siebold	*Viburnum sieboldii*	to 25	4
Tea	*Viburnum setigerum*	to 12	5
Wahoo, *see Euonymus, Burning-bush*			
Wax-myrtle	*Myrica cerifera* (native New Jersey to Florida)	10–30	6
Wayfaring-tree	*Viburnum lantana*	8–15	3
Weigela, Hybrid	*Weigela* cultivars		
	'Bouquet Rose'	to 12	5
	'Conquerant'	to 12	5
	'Seduction'	to 12	5
	and many others		

COMMON NAME	SCIENTIFIC NAME	HEIGHT (IN FEET)	HARDI- NESS ZONE
Willow, French pussy	*Salix discolor*	20	3
Willow, Shining	*Salix lucida*	20	2
Winterberry, *see Black Haw*			
Winter-hazel, Fragrant*	*Corylopsis glabrescens*	to 18	5
Witch-hazel, Common	*Hamamelis virginiana* (native Nova Scotia to Georgia)	10–15	4
Chinese*	*Hamamelis mollis*	to 30	5
Vernal	*Hamamelis vernalis* (native central USA)	10	5
Yew, Brown's (E)	x*Taxus media* 'Brownii'	15+	4
Berrybush (E)	x*Taxus media Kelseyii*	12	4
Hatfield (E)	x*Taxus media* 'Hatfieldii'	15	4
Japanese (E)	x*Taxus cuspidata* 'Hiti'	to 20+	4
Hicks (E)	x*Taxus media* 'Hicksii'	to 15	4
Shortleaf English (E)	x*Taxus baccata* 'Adpressa'	15+	6

FLOWERING SHRUBS—FRAGRANCE, COLOR, TIME OF BLOOM

Lavish in seasonal displays, flowering shrubs offer so much in the way of color that only careful thought can help the gardener to cut down the list. Select the colors with the background in mind—no garish colors that clash with backgrounds of house or fence, or vibrate unpleasantly with other blossoms at the time of bloom. Do not, for instance, place rosy purples and bluish pinks in front of a red brick house or a wall with orange or yellow tones. Oranges do not mix well with magenta pinks, if blossoming time overlaps, and orange-yellows are also less than pleasant with these shades. Sparkle the border with white flowers, creamy tones, and in shade use plenty of whites and pale pastels for best effects.

Group plants in a border, if it is large enough, so that there is continuing bloom through the season, some overlapping from early spring into mid- and late spring; early summer blossoms helped by continuing bloom of the repeat-blooming modern roses; and late summer blooms to end the season before autumn brings color to the leaves of many shrubs. Midsummer and autumn are the two times when there is likely to be little bloom possible from shrubs, but color can be maintained by perennials and annual flowers. Check the scientific names on the complete shrub lists before ordering, to be sure you get what you want.

COMMON NAME	COLOR	BLOOM TIME	FRAGRANCE
WHITE OR WHITISH			
Abelia-leaf, Korean	W	April	
Almond, Dwarf flowering	W	May	
Russian	W	May	
Andromeda, Mountain	W	April	
Formosa	Cr	April	
Himalayan	W to Pi	April	
Angelica-tree	W	August	
Apache plume	W	May	
Arrow-wood	Cr-W	June	
Azalea, species and cultivars	W	May-June	F
Barberry, Threespine	W	May	
Black-haw	W	May	
Blueberry	W to Pi	May	
Bog-rosemary	W to Pi	May	
Box-huckleberry	W or Pi	May	
Broom, Portuguese	W to Y-W	May	
White Spanish	W to Cr-W	May	
Buckeye, Bottlebrush	W	July	
Bush-cherry, Chinese	W	May	
Butterfly-bush	W	August	F
Buttonbush	Cr-W	July	
Camellia, Common and cultivars	W	October-April	
Sasanqua and cultivars	W	September-December	
Cape-jasmine (Gardenia)	W	May-September	F
Ceanothus, Inland	W	June	
Cherry-laurel	W	May	
Christmas-berry, California	W	June-July	
Cherry, Western sand-	W	May	
Purpleleaf sand-	W	May	
Clethra, Cinnamon	W	July	
Japanese	W	July	
Cotoneaster, species and cultivars	W	June	
Crab apple, Sargent	W	May	
Cranberry-bush, American	W	May	
European	W	May	
Yellow Sargent	W	May	
Daisy-bush, New Zealand	W	Summer	F

Key:
Cr = cream-white
Gr = greenish
Pi = pinkish
Si = silvery white
W = white
Y = yellowish
F = fragrant

COMMON NAME	COLOR	BLOOM TIME	FRAGRANCE
Deutzia, species, cultivars	W	May-June	
Dogwood, Gray	Pi-W	June	
Littleleaf	W	July-August	
Red osier	W	May	
Siberian	Y-W	May	
Silky	Y-W	May-June	
Elder, species, cultivars	W, Y-W	May-June	
Eleagnus, Autumn-olive	Y-W	May	F
Cherry	Y-W	May	F
Thorny	Si-W	October	F
False-spirea	W	July	
Farkleberry	W	Summer	
Fatsia	W	Autumn	
Firethorn, species, cultivars	W	May-June	
Fothergilla, Alabama	W	May	
Large	W	May	
Franklinia	W	September-October	
Fringe-tree	W	June	
Glory-bower, Harlequin	W	August	F
Hardy-orange	W	April	
Heather, some cultivars	W	May-June	
Hibiscus, Chinese	W	Summer-spring	
Hobblebush	W	May	
Honeysuckle, Amur, Arnold, Belle, Box, Morrow, Privet, Tatarian	W	May-June	some F
Winter	W	April	F
Hydrangea, Hills of snow	W	July	
Oak-leaved	W	July	
Peegee	W	August	
Jetbead	W	May-June	
Labrador-Tea	W	May	
Laurel, Alexandrian	W	Spring	
Laurel (Sweet bay)	Gr-W	June	leaf F
Laurestinus	W-Pi	Winter, spring	
Leucothoe, species	W	June	
Lilac, Common, French Hybrids	W	May	F
Japanese tree-	Cr-W	June	
Late	Pi-W	June	
Magnolia, Star	W	April	F
Sweet bay	W	May	F
Wilson	W	May	F
Mexican-orange (Choisya)	W	May	F
Mockorange, species and cultivars	W	May-June	F
Mountain-laurel	W to Pi	June	
Myrtle	Cr-W	Summer	
Nandina	W	July	

COMMON NAME	COLOR	BLOOM TIME	FRAGRANCE
Nannyberry (Shadblow)	W	May	
Natal-plum	W	May onward	F
New Jersey-tea	W	June	F
Ninebark, species	W	June	
Ocean-spray	W	July	
Oleander	W	April and summer	
Osmanthus, Fortune	W	June	F
Peony, Tree	W	May-June	F
Photinia, Chinese	W	May	
Pittosporum, Japanese	Cr-W	May	F
Plum, Beach	W	May	
Portugal-laurel	W	May	
Potentilla, cultivars	W	May onward	
Privet, most species and cultivars	W	June-July	
Quince, Flowering 'Nivalis'	W	May	
Raspberry, Boulder	W	May	
Rhododendron, Catawba cultivars	W	June	
Rock-rose cultivars	W	Summer	
Rose, species and cultivars	W	May, June	F
Hybrid	W	Recurrent	F
Rosebay (Rhododendron) 'Album'	W	June	
Rose of Sharon *see Shrub-althea*			
Sarcococca, species, cultivars	W	Spring or fall	F
Shadblow, *Amelanchier* species	W	May	
Shallon	W to Pi	June	
Serviceberry, *see Shadblow*			
Shrub-althea (Rose of Sharon)	W	August	
Skimmia, species	Y-W	May	F
Snowball, Chinese, Japanese	W	May	
Snowbell, species	W	June	F
Snow-wreath	W	May	
Spirea, many species	W	May-June	
Stephanandra, Cutleaf	Cr-W	June	
Stewartia, species	W	July	
Sweetbells	W to Pi	May	
Sweetleaf, Asiatic	W	May	F
Strawberry-tree	W	Winter	
Summersweet	W	July	
Viburnums, species and cultivars	W	Most in May-June	
Fragrant	Pi-W	April	
Japanese	W	Spring	F
Maries' doublefile	Cr-W	May	

COMMON NAME	COLOR	BLOOM TIME	FRAGRANCE
Viburnums (*cont.*)			
Sandankwa	W-Pi	June	F
Sweet	W	May	F
Tea	W	July	
Wayfaring-tree	W	May	
Wintergreen, species	W	May	
Withe-rod	Cr-W	June	
Zenobia, Dusty	W	June	

PINK, ROSE, AND OTHERS

COMMON NAME	COLOR	BLOOM TIME	FRAGRANCE
Abelia, Glossy	Pi	August	
Almond, Flowering	Pi	April	
Dwarf Flowering	Pi	April-May	
Azalea, species and cultivars			
Pinkshell	Pi	May	
Pinxterbloom	lt-Pi	May	F
Roseshell	Pi	May	F
Royal	Pi	May	F
Cultivars: Ghent, Indian, Kurume	Pi	May-June	
Beauty-berry, Japanese	Pi-W	July	
Beauty-bush	Pi	June	
Bog-rosemary	Pi-W	May	
Butterfly-bush	Pi	August	
Camellia, Common and cultivars	Pi	October-April	
Sasanqua cultivars	Pi	September-December	
Cherry, Nakai Chinese bush-	Pi-W	April	
Manchu	Pi-W	April	
Cotoneaster, species and cultivars	Pi	May-June	
Crape-myrtle	Pi	August	
Daphne, Rose	Pi	May	F
Deutzia rosea 'Eximia'	Pi	May	
Heather, many cultivars	Pi	Summer	
Hibiscus, Chinese	Pi	Summer	
Honeysuckle, Albert-thorn	dk-Pi	May	F
Belle, various	Pi	May	
Blue-leaf	R-Pi	May	
Spangle	lt, dk-Pi	May	
Tatarian	Pi	May	
Hydrangea, House (in alkaline soil)	Pi	August	

Key:

Cr = cream-white		Sc = scarlet	
Li = lilac		W = white	
O = orange		Y = yellow	
Pi = pinkish		lt = light	
R = red		dk = dark	

COMMON NAME	COLOR	BLOOM TIME	FRAGRANCE
Lilac, French hybrids	Pi-Li	May	F
Korean early	Pi	May	
Locust, Kelsey	Pi	May	
Magnolia, Star 'Rosea'	Pi	April	
Stanford	Pi	March-April	
Mountain-laurel	Pi to W	June	
Ninebark, Eastern	Pi to W	June	
Oleander	Pi	April onward	
Peony, tree	Pi	May	
Quince, Flowering, cultivars	Pi	May	
Rhododendron, species and cultivars	lt-Pi to R	May, June	some F
Rhodora (Rhododendron)	Pi-P	May	
Rose-acacia	Pi-P	June	
Roses, species and cultivars	lt, dk-Pi	May, June, July	F
Hybrid cultivars	lt, dk-Pi	June onward	F
Snowberry	Pi-W	June	
Spirea, Billiard	Pi	June-July	
Hardhack	Pi	June	
Summersweet 'Rosea'	Pi	July	F
Sweetbells (Leucothoe)	Pi-W	May	
Tamarix, species	Pi	May-July	
Viburnum, Burkwood	Pi to W	May	F
'Carlecephalum'	lt-Pi	May	F
Korean-spice (*Carlesii*)	lt-Pi to W	May	F
Leatherleaf	lt-Pi	June	
Weigela, cultivars	Pi	May	

RED AND REDDISH

R = red	Y = yellow		
Pi = pink	O = orange		
Cr = crimson	lt = light		
Sc = scarlet	dk = dark		

COMMON NAME	COLOR	BLOOM TIME	FRAGRANCE
Abelia, Mexican	R	Summer	
Allspice, Carolina	dk R	May	F
Anise-tree, Florida	R	July	leaves F
Azalea, species and cultivars (Flame, Hiryu, Ghent, Japanese Kurume)	R to Pi-R	April-June	some F
Bottlebrush	R	February-July	
Broom, cultivars:			
'Burkwoodii'	dk R	May	
'California'	Sc	May	
'San Francisco'	R	May	
'Stanford'	R to O	May	
Buckeye, Flame	R	May	
Butterfly-bush	dk R	August	
Camellia, cultivars	R to Pi	October-April	
Chokeberry, Red	R or W	May	

COMMON NAME	COLOR	BLOOM TIME	FRAGRANCE
Crape-myrtle	R	August	
Currant, Clove	R	May	F
Winter	R	May	
Enkianthus	R to Y	May	
Fuchsia, Magellan and cultivars	R	June	
Heath (*Erica*) cultivars	R	Summer	
Spring	R	April	
Heather, species and cultivars	R	Summer	
Hibiscus, Chinese	Sc, R to Pi	Summer	
Honeysuckle, Tatarian 'Pulcherrima'	R to dk Pi	May	
Oleander	R	Spring onward	
Peony, Tree-	R	May	
Rhododendron, species and cultivars	R, R-P, R to Pi	May-June	
Roses, Hybrid cultivars	Sc, R, Cr	June onward	F
Species and cultivars	R to Pi	Spring, summer	F
Sheep-laurel	lt R to Cr	June	
Shrub-althea (Rose of Sharon)	R	August	
Spirea 'Anthony Waterer'	Cr	June	
Mikado	dk Cr	June	
Weigela 'Bristol Ruby'	R	May	
Witch-hazel	R to O-Y	February	F

LAVENDER TO PURPLE

Abelia 'Edward Goucher'	La-P	July to September	
Schumann	La-Pi	June to September	
Broom, Purple	P	Mid-May	
Azalea, species and cultivars	Li, La, P	April-May	
Yodogawa and cultivars	R-P	May	
Butterfly-bush	P	August	
Chaste-tree	P, B-P	August	F
Cutleaved	Li or La	August	F
Daphne, February	Li	April	F
Winter	Li-P	March-April	F
Elscholtzia, Staunton	Li-P	August-September	
Heath, Darley	Li-Pi	November-Spring	
Heath, Mediterranean	Li-Pi	April	
Irish	P	Summer	
Honeysuckle, Lilac	Pi-Li	May	F
Tibet	La	May	F

Key:

P = purple   B = blue or bluish
Pi = pink or pinkish   R = red
Li = lilac   W = white
La = lavender

COMMON NAME	COLOR	BLOOM TIME	FRAGRANCE
Hydrangea, Oak-leaved	W then P	June	
Sargent	Li-B	July	
Indigo, Pink	Li-P	June	
Potanin	Li-Pi	June	
Judas-tree, Chinese	P-Pi	May	
Lavender, True	La	June	F
Lilac, Chinese	P-Li	May	
Lilac, French hybrids, cultivars	La, Li, P, R-P, Pi-La, B-P	May	F
Hungarian	Li-P	June	F
Littleleaf	Li	May	F
Persian	Li-P	May	F
Sweginzowi	R-Li	May-June	
Magnolia, Purple lily	P	May	
Oleander	P	April onward	
Rhododendron, Carolina	Pi-P	May	
Species and hybrids	La, Li, P	April-June	
Raspberry, Flowering	P	July	F
Rock-rose, Purple	R-P	Summer	
Whiteleaf	Pi-P	Summer	
Salt-tree	La	June	F
Shrub-althea (Rose of Sharon)	B-P	August	
Sophora, Vetch	P to W	June	
Spirea, Hardhack	Pi-P to Pi	June	

BLUE AND BLUISH

COMMON NAME	COLOR	BLOOM TIME	FRAGRANCE
Bluebeard, species and cultivars	Bl	August	
Blueblossom	Bl	March	
Ceanothus, Delisle	Bl	August	
Chaste-tree	Bl-P to Li	August	F
Hydrangea, House (in acid soil)	B	August	
Sargent	Bl-La	July-August	
Lavender, True, cultivars	dk Bl	June	F
Lead plant	Bl	July	
Leadwort, Wilmott Blue	Bl	Summer	
Lilac, French hybrids, cultivars	Bl, Bl-P	May	F
Mescal-bean	Bl-P	February-March	F
Rosemary	P-Bl	Winter-Spring	F
Shrub-althea (Rose of Sharon)	lt Bl	June	
Sophora, Vetch	Bl-P to W	June	

Key:

Bl = blue	W = white
P = purple	lt = light
La = lavender	dk = dark
Li = lilac	

109

COMMON NAME	COLOR	BLOOM TIME	FRAGRANCE
YELLOW TO ORANGE			
Azalea, Ghent cultivars	Y, Y-O, O	May-June	
Japanese cultivars	O-R,	May	
Lutea cultivars	Y-O, Y	May	
Mollis cultivars	Y to O	May	
Barberry, Bean's	Y	June	
Black	Y	May	
Cutleaf	Y	May	
Dainty	Y	May	
Darwin	Y	May	
Japanese	O and Y	May	
Longspine	Y	May	
Mentor	Y	May	
Paleleaf	Y	May	
Warty	Y	May	
Wintergreen	Y	May	
Bladder-senna	Y	May	
Broom, cultivars, species	Y	May-Summer	
Spanish (*Spartium*)	Y	Summer	
Bush-honeysuckle, Southern	dk Y	June	
Cinquefoil (Potentilla) cultivars	Y	May onward	
Cornelian-cherry	lt Y	April	
Currant, Clove	Y to R	May	F
Daphne, Giraldi	Y	May	F
Dyers-greenweed	Y	May	
Eleagnus, Autumn-olive	Y to W	May	F
Cherry	Y-W	May	F
Enkianthus, Redvein	Y-O to Y	May	
Forsythia species, cultivars	lt, dk Y	April	
Genista, species	Y	May-June	
Gorse, Spanish	Y	June	
Holly-grape, Oregon (Mahonia)	Y	May	F
Honeysuckle, Amur	W to Y	May	F
Morrow	W to Y	May	
Hypericum (St. Johnswort)	Y	Summer	
Kerria, species and cultivars	Y-O, O-Y	May	
Lavender-cotton	Y	Summer	
Mahonia species	Y	May	F
Oleander	Y	April onward	
Pea-tree, Littleleaf	Y	May	
Maximowicz	Y	May	
Siberian	Y	May	
Peony, Tree	Y, Y-O, O-Y	May	

Key: Y = yellow   W = white
O = orange   lt = light
R = red   dk = dark

COMMON NAME	COLOR	BLOOM TIME	FRAGRANCE
Quince, Flowering 'Apricot'	O-Y	May	
Flowering 'Double Orange'	O	May	
Rabbitbrush, Greenplume	dk Y	Summer	
Rhododendron, cultivars			some F
Exbury and Knaphill Series	Y, Y-O, O	May	
Rhododendron species			
Keisk	Y	May	
Fortune and hybrids	Y	May	
Roses, species and cultivars	Y, O-Y	June	
Hybrid cultivars	Y, O-Y, O, O-R	June onward	
Spice-bush	Y	April	leaves F
St-Johnswort	Y	Summer	
Viburnum, Mapleleaf	Y-W	June	
Woadwaxen *see Genista*			
Witch-hazel, Chinese	Y	March	F
Common	Y	October	F
Vernal	Y	February	F
Wintersweet	Y	August	F
Wormwood	Y	Summer	
Beach-	Y	Summer	
Winter-hazel	Y	April	F

SHRUBS WITH BERRIES OR FRUIT

Not the least virtue of shrubs is the fruit or berries that so many bear. Some of these are edible by man, some by birds only, but practically all berried shrubs are decorative in the garden. A few retain their fruits in autumn or well into winter, making a welcome contribution of color during the somber days after the leaves fall. Some evergreens and many broad-leaved evergreens are also fruit-bearing. The most commonly known, of course, is the red-berried, glossy-leaved holly we enjoy at Christmas. But there are many other colors besides red: yellow, orange-yellow, orange, orange-red, light blue, dark blue, blue-black, black, pinkish to reddish, purple and even white. All berried shrubs are good candidates for garden use while those that make a display of flowers early in the season and then have decorative fruits are doubly prized by gardeners. Some are not conspicuously flowered but the summer foliage is interesting or acceptable and the berries are the best feature. All of these categories may find a place in the home garden, the natural garden and on larger plots in many uses.

COMMON NAME	SCIENTIFIC NAME	COLOR
WHITE BERRIED (white to whitish)		
Cherry, White Manchu	*Prunus tomentosa* 'Leucocarpa'	W
Dogwood, Gray	*Cornus racemosa*	W
Red osier	*Cornus stolonifera*	W
Siberian	*Cornus alba* 'Sibirica'	W
Groundsel-bush	*Baccharis halimifolia*	W
Indian-currant, White	*Symphoricarpos orbiculatus* 'Leucocarpus'	W
Nandina, White-berried	*Nandina domestica* 'Alba'	W
Snowberry, Garden	*Symphoricarpos albus* 'Laevigatus'	W
Wintergreen, Miquel	*Gaultheria miqueliana*	W
YELLOW BERRIED		
Barberry, Cutleaf	*Berberis circumserrata*	Y
Cornelian-cherry, Yellow	*Cornus mas* 'Flava'	Y
Cranberry-bush, European	*Virburnum opulus* 'Xanthocarpum'	Y
Cranberry-bush, Yellow Sargent	*Viburnum sargentii* 'Flavum'	Y
Hardy-orange	*Poncirus trifoliata*	Y
Honeysuckle, Morrow	*Lonicera morrowii* 'Xanthocarpa'	W-Y
Tatarian	*Lonicera tatarica* 'Lutea'	Y
Olive, Russian	*Eleagnus angustifolia*	Y
Viburnum, Linden	*Viburnum dilatatum* 'Xanthocarpum'	Y
Orange-fruited Tea-	*Viburnum setigerum* 'Aurantiacum'	O-Y
Yellow Sargent	*Viburnum sargentii* 'Flavum'	Y
BLACK BERRIED (some red at first, change to black)		
Barberry, Black (BLE)	*Berberis gagnepainii*	Bl-B
Rosemary (BLE)	*Berberis stenophylla*	B
Threespine (BLE)	*Berberis tricanthophora*	Bl-B
Warty (BLE)	*Berberis verruculosa*	P-B
Wintergreen (BLE)	*Berberis julianae*	Bl-B
Black haw, *see Viburnum, Black haw*		
Buckthorn, Dahurian	*Rhamnus davurica*	B

Key:

B = black	R-O = red-orange
Bl = blue	Ro = rose-pink
BLE = broad-leaved evergreen	S = scarlet
C = crimson	SE = semi-evergreen
Cl = clusters	W = white
O = orange	Y = yellow
O-R = orange-red	Y-O = yellow-orange
O-Y = orange-yellow	* = flower and fruit sexes on separate shrubs
P = purple	
Pi = pink	x = hybrid
R = red	

COMMON NAME	SCIENTIFIC NAME	COLOR
Cherry-laurel	*Prunus laurocerasus*	P-B
Chokeberry, Black	*Aronia melanocarpa*	B
Currant, Winter, *see Winter Currant*		
Holly, Inkberry (BLE)	*Ilex glabra*	B
Japanese	*Ilex crenata*	B
Laurestinus (BLE)	*Viburnum tinus*	Bl-B
Laurel, Cherry- *see Cherry-laurel*		
Mahonia, Creeping (BLE)	*Mahonia repens*	B
Myrtle (BLE)	*Myrtus communis*	Bl-B
Nannyberry, *see Viburnum, Nannyberry*		
Osmanthus, Fortune's	x*Osmanthus fortunei*	Bl-B
Holly (BLE)	*Osmanthus ilicifolius*	Bl-B
Privet, Amur	*Ligustrum amurense*	B
Border	*Ligustrum obtusifolium*	B, Bl-B
California (SE)	*Ligustrum ovalifolium*	B
Chinese	*Ligustrum sinense*	B
Common (SE)	*Ligustrum vulgare*	B
Glossy (BLE)	*Ligustrum lucidum*	Bl-B
Henry (BLE)	*Ligustrum henryi*	B
Ibolium	x*Ligustrum ibolium*	B
Japanese (BLE)	*Ligustrum japonicum*	B
Regel	*Ligustrum obtusifolium* 'Regelianum'	B, Bl-B
Staunton	*Ligustrum sinense* 'Stauntonii'	B
Vicary	x*Ligustrum vicaryi*	Bl-B
Raspberry, Flowering	*Ribes odoratum*	B
Sand-cherry, Western	*Prunus besseyi*	P-B
Viburnum, Black haw	*Viburnum prunifolium*	Bl-B
Burkwood	*Viburnum burkwoodii*	R-B
Fragrant	*Viburnum fragrans*	R-B
Henry (BLE)	*Viburnum henryi*	R-B
Hobblebush	*Viburnum alnifolium*	R-B
Korean spice	*Viburnum carlesii*	B
Leatherleaf	*Viburnum rhytidophyllum*	R-B
Mapleleaf	*Viburnum acerifolium*	B
Nannyberry	*Viburnum lentago*	B
Siebold	*Viburnum sieboldii*	R-B
Sweet (BLE)	*Viburnum odoratissimum*	R-B
Wayfaring-tree	*Viburnum lantana*	R-B
Withe-rod	*Viburnum cassinoides*	R-B
Winter-currant*	*Ribes sanguineum*	Bl-B
Withe-rod, *see Viburnum, Withe-rod*		

113

COMMON NAME	SCIENTIFIC NAME	COLOR
PURPLE BERRIED (some purplish black or blackish purple)		
Barberry, Bean's	*Berberis beaniana*	P
Darwin	*Berberis darwinii*	P
Paleleaf	*Berberis candidula*	P
Warty	*Berberis verruculosa*	P-B
Bayberry, California*	*Myrica californica*	P
Beauty-berry, Japanese	*Callicarpa japonica*	R-P
Box-honeysuckle	*Lonicera nitida*	B-P
Cherry-laurel	*Prunus laurocerasus*	P to B
Chokeberry, Purple	*Aronia prunifolia*	P-B
Fig	*Ficus carica*	P
Honeysuckle, Privet-	*Lonicera pileata*	R-P
Pernettya, Chilean	*Pernettya mucronata*	B to P
Plum, Beach	*Prunus maritima*	P
Portugal-laurel	*Prunus lusitanica*	P
Raspberry, Boulder	*Rubus deliciosus*	P
Sand-cherry, Purple	*Prunus cistena*	B-P
Western	*Prunus besseyi*	P to B
Shadblow	*Amelanchier canadensis*	R-P
Smoke-bush, Purple hairs	*Cotinus coggygria* 'Purpureus'	P
ORANGE BERRIED		
Euonymus, Broadleaf	*Euonymus latifolia*	R-O
Firethorn, Hybrid (SE)	*Pyracantha* 'Oxford'	O-R
Laland	*Pyracantha coccinea* 'Lalandii'	O-R
Rogers (SE)	*Pyracantha rogersiana*	O-R
Honeysuckle, Blue-leaf	*Lonicera korolkowii*	R-O
Lilac	*Lonicera syringantha*	R-O
Sea-buckthorn*	*Hippophae rhamnoides*	O
Sumac, Chinese	*Rhus chinensis*	O-R
Viburnum, Orange-fruited tea	*Viburnum setigerum* 'Aurantiacum'	O to Y-O
RED BERRIED (including pink, red-orange and purplish red)		
Alexandrian-laurel	*Danae racemosa*	R
Almond, Dwarf flowering	*Prunus glandulosa*	R
Dwarf Russian	*Prunus tenella* 'Alba'	R
Ardisia, Coral	*Ardisia crispa*	R
Aucuba, Japanese*	*Aucuba japonica*	R
Barberry, Dainty	*Berberis concinna*	R
Japanese	*Berberis thunbergii*	R
Korean	*Berberis koreana*	R, Cl.
Longspine	*Berberis potanini*	R
Mentor	x*Berberis mentorensis*	R
Black alder (Winterberry)	*Ilex verticillata*	R
Buffaloberry, Russet*	*Shepherdia canadensis*	R, Cl.
Bush-cherry, Nakai Chinese	*Prunus japonica* 'Nakai'	R
Ceanothus, Island	*Ceanothus ovatus*	R
Cherry, Manchu	*Prunus tomentosa*	S

COMMON NAME	SCIENTIFIC NAME	COLOR
Chokecherry, Red	*Aronia arbutifolia*	R
Christmas-berry, California	*Heteromeles arbutifolia*	R
Crab apple, Sargent	*Malus sargentii*	R
Coralberry, Chenault	x*Symphoricarpos chenaultii*	Pi-R
Cornelian-cherry	*Cornus mas*	S
Cotoneaster, Bearberry	*Cotoneaster dammerii*	R
Creeping rockspray	*Cotoneaster adpressa*	R
Henry	*Cotoneaster henryi*	C
Himalayan	*Cotoneaster frigida*	R
Rock-spray	*Cotoneaster horizontalis*	R
Showy	*Cotoneaster multiflora* 'Calocorpa'	R to Pi
Simon's	*Cotoneaster simonsii*	S
Small-leaved	*Cotoneaster microphylla*	R
Spreading	*Cotoneaster divaricata*	R
Vilmorin	*Cotoneaster bullata* 'Floribunda'	S
Willowleaf	*Cotoneaster salicifolia* 'Floccosa'	R
Cotoneaster, Cultivar	*Cotoneaster* 'Autumn Fire'	R
Cranberry-bush, American	*Viburnum trilobum*	S
European	*Viburnum opulus*	R
Currant, Alpine*	*Ribes alpinum*	S
Dahoon*	*Ilex cassine*	R
Daphne, February	*Daphne mezereum*	S
Giraldi	*Daphne giraldii*	S
Elder, European red	*Sambucus racemosa*	S
Golden American	*Sambucus canadensis* 'Aurea'	R
Scarlet	*Sambucus pubens*	S
Eleagnus, Autumn-olive	*Eleagnus umbellata*	S
Cherry	*Eleagnus multiflora*	R
Euonymus, Broadleaf	*Euonymus latifolia*	R-O-R
Dwarf	*Euonymus nana*	Pi
Evergreen	*Euonymus japonica*	Pi-O
Yeddo	*Euonymus yedoensis*	R
Firethorn, Gibbs	*Pyracantha atlantoides*	S-C
Scarlet	*Pyracantha coccinea* and cultivars	R-R-O
Holly, Chinese*	*Ilex chinensis* and cultivars	R
Burford*	*Ilex chinensis* 'Burfordii' and cultivars	R
Longstalk*	*Ilex pendunculosa*	R
Perny*	*Ilex pernyi*	R
Honeysuckle, Albert-thorn	*Lonicera spinosa* 'Albertii'	R
Amur	*Lonicera maackii*	R
Arnold	x*Lonicera amoena* 'Arnoldiana'	R
Belle	x*Lonicera* 'Bella' and cultivars	R
Morrow	*Lonicera morrowii*	R
Spangle	*Lonicera gracilipes*	S
Tatarian	*Lonicera tatarica*	R
Winter	*Lonicera fragrantissima*	R
Indian-currant (Coralberry)	*Symphoricarpos orbiculatus*	Pi-R

115

COMMON NAME	SCIENTIFIC NAME	COLOR
Laurel, Alexandrian-, *see* Alexandrian-laurel		
Locust, Kelsey	*Robinia kelseyi* (hairy pods)	R
Magnolia, Purple lily	*Magnolia liliflora* 'Nigra' (pods)	R
Star	*Magnolia stellata* (pods)	R
Sweet bay	*Magnolia virginiana* (pods)	R
Wilson	*Magnolia wilsonii* (pods)	R
Maples, various	*Acer*, species	R
Nandina	*Nandina domestica*	R-P
Photinia, Chinese	*Photinia serrulata*	R
Oriental	*Photinia villosa*	R
Plum, Beach-	*Prunus maritima*	often C-P
Possum-haw*	*Ilex decidua*	S-O
Raspberry, Flowering	*Rubus odoratus*	R
Rose	*Rosa* species, cultivars (especially native kinds)	R
Sarcococca, Fragrant	*Sarcococca ruscifolia*	S
Serviceberry, Allegheny	*Amelanchier laevis*	R
Apple	x*Amelanchier grandiflora*	Pi-R-B
Skimmia, Japanese*	*Skimmia japonica*	R
Reeves*	*Skimmia reevesiana*	R
Smoke-bush	*Cotinus coggygria*	Pi
Spice bush	*Lindera benzoin*	R
Spindletree, Aldenham	*Euonymus europaea* 'Aldenhamensis'	Pi-R
Winged	*Euonymus alata*	S
Dwarf winged	*Euonymus alata* 'Compacta'	S
Strawberry-tree	*Arbutus unedo*	R-R-O
Sumac, Fragrant	*Rhus aromatica* (hairy)	R
Shining*	*Rhus copallina* (hairy)	R
Smooth*	*Rhus glabra* (hairy)	S
Staghorn*	*Rhus typhina* (hairy)	C
Viburnum, Doublefile	*Viburnum tomentosum*	R
Japanese	*Viburnum japonicum*	R
Leatherleaf	*Viburnum rhytidophyllum*	R-B
Maries' doublefile	*Viburnum tomentosum* 'Mariesii'	R
Sandankwa	*Viburnum suspensum*	R
Wayfaring-tree	*Viburnum lantana*	R-B
Yew, Several	*Taxus*, species and cultivars	Pi-R

BLUE BERRIED (some changing to black, some whitish to light blue)

Arrow-wood	*Viburnum dentatum*	Bl
Barberry, Black (BLE)	*Berberis gagnepainii*	Bl to B
Threespine (BLE)	*Berberis tricanthophora*	B-B
Wintergreen (BLE)	*Berberis julianae*	Bl-B
Black haw, Southern	*Viburnum rufidulum*	dk-Bl
Blueberries, various	*Vaccinium species* and cultivars	Bl
Box-huckleberry	*Gaylussacia brachycera*	Bl
Dogwood, Siberian	*Cornus alba* 'Sibirica'	W to Bl
Silky	*Cornus amomum*	Bl
Elder, American	*Sambucus canadensis*	Bl to B
Blueberry	*Sambucus caerulea*	Bl to B

COMMON NAME	SCIENTIFIC NAME	COLOR
Farkleberry (BLE)	*Vaccinium arboreum*	Bl
Fatsia (BLE)	*Fatsia japonica*	lt-Bl
Fringe-tree	*Chionanthus virginicus*	dk-Bl
Glory-bower, Harlequin	*Clerodendron trichotomum*	Bl
Juniper, Chinese (E)	*Juniperus chinensis* and cultivars	Bl
Common (E)	*Juniperus communis* and cultivars	Bl
Creeping (E)	*Juniperus horizontalis* and cultivars	Bl
Eastern Red-cedar	*Juniperus virginiana* and cultivars	Bl
Laurestinus (BLE)	*Viburnum tinus*	Bl then B
Mahonia, Leatherleaf (BLE)	*Mahonia bealii*	Bl-B
Oregon holly-grape (BLE)	*Mahonia aquifolium*	Bl-B
Privet, Glossy	*Ligustrum lucidum*	Bl-B
Regel	*Ligustrum obtusifolium* 'Regelianum'	Bl-B to B
Vicary	*Ligustrum vicaryi*	Bl-B
Red-cedar, *see Juniper, Eastern Red-cedar*		
Sweetleaf, Asiatic	*Symplocos paniculata*	lt-Bl
Viburnum, David	*Viburnum davidii*	lt-Bl
Wintergreen, Veitch (BLE)	*Gaultheria veitchiana*	dk-Bl

COLORFUL BARK ON TRUNK OR TWIGS

COMMON NAME	SCIENTIFIC NAME	HEIGHT (IN FEET)	HARDI-NESS ZONE
Blueberry, Highbush	*Vaccinium corymbosum*	12	3
Dogwood, Greentwig	*Cornus stolonifera* 'Nitida'	6–7	2
Red osier	*Cornus stolonifera*	7	2
Siberian	*Cornus alba* 'Sibirica'	9	2
Silky	*Cornus amomum*	9	5
Tatarian	*Cornus alba*	9	2
Yellowtwig	*Cornus stolonifera* 'Flaviramea'	6–7	2
Huckleberry, Box-	*Gaylussacia brachycera*	1½	5
Leucothoe, Sweet bells	*Leucothoe racemosa*	1	5
Maple, Japanese	*Acer palmatum*	20	5
Rose, Dog	*Rosa canina*	8	4
Japanese	*Rosa multiflora*	10	5
Prairie	*Rosa setigera*	to 15	4
Virginia	*Rosa virginiana*	6	3
Snowball, Dwarf European	*Viburnum opulus* 'Nana'	2	3
Willow, Corkscrew (Contorted)	*Salix matsudana* 'Tortuosa'	to 30	4
Redstem	*Salix alba* 'Chermesina'	to 70	2

Note: Some of this listing are actually trees, but do not always grow as tall as mature height given. The same is true of shrubs, for soils and climate conditions affect growth. The height given is the maximum mature height, and this may take many years to achieve. Tall subjects can also be kept lower by pruning, and in most cases the new wood induced is the most colorful.

SHRUBS FOR SHADY SPOTS

It is surprising how many shrubs enjoy shady conditions—probably because in the wild they come from such a habitat, or will adjust to and tolerate varying amounts of shade. That is the important thing—varying amounts. Shade is not an absolutely rigid or distinctly defined condition. There are several degrees and kinds.

FULL SHADE: This occurs under heavy-foliaged trees, usuallly of low-branching habit of growth. Because of this, and because tree roots may take a good bit of sustenance from the shrub root area, it pays to be careful in planting under trees with such rigorous conditions.

LIGHT SHADE or HIGH SHADE: Open-branching trees and high-branching ones that have light foliage allow light and sunlight to filter through, producing light shade conditions.

HALF SHADE: Areas that receive direct sunlight in the morning or afternoon (or possibly some in the middle of the day) but are shaded the rest of the day qualify for this category. They may be open to the sky and receive some light.

OPEN SHADE: Spots alongside a house wall or a high garden wall or that are shaded by trees placed outside the immediate area so that they do not overhang the bed meet the specifications for this category. Because they are open to the sky, they get some light but not direct sunlight.

Low-growing shrubs that will endure or demand shade are an interesting ground cover category, one useful to the gardener.

COMMON NAME	SCIENTIFIC NAME
Abelia, Glossy (SE)	*Abelia grandiflora*
Aralia	*Acanthopanax sieboldianus*
Alder, various	*Alnus*, species
Ardisia, Coral	*Ardisia crispa*
Andromeda (BLE)	*Pieris*, species
Arborvitae (E)	*Pseudotsuga*, dwarf cultivars
Aucuba, Japanese (BLE)	*Aucuba japonica*
Azalea	*Rhododendron (Azalea)* species and cultivars

Key:
BLE = Broad-leaved evergreen
  E = Needled evergreen
 SE = Semi-evergreen

COMMON NAME	SCIENTIFIC NAME
Barberry, Japanese	*Berberis thunbergii*
Three-spine (BLE)	*Berberis tricanthophora*
Warty (BLE)	*Berberis verruculosa*
Wintergreen (BLE)	*Berberis julianae*
Bayberry (SE)	*Myrica* species
Bladder-senna	*Colutea arborescens*
Blueberry	*Vaccinium* species
Bog-rosemary (BLE)	*Andromeda polifolia*
Box, various (BLE)	*Buxus* species
Box-huckleberry, Southern (BLE)	*Gaylussacia brachycera*
Buckthorn, various	*Rhamnus* species
Bush-honeysuckle	*Diervilla sessilifolia*
Butchers-broom (BLE)	*Ruscus aculeatus*
Camellia, Common (BLE)	*Camellia japonica* and cultivars
Sasanqua (BLE)	*Camellia sasanqua*
Chokeberry, Black	*Aronia melanocarpa*
Purple	*Aronia prunifolia*
Red	*Aronia arbutifolia*
Cinquefoil	*Potentilla fruticosa*
Coontie	*Zamia integrifolia*
Coralberry	*Symphoricarpos chenaultii* and *orbiculatus*
Cornelian-cherry	*Cornus mas*
Cotoneaster	*Cotoneaster* species
Rockspray (SE)	*Cotoneaster horizontalis*
Willowleaf (SE)	*Cotoneaster salicifolia*
Dogwood, Gray	*Cornus racemosa*
Red Osier	*Cornus stolonifera*, and cultivars
Silky	*Cornus ammomum*
Tatarian	*Cornus alba* and *C. a.* 'Sibirica'
Elder, Blueberry	*Sambucus caerulea*
Scarlet	*Sambucus pubens*
False cypress (E)	*Chamaecyparis* species, cultivars
Fatsia	*Fatsia japonica*
Firethorn	*Pyracantha* species and cultivars
Fothergilla	*Fothergilla* species
Fringe-tree	*Chionanthus virginicus*
Hazel	*Corylus* species
Hemlock (E)	*Tsuga* species and cultivars
Hollies (BLE)	*Ilex* most species and cultivars
Honeysuckle	*Lonicera* species and cultivars
Hydrangea, House	*Hydrangea macrophylla* 'Hortensia'
Oak-leaved	*Hydrangea quercifolia*
Hypericum, *see St. Johnswort*	
Jetbead	*Rhodotypos scandens (kerriodes)*
Judas-tree, Chinese	*Cercis chinensis*
Laurel (Sweet bay) (BLE)	*Laurus nobilis*
Laurel, Mountain-, *see Mountain-laurel*	
Laurel, Sheep-, *see Sheep-laurel*	

119

COMMON NAME	SCIENTIFIC NAME
Laurestinus (BLE)	*Viburnum tinus*
Leucothoe (BLE)	*Leucothoe* species
Magnolia, Sweet bay (SE)	*Magnolia virginiana*
Mahonia (BLE)	*Mahonia* species
Mockorange, Sweet	*Philadelphus coronarius*
Mountain-laurel (BLE)	*Kalmia latifolia*
Myrtle (SE to E)	*Myrtus* species
Nandina	*Nandina domestica*
Osmanthus (BLE)	*Osmanthus* species
Pachistima, Canby	*Pachistima canbyi*
Photinia	*Photinia* species
Pittosporum, Japanese (BLE)	*Pittosporum tobira*
Privet (S-E to E)	*Ligustrum* species
Raspberry, Flowering	*Rubus odoratus*
Rhododendrons (BLE)	*Rhododendron* many species
Sarcococca, Fragrant (BLE)	*Sarcococca ruscifolia*
Hooker's (BLE)	*Sarcococca hookeriana* 'Humilis'
Serviceberry, various	*Amelanchier* species
Shallon, Salal (BLE)	*Gaultheria shallon*
Sheep-laurel (BLE)	*Kalmia angustifolia*
Skimmia (BLE)	*Skimmia* species
Snowbell, various	*Styrax* species
Snowberry	*Symphoricarpos* species
Stephanandra, Cutleaf	*Stephanandra incisa*
St. Johnswort, Aaronsbeard	*Hypericum calycinum*
Goldflower	*Hypericum moserianum*
Henry	*Hypericum patulum* 'Henryi'
Hidcote	*Hypericum hookerianum* 'Hidcote'
Kalm	*Hypericum kalmianum*
Summersweet	*Clethra alnifolia*
Viburnum, Arrow-wood	*Viburnum dentatum*
Black haw	*Viburnum prunifolium*
Hobblebush	*Viburnum alnifolium*
Mapleleaf	*Viburnum acerifolium*
Nannyberry	*Viburnum lentago*
Sandankwa	*Viburnum suspensum*
Siebold	*Viburnum sieboldii*
Withe-rod	*Viburnum cassinoides*
Wintercreeper (BLE)	*Euonymus fortunei* and cultivars
Witch-hazel	*Hamamelis* species
Yellow-root	*Xanthoriza simplicissima*
Yew, various (E)	*Taxus* species and cultivars
Zenobia, Dusty	*Zenobia pulverulenta*

SHRUBS DEMANDING OR TOLERANT OF ACID SOIL

Andromeda
Anise-tree, Florida
Azalea (*Rhododendron* species)
Bayberry (*Myrica* species)
Blueberry (*Vaccinium* species)
Bog-rosemary
Broom (*Cytisus* species)
Clethra (*Clethra* species)
Enkianthus
Fothergilla
Heath (*Calluna* species)
Heather (*Erica* species)
Hobblebush
Holly (*Ilex* species)

Juniper, Common
Leucothoe (*Leucothoe* species)
Magnolia, Sweet Bay
Mountain-laurel
New Jersey-Tea
Raspberry (*Rubus* species)
Rhododendron (*Rhododendron* species)
Spicebush
Strawberry-tree
Summersweet (*Clethra* species)
Sweetspire
Teaberry
Yellow-root
Yew

SHRUBS THAT MOST LIKELY WILL SURVIVE IN THE CITY

COMMON NAME	SCIENTIFIC NAME	HEIGHT* (IN FEET)	ZONE**
Acanthopanax	*Acanthopanax sieboldianus*	9	4
Andromeda	*Pieris*, species	6–12	4–7
Aralia, Devil's-walking-stick	*Aralia*, species	var.	3–4
Arrowwood	*Viburnum dentatum*	15	2
Azalea, Hiryu	*Rhododendron obtusum*, and cultivars	3	6
Barberry, Japanese	*Berberis thunbergii*	7	5
Bayberry	*Myrica pennsylvanica*	9	2
Buckthorn	*Rhamnus*, several species	18	2
Cherry, Cornelian	*Cornus mas*	to 20	4
Higan	*Prunus subhirtella*	10–15	5
Chokeberry, Red	*Aronia arbutifolia*	9	2

Key:
var. = variable

* Height: Many species and varieties here given at normal height will be stunted by city conditions or can be kept lower by judicious pruning. Also life expectancy is less in the city, so that replacement might become necessary from time to time if pollution is severe. Cultivars of species shown may or may not be hardier, but are worth exploring.

** Zone of Hardiness: In cities, due to pollution pall and reflected heat, the temperatures may be a bit warmer than on open ground outside the city. The hardiness-zone numbers here are for normal conditions. In protected and warm spots plants might grow a half to a full zone north of the normal zone.

COMMON NAME	SCIENTIFIC NAME	HEIGHT* (IN FEET)	ZONE**
Cinquefoil, Bush	*Potentilla fruticosa*	to 4	2
Coralberry	*Symphoricarpos orbiculatus*	3–6	2
Chenault	*Symphoricarpos chenaultii*	3	5
Crab apple	*Malus*, smaller species	var.	4
Cranberry-bush, European	*Viburnum opulus*	12	3
Crape-myrtle	*Lagerstroemia indica*	20	7
Deutzia, Snowflake	*Deutzia scabra*	8	5
Dogwood, Bloodtwig	*Cornus sanguinea*	12	4–5
Gray	*Cornus paniculata*	3–8	3
Red osier	*Cornus stolonifera*	7	2
Silky	*Cornus amomum*	9	5
Tatarian	*Cornus alba*	9	2
Elder, American	*Sambucus canadensis*	12	3
Eleagnus, Autumn-olive	*Eleagnus umbellata*	12	3
Euonymus	*Euonymus*, several species (except evergreen kinds)	var.	var.
False-spirea	*Sorbaria*, species	var.	5–6
Fatsia	*Fatsia japonica*	to 15	7
Firethorn, Laland	*Pyracantha coccinea* 'Lalandii'	10	5–6
Forsythia, various	*Forsythia*, species	var.	4–5
Fringe-tree	*Chionanthus virginicus*	to 30	4
Hawthorn, Washington	*Crataegus phaenopyrum*	to 25	4
Hibiscus, Chinese	*Hibiscus rosa-sinensis*	to 25	9
Holly, Japanese	*Ilex crenata*	20	6
Holly-grape, Oregon	*Mahonia aquifolium*	3–5	5
Honeysuckle	*Lonicera*, species	4–15	2–7
Hydrangea	*Hydrangea*, species	4–8	4–7
Indigo-bush (False-indigo)	*Amorpha fruticosa*	20	4
Inkberry	*Ilex glabra*	20	3
Jetbead	*Rhodotypos scandens*	7	5
Juniper, Pfitzer's	*Juniperus chinensis* 'Pfitzeriana'	to 10	4
Kerria	*Kerria japonica*	4–6	4
Leucothoe, Drooping	*Leucothoe catesbaei*	6	4
Lilac, Common	*Syringa vulgaris*	to 15	3
Hybrids	*Syringa*, various	6–15	2–5
Magnolia, Saucer	*Magnolia soulangiana*	to 25	5
Star	*Magnolia stellata*	to 20	5
Maple, Amur	*Acer ginnala*	20	2
Matrimony-vine	*Lycium chinense*, and vars.	2–5	4
Mockorange, Sweet	*Philadelphus coronarius*	9	4
Nannyberry	*Viburnum lentago*	to 30	2
Ninebark, Eastern	*Physocarpus opulifolius*	9	2
Olive, Russian	*Eleagnus angustifolia*	20	2
Pea-tree, Siberian	*Caragana arborescens*	18	2
Pittosporum, Japanese	*Pittosporum tobira*	10	8
Privet	*Ligustrum*, species	var.	3–7
Quince, Japanese	*Chaenomeles japonica*	4	4
Rose, Memorial	*Rosa wichuriana*	prostrate	5
Rugosa	*Rosa rugosa*	6	2

COMMON NAME	SCIENTIFIC NAME	HEIGHT* (IN FEET)	ZONE**
Sea-buckthorn	*Hippophae rhamnoides*	to 30	3
Serviceberry	*Amalanchier laevis*	25	4
Shrub-althea	*Hibiscus syriacus*	15	5
Snowball, Chinese	*Viburnum macrocephalum* 'Sterile'	12	6
Japanese	*Viburnum tomentosum* 'Sterile'	10	5
Snowberry	*Symphoricarpos albus* 'Laevigatus'	6	3
Spicebush	*Lindera benzoin*	to 15	4
St. Johnswort, Golden	*Hypericum frondosum*	3	5
Spirea, 'Anthony Waterer'	*Spiraea bumalda*, cultivar	3	5
Vanhoutte	*Spiraea vanhouttei*	7	4
Sumac	*Rhus*, species	var.	2–5
Wayfaring tree	*Viburnum lantana*	15	3
Witch-hazel	*Hamamelis*, species	var.	4–5
Yellow-root	*Xanthoriza simplicissima*	2	4
Yew, English	*Taxus baccata*	to 50	6
Japanese	*Taxus cuspidata*	to 50	4

THE REASON FOR ROSES

Time after time the popularity contest for garden plants is won by roses, and this is understandable, for roses are generally rewarding, offering splendid dividends to the gardener. Anyone can grow roses, it is said, and this is more or less true in every region provided proper care is given. Those, by the way, are the key words: proper care. This is the rock on which the hopes of many gardeners are wrecked. Lured by enticing pictures, people often rush into buying and planting without considering what is needed for success with roses. Along with disappointment comes disenchantment, and the blame often falls on the roses.

Roses are such wonderful plants, so varied, so colorful, and they make such a contribution to the garden that a little forethought is needed to get the full value in return for one's investment of money and labor. Roses will grow in such widely varying conditions that there seems to be little reason why every garden cannot accommodate a few. The point is that you must know what kind of roses will do best for you, for the rose family is a large and very rich one, offering myriads of choices.

What do you mean by choices?

There are two broad categories: the species roses and the modern hybrids. The species roses are the native roses gathered from all over the world, though there may be named hybrids or cultivars of them offered in the trade. For example, the rugosa rose (*Rosa rugosa*), with thorny canes and rugose (rough or wrinkled) leaves has some excellent cultivars that offer larger flowers, longer periods of bloom, and other desirable qualities. Its innate vigor and hardiness make it possible to grow it in Maine or in California, in sandy or in heavy soils. Although it is not usually considered a good companion for the more refined hybrid teas and floribundas, it can be planted with other shrubs and in places where the beautiful but effete hybrids will not thrive. Other species roses, often found listed in catalogs as "old roses," may also be suited to your particular conditions, particularly if they are native to your region or to similar regions. They are well worth considering.

The modern hybrids (modern meaning within the last fifty to one hundred years) have considerable interest, particularly today when people all over the country are growing roses. Fascinating new developments in crossing and breeding have brought new colors, new vigor, and other new desirable qualities to the category. There are three divisions under this heading:

Hybrid tea roses are similar to the so-called florist's roses, with large flowers, pointed buds, and multiple petals.

Floribunda roses are a development that brought greater hardiness to the category by bringing in certain qualities from the polyantha-rose parent while keeping a good many of the splendid attributes of the hybrid-tea parent. They are smaller-flowered than hybrid teas but occur in clusters, often as many as twenty or more flowers to the cluster.

Grandiflora roses are tall and robust, with blooms similar to hybrid teas but not always produced singly. Some candelabra-branching growths, as with floribundas, present multiple blooms, though they are fewer than floribundas. There is some argument in the trade as to whether this should be a separate category. Pending the settlement, if any, many catalogs list them as a separate category, leaving the argument to the rosarians, since gardeners usually feel like Juliet in Shakespeare's immortal play: "What's in a name? That which we call a rose / By any other name would smell as sweet. . . ." They feel that its grace and color, as well as its fragrance, makes noble any garden bed in which it is placed.

How can you be sure that the rose you choose will be hardy and grow well?

Since about 1940 there has been a system that is a boon to the amateur and, for gardeners all over America, a distinct aid in choosing roses that will produce blossoms wherever they are planted. This is the All-America Rose Selections program. New introductions are submitted by breeders and growers for testing and trial in twenty-four gardens all over the country, strategically located in every climate and condition. After two years of close observation competent judges rate them according to vigor, habit of growth, hardiness, disease resistance, foliage and flower

A ROSE BED burgeons with color all summer, but to enhance its garden effect, plant a good climbing rose with blooms similar to those in the bed and harmonious in color. Train it on a trellis, as here, let it clamber on a house wall, or spill its freshet of color over a fence. (*Courtesy of Jackson & Perkins Company*)

production, form of bud and flower, color at opening of bud and through-out bloom, quality of stem, degree of fragrance, and, finally, novelty. Some roses perform well in certain regions but do not measure up in others. Some may do well initially but less well later on. These are eliminated, and only the best of the best remain with their top ratings in all respects and good performance in every region. These may become All-America Selections for the following season when enough stock has been propagated to meet the demand.

Some years five or six roses may be chosen after passing the rigorous tests and rigid standards. On one occasion no rose was deemed worthy of the high accolade, but most years see two, three, or four selections awarded the honor and offered in nurseries, garden centers, or by mail. You will recognize these plants by the small white seal bearing the inscription AARS and the name of the selection fastened loosely to the plant by a wire. There are, of course, other roses that may do very well indeed for you in your garden, but the surest way to probable success is to depend on these tested roses. Plant them properly, tend them correctly, give them the yearly main-tenance they need, and you will have the fine roses you deserve.

What about climbing roses? How do we choose them?

Some roses "climb," though not in the way that most vines do. Some are sprawlers, covering the ground or enhancing a trellis over a gateway or door, depending on the support offered or the lack of it. The best way to choose a climbing rose is to visit a rose garden in June and note the name of the best ones. If that is not possible, the All-America Rose Selec-tions list has some excellent climbers to choose from.

The hybrid climbers of today are superior to those of the recent past, as breeders combine strains or qualities from roses across the world. To produce hardiness, better color, larger blooms, fragrance, and other wanted characteristics, such as long season of bloom, growers have worked un-ceasingly and with some splendid results.

What are pillar roses and how do they differ from regular climbers?

This is a term that causes much confusion. Ideally, a pillar rose would be one that could be kept to about eight to ten feet, while a climber would be any rose that grew more rampantly. However, many that are called by one name or the other in catalogs and even in the literature do not fit easily into either description. For most of us, the average height listed should be our guide, whatever the nomenclature may be.

What are rambler roses?

The true rambler rose is characterized by flexible long canes, growing from fifteen feet to as much as thirty feet, but having insufficient stiffness to grow upright without support. Most are once-a-season bloomers, producing flowers only on last-year's wood. Each year new canes shoot up from the roots to arch and sprawl and ramble, thus needing more care in the pruning, directing, and support of these new growths. Ramblers are little grown, in general, probably because of this latter factor and also because of the short blooming time, but they are charming roses, and where available they might still be used to cover a sunny bank or to ramble over protected dunes in oceanside gardens. Some rose fanciers collect them and grow them with other "old roses." Less enthusiastic rose growers will content themselves with the hybrids that include rambler "blood" in the family tree but are less demanding of care and pruning, are longer blooming, and may offer other qualities.

Where should roses be planted—in beds with other shrubs or alone?

On the whole, hybrid roses are best placed in beds separated from other shrubs and trees so that root competition is avoided. A root barrier

HYBRID ROSES are best grown in separate beds where they may be properly tended with greater ease. All need much the same conditions—sun, good drainage, spraying to combat pests and diseases, winter protection, and seasonal pruning. Where drainage in the garden soil is poor, a raised bed like the masonry-edged one here solves the problem beautifully. A separate bed also ensures that no other plant roots interfere with the rose roots or rob them of nutrition. (*Courtesy of Jackson & Perkins Company*)

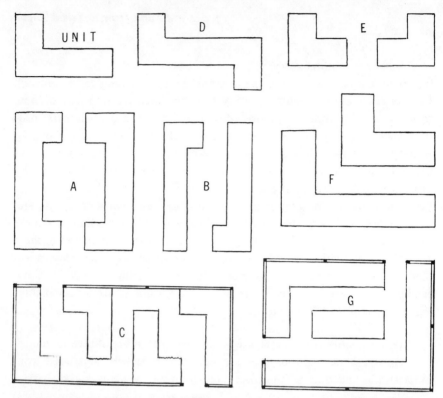

A MODULAR UNIT FOR ROSE BEDS. Roses, particularly modern hybrids, are best grown in separate beds away from other shrubs and trees so that they may be easily tended. A simple modular unit like this L-shaped bed can be adapted in dozens of ways to fit your plan. It may be formal or semiformal in aspect, placed in the open or fenced as a little private garden (*C, G*), set beside a wall, a driveway, or a fence. Units may be bisymmetrical (*A, B, E*), asymmetrical (*C, D, F, G*), extended (*D, B, F, G*), compressed (*E, G*), reversed (*A, B, C, D, E, G*), or adapted in any number of ways according to the space available and its shape.

can be placed deeply in the soil, of course, to discourage competition, but this is not always totally successful.

In general, roses need sun for at least half a day; six hours or more are usually needed. In hot climates, some light shade at midday and the hottest hours of the afternoon will be appreciated. Air circulation is also mandatory to keep down fungus diseases and prevent mildewing of the foliage. Good drainage, both surface and below ground, will provide water at the roots but not so much that the soil becomes waterlogged. Deep, well-prepared soil will give roses proper nutrition and a good start in life.

Proper spacing will allow roses to develop normally (see the chart-sketch on page 128) according to the climate yet allow the gardener to maintain them with sprays, pruning, and other care. Watering and feeding are also accomplished more easily in beds.

To sum up, the recommended location for rose beds is separate from other plant beds, in full sun for half a day or more, with good air circulation, provided with good drainage and deep, well-prepared soil, and, finally, properly spaced according to growth expected in your climate.

Can any roses be grown successfully with other shrubs?

Certain of the species roses can be planted in shrubbery beds provided they have enough room to spread, are not shaded out by encroaching shrubs and trees, and have suitable soil. Rugosa roses, China roses, and centifolia roses have been successfully combined with other shrubs, while climbing roses can be trained on fences beside shrubbery borders provided soil and sun, as well as other conditions are satisfactory. Hybrid varieties are best cultivated in separate beds where they are easily tended, and similar conditions are required for all or most of them.

What kinds of soils are best for growing roses?

Roses are rather tolerant of soils, judging by the locations in which I have observed them, but like all plants, they appreciate the best conditions available. Plenty of organic humus in the soil at planting time aids in aerating the soil, providing drainage with some retention of moisture. In sandy soils—such as at the seaside—much organic humus will be needed to retain sufficient moisture for the roses to thrive. A slightly acid reaction is preferable, between pH 6 and 7 on the testing scale. (See section on soils, Chapter 7.) Roses are known to do rather well in soils somewhat above and below these figures, but not in conditions that are overly acid or too alkaline. If roses grow in your neighborhood in soils similar to your own (untreated soils, that is), then you will probably find your soil is suitable without further adjustment.

What do you mean by adjustment of the soil?

To adjust the soil is to add a specific amount of some component that is needed to bring it to optimum condition. Sandy soils need to be made heavier with organic humus, such as peat moss, leaf mold, animal manure, or compost. Heavy or clay soils need opening up by adding sand and humus to permit drainge and allow air to get to the plant's roots. Acid soil can be

129

made less acid and overly alkaline soil can be made to approach neutral by adding certain ingredients. For roses, for instance, making a bed of 50 square feet (5 feet $\times$ 10 feet) less acid would require adding and mixing in 4 to 8 pounds of agricultural lime (ground raw limestone) and making sure that any compost or leaf-mold humus added was not made from oak or other acid-producing leaves. Acid leaf mold or compost would tend to neutralize the alkaline content of the soil. Similarly, to neutralize an alkaline soil we would mix in 2 to 2½ pounds of aluminum sulfate. Or 1 pound of either garden sulfur or ammonium sulfate might be used instead. See pages 319–321 for a further explanation of soil adjustment.

Do roses need a lot of water or very little?

Roses need plenty of water but not too much. This may sound vague and indefinite, but it is actually the case. Enough water will enable the natural elements and foods in the soil to be taken up by the roots, keeping the plants healthy and promoting good growth. Insufficient moisture means starving the plants, and neglect may mean death for them. On the other hand, too much water does not allow for air penetration to the roots, something that is also necessary for healthy plants. Good drainage (as answered in the question about soil for roses) will permit water to pass through the soil, lingering just long enough to put foods into solution so that the questing roots can absorb and transport the necessary building material for above-ground growth.

When and how much should we feed our roses?

Feedings several times a season are more successful than one or two heavy applications. At a flower show some time ago I heard someone quoting a famous lady who grew superb roses: "I fed 'em like hogs and I water 'em like elephants." This may be taken as a precept, although with some reservations. Too much fertilizer or foods can cause trouble and actually retard growth. Root "burn" may come from heavy applications of commercial fertilizer mixed in the planting soil. Heavy applications of high-nitrogen plant foods may cause excessive leaf growth but lower production of flowers. As with human beings, a balanced diet is recommended.

What is a balanced fertilizer for roses?

The special-formula rose foods offered widely are usually in a ratio of 6-10-4. However, a 5-10-5 formula, the usual garden fertilizer mixture, will suffice. Animal manures may be too high in nitrogen, although they are slower acting and help to add humus to the soil. Compost, with its natural plant foods, is always a good addition, and mulches break down slowly to add fertility as well as humus to the soil.

How much fertilizer is needed, and how often?

For northern gardens (Zones 6 and north) two to three feedings a season are usually sufficient. Suggested times are March 1–15, May 15, and July 15. For gardens south of Zone 6 one to three extra feedings may be in order, and for really warm areas a monthly or six-week feeding program is suggested, slacking off in the winter season to allow plants to rest and go dormant. Feedings in warm areas may be begun earlier—a month before new growth normally occurs—and applied later in the summer or early autumn. In cold areas no feeding beyond midsummer is warranted, for new growth may be forced that would later be killed by frost.

Use no more than a half-cupful of commercial plant or rose food per plant. Distribute it atop the soil about 9 inches out from the base of the rose and cultivate it into the soil well. Then water well, soaking the bed each morning for two or three days. Remember that plants can absorb foods only in liquid form.

How about the foliar feedings one hears about for roses?

Liquid formulae plant foods may be diluted according to directions and sprayed on the leaves of the roses where it will be absorbed directly into the plants. Avoid feeding after August 1 in Zones 5, 6, and 7; but southward, feeding may continue for two to four weeks. Foliar feedings may not be satisfactory when plants are in full flower, since the spray may hit the petals making them unsightly. Rains or watering might wash off foliar foods, but the foods would fall to the soil and eventually be absorbed.

Is there a special time for watering and how often should it be done?

The best time to water is in the early morning. This will give the leaves time to dry off during the sunny part of the day. Wet leaves at night may foster mildew and fungus growth, blackspot, and other troubles. You will be amazed at how much water the soil can absorb. Most rains or showers will wet only the top inch or so of soil, while below that it may be quite dry. Therefore, soak the soil well each time you water, but in that case remember to water less often. Surface sprinkling encourages shallow rooting, which may cause trouble in prolonged hot and dry spells.

A subsurface watering pipe with holes in it for depth irrigation may be a help, particularly in dry climates. Subsurface watering saves water two ways: it prevents evaporation of the sort that occurs each time the surface is watered and it sends water directly to the roots where it can be utilized. Deeper rooting is thereby encouraged, with consequent promotion of growth. Periodic deep soakings or subsurface irrigation will conserve moisture and save time and money.

How deep should the beds be dug and how should they be prepared?

Advance preparation and adequate digging in the beginning will prevent disappointment later. Most soils are average and need no preparation or adjustment beyond digging and some additives to ensure fertility. Some others—sandy or clay soils—require more effort to provide optimum conditions. All rose beds should be dug to at least 18 inches. Removing all soil from the bed and taking out rocks, bits of wood, old roots, brick, plaster and wood chips from building operations, or whatever is encountered must be done before refilling the bed. This is a great deal of work, admittedly, but by doing it before planting you will give the roses the best possible start in their new home. It is even more arduous and expensive later on, and there would be a chance of killing some of the rose plants if piecemeal digging and soil preparation were attempted.

The soil is somewhat acid and rather heavy. What should I do?

Add the following to lighten, open up, and enrich average soil while making it somewhat less acid: Up to 20 percent by volume of peat moss or other humus; 1 pound of ground limestone per bushel of soil (more if the soil is more acid, none if it is alkaline); up to 50 percent by volume of sand; 1 to 2 cupfuls of commercial plant or rose food per bushel of soil. Thoroughly mix in all of this with a spading fork and a shovel before refilling the hole.

Our soil is light and on the alkaline side. How can I adjust it?

Add humus up to half the volume of the soil (most slightly sandy to moderately sandy soils will need only 20 to 25 percent) and adjust it to the neutral area by adding aluminum sulfate, sulfur, or ammonium sulfate (see page 319). Mix thoroughly and refill hole. Water, let settle, and add more of the mixture if it settles below the surface. After a few days dig out planting holes.

How far apart should I plant my roses?

In mild climates, where roses grow larger and spread wider, up to 3 feet between plants is needed, while in cooler to cold climates, 18 inches to 2 feet is sufficient. (See bed sketch here.)

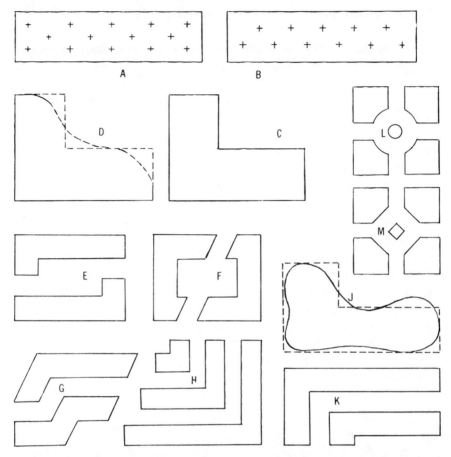

LAYING OUT BEDS. Roses should be planted the proper distance apart: (*A*) in cold climates, 18 inches to 2 feet apart, (*B*) in warm climates, 3 feet apart. Bed shape will vary according to space available and desires of the gardener. L-shapes are convenient, provide easy access for maintenance, and are adjustable in length of arms. Square-edged beds (*C, E, F, G, H, K*) are easiest to lay out, but flowing curves can be built on L-shaped areas for freer form. Classic formal beds (*L* and *M*) feature either round or square centers with access paths from all four sides.

What is the best time for planting roses, spring or autumn?

Either late autumn or early spring planting is best, but in autumn you must make sure to get roses that are already dormant, something that is not always easy to accomplish. Late-season or early-spring planting means that even though nothing seems to be happening above ground, roots are already at work below the surface. Late-spring planting is usually less successful, because there is less time for proper root growth before the roots are called on to send food to the superstructure.

Planting in very cold climates (Zone 5 and north): Because of deep frozen soil and early winters, spring planting is indicated. Plant in the spring as soon as the soil is warm enough to be worked.

Planting in warm climates (Zone 8 and south): Spring planting is suggested here, too, where growth can proceed unimpeded. Spring comes early—January to February—and warm to hot sun means plants should be shaded until the leaves are well started.

Planting in the in-between climates (Zones 5 to 8): Either spring or autumn planting will suffice in most places.

Are container-grown roses all right to plant, and if so, when?

Roses grown in soil in pots or cans, plastic or fiber containers may be planted almost any time, even when in full leaf and flower. Some gardeners prefer to plant them this way, for they can tell where to place them according to color in the bed and also they are sure of what they are buying, although nurseries of reputation supply good dormant plants properly marked. So planted, they are usually a bit more expensive than bare-rooted dormant plants, due to the extra care needed. See Chapter 7 for methods of removing from containers and planting. No cutback is necessary except for broken or dead wood.

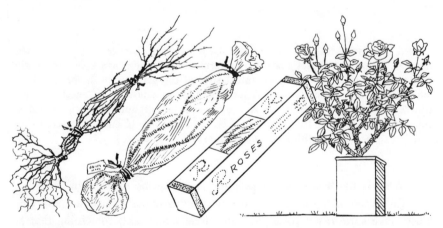

BUYING ROSES. *Left to right,* bare-rooted, sometimes trimmed back, often waxed to prevent canes drying out in storage; bare-rooted in plastic bag, usually with moist sawdust or peat moss around roots; boxed roses, sometimes sealed (superior plants are sold like this). All three of these are ways roses are shipped by mail. *At right,* rose in container (tin, plastic, fiber) is in soil, usually leafed out and often in bloom. Available at nurseries, garden centers, ready to plant.

What are bare-rooted roses and can I plant them with assurance of success?

Bare-rooted rose plants are the usual offerings, whether bought through the mail from a rose grower or purchased in a garden center. These are dormant plants (when offered in spring) that were dug at the end of the season and stored over the winter in a cold-storage house. Often the canes, after being cut back, were wax coated to preserve moisture in the wood, and the roots were trimmed moderately and inserted in a plastic bag that contains moistened peat moss and sometimes wet wood chips. Some companies also offer them in a cardboard box with a plastic window in the side to show the plumpness of the canes and size of the plant. All of these forms are quite usual, and they obviously keep plants alive long enough to be replanted. However, a word of caution might be in order here: Roses, even though bagged about the roots and waxed on the canes, cannot be set in the hot sun outside a garden center or placed in a heated supermarket and live for long. Sometimes one sees roses quite dried out, with dead shoots on the canes still being offered for sale to the unwary. Buy early or not at all, or better still, buy only from professional nurseries that know how to treat plants or by mail from reputable rose growers.

How do I plant roses once I have them in hand?

Assuming that adequate soil preparation has already taken place, plant bare-rooted plants immediately. If you are unable to do so, then heel them someplace in the shade until you can (see pages 307–308). Unwrap them first so that the roots will have contact with the moist soil. Do not delay transplanting too long or root growth may be set back.

For immediate planting, unwrap the roses and put the roots in a pail with enough water to cover them completely. Dig holes 18 inches deep at the proper distance apart. As you plant each rose, take it from the pail, cut off any broken or dead wood from the top, trim back straggly roots and remove broken ones. Follow the procedures shown in the sketches, filling in around the roots with the prepared enriched and adjusted soil. End the procedure by hilling up the soil around the canes to about 8 to 10 inches.

If planting in spring: Keep the soil mound intact until growth appears on the exposed wood, thus allowing sufficient root growth to begin. Reduce the mound a little at a time—say, a couple of inches—until ground level is reached. Then form the soil into a saucerlike depression to contain the water when you soak the plants.

135

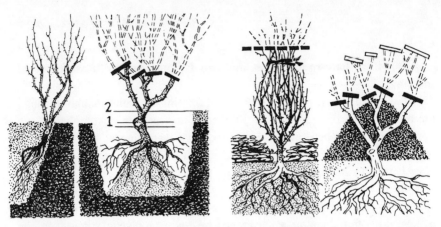

PLANTING BARE-ROOTED ROSES. Remove wrappings on arrival. Soak roots at least an hour in a bucket of water before planting. If immediate transplanting is impossible, heel in, *left,* in a shaded spot. Cover roots and graft knob with soil. *To plant:* Dig holes of adequate depth and width to accommodate roots without cramping. Enrich dug-out soil. Cut back hybrid roses drastically before planting (*sketch*), removing breakage and trimming straggly roots. Make a cone of soil and spread roots around it in the hole, cutting back any that are cramped. In mild climates keep graft knob a little above ground level (*1*); in cold areas, cover it 1 to 3 inches (*2*). Fill hole with soil by stages, tamping, watering, and settling soil each time to prevent air pockets. Make "saucer" of mounded soil to hold water and mound up soil around canes 8 to 10 inches. Leave over winter for fall-planted roses; for spring-planted, leave until growth begins, then remove. *Winter care:* In mild climates, tie canes and cut back a little to prevent whipping by winter winds; mulch deeply with wood chips or other open materials. In cold climates, tie and cut back about half, *top of dotted lines, right,* and mound up soil around canes 8 to 10 inches each year. Cut back dead, damaged canes to live green wood, *black lines,* in spring, and remove soil mound as growth begins.

SPECIES OR OLD ROSES. In general, plant as above but cut back only about one-third. Mulch each winter (leave mulch in summer, too), and each spring cut back dead, damaged, or oldest wood.

If planting in autumn: Keep the soil mound intact all winter. In spring when growth appears on exposed canes, cut back dead wood to strong green growing wood on the canes. Reduce the soil mound in spring as above.

Note: In warm, dry climates plastic bags are sometimes used instead of soil mounds to cover the tops, or canes may be sprayed with wilt-proofing material (obtainable at garden centers) to retain the cane moisture. As growth begins to show, the bag is slit to admit air, and as growth advances, the bag may be removed, usually within a week or so.

In a cold climate, is winter protection needed?

In all areas it is wise to use some kind of winter protection. Roses are vulnerable not only to cold, but also to sudden warming and the cold that follows.

For cold areas: In Zone 5 and northward, after the first frosts, cut back all dead wood, removing completely all wood that shows disease or damage. Tie all canes together about 12 to 18 inches above ground (depending on habit of growth of the plant) with a soft cloth or old nylon stocking. Cut off the canes 4 to 6 inches above the tied area. This will prevent winter winds from whipping the canes about and causing damage to them and adjacent plants. Clean up all dead leaves, weeds, and any debris around the base of the plants, and if you mulch your roses, remove it for the moment. Bring in some clean soil from another part of the garden and mound up each rose to a depth of 8 to 10 inches. The mulch can be replaced between mounds.

In very cold areas, it is wise to add about 6 inches of clean straw or sale hay if it is available or a hefty layer of evergreen boughs. Anchor the layer to prevent dislodgement by winter winds. *Do not use peat moss* or other moisture-retentive materials for mounding up around the canes or they may become diseased by spring, if conditions exist for mold or spores to flourish.

In warm areas: Because "warm" can mean anything from a somewhat mild winter to the truly warm temperatures of Florida and other subtropical temperature areas, no set rule can be given for winter protection. We suggest that you inquire locally, either from the nursery where you purchase your plants or from the county agent or other reliable source for advice.

General practices offered by southern gardeners include cutting back plants in November or December as growth ceases, removing up to one-third the top growth. In really warm areas up to six prunings of the tops are needed yearly in order to prevent overgrowth and distorted plants. Feeding should stop no later than October 1, earlier in cooler sections, so that plants can rest and to arrest new growth that might be injured if the winter proves to be cold and damp. Mulching is recommended all year long to keep soil moist and cooler than the air. Cocoa hulls, bagasse, wood chips, shredded bark, or other organic materials coarse enough to allow rain and water to penetrate to the soil should be used.

MINIATURE ROSES make a big success in the garden, whether filling a bed of their own, edging a bed of full-sized roses, or used in a dozen other ways. They are always garden favorites. Some of the newer varieties ape the tea rose or floribundas in flower form and rival them in color. Crimson Gem, a free-blooming, bushy rose carries some flowers one to a stem, others in clusters. The thimble and needle give the scale of the 1- to 1¼-inch blooms. (*Mateja Assoc.*)

Is it possible to grow roses in hot climates such as Florida?

It is possible to grow hybrid roses in relatively hot climates, even in sandy soils, salt-air conditions, and with brackish water. At the Cape Coral Gardens near Fort Myers, Florida, a large rose garden was established by adjusting maintenance and care to what, for roses, were difficult conditions. The ravages of sun, hot weather, little or no resting time during dormancy, plus other adverse growing conditions were all coped with and overcome. If you live in a similar area, you might wish to visit the gardens and see how this was accomplished.

Are roses subject to pests and diseases and how do you conquer these troubles?

Hybrid roses particularly are subject to insect damage and certain diseases, but the degree will vary with the climate and the location. In

138

most areas pests are not serious enough to warrant much worry. Special formulations in the form of dusts and sprays that contain a combination of control materials aimed at the specific problems of roses are offered at garden centers and nurseries. Where pests and diseases are troublesome, application of sprays or dusts every week to ten days from the first full leafage until the first frost will provide control during the summer and, with a good fall cleanup of the beds, prevent spores and fungi as well as pests from wintering over.

Aside from the hybrid roses, what others are available for modern gardeners?

While the modern hybrids are magnificent and distinctly a step forward from the hybrids of the recent past, many of the old roses are of interest to the plantsman. They are usually grown more for garden display than for cutting and exhibition, although they are very beautiful, intensely fragrant, and often offer attractive foliage even when not in bloom. The "old roses" previously mentioned are one category, while the native roses growing in the wild are certainly hardy and would fit well into gardens of informal, natural character. You would have to get permission, of course, to dig them up. It is better to use small plants rather than the large, older ones that may have extensive roots that might be damaged or cut beyond redemption while being dug.

Another category is the miniature rose. These grow only a foot to a foot and a half tall, have lovely flowers that are in scale with the bushes, and are perfectly hardy in the same way that the hybrids are hardy, requiring similar care and winterizing. They may be used to edge beds, as charming small plants in planters or terrace beds, or any place where their flowers and fine foliage can be admired.

A category called Hedge Roses has become popular lately. These are inexpensive, free-flowering roses that are planted as informal, unclipped hedges alongside driveways, on property borders, or wherever a wide-spreading hedge might fit. However, one rose advertised for hedges is a menace on small properties. This is the multiflora rose, billed in the advertisements as "A Bower of Bloom," and it is—ten to fifteen feet wide—but only in early summer. It is hardy, and its seeds are constantly distributed by birds, so that it is something of a weed plant that must be watched for and eradicated. I can think of only one place where it would be a good hedge and that is on a farm or large estate. But the rugosa rose is one to be recommended highly. It is hardy with little or no protection, full-foliaged, and because of its many-spined stems animals and children will find it unpleasant to try to cross once it is established and throws up many canes. Its handsomely creased bright green leaves are fragrant, as are the flowers. Recurrent-blooming rugosas will produce flowers throughout the season, while the species *Rugosa* will bloom well in only early summer, with perhaps a stray bloom later on now and then. Named cultivars have large blossoms, some are semidouble, and a variety of colors is available. The rugosa rose is desirable and seems to thrive particularly near the sea.

What are some good species roses to consider?

There are a great many, so many that only a brief summary of those that are particular favorites of mine can be presented here, though the list will give indications of others that might fit in other areas.

Many of the species have crossbred or selected cultivars that contribute the vitality and hardiness of the species but give improved color, size of blossom, habit of growth, or some other desirable quality for garden use. Most bloom but once a season, while hybrid teas and floribundas bloom recurrently from June onward until frost (though less vigorously as the season progresses). Some of the species will put forth stray blooms even after the time that they are supposed to be finished blooming.

A favorite of mine is the Cabbage rose, also called Centifolia or Hundred-petal rose (*Rosa centifolia*), first mentioned in 410 B.C. by Herodotus, the Greek historian, as blooming sweetly in the gardens of Midas. The Centifolia's origin is mysterious, though it is believed by some rosarians to be a hybrid or mutation. Known to have reached America in 1633, it has been grown in our gardens ever since. In addition to being a beautiful, fragrant rose, many other old roses stem from its parentage.

Other old roses to consider include Moss, Damask, China, Musk, Alba, and *spinossima*, or Scotch rose. The Gallica is another rose with many progeny. Among the American natives, *R. carolina* and *R. virginiana* are eastern natives, while West Coast roses include *R. californica* and *R. gratissima*. The Swamp rose (*R. palustris*) not only inhabits moist-soil areas, where it grows to as much as eight feet, but is also found on dry hillsides, where it grows only to a moderate two feet or so. It is found from Quebec to Florida and as far west as Iowa. Other native midland roses are *R. macounii*, South Dakota; *R. arkansana*, Wisconsin to Kansas and Colorado; and *R. acicularis bourgeauiana*, a cold-weather type related to the Arctic rose and found from Ontario to British Columbia and as far south as Colorado.

Around old farmhouses or the foundations of burned or razed houses, as well as in nearby woods, where birds have seeded them, old roses may occasionally be found. Cuttings of old roses may be successfully propagated, as I once proved by obtaining some wood from an old rose growing by a nineteenth-century house. As yet not completely identified, it would seem from the blossom to be a kind of miniature damask rose, though the leaves are not characteristic. It has sufficed to grow it, to enjoy it, and to treasure it, because it is truly our own, since we propagated it. Another of our collected roses is *R. virginiana,* "liberated" from the staked-out path of a new road near the seashore over twenty-five years ago. It has been divided and subdivided, planted in sun as well as part shade, and it seems to thrive in both places, even though the soil is not at all sandy as in its original habitat.

Old roses can become a completely absorbing hobby or they can be merely pleasant additions and variations to your plantings. However, two things are sure: they will never be dull, and unless you have a large estate, you will never have room to collect all of them for your garden.

ROSE MAINTENANCE

Aside from the winter protection, the watering, feeding, and general month-to-month care that have already been covered, a yearly pruning program should be part of the care of roses. Pruning is covered in Chapter 7, along with the pruning of shrubs and trees, since they are similar in many ways. However, the old roses require a different pruning program that that of the hybrid teas and other modern roses. Be sure to note this distinction when you read the pruning notes and answers. Also, the miniature roses, which may be grown as pot or house plants, need only occasional heading back to keep them compact and in good health.

ROSE LISTS

ALL-AMERICA ROSE SELECTIONS

These are the roses, year by year, that were chosen after having been grown in trial gardens in all sections of the country as qualified for home gardens in every corner of the land. As nearly as this is possible, these roses will succeed, given normal care and conditions.

YEAR AND WINNER	FLOWER COLOR	CLASS
1975 Arizona	bronze-copper	Gr.
Oregold	pure yellow	Ht.
Rose Parade	pink	Fl.
1974 Bahia	orange-pink	Fl.
Bon Bon	pink and white bicolor	Fl.
Perfume Delight	clear pink	Ht.
1973 Electron	rose-pink	Ht.
Gypsy	orange-red	Ht.
Medallion	apricot-pink	Ht.
1972 Apollo	sunrise yellow	Ht.
Portrait	pink	Ht.
1971 Aquarius	pink blend	Gr.
Command Performance	orange-red	Ht.
Redgold	yellow, red-edged	Fl.
1970 First Prize	rose-red	Ht.
1969 Angel Face	lavender	Fl.
Comanche	scarlet-orange	Gr.
Gene Boerner	pink	Fl.
Pascali	white	Ht.
1968 Europeana	red	Fl.
Miss All-American Beauty	pink	Ht.
Scarlet Knight	scarlet-red	Gr.
1967 Bewitched	clear phlox-pink	Ht.
Gay Princess	shell pink	Fl.
Lucky Lady	creamy shrimp-pink	Gr.
Roman Holiday	orange-red	Fl.
1966 American Heritage	ivory, carmine-tinged	Ht.
Apricot Nectar	apricot	Fl.
Matterhorn	white	Ht.
1965 Camelot	shrimp pink	Gr.
Mister Lincoln	deep red	Ht.
1964 Granada	scarlet, nasturtium, yellow	Ht.
Saratoga	white	Fl.
1963 Royal Highness	clear pink	Ht.
Tropicana	orange-red	Ht.
1962 Christian Dior	crimson-scarlet	Ht.
Golden Slippers	orange-gold	Fl.
John S. Armstrong	deep red	Gr.
King's Ransom	chrome yellow	Ht.
1961 Duet	salmon-pink and orange-red	Ht.
Pink Parfait	dawn pink	Gr.
1960 Fire King	vermilion	Fl.
Garden Party	white	Ht.
Sarabande	scarlet-orange	Fl.

Key:
Ht. = hybrid tea   Gr. = grandiflora
Fl. = floribunda   Cl. = climber

* No longer generally available
† Denotes sectional recommendation, not general

YEAR AND WINNER	FLOWER COLOR	CLASS
1959 Ivory Fashion	ivory	Fl.
Starfire	cherry-red	Gr.
1958 Fusilier	orange-red	Fl.
Gold Cup	golden-yellow	Fl.
White Knight	white	Ht.
1957 Golden Showers	daffodil yellow	Cl.
White Bouquet	white	Fl.
1956 Circus	multicolor	Fl.
1955 Jiminy Cricket	coral-orange	Fl.
Queen Elizabeth	clear pink	Gr.
Tiffany	orchid-pink	Fl.
1954 Lilibet*	dawn pink	Fl.
Mojave	apricot-orange	Ht.
1954 Chrysler Imperial	crimson red	Ht.
Ma Perkins	coral-shell pink	Fl.
1952 Fred Howard*	yellow, penciled pink	Ht.
Helen Traubel	apricot-pink	Ht.
Vogue	cherry-coral	Fl.
1951—(No introductions met rigid AARS standards)		
1950 Capistrano	pink	Ht.
Fashion	coral-pink	Fl.
Mission Bells*	salmon	Ht.
Sutter's Gold	golden yellow	Ht.
1949 Forty-niner	red and yellow	Ht.
Tallyho*	two-tone pink	Ht.
1948 Diamond Jubilee	buff	Ht.
High Noon†	yellow	Cl. Ht.
Nocturne	dark red	Ht.
Pinkie	light rose-pink	Fl.
San Fernando*	currant-red	Ht.
Taffeta	carmine	Ht.
1947 Rubaiyat	cerise-red	Ht.
1946 Peace	pale gold	Ht.
1945 Floradora	salmon-rose	Fl.
Horace McFarland*	buff-pink	Ht.
Mirandy	crimson-red	Ht.
1944 Fred Edmunds†	apricot	Ht.
Katherine T. Marshall	deep pink	Ht.
Lowell Thomas	butter yellow	Ht.
Mme. Chiang Kai-Shek*	light yellow	Ht.
Mme. Marie Curie*	golden yellow	Ht.
1943 Grand Duchesse Charlotte*	wine-red	Ht.
Mary Margaret McBride	rose-pink	Ht.
1942 Heart's Desire	deep rose-pink	Ht.
1941 Apricot Queen*	apricot	Ht.
California*	golden yellow	Ht.
Charlotte Armstrong	cerise-red	Ht.
1940 Dickson's Red	scarlet-red	Ht.
Flash*	oriental red	Cl. Ht.
The Chief*	salmon-red	Ht.
World's Fair	deep red	Fl.

LIST OF OLD ROSES

Old roses include many that are quite ancient—*R. centifolia*, for instance—and others that are hybrids of the old with the native or species roses, some of which go back to about the eighteenth or early nineteenth centuries. A few are of more recent introduction, for old roses have a fascination for the true plantsman, and crossbreeding and improvement of various qualities is a challenge hard to resist. Wherever possible we have inserted the date of introduction, but in many cases it is either unclear or not known.

Colors vary in descriptions, possibly because of variations in the color vocabulary of different observers and probably due to some difference in growing conditions—soil, amount of sun or shade, moisture, and fertilizers used. Where a particular variety was known to the author, it was possible to verify or modify the description of color.

Height is also understandably variable. Where climates are mild but not hot, or favorable in some way, old roses respond quite vigorously, though in other regions their height might be much less. Hence, the wide variations in height in this list. The height of some of the taller roses can be controlled by vigorously cutting back and by yearly pruning. Some of the tall ones might also be espaliered on a wall (see pages 273–281), making use of them as a decorative blossoming feature.

Climbers have been rather sparingly listed here. A few are noted that are not rampant growers and can be kept to shrublike proportions. The newer hybrid climbers, in general, will serve the average gardener better, though the old-rose hobbyist will wish to look up the ramblers and the old climbers in other categories and grow them.

There are many, many more old roses that are quite worthwhile, but this selected list (all specimens of which at the time of writing are available from nurseries specializing in old roses) will serve as a basic, practical guide.

CATEGORY AND COMMON NAME	HEIGHT (IN FEET)	FLOWER FORM	COLOR	ODOR	BLOOM TIME
Rosa alba and hybrids					
Maiden's Blush, before 1800	4–5	db.	white, blush tinge	fr.	spring
Queen of Denmark (Damask hyb.) (also listed Koenigen von Daenemarck)	4–6	db.	pink to light blush pink	fr.	spring
Rosa centifolia, Cabbage, Provence, or Hundred-petal rose					
Rosa centifolia, ancient	5–6	v-db.	pale to rosy pink	v-fr.	June
Rosa centifolia bullata, 1815	4–6	db.	lg. clear pink	fr.	June
de Meaux, before 1800	2–3	s-db.	1″ clear pink	fr.	June
Petite de Hollande	4–5	db.	2″ clear pink	v-fr.	May to June
Tour de Malakoff, 1856	to 7	db.	lilac pink with Parma violet	fr.	June
Variegata de Bologna, 1909	4–8	db.	pink-striped magenta	fr.	early, some recurring
Rosa chinensis, China rose					
Archduke Charles, about 1840	3–4	db.	rose to red	fr.	spring, warm climates only
Gruss an Teplitz, 1894	3–4	db.	dusky scarlet	fr.	recurrent
Old Blush, 1752	3–5	s-db.	clear pink	fr.	recurrent
Rosa chinensis bourboniana, Bourbon rose					
Adam Messerich	4–5	s-db.	bright rose red	fr.	recurrent
Coquette des Alpes, 1867	to 7	v-db.	blush pink	fr.	recurrent, profuse
La Reine Victoria, 1872	4–6		rosy pink	v-fr.	recurrent
Mme. Pierre Oger, 1878	6–7	db.	blush with lilac tinge	fr.	recurrent
Souvenir de la Malmaison, 1843	2½–4	db.	pearly flesh pink	fr.	recurrent

Key:

db. = double	sg. = single
fr. = fragrant	v-db. = very double
s-db. = semi-double	v-fr. = very fragrant

CATEGORY AND COMMON NAME	HEIGHT (IN FEET)	FLOWER FORM	COLOR	ODOR	BLOOM TIME
Rosa damascena, Damask rose					
Celsiana, before 1750	4–5	db.	warm light pink	fr.	May to June
Leda	4–5	db.	blush, red-violet edged	fr.	recurrent
Mme. Hardy, 1832	4–6	db.	large white	fr.	spring
R. damascena bifera, ancient	3–4	v-db.	pink to blush	fr.	recurrent
Rose de Rescht	2½–3	s-db.	deep violet rose	fr.	recurrent
Rose du Roi, 1812	3–4	s-db.	bright to blackish red, light-red reverse	fr.	recurrent
Rosa gallica (provincialis), French rose					
Belle de Crecy, before 1848	4–5	s-db.	cerise pink to violet	fr.	spring
Belle des Jardins, 1872	4–5	s-db.	deep royal purple, lavender reverse	fr.	spring
Camaieux (Cameo), 1830	3–5	db.	white, striped blush	fr.	spring
Empress Josephine, before 1770	4–5	db.	silvery pink	v-fr.	spring
R. gallica grandiflora, Alikan, 1906	3–5	s-db.	large brilliant red	fr.	spring
Rosa hugonis, Father Kugo's rose					
Father Kugo's rose, 1899	6–8	sg.	light bright yellow		May, June
Rosa moschata, Musk rose					
Belinda, 1936	4–7	db.	soft pink, clusters		spring
Buff Beauty, 1939	4–6	db.	cream to yellow-gold	fr.	recurrent
Cornelia, 1925	5–8	s-db.	salmon to strawberry pink	fr.	recurrent
Danae	4–6	db.	large pale yellow	fr.	spring
Pax, 1918 (somewhat climbing)	4–8	s-db.	large ivory to white	fr.	recurrent
Vanity, 1920	6–8	sg.	bright rose pink	fr.	recurrent
Will Scarlet, 1950 (blooms in part shade)	5–7	s-db.	red	fr.	recurrent
Rosa (centifolia) muscosa, Moss rose					
Alba, 1810	4–5	db.	white	v-fr.	spring
Alfred de Dalmas, 1855	2–3	db.	blush pink to white	fr.	recurrent

CATEGORY AND COMMON NAME	HEIGHT (IN FEET)	FLOWER FORM	COLOR	ODOR	BLOOM TIME
Rosa (cont.)					
Common Moss (*R. centifolia muscosa*), 18th century	4–6	db.	clear rose pink	fr.	recurrent
Comtesse de Murinaise	5–6	db.	faint blush white	fr.	spring
Crested Moss, (Chapeau de Napoleon), 1827	4–5	db.	large clear pink	fr.	recurrent
Deuil de Paul Fontaine, 1873	3–4	db.	crimson-black, purple, brownish red tones	fr.	recurrent
Gabriel Noyelle, 1933	4–5	s-db.	salmon pink	fr.	recurrent
Gloire de Mousseux, 1852	4–5	db.	flesh pink	fr.	spring
Mme. Louis Leveque, 1874	4–5	db.	soft salmon pink	fr.	recurrent
Marie de Bloís, 1852	4–5	db.	deep rose pink	fr.	recurrent
Salet, 1854	3–4	db.	bright rose, blush edge	v-fr.	recurrent
Striped Moss, before 1820	3–5	s-db.	crimson and white or pink	fr.	spring
Rosa rugosa, Rugosa rose					
Agnes, 1900	4–6	db.	pale amber	fr.	recurrent
Belle Poitevine, 1894	4–8	db.	lilac pink	fr.	recurrent
Blanc Double de Coubert, 1892	5–7	s-db.	warm cream to white	fr.	June to August
Delicata, 1898	3–4	s-db.	mauve pink	fr.	recurrent
Frau Dagmar Hastrup, 1914	3–5	sg.	soft pink	fr.	recurrent
Hansa	4–8	s-db.	violet red	fr.	recurrent
Rosa rugosa 'Rubra'	5	sg.	light red	fr.	recurrent
Rose à Parfum de l'Hay	4–5	db.	cherry red	fr.	June and July
Roseraie de l'Hay, 1901	4–6	db.	wine red	fr.	recurrent
Ruskin, 1928	4–5	s-db.	brilliant red	fr.	recurrent
Schneezwerg	4	s-db.	white	fr.	recurrent
Will Alderman, 1949	3–5	db.	deep rose pink	fr.	recurrent
Rose, Polyantha, a class somewhat loosely defined					
Gruss an Aachen, 1909	2–3	db.	pink, in clusters	fr.	recurrent
Happy, 1954	1–1½	db.	currant red		recurrent
Orange Triumph, 1937	2½–4	db.	scarlet orange		recurrent
Perle d'Or, 1884	3	db.	pinkish gold		spring
The Fairy, 1941	2–3½	db.	pink		recurrent
White Pet, 1879	2–2½	db.	pinkish white		spring

147

CATEGORY AND COMMON NAME	HEIGHT (IN FEET)	FLOWER FORM	COLOR	ODOR	BLOOM TIME
Rose, Trailing, Rosa wichuriana,					
Memorial Rose, 1880 (grows flat on ground)	—	sg.	white	fr.	July
R. wichuriana 'Max Graf', 1919	—	sg.	pink		June
R. wichuriana 'May Queen', 1898	—	s-db.	dusky pink		recurrent
Rose, Old Climbing, some are climbing types of bush roses					
American Beauty Climber, 1919	to 14	db.	carmine rose	fr.	recurrent
Cecile Brunner, 1894	to 20	db.	pink, clusters		recurrent
Devoniensis, 1858	to 15	db.	creamy white	fr.	recurrent
Dr. W. Van Fleet, 1910	to 20	db.	light pink	fr.	spring
Etain, 1953	to 12	db.	clear pink, clusters		recurrent
Gloire de Dijon, 1835	to 20	db.	white to amber-blush	fr.	recurrent
Shot Silk, 1931	to 15	db.	cherry-cerise with gold	fr.	recurrent

5

Trees and How to Select Them

What would a garden be like without trees? Even though shrubs and flowers were well integrated into the general design, even if the basic pattern had been attractively adapted to the terrain and harmonized with the architecture of the house, wouldn't something still be lacking? Definitely.

The composition of a garden is a three-dimensional art, with an up-and-down-and-sideways thrust to it, cleverly put together by the garden artist working hand-in-hand with nature. If the garden had only horizontals, with minor swells and depressions, the composition would be less interesting—in fact, rather dull. Trees add verticals and upward thrusts for emphasis and accent, while unobtrusively enhancing and pointing up the flow of the lines in the plan in a most telling fashion. And a particular tree, well chosen and admirably placed, is far more than a mere component or ingredient. Like certain herbs in cookery, a tree can be the one element that gives flavor to the entire result and makes it memorable even if the beholder is not conscious of its subtle contribution.

Certainly the Joyce Kilmer line, "I think that I shall never see / A poem lovely as a tree," is overly familiar and has become so trite that people smirk as they quote it, yet it has a valid point. Whatever one may think of Kilmer's poetry, most trees are able to hold their own with any poem. Only those people whose artificial sophistication makes them view life through twin lenses of prejudice and boredom miss the point. There are, naturally, degrees of beauty in trees as there are levels of art in poetry. Much depends upon the experience and judgment of the beholder.

There have been fads in trees for many generations. What was popular in one era becomes tiresome in the next, often for no good reason. Today may be something of an exception, for in recent years there has been a radical change in the way we look at gardens. Whereas gardens in the past were often designed and planted for show, to lend luster and prestige to the owner, today's gardens are planned for intimate use by the family. The plantings combine utility with as much grace and beauty as possible. As with architecture, form follows function, but, unlike houses, where this precept may result in austerity and sterility, the garden's living, growing, and changing qualities tend to soften and bring into harmony the diverse, stiff lines of architectural elements.

Trees are a kind of kingpin around which the rest of the garden can be planned. They serve a number of useful and aesthetic functions, and in order to perform their tasks well they must be thoughtfully chosen. If the proper questions are posed and answered before the gardener sets out to acquire the trees, the sums of money spent will not be wasted nor the labor of planting regretted. Intelligent thinking is the most vital concern at this point, because trees may be the most permanent part of the whole scheme. Some of the questions that might be asked follow, and the answers set up a kind of yardstick by which the gardener can measure the performance of the trees to be considered.

CHOOSING TREES

How many trees should be planted around the house?

The simple answer to this is: as many as are needed. Which is to say that there is no single answer. It will depend on many factors: The climate, the need for shade, the kind of house, and most of all, the size and kind of tree required to fulfill these functions must enter into the considerations.

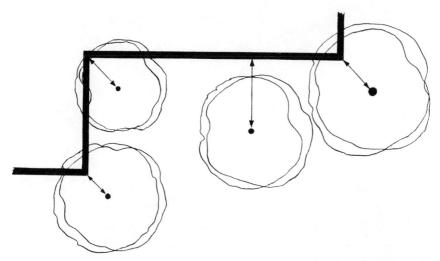

WHERE TO PLACE TREES. *Left,* small trees on a corner may be planted out from the house so that both facades are enhanced by the placement. *Right,* similarly, a larger tree should be placed so that it can cast its shade on the house without being in danger of rubbing limbs on the roof. The distances shown are minimum for small trees, *left,* larger ones, *right,* so as not to interfere with the walls or roof. Tall vase shapes may be planted closer than oval or round shapes; columnar also may be placed nearer walls.

How does one determine these needs in order to choose the proper trees?

First of all ask yourself what is the reason you need a tree—what do you want it to do for you and your garden? Is it to be a shade tree, one to break the hot rays of the sun and keep the roof and walls of the house cooler in summer? a tree to be an umbrella over the outdoor sitting-out place? a tree to block out an unsightly view—a utility pole or some unpleasant eyesore on another property? a tree to give privacy overhead from neighboring houses or a street above the private garden? a tree or trees to form a windbreak so that gales do not sweep unhampered through the garden and dry out or damage shrubbery and make sitting-out less than a pleasure? a tree or trees to frame the house or the doorway, helping to anchor the building visually to its setting and giving height to the plantings of shrubs? These are some of the questions that should be posed before rushing out to purchase a tree.

SHADE AND TREES. If the tree is placed some distance from the house, the nearly vertical summer sun may fall on the roof and heat up the house. On the other hand, in cool climates it may be desirable to have winter sun on the roof and place the shade tree some distance away to shade the terrace or outdoor living space. The chart illustrates how shade is cast at relative distances, using tall and small trees.

TREES FOR WIND PROTECTION. Garden living is more pleasant when the force of prevalent winds is broken. *Left,* a tall, open-branched tree allows wind to sift through, somewhat diminished. *Center,* a tree with heavier leafage will break the force still more, while some winds must climb over if slowed that much. *Right,* heavy, dense-branching types nearly stop wind, giving year-round protection if they are evergreen.

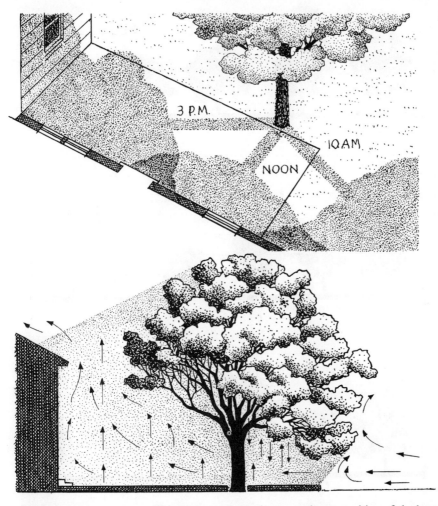

SHADE THROUGH THE DAY. This diagram shows the approximate position of shade at various times of day. According to when you wish to have shade, morning or afternoon, place the tree in proper relation to the terrace or the house. Afternoon sun is usually hottest, and a certain amount of heat is absorbed and retained by paving, house walls, and even soil long after the sun has set. A shaded pavement will naturally exude less heat.

What should one look for in trees after deciding where the tree is to be planted?

The first point to consider is height: how tall will the tree be at maturity? Next is how long does the tree take to mature? What is the habit of growth? These are basic questions.

153

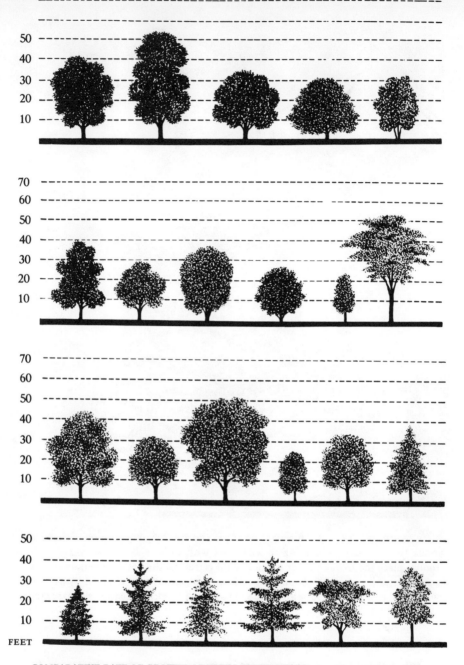

COMPARATIVE RATE OF GROWTH OF TREES IN TEN YEARS

Top row, left to right: American ash, green ash, Amur cherry, European beech, canoe birch, buckeye, American elm, Chinese elm, moline elm, ginkgo, sour gum.

Second row, left to right: sweet gum, hackberry, Washington hawthorn, English hornbeam, shagbark hickory, thornless honey locust, horse chestnut, Kentucky coffee tree, basswood (American linden), littleleaf linden, cucumber tree.

Third row, left to right: sugar maple, Norway maple, silver maple, bur oak, English oak, pin oak, red oak, white oak, sycamore, tulip tree, black walnut.

Fourth row, left to right: white fir, Douglas spruce, hemlock, European larch,

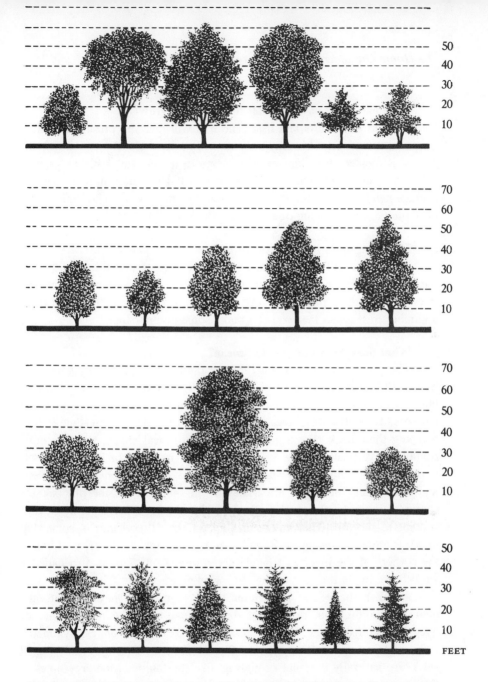

Austrian pine, red pine, Scotch pine, white pine, Black Hills spruce, Norway spruce, Serbian spruce, white spruce.

These silhouettes of trees give the approximate sizes ten years after planting. Each dotted line signifies ten feet, and thus it is seen that there is a considerable variation in growth rates. These growths were computed from actual measurements and are optimum growths, where trees were given their best possible conditions. Growth rates will vary in other climates and in different conditions.

155

How can you know how tall the tree may grow?

Consult our charts and lists. The lists will give the presumed mature height, the average. This may vary according to the section in which the garden is located, for climates may be more or less favorable to growth. Soils, moisture, and other considerations will also enter into it, but the average height gives you an idea of whether or not you are choosing a tall-, medium-, or low-growing tree, which is the basic question.

How long does it take trees to mature?

Again this will vary somewhat with the climate and local conditions, but the lists will guide you to choose slow-, quick-, and moderate-growth trees. The chart on pages 154–155 shows the average growth rate of quite a number of trees so that you can make some comparisons.

What does "habit of growth" mean?

The general form or outline and the direction of growth by which the tree is formed is called habit of growth. For instance, some trees are very tall and narrow, like exclamation points. Others may not grow very tall but spread widely. Most trees at maturity and for quite some time before reaching their peak take a vaguely circular or oval shape, whether horizontally or vertically. Some may be somewhat irregular or flat on the bottom above the trunk but be round topped. And, of course, many evergreens and some deciduous trees are triangular in shape. Take the pin oak for example: it sits on the trunk with the limbs and branches tapering toward a point at the top. The American elm, on the other hand, is somewhat like a triangle balancing on its point atop the trunk of the tree, although the corners of the inverted triangle are rounded off. This is also called a vase shape, or, in the case of the elm, wine glass.

Another shape that is popular today in modern gardens that take their inspiration from the Orient or from nature is the picturesque, or irregular habit of growth. While most trees grow more or less symmetrically, certain types, even if given sufficient room to develop evenly on all sides, are naturally irregular or zig-zag, like the famous Monterey pines in California. Some gardeners carefully train and prune trees to achieve this asymmetrical effect, but there is a danger inherent in this practice: It is easy to get carried away and produce something more grotesque than picturesque, a tree that looks tortured and unnatural.

HABIT OF GROWTH OF TREES. (A) Round. Ball to upright oval. (B) Pyramidal, cone or triangular. (C) Vase shaped. (D) Columnar or upright. (E) Pendulous or weeping. (F) Picturesque or irregular. Sometimes trees will reach these ideal shapes only when mature, while other trees shape up very early. Occasionally one finds a tree changing from one shape to another, or within the genus there may be two or more habits of growth. Example: A weeping tree may be a sport or selection from a tree that grows otherwise.

Wouldn't faster-growing trees be a better choice in order to get the effect sooner?

Unfortunately, most fast-growing trees are poor choices because they do not live very long. Some also have undesirable side effects—brittle wood that gets strewn about on the lawn as it snaps off in winter gales or summer storms, roots that enter sewer pipes in quest of water and nutrients to sustain their quick growth, soft growth subject to injury and disease, and other troubles that cancel out the gains of quick growth.

157

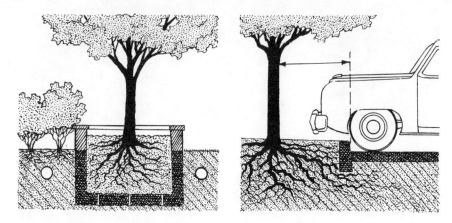

PROTECT PIPES and insulate them from encroaching tree roots that may cause trouble in sewage and drainage lines. Build a planting box for the tree of concrete with drainage holes only in the bottom. This can be a pleasant raised feature, with seats on the sides, or simply made of masonry.

PARKING AREAS are hazards for trees. Keep trees well back from the curb, at least 4 to 5 feet. Remember that wheels are set far behind bumpers.

Couldn't shrubs be planted first and trees put in later?

If a choice must be made, it is a better plan to plant trees first, because they are usually slower growing, and it takes them longer to approach maturity than it does for shrubs to fill out. Also, the placement of shrubs and even their choice may depend upon placement of the trees. Some trees, such as maples, are shallow rooted, so that shrubbery planted under them may have to compete with the roots of the tree for sustenance. It therefore is safer to plant shrub borders under oaks and other deep-rooted trees. Borders incorporating trees will help to cut maintenance time when lawns are mowed, so that this is also a factor to consider.

One piece of advice from professional designers and landscape gardeners is to postpone buying shrubs if you must, but buy as large a tree as possible. This applies mainly to the bigger shade trees, not the smaller flowering ones, although here, too, it is well to buy older trees for a quicker effect. The old idea that a smaller tree would soon catch up with a bigger one that suffers more transplanting shock is now outmoded due to better nursery practices. In fact, "instant" gardens may be planted if one is rich enough to do it all at one time, using older trees and shrubs so that a reasonably mature planting effect is achieved within a couple of years when they are established. For those of us who are not blessed with a fortune, a big tree, with later plantings of moderate-sized shrubs, is the answer.

158

If a lot of fertilizer were given to trees at planting and afterward, wouldn't that make them grow faster and taller?

While this would seem to be logical, it does not always follow. Trees are like other living things. They can utilize only as much food as they can absorb and transform for the work of building cells. Too much fertilizer may cause "indigestion" or foster quick and weak growth that is likely to fall prey to disease or damage by winds and weather. If too much fertilizer is applied and the weather is dry early in the season but gets more moist late in summer, the food will be made available, and late soft growth will result, making it susceptible to winterkill. Much will depend, too, upon how much moisture is available in the soil for food to be dissolved and

LEAF SIZE AFFECTS TEXTURE. Large coarse leaves, tiny refined ones, fluttery compound leaves composed of numerous leaflets on a stem—these are the main ingredients of garden-leaf texture. All trees are variations of these three major types, most falling between the first two. Textural effects of trees as well as that of shrubs should be taken into consideration when the gardener is planning in addition to the color and seasonal effects. Contrast and harmony can be achieved by careful planning. *Left,* large-leaved tulip tree may be out of scale for small areas. *Center,* littleleaf linden gives a pleasant scale, a finer texture. *Right,* compound leaves of thornless honey locust give a lacy, open texture, light-dappled shade, and good ventilation.

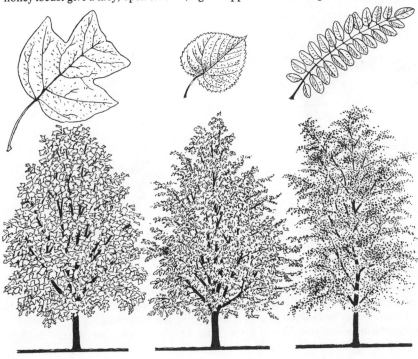

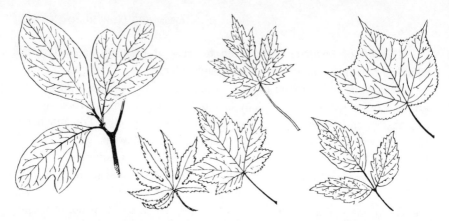

LEAF FORMS VARY. Within the genus the forms may vary considerably, and even on the same tree there may be some variations from what is considered to be the general description. *Left,* sassafras, often described as a "mitten leaf," may have one lobe generally, two lobes occasionally, and even no lobes, all on one branch. *Right,* maples vary within the genus, though most are divided into lobes. *Bottom, reading up,* Japanese maple is sharply divided, some more than others; red maple is less sharply lobed; silver maple is in between; striped maple is distinctive for rounded divisions, showing why a common name is goosefoot maple; box elder is of the maple genus, and seldom lobed at all.

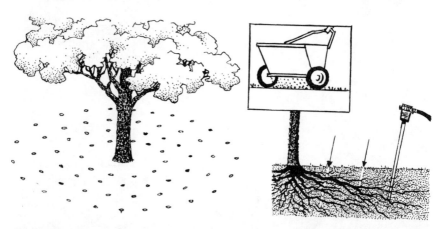

FERTILIZING TREES. Large trees as well as young ones need nutrients. A spreader, *center,* distributes plant foods on lawns beneath trees, and tree may get some food but may need more and deeper fertilizing. *Left,* starting 2 or 3 feet out from the trunk, punch crowbar holes a foot or more deep. Fill with plant food, water in well, then fill with soil or replace grass displaced. *Right,* another method of deep feeding is the root feeder, a hose attachment with long metal rod pierced with holes to poke into soil to root level. Water flows through a receptacle at the top containing soluble fertilizer of specific formula and goes directly to root area. This is best used in shrub or rose beds, not so good on lawns.

160

taken up in solution by the roots and the small feeding root hairs for use in building above-ground structure. The climate, too, influences growth. Mild, long-season growing periods may give greater growth, while cooler, shorter seasons will possibly shorten the time and means of producing growth.

All in all, however, the growing factor is nature. Some trees will grow faster than others and some will grow faster than the same genus and variety when conditions are more acceptable and favorable. In general, the rule is not to overfeed, and when fertilizer is applied, be sure that enough moisture is applied soon after feeding and periodically thereafter according to the climate to leach the nutrients into the soil where the roots can reach them. See the sketch on the opposite page on fertilizing trees.

How tall should a mature tree be for a small property?

Height of trees to be chosen will be governed somewhat by the size of the house or building as well as by the space around where the tree is to be planted. Examine the sketch here that demonstrates how a forest giant of a tree can make a one-story house look even lower and more insignificant while a house with smaller—medium to small—trees can be made to look important and most pleasant when the scale of the trees is right. Similarly, a two-story house looks better with a medium-tall to tall tree nearby. As to horizontal scale, consider the "wing-spread" of the mature tree and plant it far enough out from a building. Or, if as it matures it will become higher branched, let it overhang the roofline a little. But in either case, do not cramp it. Give it room to develop its full beauty and save yourself a good bit of pruning work keeping it within bounds.

What kind of trees should be planted along the street?

Street-side trees are not always a blessing, as more and more home-owners are finding to their sorrow. The case for no trees or for only certain kinds is a good one. Here are some of the drawbacks to trees planted outside the property line: The gardener has little control over what will happen to them, since they are technically not his property, even though he has bought and planted them. Utility companies and town street workers are well known for the butchery they wreak on trees. If any tree has to be planted under utility lines, be sure it is a low-growing type that will not interfere with the wires when it matures, or you are asking for the tops to be amputated or butchered.

161

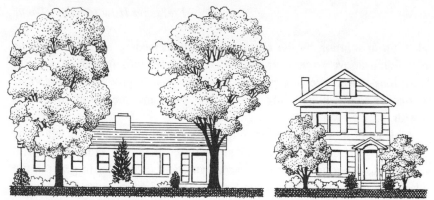

WRONG: Tall trees dwarf a low house, and short small trees make a tall house look even taller. Occasionally, of course, taller trees will be needed to shade the roof of the house in summer, but in general a medium-sized to low-growing tree is better for long low houses, taller ones are in better scale with two-story houses. In the house at left, a tall evergreen between windows cuts the house in two and further compounds the problem.

RIGHT: Medium-sized shade trees and small flowering trees relate better to the lines of long low houses. Unless the layout of the garden is formal, and particularly if the front door is not in the center, there is little reason to put two shade trees in the front in bisymmetrical form. With a two-story house a tall shade tree can be balanced by a sizable columnar or narrow-growing tree, allowing for air circulation and views from windows.

Cars on the street frequently bang into tree trunks and injure them, even break them off and kill them. On major streets exhaust fumes are heavier along the street than even ten to twenty feet away. Pollution is a factor in diseased and damaged trees. In cold-winter areas, it has lately been found that trees, particularly shallow-rooted ones, suffer from salt damage. Streets are salted to melt the snow and ice, then snow plows pile up the briny residue on the curbside areas, and the melting and moisture carry the death-dealing salt to the root areas.

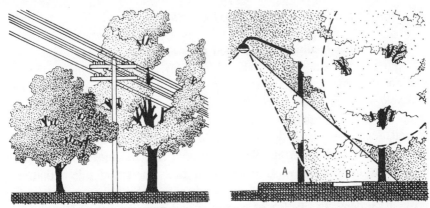

UTILITY LINES will not tolerate tall trees that interfere with wires, and trees are frequently butchered as a result. Avoid trouble by planting small trees below wires or, better still, nowhere near them. *At right,* trees should not obscure sidewalks by cutting off rays of street lights (*A*) when trees of oval or narrow habit (*B*) will permit light to enter under them.

STREET OR DRIVEWAY TREES. *Left:* Avoid low wide-branching types that are likely to interfere with street and sidewalk traffic. On the street, cars and tall vehicles (trucks and buses) will scrape and break branches and limbs. *Center:* Columnar or vase-shaped trees not only give vehicles street room but will permit freer passage to pedestrians on the walk, and require less pruning to stay within bounds. *Right:* Plan shows comparative approximate diameters of too wide types, top, and narrower growing sorts, below. The shaded areas indicate on the plan the curb and the sidewalk.

Note the sketch, which shows the eventual spread of the trees and the effects of low branching on foot traffic and lighting of the walkways. Often a medium-tall or medium tree can be planted within the property area and give much the same effect as one planted on the street.

What other qualities should good trees have?

First and foremost, a tree should be hardy. This usually means that it will not be winter-killed, and that implies that it is either a native tree or a development of one or that it grows naturally in a climate similar in temperature to your garden. A point sometimes overlooked is the question of soil, for certain trees do best only in soil similar to their native one. Some like an acid soil, some like an alkaline soil, but most prefer a soil somewhere in a neutral range between the two. The bright side is that an astounding number of trees are quite tolerant of the soils in which they grow in gardens. In our list of trees you will note the zone of hardiness and the soil preferences of the trees covered wherever this latter information was available and reliable. Some trees will either endure moist to wet soils or they grow most happily in them, while others insist on well-drained, even dry soils. You can see that nature has provided for every contingency that a gardener may encounter.

What should a gardener be most wary of in choosing trees?

Some trees are brittle, and twigs and limbs or branches are likely to snap off in wind storms, not only making the trees look ill shaped, but their debris must be cleaned up and disposed of constantly. Others are

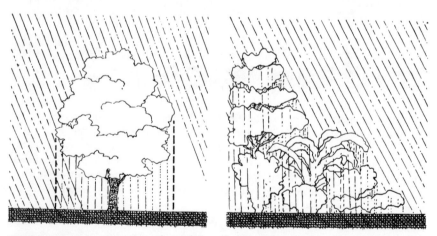

WATER AND RAIN may not get through heavily foliaged trees, even in a heavy shower. *Left,* note area protected from rain by the tree; only some rain drips from leaves. *Right,* overhanging trees or large shrubs may deflect or stop rain in the same way, preventing moisture from reaching the soil below. Both sketches indicate why, even if there is normal rain, areas below heavily leaved plants may need additional watering from hoses and occasional deep soakings.

rather messy in that they are likely to discard pods, seeds, and unwanted and inedible fruit. And, if the seeds are allowed to sprout, they may cause dozens of little seedling trees to spring up that must be disposed of. All trees that are deciduous shed their leaves, as we well know, and this is a seasonal and acceptable quality. However, evergreens also shed their needles periodically, with new ones replacing them, though not all the needles drop at once unless disease, drought, or other disturbances cause the tree to dispose of them. Most evergreen needles are a minor problem and can be raked off the lawn or allowed to remain below the tree if it is on bare ground or underplanted with shrubs, so that they act as a mulch. In fact, many gardeners gather needles and use them as a mulch or compost them separately to obtain acid-type soil.

If trees sometimes shed leaves in midsummer, should such trees be avoided?

Oftentimes trees will make lush leaf and twig growth during a wet spring and early summer, but when hot weather comes, dry weather also arrives. The tree cannot support the leafage it so gaily put forth in the good growing season, so it disposes of the weaker leaves until it has what can be supported. Watering the soil may retard this, though if it is already started, some leaves are bound to be discarded. In drought periods leaves are likely to dry up and fall from trees, too, and only deep watering can prevent damage to the tree.

If many trees in the neighborhood discard their leaves in summer, you may be fairly sure it is due to the causes described, but if only one tree does it, then there is some other cause, and advice should be sought about how to correct it.

Is it true that weed killers on the lawn can kill trees?

While this is not universally the case, there are documented instances in which concentrations of weed killers have injured and even killed shallow-rooted trees, especially young ones. A known case involved a sloping lawn with a slight depression at the base of it in which a dogwood tree planted a dozen years before had flourished. Suddenly it began to sicken and finally died despite all efforts to save it. The cause was a weed-feed formula that had been spread on the lawn but not watered in, and when a heavy shower came within a few days, the weed killer apparently washed down to concentrate in the area where the dogwood tree stood and was leached into the root area in the soil. Ordinarily such a combination for killing broad-leaved weeds in lawn grasses would cause little or no trouble, but it emphasizes the need for watering in well after applications of such formulae and even of fertilizer, which in large concentrations may cause root burn and other troubles.

Can trees make a garden cooler, aside from the shade they cast?

Most certainly they can and do. A medium-sized tree will draw up dozens of gallons of water from its roots in the course of a day and by transpiring it make the surrounding air cooler by several degrees, day or night. At night the transpiration process is slowed or even ceases since it is sun and light that brings this about. Evaporation of moisture is well known to be a cooling process, as desert dwellers and travelers have long since learned. The whole ecology of a region is affected by this moisturizing process, and trees, with their immense quantity of leaves, are the prime movers.

Should all the major trees on the street side be the same kind?

Not unless a formal symmetrical effect is desired. With bisymmetrical houses it has been the custom in the past to flank the front walk with two identical trees, placed in the middle or to the sides of the yard. This is

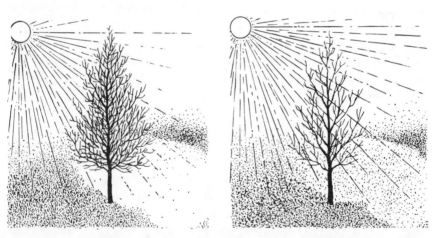

BRANCHING AND WINTER SUN. Depending on the habit of branching, light or heavy, considerable sun can be admitted to the winter garden, or the rays obscured and broken by heavy twig growth, even though the tree is leafless. *Left,* rays are deflected, spring warming of the soil may be delayed, and snow will lie longer on the ground. *Right,* open-branching trees permit rays to pass through, fewer are inhibited or detoured, allowing warmth and light to enter the house as well as the garden.

166

still quite acceptable, though no longer done so much as it was. On the other hand, too many different kinds of tree and shrub varieties may give the impression of a hodgepodge planting, unless it is carefully designed and plants cleverly arranged. An outdoor botanical whatnot may be satisfying because of the diverse elements it contains, but it will not give a serene, natural effect. In a woodland garden, made from existing woodland where the trees have already grown to sizable proportions, thinning out the trees a bit will give each more light and nutrition. Here, of course, you are likely to find a number of trees of the same sort, possibly children of one or two magnificent old specimens. It is acceptable to keep several but in thinning out, always keep in mind that a natural effect is the idea. You may fill in under the higher shade with shade-tolerant small flowering trees or tall treelike shrubs to give variety and interest and to enhance outcroppings of stone or other natural features. Many of these plants are woodland trees in their native area of growth, edging woodlands or filling in under tall trees with high broken shade. Therefore they will fit very well into the scheme.

SPECIAL ENVIRONMENTAL CONSIDERATIONS

What kinds of trees are best for seashore plantings?

Because of the peculiar conditions encountered on most seashores it is difficult to set any rules. The winds that are likely to sweep in are unbroken by any natural features, such as mountains or hills, and the salt spray that may be brought with the wind adds another plant hazard. Then, too, the soils are frequently sandy or pure sand, which means that only deep-rooted trees should be considered so that there will be all possible anchorage against gales and sudden gusts. Tall-growing evergreens, particularly the close-growing kinds, such as spruces, firs, and close-growing pine are not good choices. Open-limbed pines seem to do well, however, and on sandy Cape Cod there was once a great natural forest of Eastern white pine, long since cut off and gone. The sandy soil now supports various kinds of scrub pines, notably the pitch pine (*P. rigida*), which is somewhat dwarfed near the sea but grows taller inland. In the South along the shore, in Zone 7 and south, live oak and the Southern magnolia will do well even fairly close to the sea, as well as inland. On the West Coast a variety of plant material, much of it native, seems to endure the conditions very well. Wherever the garden is to be, it is well to explore a bit and question local sources to augment your list and to avoid failure.

What trees are good for gardens in desert and semi-arid areas?

Something of the same problem exists here that is encountered in seashore gardens, but with added hazards. In general it is best to keep to plants that originated in arid regions so that little or no watering is needed. Desert soils, though variable to some degree, are sandy in general, often highly alkaline, with salts building up in the surface soil and remaining there. Water is also likely to be alkaline or salty, and if this is applied, the problem is compounded. It is recommended that shade be created by lattice coverings over terraces rather than to depend on trees. In semi-arid regions of the Southwest and some High Prairie locations various native trees and others may be considered. Deserts have extremes of temperature—high in the daytime and often quite cold at night. In some land considered desert, there is snow and freezing cold in winter. Therefore, heat-hardiness as well as frost-hardiness are factors to consider. See Chapter 6 for a more complete picture of desert gardening.

If some of the land is boggy or swampy or borders a stream, what trees will endure these wet or moist conditions?

Any of the trees that grow naturally in moist soil, such as swamp maple, swamp oak, the willows, or black birch, would be suitable. Some that grow elsewhere are also tolerant of moist soil. The tupelo or sour gum, and sweet gum are able to take either moist soil or moderately dry soils. *Magnolia virginiana*, the sweet bay, and the Southern live oaks seem to do well in rather moist soil. Among the smaller trees or treelike shrubs there are a number that are either naturally moist-soil plants or are tolerant of moisture: Viburnums *V. alnifolium trilobum, opulus, dentatum* are all recommended in their hardiness zones, and among the hollies, inkberry (*Ilex glabra*), dahoon (*Ilex cassine*), and the longstalk holly (*Ilex pedunculosa*) are possible subjects. Then the alders, hazels, Southern wax-myrtle (*Myrica cerifera*), and an evergreen or two may be considered. *Thuja occidentalis,* the American arborvitae, and the California incense-cedar (*Libocedrus decurrens*) are two such evergreens, and Eastern larch or tamarack (*Larix laricina*), a deciduous coniferous tree, is also moisture tolerant to moisture demanding.

Are there trees tough enough to withstand dry, poor soils?

There are always trees that will grow in any particular place, provided the soil is not loaded with salts or other materials inimical to good growth. The alkaline soils of the West oftentimes fall into this category, and watering the soil only seems to compound the problem as the salts are brought near the surface and remain there. This is very hard to correct. However, many poor soils are dry because they are sandy, a condition that can be corrected. See Chapter 7 for tips on soil improvement. But there are other places where rainfall is light and the soil is reasonably good. Choosing trees that do not ordinarily demand much water and occasionally adding a bit of hose water should bring good results in these cases. See the list of dry-soil trees at the end of the chapter. See also the section on desert gardening in Chapter 6.

What trees are able to withstand city conditions and pollution?

More than air pollution must be endured by plants in the city, for poor and often sour soil and not enough water or sunlight, in addition to the gases and smoke, the dust, and other particles that make city air thick, are among the hazards they face. Noxious gases are emitted by cars and trucks, and the salt used to de-ice streets and sidewalks is often piled along with the snow and partly melted ice on top of the soil trees depend upon for life. Still, there are a number of trees that may withstand these unusual conditions well enough to live and put forth leaves. Not only deciduous trees, which can rid themselves of dust and soot yearly by discarding their leaves, but also some evergreens fit into this category.

What are some of the best trees to go with small houses and grounds?

This will naturally depend on the climate, altitude, soil, and other conditions, but lists of possible trees to explore are placed at the end of the chapter. There are probably others available locally, but the "best" are of medium height and will serve as shade trees. The smaller trees, flowering trees, and tall-shrub trees are in a separate list. Some of the latter may be shrubby in the North, full height and tree-like to the South.

TREE COLOR AND TEXTURE

What are some trees with interesting branches that would look well in winter when they have no leaves?

Most trees are interesting if you examine them closely, but some are more spectacular than others. The birches are interesting because of the gray or white bark; the canoe or paper birch in particular is an off-season tree because of the peeling outer layers of bark and the vivid black markings where branches have been discarded. *Prunus serrula*, a cherry tree, has glossy dark red bark with conspicuous horizontal markings. It is not widely obtainable but is worth the pursuit. Striped maple or moosewood (*Acer pennsylvanicum*) has vertically striped green and white bark on limbs and branches. The beeches, with rather smooth sculptural lines and warm gray bark, make a display in winter that is particularly attractive, since the dry apricot-colored leaves stay on for a good part of the season. Many trees have interesting structures, and one of the most picturesque is the wide-spreading limbs of the Amur cork tree, with corklike, deeply fissured bark on the trunk. The Russian olive, iron-hardy and picturesque in form, has brown bark that shreds off in long strips. The plane trees and sycamores are interesting in winter, too, with dappled grays and greens of various hues where the bark sheds and new bark shows on the trunk and larger limbs. Tulip trees, though possibly too large for most gardens, hold their dried seed pods, and against a cold blue winter sky these ivory to pale yellow pods gleam in the sun all winter.

Many fruiting trees keep their berries or fruits for some time, and some, such as the flowering dogwood (*Cornus florida*), are most colorful in early autumn, with clusters of bright red berries. The hawthorns often retain their fruits into early winter or even longer, provided the birds do not make off with them, and some are quite colorful indeed. Katsura (*Cercidiphyllum japonicum*) is of interest all year round, with structural interest in winter when the spreading boughs and limbs are exposed after the leaves drop. Interesting in autumn color, too, are the yellow to scarlet leaves. The silk tree (*Albizia julibrissin*) may take a picturesque spreading form as it develops if it is not pruned too severely, but it has no fruit. The chinaberry, much planted in the South, has yellow berries that are attractive to birds, but it may be a nuisance because it drops fruit and leaves, making a lawn look messy unless constantly cleaned up.

Evergreens, of course, are good winter subjects, and some of them are picturesque in form, especially as they mature. Widely available now is the Atlantic cedar (*Cedrus atlantica*) also called Atlas cedar, which grows slowly, putting forth silvery to pale green needles and maturing upright cones on its branches. Cedar of Lebanon and the deodar cedar have similar characteristics but darker green needles, and their cones, like the Atlas, require two years to mature. Of the three, deodar is the most graceful but can be planted only in mild climates. Colorado blue spruce, hardy practically everywhere, has many selections and cultivars that present silvery blue to electric-blue stiff needles on thickly covered branches. Some of the cultivars are less tall at maturity than the species.

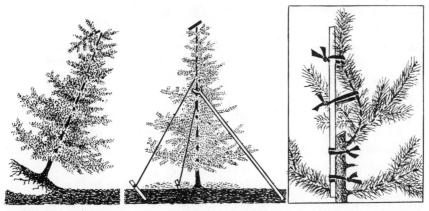

REPAIRING EVERGREEN DAMAGE. Sometimes shallow-rooted evergreens are detached by high winds, tilted, tops often broken. Although big trees may be too severely injured to recover, small to medium height ones may be saved. *Center,* if carefully raised upright, broken roots cleanly cut back, trunk braced with wires through hose and securely staked (see page 305), the lee side braced with a padded forked pole, they may recover in time. Feed moderately several times up to midsummer and keep soil moist. *Right,* to repair tops, cut back just above a strong side branch. Bind a short pole to the trunk top and fasten the branch lightly to it. Later tighten these bindings to secure branch upright. When it has grown for a year or two, the pole can be removed as the new top grows and replaces the old one.

A few evergreens change color in winter, notably some of the low-growing junipers, which become purplish or pinkish, though green to gray-green in the growing season.

How do trees give texture to a garden?

By the number of branches and their placement, by the leaves on them and most of all by the size and shape of the leaves, trees are able to make a major contribution to the textural effects in all gardens. Some leaves are large and coarse. For example, leaves of cucumber magnolia trees and catalpas may reach ten to twelve inches in length. They are overpowering in a small garden. Other trees may have rather fine and small leaves such as are found on the English hawthorn and the Southern live oak. Shape is important, too, for pointed leaves make a sharper and more exciting effect than rounded ones, triangular or heart-shaped leaves present a totally different aspect from long narrow leaves.

If the leaves are thin and delicate they will give a different general appearance than those that are thick and leathery. And if the tree bears multiple-leaved stems, with numerous leaflets placed on either side of a long stem, there is likely to be a fluffy or feathery texture. Similarly the multiple needles on needled evergreens may give a soft or stiff texture, according to the length and placement of the needles. Broad-leaved evergreen trees are generally furnished with rather thick, leathery leaves. These range in size from the magnificent big ones on the Southern magnolia or bull bay, to rather small ones on Holly or Holm oak. The former grow to eight to ten inches while the latter are more likely to be nearer one inch than the maximum of three inches long.

In general, for small gardens it is better to choose trees with medium leaf texture or fine-textured foliage which will fit better with the shrubs that are nearby and also will be in better scale with the house and the entire garden.

Are there any large shade trees that also blossom?

Medium to large trees blossom at various times through the year, according to climate and the nature of the tree. The sorrel or sourwood has white blossoms in midsummer, while the pendulous clusters of white wisterialike blossoms of the yellowwood appear in early June in the North. The Southern magnolia or bull bay, a magnificent, really tall tree blooms in May and into the summer where it is hardy, with blooms often spectacularly large and quite fragrant. The castor-aralia (*Kalopanax pictus*) produces blooms in late midsummer among its large maplelike leaves. The pagoda tree (*Sophora japonica*) sports its blossoms in August, a month later than the Japanese stewartia (*S. pseudo-camellia*), whose white flowers indeed resemble camellias and whose flaking bark peels to reveal lighter colored bark below. The sweet bay (*Magnolia virginiana*) may grow forty to sixty feet tall in its southern growth area, but as it goes north, it becomes progressively shorter, though its waxy two- to three-inch blooms will still appear in late spring. Golden-rain tree flaunts its small flowered, upright, pyramidal clusters in early summer, but it does not live as long as some other flowering trees.

Although not generally thought of as flowering trees, the maples make quite a display of small flower clusters in early spring along their bare branches. Norway maples (*Acer platanoides*) have yellow flowers in conspicuous clusters in April, while the red or swamp maple has smaller but very profuse bright red flowers that give a lacy aspect to the tree.

All of the horse-chestnuts, red, white, and the named cultivars, have spectacular upright flower clusters in white or pink to red.

GOLDEN-RAIN tree sports upright clusters of yellow flowers in early summer. A columnar form would fit better into small spaces than this spreading type. (*Paul E. Genereux*)

What are some good small flowering trees?

There are so many we shall not attempt to list or describe them here but will present them in a list at the end of this chapter.

What are the best trees for leaf color in autumn?

This will depend a great deal on the conditions existing where the trees are planted, though certain species are naturally more colorful in most places than other species. All leaves will eventually become some shade of brown, but early in the process of turning color they may be many shades of yellow, orange, and red. Some kinds in certain places may have only a branch or two of vivid color at first or the leaves may be green mottled with red or yellow before turning color completely. The conditions of temperature and light are mostly responsible for producing vivid colors, particularly reds. On warm, sunny days in autumn, the leaves make a great deal of sugar with the aid of bright sun. During the summer this would ordinarily be transported back into the tree; but in autumn, when temperatures drop quickly at night to 45 degrees F. or less, sugars are trapped in the leaves. Somehow this causes the chlorophyll (green) coloring to become subordinate to red or orange coloring matter. Because sugar is manufactured partly by using sunlight, the sunny side of a tree may be more colorful than the shady side. Low-lying plantings, valleys, or swampy areas often have the earliest and most vivid color. This is not due to the moisture but to the fact that frost drains down hillsides and settles in such places. For a list of trees with various autumn coloration, see the end of this chapter.

What trees have colorful leaves or different-colored leaves in summer?

Where there are many trees, either in a garden or in the immediate background of the garden, some trees with colored leaves provide welcome contrast. However, several trees of diverse colors can create a disturbing effect, and you will lose the serenity that is so desirable in a garden, obtaining only novelty and oddity.

There are many colors to choose from, some being subtle in hue and others more vivid. Some are naturally colored and are likely to be the less vivid colors, while their hybrids have been selected for the brighter colors. Take the beech, for instance. The European beech normally has dark green leaves but it is also the parent of the copper beech, with rich reddish bronze foliage that varies in intensity of color. Also, over a century ago a purple-leaved variety was produced that is reddish as the leaves appear but turns purplish for the summer. Several offshoots of this have been selected, some of them producing glossy, deep purplish-black foliage that contrasts interestingly with the gray bark of the trunk.

Foliage may also be silvery, bluish-silver, yellow or yellow-green, blue-green, as well as reddish to purplish. A few specimens offer foliage margined with white or yellow, an accent, again, that can be effective when carefully used. Needled evergreens offer some exciting color, too, ranging from whitish to near blue, yellowish to creamy yellow, and a few have mixtures of colors in a kind of variegated effect.

Among the species to look for in the list are: maples, for reds and yellows particularly the Japanese and the Norway maple 'Crimson King'. Gray-leaved types include Russian olive, eucalyptus, olive, silver poplar, silver linden, and the sea buckthorn. Some needled evergreens also are grayish to bluish, notably the juniper tribe. Yellows to yellow-greens are found in speckled alder, honey locust 'Sunburst,' white poplar 'Richardii,' English oak 'Concordia,' and bigleaf linden 'Aurea.'

Reds include, in addition to the above mentioned, some reddish purple kinds: Blireiana plum, Pissard plum, and some crab apples, which have reddish tones in the hybrids. Look for blue to blue-greens in the white firs and their cultivars and in Colorado spruce, especially in *Picea pungens*

'Glauca' and its hybrids or selections. The blue-white pine is another interesting evergreen, while the Atlas cedars offer short-needled blue-green tufts of great beauty. The Arizona cypress 'Bonita' and cultivars of Lawson false-cypress also have blue-green foliage. Some of the eucalyptus family are also blue-green leaved.

Bronzy purple leaves are found on the sycamore maple, as well as on some of the European beech varieties. The color-margined species include box elder, flowering dogwood, and cornelian cherry.

TREE SHAPES FOR SPECIAL PURPOSES

Are there some medium to tall trees that are narrow growing so as to create some shade but also fit into a constricted area?

Aside from poplars and the narrow-growing tall evergreens that are naturally upright in growth, there are many cultivars and selections that are columnar in growth. Some excellent varieties will be found in the list at the end of this chapter, which includes both evergreens and deciduous columnar trees.

Are there any trees with weeping habit, aside from willows?

Quite a number of weeping forms exist in the various genera, some blossoming, some evergreen, and all of interest when used sparingly and in the proper setting. Willows should be used with care because of their searching roots, which may be troublesome as they seek and enter sewer pipes.

Among deciduous trees, adapted to many regions, look for: weeping birch, 'Tristis' or 'Youngii' or the cutleaf European birch 'Gracilis,' all of which are hardy. A small tree, the weeping boree acacia, is a possible tree for very warm areas, while the European ash 'Pendula' is hardy to the northern states into Canada and grows much lower than the rest of the species. Weeping beeches are well known, 'Pendula' is green-leaved, and 'Purpureo-pendula' is a weeping form of purple beech. Flowering dogwood 'Pendula' and crab apple 'Red Jade' are both flowering trees of merit. A weeping hornbeam 'Pendula' and the following three elms complete the recommendations in the deciduous category: Scotch or wych elm 'Camperdownii' and 'Pendula'; and Siberian elm 'Pendula.'

Evergreens include deodar cedar, which has a natural pendulous branch habit, Lawson false-cypress 'Pendula' and the even more graceful form 'Gracilis Pendula,' the weeping red cedar (*Juniperus virginiana* 'Pendula'), weeping Eastern white pine 'Pendula,' weeping Douglas fir 'Pendula,' a bald cypress 'Pendens,' and perhaps most beautiful of all, weeping Colorado spruce 'Pendens,' which is sometimes offered as Koster weeping blue spruce.

What trees can be grown against walls?

Because fruit trees are frequently espaliered against walls (see page 271) where the warmth may help to ripen fruit or the wall may at least protect the tree from wind and cold, it is often believed that only fruit trees can be espaliered. Not at all. Many small trees, particularly those of low-branching habit may be trained either on frames or directly on walls, even trained in the open on frames or wires strung between sturdy posts. Dogwood, as well as many other flowering trees of small stature, and the Southern and other magnolias are all possible subjects. Any tree with horizontal branching may be easily trained. The tupelo or sour gum may be grown away from walls, with young branches on both sides pruned off so that only opposite branches or those nearly opposite remain. It will, of course, eventually grow to a great height, but could be kept lower by topping and judicious yearly pruning to keep only side branches growing. See dogwood photograph, page 273.

Evergreens of various sorts may be espaliered, needled evergreens as well as the broad-leaved sorts. Yew is a favorite subject, as are certain kinds of juniper, while the evergreen magnolias, hollies, and figs can also be wall trained.

How are dwarf trees produced? Are they natural or man made?

Many trees are naturally kept to a low height by wind and other conditions, though their seeds when planted in normal conditions elsewhere produce trees as large as the species. And then there are the natural sports that for some genetic reason became dwarfed, the characteristic having become set.

However, many trees are artificially dwarfed by being grafted onto dwarfing rootstocks. These are roots that will starve or diet the upper part of the plant so that it will grow only to a certain maximum height, though leaves and fruits may be perfectly normal in size. Notable among these are the dwarf apples grafted onto East Malling rootstocks of various numbers that gear them to grow to certain heights and possess other characteristics. The dwarfing stock must be a compatible genus that will not be rejected by, or reject, the desired tree stock. In catalogs you will find apple trees on dwarf rootstocks that will grow only ten or twelve feet tall, perhaps even less, while the parent tree from which stock was taken for grafting would grow twenty to thirty feet tall and just as broad.

Some grafting is done, of course, not for dwarfing but for propagating plant material in short supply, for propagating material that might be weaker or less desirable in some way onto a sturdier or better rootstock, or for other sufficient reason. Often the prime reason is that the variety will not "come true" from seed but will revert to a less desirable form, color, fruit, or other characteristic of the genetic parent. Do not, therefore, assume that a grafted tree is a dwarf type.

TREES RECOMMENDED FOR SPECIFIC REGIONS

Even though this can hardly claim to be a comprehensive list of trees known to grow and thrive in the various regions (see Plant Hardiness Zone Map, page 18), it may be useful to the average home gardener. It concentrates on trees available and noted for growing well in each region. However, let it be emphasized that this is no "guaranteed list." Differences in soil, moisture, weather, and winds that may be encountered in the mini- or microclimates within these broad regions would invalidate any pretensions to infallibility. Nevertheless, it is a starting point for the gardener, whether he be a beginner or is more experienced, and it will give him many possibilities to explore.

USE THE ZONAL FIGURES

Following the plant names, the figures representing the hardiness zones will be the key to what part of each region in which it may be expected that the trees named will be hardy according to the minimum temperatures represented by the zones. In some cases you will find a range of hardiness zones—3–8, for example. This means that in researching hardiness, we have found that the several reliable authorities consulted have given a variety of hardiness figures, all of which are probably correct for the areas in which the hardiness was tested. Therefore, it would be well for the gardener to consult either local nurseries or his county agent for further information. If a nursery stocks a plant, it is fairly certain that it will grow in that region, given reasonable care.

In some cases, notably those asterisked in the list, there are factors of disease or difficulties to inquire about locally before purchasing. In comparing these trees with the Height Lists it will be noted that we have included many trees that are taller and more spreading than we recommend for the average small-home garden and particularly for use with one-story houses. The reason for this is that many readers may have large properties where such trees would be in scale, or else such trees may be so slow growing that they would fit in with the plans of the gardener for many years to come as we have suggested elsewhere.

REGIONAL MAP OF THE UNITED STATES

For convenience in providing lists of trees for the varying climates, the country is divided into nine regions. The various plant hardiness zones, of course, overlap these areas because they are based on temperature, not climate. The regions, though roughly subdivided into climate-based sections, embrace within themselves differing temperatures, rainfall, soils, and other conditions. Therefore it is also suggested that the temperatures indicated by the zonal numbers also be considered, bolstered, if necessary, by inquiries from the state college of agriculture or the local county agent, a good nurseryman or other local authority. If in doubt as to cold-hardiness, it is always safer to use a zone to the north as a guide in selection, assuring survival of the tree.

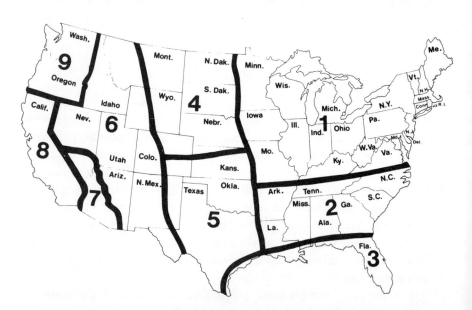

Compiled by the United States Department of Agriculture.

TREE LISTS
TREES LISTED ACCORDING TO REGION

COMMON NAME	SCIENTIFIC NAME AND COMMENTS	HARDINESS ZONE
	REGION I	
BROAD-LEAVED EVERGREENS:		
Box, Tree	*Buxus sempervirens* 'Arborescens'	5
Holly, American	*Ilex opaca*	5
Longstalk	*Ilex pedunculosa*	5
Magnolia, Southern	*Magnolia grandiflora*	7
NEEDLED EVERGREENS:		
Arborvitae, American	*Thuja occidentalis*	2˙
Giant	*Thuja plicata*	5
Japanese	*Thuja standishii*	5–6
Cedar, Deodar	*Cedrus deodara*	7
Eastern red-	*Juniperus virginiana*	2
of Lebanon	*Cedrus libani* 'Stenocoma'	5–6
Cryptomeria	*Cryptomeria japonica*	5–6
Cypress, Lawson false	*Chamaecyparis lawsoniana*	5–6
Fir, White	*Abies concolor*	4–5
Hemlock, Canadian	*Tsuga canadensis*	3
Juniper, *see Cedar, Eastern red-*		
Pine, Eastern white	*Pinus strobus*	3
Red	*Pinus resinosa*	2
Swiss stone	*Pinus cembra*	2
Spruce, Colorado blue	*Picea pungens*, and varieties	2
White	*Picea glauca*	2
Yew, Intermediate	*Taxus media*	4
Japanese	*Taxus cuspidata*	4
DECIDUOUS TREES:		
Ash, Green	*Fraxinus pensylvanica* 'Lanceolata'	2
Mountain, *see Mountain-ash*		
White	*Fraxinus americana*	3
Aspen, Quaking	*Populus tremuloides*	1–2
Bald cypress	*Taxodium distichum*	4–5
Basswood, *see Linden, American*		
Beech, American	*Fagus grandifolia*	3
European	*Fagus sylvatica* and cultivars	5
Birch, Canoe or Paper	*Betula papyrifera*	2
Cutleaf European	*Betula pendula*	2
White	*Betula alba*	2
Black-haw	*Viburnum prunifolium*	3
Buckeye, Ohio	*Aesculus glabra* (best in southern and western areas)	3–4
Catalpa, Northern	*Catalpa speciosa*	3–4
Southern	*Catalpa bignonioides*	4–5

179

COMMON NAME	SCIENTIFIC NAME AND COMMENTS	HARDINESS ZONE
DECIDUOUS TREES (*cont.*)		
Cherry, Cornelian	*Cornus mas*	4
Flowering named varieties		3–6
Coffee-tree, *see Kentucky coffee-tree*		
Cork tree, Amur	*Phellodendron amurense*	3–4
Crab apple, many named varieties		2–5
Cucumber tree, *see Magnolia, Cucumber tree*		
Elm, American	*Ulmus americana**	2–3
English	*Ulmus procera*	5–6
European field (Smooth-leaved)	*Ulmus carpinifolia*	5
Scotch (Wych)	*Ulmus glabra*	5
Ginkgo	*Ginkgo biloba*	4–5
Golden-rain tree	*Koelreuteria paniculata*	5
Gum, Black, *see Sour gum*		
Sour, *see Sour gum*		
Sweet, *see Sweet gum*		
Hackberry, Eastern	*Celtis occidentalis**	3
Sugarberry or Western	*Celtis laevigata*	5
Hawthorn	*Crataegus*, many named varieties	3–5
Hickory, Bitternut	*Carya cordiformis*	4–5
Mockernut	*Carya tomentosa*	4–5
Pignut	*Carya glabra*	4–5
Shagbark	*Carya ovata*	4–5
Honey locust, Thornless	*Gleditsia triacanthos* 'Inermis'	3–4
Hornbeam, American	*Carpinus caroliniana*	2–3
European	*Carpinus betulus*	5–6
Hop-	*Ostrya virginiana*	4–5
Horse-chestnut, Red	*Aesculus carnea*	3
White	*Aesculus hippocastanum* 'Baumannii'	3
Japanese pagoda tree (*see Pagoda tree*)		
Kalopanax (Castor aralia)	*Kalopanax pictus*	4–5
Katsura	*Cercidiphyllum japonicum*	4–5
Kentucky coffee-tree	*Gymnocladus dioica*	4–5
Laburnum, Scotch	*Laburnum alpinum*	4
Waterer	*Laburnum watereri*	5
Larch, European	*Larix decidua*	2–3
Japanese	*Larix leptolepis*	4
Linden, American (Basswood)	*Tilia americana*	2–3
Littleleaf	*Tilia cordata*, and varieties	3
Silver	*Tilia tomentosa*	4–5
Locust, Black	*Robinia pseudoacacia*	3

COMMON NAME	SCIENTIFIC NAME AND COMMENTS	HARDINESS ZONE
DECIDUOUS TREES (*cont.*)		
London plane	*Platanus acerifolia*	5–6
Magnolia, Cucumber tree	*Magnolia acuminata*	4–5
Saucer	*Magnolia soulangeana*	5
Star	*Magnolia stellata*	5
Sweet bay	*Magnolia virginiana* (shrublike, North, deciduous)	5
Maple, Norway	*Acer platanoides*, and varieties	3–4
Red	*Acer rubrum*	3
Sugar	*Acer saccharum*	3
Sycamore	*Acer pseudoplatanus*	5–6
Mimosa (Silk-tree)	*Albizzia julibrissin**	7
Mountain-ash, European	*Sorbus aucuparia*	3
Korean	*Sorbus alnifolia*	4
Nannyberry	*Viburnum lentago*	2
Oak, Black	*Quercus velutina*	4–5
Burr	*Quercus macrocarpa*	3
Chestnut	*Quercus prinus*	5
Northern red	*Quercus rubra* 'Borealis'	4
Pin	*Quercus palustris*	4
Scarlet	*Quercus coccinea*	4
Shingle	*Quercus imbricaria*	5–6
Spanish	*Quercus falcata*	5–6
Turkey, *see Oak, Spanish*		
White	*Quercus alba*	4–5
Willow	*Quercus phellos*	5–6
Yellow	*Quercus muehlenbergii*	5
Osage-orange	*Maclura pomifera* (Western sections)	5
Pagoda-tree, Japanese	*Sophora japonica*	4–5
Pawlownia, Royal	*Pawlownia tomentosa*	5
Pear, Bradford	*Pyrus calleryana* 'Bradford'	4–5
Pepperidge, *see Sour gum*		
Poplar, Tulip or Yellow, *see Tulip tree*		
Red-bud, Eastern	*Cercis canadensis*	4–5
Sassafras	*Sassafras albidum*	4–5
Silk-tree, *see Mimosa*		
Silverbell, Carolina	*Halesia carolina*	5
Mountain	*Halesia monticola*	5
Smoke tree, American	*Cotinus americanus*	5
Sorrel tree, *see Sourwood*		
Sour gum (Pepperidge, Tupelo)	*Nyssa sylvatica*	4–5
Sourwood	*Oxydendrum arboreum*	5
Stewartia	*Stewartia koreana*	5
Japanese	*Stewartia pseudo-camellia*	5
Sweet gum	*Liquidambar styraciflua*	5

181

COMMON NAME	SCIENTIFIC NAME AND COMMENTS	HARDINESS ZONE
DECIDUOUS TREES (*cont.*)		
Sycamore	*Platanus occidentalis**	5
Tamarack	*Larix laricina*	1–2
Tulip tree (Tulip poplar)	*Liriodendron tulipifera*	4–5
Tupelo, Black, *see Sourgum*		
Viburnum, Siebold	*Viburnum sieboldii*	4
Walnut, English or Persian	*Juglans regia*	5–6
Willow, Corkscrew	*Salix matsudana* 'Tortuosa'	4–5
Weeping	*Salix babylonica*	6
Yellow poplar, *see Tulip tree*		
Yellowwood	*Cladrastis lutea*	4
Zelkova, Japanese	*Zelkova serrata*	5

REGION 2

BROAD-LEAVED EVERGREENS:

COMMON NAME	SCIENTIFIC NAME AND COMMENTS	HARDINESS ZONE
Camphor tree	*Cinnamomum camphora*	9
Dahoon	*Ilex cassine*	7
Holly, American	*Ilex opaca*	5
Chinese	*Ilex cornuta*	6–7
English	*Ilex aquifolium*	6–7
Longstalk	*Ilex pedunculosa*	5
Holly oak or Holm oak	*Quercus ilex*	8–9
Juniper, West Indies	*Juniperus lucayana*	9
Laurel, *see Sweet bay*		
Laurel cherry	*Prunus laurocerasus*	7
Loquat	*Eriobotrya japonica*	7
Magnolia, Southern	*Magnolia grandiflora*	7
Oak, Laurel	*Quercus laurifolia*	7–9
Live	*Quercus virginiana*	7–8
Sweet bay (Laurel)	*Laurus nobilis*	
Wax myrtle	*Myrica cerifera*	9
Yaupon	*Ilex vomitoria*	7

NEEDLED EVERGREENS:

COMMON NAME	SCIENTIFIC NAME AND COMMENTS	HARDINESS ZONE
Arborvitae, American	*Thuja occidentalis*	2
Oriental	*Thuja orientalis*	6
Cedar, Atlas	*Cedrus atlantica*	6
Deodar	*Cedrus deodara*	7
California incense	*Libocedrus decurrens*	5–6
Eastern red-	*Juniperus virginiana*	2
of Lebanon	*Cedrus libani* 'Stenocoma'	5–6

* Subject to insect or disease damage in certain areas. Check locally to see if trouble exists before purchasing and planting.

COMMON NAME	SCIENTIFIC NAME AND COMMENTS	HARDINESS ZONE
NEEDLED EVERGREENS (*cont.*)		
Cryptomeria	*Cryptomeria japonica*	5–6
Hemlock, Carolina	*Tsuga caroliniana*	4–5
Pine, Eastern white	*Pinus strobus*	3
Loblolly	*Pinus taeda*	7
Longleaf	*Pinus palustris*	8
Shortleaf	*Pinus echinata*	7
Slash	*Pinus caribea*	8–9
Spruce, Colorado blue	*Picea pungens*, and cultivars	2
Red	*Picea rubens*	7
DECIDUOUS TREES:		
Ash, Moraine	*Fraxinus holotricha* 'Moraine'	5
White	*Fraxinus americana*	3
Bald cypress	*Taxodium distichum*	4–5
Basswood, *see Linden, American*		
Beech, American	*Fagus grandifolia*	3
European	*Fagus sylvatica* and cultivars	3
Birch, Cutleaf European	*Betula pendula*	2
Blackhaw, Southern	*Viburnum rufidulum*	5
Buckeye, Ohio	*Aesculus glabra* (western areas)	3–4
Catalpa, Northern	*Catalpa speciosa*	3–4
Southern	*Catalpa bignonioides*	4–5
Cherry, Black	*Prunus serotina*	3
Flowering, many cultivars (northern sections best)		3–6
Chinaberry	*Melia azedarach*	7
Coffee-tree, *see Kentucky coffee-tree*		
Crab apple, many varieties (mid to northern sections best)		2–5
Crape-myrtle	*Lagerstroemeria indica*	7
Cucumber tree or Cucumber magnolia, *see Magnolia, Cucumber tree*		
Dove tree	*Davidia involucrata*	6
Elm, American	*Ulmus americana**	2–3
Cedar	*Ulmus crassifolia*	7
English	*Ulmus procera*	5–6
Winged	*Ulmus alata*	7
Farkleberry	*Vaccinium arboreum*	7
Franklinia	*Franklinia alatamaha*	5
Ginkgo	*Ginkgo biloba*	4–5
Golden-rain tree	*Koelreuteria paniculata*	5
Gordonia (Loblolly bay)	*Gordonia lasianthus*	8
Hackberry, Eastern	*Celtis occidentalis**	3
Sugarberry or Western	*Celtis laevigata*	5

COMMON NAME	SCIENTIFIC NAME AND COMMENTS	HARDINESS ZONE
DECIDUOUS TREES (*cont.*)		
Hawthorn	*Crataegus*, many cultivars	3–5
Hickory, Bitternut	*Carya cordiformis*	4–5
Mockernut	*Carya tomentosa*	4–5
Pignut	*Carya glabra*	4–5
Shagbark	*Carya ovata*	4–5
Honey locust, Thornless	*Gleditsia triacanthos* 'Inermis'	3–4
Hornbeam, American	*Carpinus caroliniana*	2–3
Hop-	*Ostrya virginiana*	4–5
Japanese pagoda tree, *see Pagoda tree*		
Judas-tree, *see also Red-bud*	*Cercis siliquastrum*	6
Katsura	*Cercidiphyllum japonicum*	4–5
Kentucky coffee tree	*Gymnocladus dioica*	4–5
Linden, American (Basswood)	*Tilia americana*	2–3
Littleleaf	*Tilia cordata*	3
London plane	*Platanus acerifolia*	5–6
Magnolia, Cucumber tree	*Magnolia acuminata*	4–5
Sweet bay	*Magnolia virginiana* (semideciduous in north)	5
Maple, Norway	*Acer platanoides*, and varieties	3–4
Red	*Acer rubrum*	3
Sugar	*Acer saccharum*	3
Sycamore	*Acer pseudoplatanus*	5–6
Mimosa	*Albizzia julibrissin**	7
Mulberry, Paper	*Broussonetia papyrifera*	6
Oak, Black	*Quercus velutina*	4–5
Burr	*Quercus macrocarpa*	3
Cork	*Quercus suber*	7
Chestnut	*Quercus prinus*	5
Holly or Holm	*Quercus ilex* (usually evergreen)	8–9
Laurel	*Quercus laurifolia*	7
Live, *see* BROAD-LEAVED EVERGREENS		
Pin	*Quercus palustris*	4
Post	*Quercus stellata*	7
Scarlet	*Quercus coccinea*	4
Shingle	*Quercus imbricaria*	5
Southern red	*Quercus rubra*	7
Water	*Quercus nigra*	5–7
White	*Quercus alba*	4–5
Willow	*Quercus phellos*	5–6
Pagoda tree, Japanese	*Sophora japonica*	4–5
Pear, Bradford	*Pyrus calleryana* 'Bradford'	4–5
Pecan	*Carya illinoiensis*	5–7
Pepperidge, *see Sour gum*		
Persimmon	*Diospyros virginiana*	5–7

COMMON NAME	SCIENTIFIC NAME AND COMMENTS	HARDINESS ZONE
DECIDUOUS TREES (*cont.*)		
Plum, Flowering, many cultivars		4–5
Poplar, Tulip or Yellow, see Tulip tree		
Privet, Glossy	*Ligustrum lucidum*	7
Red-bud, Eastern, *see also* Judas-tree	*Cercis canadensis*	4–6
Sassafras	*Sassafras albidum*	4–5
Silk-tree, *see Mimosa*		
Silverbell, Carolina	*Halesia carolina*	5
Mountain	*Halesia monticola*	5
Smoke tree, American	*Cotinus americanus*	5
Sorrel tree, *see Sourwood*		
Sour gum (Pepperidge or Tupelo)	*Nyssa sylvatica*	4–5
Sourwood	*Oxydendrum arboreum*	5
Sweet gum	*Liquidambar styraciflua*	5
Sycamore	*Platanus occidentalis**	5
Tamarack	*Larix laricina*	1–2
Tulip tree	*Liriodendron tulipifera*	4–5
Tupelo, *see Sour gum*		
Umbrella tree, *see Chinaberry*		
Walnut, English or Persian	*Juglans regia*	5–6
Yellowwood	*Cladrastis lutea*	4
Zelkova, Elm	*Zelkova carpinifolia*	6
PALMS:		
Palmetto, Cabbage	*Sabal palmetto*	8

REGION 3

BROAD-LEAVED EVERGREENS:		
African tulip tree (Bell flambeau)	*Spathodea campanulata*	10
Brazilian pepper	*Schinus terebinthifolius*	9–10
Brush-cherry eugenia	*Eugenia paniculata*	9
Cajeput	*Melaleuca leucadendron*	10
Camellia, Common	*Camellia japonica*, and hybrid varieties	9
Cherry-laurel, *see Laurel, Cherry-*		
Cocoplum	*Chrysobalanus icaco*	10
Cypress-pine	*Callistris robusta*	9
Fig, Fiddleleaf	*Ficus lyrata*	10
India laurel	*Ficus retusa*	10
Lofty	*Ficus altissima*	10
Franklinia	*Franklinia alatamaha*	5
Geiger tree	*Cordia sebestena*	10

* Subject to insect or disease damage in certain areas. Check locally to see if trouble exists before purchasing and planting.

185

COMMON NAME	SCIENTIFIC NAME AND COMMENTS	HARDINESS ZONE
BROAD-LEAVED EVERGREENS (*cont.*)		
Holly, American	*Ilex opaca*	5
Chinese	*Ilex cornuta*	6–7
India laurel, *see Fig, India laurel*		
Indian rubber tree	*Ficus elastica*	10
Jacaranda	*Jacaranda acutifolia*	9–10
Juniper, West Indies	*Juniperus lucayana*	9
Laurel, Cherry-	*Prunus laurocerasus*	7
Magnolia, Southern	*Magnolia grandifolia*	7
Mahogany, Swamp	*Swietenia mahagonii*	10
(West Indies mahogany)		
Oak, Laurel	*Quercus laurifolia*	7–9
Live	*Quercus virginiana*	7–8
Oxhorn bucida	*Bucida buceras*	10
Pigeon plum	*Coccoloba diversifolia*	10
Silk-oak	*Grevillea robusta*	10
Silver trumpet	*Tabebuia argentea*	10
Surinam-cherry	*Eugenia uniflora*	10
Wax-myrtle	*Myrica cerifera*	9
NEEDLED EVERGREENS:		
Pine, Longleaf	*Pinus palustris*	8
Slash	*Pinus caribea*	8–9
Spruce	*Pinus glabra*	9
DECIDUOUS TREES:		
Bald cypress	*Taxodium distichum*	4–5
Basswood, *see Linden, American*		
Bo tree	*Ficus religiosa*	10
Crape myrtle	*Lagerstroemia indica*	7
Cucumber tree, *see Magnolia*		
Fig, Benjamin	*Ficus benjamina*	10
Flame tree, *see Poinciana, Royal*		
Golden-rain tree	*Koelreuteria paniculata*	5
Judas-Tree, *see Red-bud, Eastern*		
Linden, American (Basswood)	*Tilia americana*	2–3
Magnolia, Cucumber tree	*Magnolia acuminata*	4–5
Maple, Red	*Acer rubrum*	3
Mimosa (Silk-tree)	*Albizia julibrissin**	7
Lebbek	*Albizia lebbek*	9
Oak Holly or Holm	*Quercus ilex*	8–9
Water	*Quercus nigra*	5–7
Orchid tree	*Bauhinia*, species	9–10
Pecan	*Carya illinoiensis*	5–7
Poinciana, Royal (Flame tree)	*Delonix regia*	9–10
Red-bud, Eastern (Judas-tree)	*Cercis canadensis*	4–6
Silk-tree, *see Mimosa*		
Sophora, New Zealand	*Sophora tetraptera*	9
Sweet gum	*Liquidambar styraciflua*	5

COMMON NAME	SCIENTIFIC NAME AND COMMENTS	HARDINESS ZONE
PALMS:		
Coconut	*Cocos nucifera*	10
Cuban royal	*Roystonea regia*	10
Fishtail	*Caryota mitis*	10
Florida royal	*Roystonea elata*	10
Manila	*Veitchia merillii*	10
Mexican fan (Washington)	*Washingtonia robusta*	9–10
Palmetto, Cabbage	*Sabal palmetto*	8
LEAFLESS TREES:		
Beefwood (Horsetail-tree)	*Casuarina equisetifolia*	9–10
Cunningham	*Casuarina cunninghamiana*	10
Scalybark	*Casuarina lepidophloia*	9–10

REGION 4

BROAD-LEAVED EVERGREENS:
None recommended

NEEDLED EVERGREENS:		
Arborvitae, American	*Thuja occidentalis*	2
Oriental	*Thuja orientalis*	6
Cedar, California incense-	*Libocedrus decurrens*	5–6
Eastern red-	*Juniperus virginiana*	2
Western red-	*Juniperus scopulorum*	4–5
Fir, Douglas	*Pseudotsuga menziesii*	4–6
Hemlock, Canadian	*Tsuga canadensis*	4–5
Pine, Austrian	*Pinus nigra* 'Austriaca'	3–4
Ponderosa	*Pinus ponderosa*	3–5
Scotch	*Pinus sylvestris*	2–3
Spruce, Colorado blue	*Picea pungens*, and cultivars	2
DECIDUOUS TREES:		
Ash, Black	*Fraxinus nigra*	3
Green	*Fraxinus pensylvanica* 'Lanceolata'	2
White	*Fraxinus americana*	3
Basswood, *see Linden American*		
Birch, Canoe or Paper	*Betula papyrifera*	2
Cutleaf European	*Betula pendula*	2
White	*Betula alba*	2
Catalpa, Northern	*Catalpa speciosa*	3–4
Cherry, Black	*Prunus serotina*	3
Cottonwood	*Populus*, seedless hybrids	3

* Subject to insect or disease damage in certain areas. Check locally to see if trouble exists before purchasing and planting.

COMMON NAME	SCIENTIFIC NAME AND COMMENTS	HARDINESS ZONE
DECIDUOUS TREES (*cont.*)		
Elm, American	*Ulmus americana**	2–3
Siberian	*Ulmus pumila*	3
Hackberry, Eastern	*Celtis occidentalis**	3
Sugarberry or Western	*Celtis laevigata*	5
Honey locust, Thornless	*Gleditsia triacanthos* 'Inermis'	3–4
Katsura	*Cercidiphyllum japonicum*	4–5
Larch, Siberian	*Larix sibirica*	3
Linden, American (Basswood)	*Tilia americana*	2–3
Littleleaf	*Tilia cordata*, and cultivars	3
Maple, Silver	*Acer saccharinum*	3
Oak, Burr	*Quercus macrocarpa*	3
Northern red	*Quercus rubra* 'Borealis'	4
Pin	*Quercus palustris*	4
Scarlet	*Quercus coccinea*	4
Poplar, Plains, *see Cottonwood*		
Sugarberry, *see Hackberry*		
Zelkova, Japanese	*Zelkova serrata*	5

REGION 5

BROAD-LEAVED EVERGREENS:		
Loquat	*Eriobotrya japonica*	7
Oak, Live	*Quercus virginiana*	7–8
Yaupon	*Ilex vomitoria*	8
NEEDLED EVERGREENS:		
Arborvitae, Oriental	*Thuja orientalis*	6
Cedar, Atlas	*Cedrus atlantica*	6
Eastern red-	*Juniperus virginiana*	2
Cryptomeria	*Cryptomeria japonica*	5–6
Cypress, Arizona	*Cupressus arizonica*	7
Juniper, *see also Cedar,* *Eastern red-*		
Rocky Mountain	*Juniperus scopulorum*	3
Pine, Austrian	*Pinus nigra* 'Austriaca'	3–4
Loblolly	*Pinus taeda*	7
Ponderosa	*Pinus ponderosa*	3–5
Spruce, Colorado blue	*Picea pungens*, and cultivars	2

* Subject to insect or disease damage in certain areas. Check locally to see if trouble exists before purchasing and planting.

COMMON NAME	SCIENTIFIC NAME AND COMMENTS	HARDINESS ZONE
DECIDUOUS TREES:		
Ash, Green	*Fraxinus pensylvanica* 'Lanceolata'	2
Bald cypress	*Taxodium distichum*	4–5
Beech, European	*Fagus sylvatica*	3
Buckeye, Ohio	*Aesculus glabra* (northern areas)	3–4
Catalpa, Northern	*Catalpa speciosa*	3–4
Southern	*Catalpa bignonioides*	4–5
Chinaberry	*Melia azedarach*	7
Coffee-tree, *see Kentucky coffee-tree*		
Desert-willow, *see Willow*		
Elm, American	*Ulmus americana**	2–3
Chinese	*Ulmus parvifolia*	5
Siberian	*Ulmus pumila*	4
Golden-rain tree	*Koelreuteria paniculata*	5
Gordonia, Loblolly-bay	*Gordonia lasianthus*	8
Hackberry, Eastern	*Celtis occidentalis**	3
Sugarberry or Western	*Celtis laevigata*	5
Honey locust, Thornless	*Gleditsia triacanthos* 'Inermis'	3–4
Huisache	*Acacia farnesiana*	9
Japanese pagoda-tree, *see Pagoda-tree, Japanese*		
Judas-tree (Red-bud)	*Cercis siliquastrum*	6
Katsura	*Cercidiphyllum japonicum*	4–5
Kentucky coffee-tree	*Gymnocladus dioica*	4–5
Loquat	*Eriobotrya japonica* (evergreen in warmer areas)	7
Maple, Silver	*Acer saccharinum*	3
Sycamore	*Acer pseudoplatanus*	5–6
Mesquite	*Prosopis*, species	8–9
Mulberry, Paper	*Broussonetia papyrifera*	6
Russian	*Morus alba* 'Tatarica'	4–5
Oak, Burr	*Quercus macrocarpa*	3
Chestnut	*Quercus prinus*	5
Pin	*Quercus palustris*	4
Post	*Quercus stellata*	7
Scarlet	*Quercus coccinea*	4
Shumard	*Quercus shumardii*	5
Spanish	*Quercus texana* (or *falcata*)	7–8
Texas (*see Oak, Shumard*)		
Yellow	*Quercus muehlenbergii*	5
Osage-orange	*Maclura pomifera*	5
Pagoda-tree, Japanese	*Sophora japonica*	4–5
Pecan	*Carya illinoiensis*	5–7
Pistache, Chinese	*Pistacia chinensis*	8–9

COMMON NAME	SCIENTIFIC NAME AND COMMENTS	HARDINESS ZONE
DECIDUOUS TREES (*cont.*)		
Red-bud, Chinese	*Cercis chinensis*	6
Eastern Judas-tree	*Cercis canadensis*	4–5
Retama	*Parkinsonia aculeata*	9
Sassafras	*Sassafras albidum*	4–5
Soapberry, Western	*Sapindus drummondii*	6
Sugarberry, *see Hackberry*		
Sycamore	*Platanus occidentalis**	5
Umbrella-tree, *see Chinaberry*		
Willow, Desert-	*Chilopsis linearis*	7
Zelkova, Japanese	*Zelkova serrata*	5

REGION 6

BROAD-LEAVED EVERGREENS:		
Olive	*Olea europaea*	9
Russian	*Eleagnus angustifolia*	3–5
NEEDLED EVERGREENS:		
Arborvitae, Giant	*Thuja plicata*	5–6
Oriental	*Thuja orientalis*	3–6
Cedar, Atlas	*Cedrus atlantica*	6
California incense-	*Libocedrus decurrens*	5–6
Eastern red-	*Juniperus virginiana*	2
Fir, Douglas	*Pseudotsuga menziesii*	4–6
White	*Abies concolor*	4–5
Juniper, *see also Cedar,*		
Eastern red-		
Rocky Mountain	*Juniperus scopulorum*	3
Pine, Austrian	*Pinus nigra* 'Austriaca'	3–4
Ponderosa	*Pinus ponderosa*	3–5
Spruce, Colorado blue	*Picea pungens*, and cultivars	2
DECIDUOUS TREES:		
Ash, Arizona (Modesto or Velvet)	*Fraxinus velutina*	5–7
European	*Fraxinus excelsior*	3
Green	*Fraxinus pensylvanica* 'Lanceolata'	2
Beech, European	*Fagus sylvatica*	3
Buckeye, Ohio	*Aesculus glabra*	3–4
Catalpa, Northern	*Catalpa speciosa*	3–4
Coffee-tree, *see Kentucky coffee-tree*		

* Subject to insect or disease damage in certain areas. Check locally to see if trouble exists before purchasing and planting.

190

COMMON NAME	SCIENTIFIC NAME AND COMMENTS	HARDINESS ZONE
DECIDUOUS TREES (*cont.*)		
Cottonwood	*Populus*, seedless hybrids	3
Elm, American	*Ulmus americana***	2–3
Chinese	*Ulmus parvifolia*	5
European field (Smooth-leaved)	*Ulmus carpinifolia*	5
Siberian	*Ulmus pumila*	4
Ginkgo	*Ginkgo biloba*	4–5
Golden-rain tree	*Koelreuteria paniculata*	5
Hackberry, Eastern	*Celtis occidentalis***	3
Horse-chestnut, Red	*Aesculus carnea*	3
White	*Aesculus hippocastanum* 'Baumannii'	3
Japanese pagoda-tree, *see* Pagoda tree		
Katsura	*Cercidiphyllum japonicum*	4–5
Kentucky coffee-tree	*Gymnocladus dioica*	4–5
Linden (American Basswood)	*Tilia americana*	2–3
Littleleaf	*Tilia cordata*	3
London plane	*Platanus acerifolia*	5–6
Maple, Bigleaf	*Acer macrophyllum*	6–7
Norway	*Acer platanoides*	3–4
Sugar	*Acer saccharum*	3
Mulberry, Russian	*Morus alba* 'Tatarica'	4–5
Oak, Burr	*Quercus macrocarpa*	3
Northern red	*Quercus rubra* 'Borealis'	4
Pin	*Quercus palustris*	4
White	*Quercus alba*	4–5
Pagoda-tree, Japanese	*Sophora japonica*	4–5
Poplar, Plains, *see Cottonwood*		
Sweet gum	*Liquidambar styraciflua*	5
Zelkova, Japanese	*Zelkova serrata*	5

REGION 7

BROAD-LEAVED EVERGREENS:		
Carob	*Ceratonia siliqua*	9–10
Eucalyptus	*Eucalyptus*, species	10
Gum tree, *see Eucalyptus*		
Olive	*Olea europaea*	9
Russian	*Eleagnus angustifolia*	3–5
Palo verde, Blue	*Cercidium floridum*	7

* Subject to insect or disease damage in certain areas. Check locally to see if trouble exists before purchasing and planting.

191

COMMON NAME	SCIENTIFIC NAME AND COMMENTS	HARDINESS ZONE
NEEDLED EVERGREENS:		
Cedar, Atlas	*Cedrus atlantica*	6
Deodar	*Cedrus deodara*	7
Eastern red	*Juniperus virginiana*	2
Cypress, Arizona	*Cupressus arizonica*	7
Italian	*Cupressus sempervirens*	7
Fir, Douglas-	*Pseudotsuga menziesii*	4–6
Silver	*Abies alba*	5
Juniper, *see Cedar, Eastern red-*		
Rocky Mountain	*Juniperus scopulorum*	3
Pine, Aleppo	*Pinus halepensis*	9
Austrian	*Pinus nigra* 'Austriaca'	3–4
Canary Island	*Pinus canariensis*	8
DECIDUOUS TREES:		
Acacia, Bailey's, *see Wattle, Bailey's*		
Ailanthus, *see Tree of heaven*		
Chinaberry	*Melia azdarach*	7
Cottonwood	*Populus*, seedless hybrids	3
Desert-willow, *see Willow, Desert-*		
Elm, Cedar	*Ulmus crassifolia*	7
Chinese	*Ulmus parvifolia*	5
Siberian	*Ulmus pumila*	4
Ginkgo	*Ginkgo biloba*	4–5
Golden-rain tree	*Koelreuteria paniculata*	5
Hackberry, Eastern	*Celtis occidentalis**	3
Sugarberry or Western	*Celtis laevigata*	5
Honey locust, Thornless	*Gleditsia triacanthos* 'Inermis'	3–4
Huisache	*Acacia farnesiana*	9
Linden, Littleleaf	*Tilia cordata*	3
Locust, Black	*Robinia pseudoacacia*	3
London plane	*Platanus acerifolia*	5–6
Maple, Silver	*Acer saccharinum*	3
Mesquite	*Prosopis*, species	8–9
Mulberry, Russian	*Morus alba* 'Tatarica'	4–5
Oak, Pin	*Quercus palustris*	4
Southern Red (Spanish)	*Quercus falcata*	6–7
Pecan	*Carya illinoiensis*	5–7
Poplar, Carolina	*Populus canadensis* 'Eugenei'*	4
Plains, *see Cottonwood*		
White (Bolleana)	*Populus alba* 'Nivea Pyramidalis'	3
Sugarberry, *see Hackberry,*		
Sweet gum	*Liquidambar styraciflua*	5
Tree of heaven	*Ailanthus altissima*	4–5
Umbrella tree, *see Chinaberry*		
Wattle, Bailey's	*Acacia baileyana*	9–10
Sydney	*Acacia longifolia*	10
Willow, Desert-	*Chilopsis linearis*	7

COMMON NAME	SCIENTIFIC NAME AND COMMENTS	HARDINESS ZONE
PALMS:		
Canary date	*Phoenix canariensis*	9

REGION 8

BROAD-LEAVED EVERGREENS:		
Brush-cherry	*Eugenia paniculata*	9
Australian	*Eugenia australis*	8
Cajeput	*Melaleuca leucadendron*	10
Camellia	*Camellia*, species and hybrids	8
Camphor tree	*Cinnamomum camphora*	9
Carob	*Ceratonia siliqua*	9–10
Coral tree	*Erythrina caffra*	10
Dove tree	*Davidia involucrata*	6
Eucalyptus	*Eucalyptus*, species	10
Fig, Fiddleleaf	*Ficus lyrata*	10
India laurel	*Ficus retusa*	10
Moreton Bay	*Ficus macrophylla*	10
Gum tree, *see Eucalyptus*		
Jacaranda	*Jacaranda acutifolia*	9–10
Laurel, California	*Umbellularia californica*	7
Grecian (or Sweet bay)	*Laurus nobilis*	6
Laurel-cherry	*Prunus laurocerasus*	7
Lily-of-the-valley tree	*Crinodendron dependens*	10
Live oak, *see Oak, Live*		
Loquat	*Eriobotrya japonica*	7
Magnolia, Southern	*Magnolia grandiflora*	7
Oak, California live	*Quercus agrifolia*	9
Canyon	*Quercus chrysolepis*	7
Holly or Holm	*Quercus ilex*	9
Live	*Quercus virginiana*	7–8
Tan-, *see Tan-oak*		
Palo verde, Blue	*Cercidium floridum*	7
Pittosporum, Diamond-leaf	*Pittosporum rhombifolium*	10
Sweet Bay, *see Laurel, Grecian*		
Tan-oak (Tanbark oak)	*Lithocarpus densiflorus*	7–8
NEEDLED EVERGREENS:		
Arborvitae, Giant	*Thuja plicata*	5
Oriental	*Thuja orientalis*	3–6
Cedar, Atlas	*Cedrus atlantica*	6
California incense-	*Libocedrus decurrens*	5–6
Deodar	*Cedrus deodara*	7
of Lebanon	*Cedrus libani* 'Stenocoma'	5–6

* Subject to insect or disease damage in certain areas. Check locally to see if trouble exists before purchasing and planting.

COMMON NAME	SCIENTIFIC NAME AND COMMENTS	HARDINESS ZONE
NEEDLED EVERGREENS (*cont.*)		
Cryptomeria	*Cryptomeria japonica*	5–6
Cypress, Arizona	*Cupressus arizonica*	7
Italian	*Cupressus sempervirens*	7
Lawson false-	*Chamaecyparis lawsoniana*	5–6
Monterey	*Cupressus macrocarpa*	7
Cypress pine	*Callistris robusta*	9
False-cypress, *see Cypress,* *Lawson false-*		
Pine, Aleppo	*Pinus halepensis*	9
Canary Island	*Pinus canariensis*	8
Norfolk Island	*Araucaria excelsa*	10
Spruce, Colorado blue	*Picea pungens*, and cultivars	2
DECIDUOUS TREES:		
Almond	*Prunus amygdalus*	6
Apricot	*Prunus armeniaca*	5
Ash, Arizona (Modesto, Velvet)	*Fraxinus velutina*	5–7
Banana, Abyssinian	*Musa ensete*	9
Bayberry, California	*Myrica californica*	7
Chinaberry	*Melia azedarach*	7
Cherry, Flowering, many hybrid cultivars		3–6
Chinese flame tree	*Koelreuteria formosana*	9
Chinese lantern tree	*Koelreuteria bipinnata*	6
Cottonwood	*Populus*, seedless hybrids	3
Desert Willow, *see Willow, Desert*		
Elm, American	*Ulmus americana**	2–3
Chinese	*Ulmus parvifolia*	5
Siberian	*Ulmus pumila*	4
Ginkgo	*Ginkgo biloba*	4–5
Golden-rain tree	*Koelreuteria paniculata*	5
Hackberry, Eastern	*Celtis occidentalis**	3
Honey locust, Thornless	*Gleditsia triacanthos* 'Inermis'	3–4
Japanese pagoda-tree (*see Pagoda-tree*)		
Locust, Black	*Robinia pseudoacacia*	3
London plane	*Platanus acerifolia*	5–6
Loquat	*Eriobotrya japonica* (evergreen in warmer areas)	7
Maple, Bigleaf	*Acer macrophyllum*	6–7
Norway	*Acer platanoides*	3–4
Red	*Acer rubrum*	3
Mimosa (Silk-tree)	*Albizia julibrissin** (grows only in southern areas)	7
Mulberry, Russian	*Morus alba* 'Tatarica'	4–5

COMMON NAME	SCIENTIFIC NAME AND COMMENTS	HARDINESS ZONE
DECIDUOUS TREES (*cont.*)		
Oak, Burr	*Quercus macrocarpa*	3
English	*Quercus robur*	5
Northern red	*Quercus rubra* 'Borealis'	4
Pin	*Quercus palustris*	4
Scarlet	*Quercus coccinea*	4
Valley	*Quercus lobata*	9
Olive	*Olea europaea*	9
Orchid tree	*Bauhinia*, species	9
Pagoda-tree, Japanese	*Sophora japonica*	4–5
Pepper-tree, California	*Schinus molle*	9
Pistache, Chinese	*Pistacia chinensis*	8–9
Sweet gum	*Liquidambar styraciflua*	5
Sweet-shade	*Hymenosporum flavum*	10
Tulip tree, Tulip poplar	*Liriodendron tulipifera*	4–5
Umbrella tree, *see Chinaberry*		
Walnut, English or Persian	*Juglans regia*	5–6
Willow, Desert-	*Chilopsis linearis*	7
PALMS:		
Canary date	*Phoenix canariensis*	9
Mexican fan (Washington)	*Washingtonia robusta*	9–10
LEAFLESS TREES:		
Beefwood, Horsetail-tree	*Casuarina equisetifolia*	9–10

REGION 9

BROAD-LEAVED EVERGREENS:		
Holly, American, Chinese, and other species		
English	*Ilex aquifolium*	6
Perny	*Ilex pernyi*	6
Madrone	*Arbutus menziesii*	7
Magnolia, Southern	*Magnolia grandiflora*	7
Tan-oak (Tanbark oak)	*Lithocarpus densiflorus*	7–8
Rhododendron, Rosebay	*Rhododendron maximum*	3
Many other Rhododendron species and cultivars		3–6
NEEDLED EVERGREENS:		
Arborvitae, Giant	*Thuja plicata*	5
Oriental	*Thuja orientalis*	6
Cedar, Atlas	*Cedrus atlantica*	6
California incense-	*Libocedrus decurrens*	5–6
Deodar	*Cedrus deodora*	7

* Subject to insect or disease damage in certain areas. Check locally to see if trouble exists before purchasing and planting.

195

COMMON NAME	SCIENTIFIC NAME AND COMMENTS	HARDINESS ZONE
NEEDLED EVERGREENS (*cont.*)		
Cryptomeria	*Cryptomeria japonica*	5–6
Cypress, Lawson false-	*Chamaecyparis lawsoniana*, and cultivars	5–6
Sawara false-	*Chamaecyparis pisifera*, and cultivars	3
Pine, Austrian	*Pinus nigra* 'Austriaca'	3–4
Ponderosa	*Pinus ponderosa*	3–5
Spruce, Colorado blue	*Picea pungens*, and cultivars	2
DECIDUOUS TREES:		
Ash, European	*Fraxinus excelsior*	3
Green	*Fraxinus pensylvanica* 'Lanceolata'	2
Oregon	*Fraxinus oregana*	6
White	*Fraxinus americana*	3
Bayberry, California	*Myrica californica*	7
Beech, European	*Fagus sylvatica*	5
Birch, White	*Betula alba*	2
Buckeye, Ohio	*Aesculus glabra* (limited use)	3–4
Coffee-tree, *see Kentucky coffee-tree*		
Cork tree, Amur	*Phellodendron amurense*	3–4
Dogwood, Pacific	*Cornus nuttallii*	7
Elm, American	*Ulmus americana**	2–3
Chinese	*Ulmus parvifolia*	5
English	*Ulmus procera*	5–6
Scotch or Wych	*Ulmus glabra*	5
Siberian	*Ulmus pumila*	4
Ginkgo	*Ginkgo biloba*	4–5
Golden-chain tree	*Laburnum anagyroides* and *L. watererii*	5–7
Golden-rain tree	*Koelreuteria paniculata*	5
Honey locust, Thornless	*Gleditsia triacanthos* 'Inermis'	3–4
Hornbeam, American	*Carpinus caroliniana*	2–3
Horse-chestnut, Red	*Aesculus carnea*	3
White	*Aesculus hippocastanum* 'Baumannii'	3
Japanese pagoda-tree, *see Pagoda-tree*		
Kentucky coffee-tree	*Gymnocladus dioica*	4–5
Linden, American	*Tilia americana*	2–3
Littleleaf	*Tilia cordata*, and varieties	3
London plane	*Platanus acerifolia*	5–6
Maple, Bigleaf	*Acer macrophyllum*	6–7
Norway	*Acer platanoides*	3–4
Red	*Acer rubrum*	3
Sugar	*Acer saccharum*	3

COMMON NAME	SCIENTIFIC NAME AND COMMENTS	HARDINESS ZONE
DECIDUOUS TREES (*cont.*)		
Mimosa (Silk-tree)	*Albizia julibrissin**	7
Oak, Northern red	*Quercus rubra* 'Borealis'	4
Oregon white	*Quercus garryana*	6
Pin	*Quercus palustris*	4
Scarlet	*Quercus coccinea*	4
White	*Quercus alba*	4–5
Pagoda-tree, Japanese	*Sophora japonica*	4–5
Silverbell	*Halesia carolina*	5
Sourwood	*Oxydendrum arboreum*	5
Sweet gum	*Liquidambar styraciflua*	5
Tulip tree (Tulip poplar)	*Liriodendron tulipifera*	4–5
Yellowwood	*Cladrastis lutea*	4

* Subject to insect or disease damage in certain areas. Check locally to see if trouble exists before purchasing and planting.

DRY-SOIL TREES

This list embraces trees known to grow and survive in various conditions of dry soil. Not all will do well in every dry soil, for the range is from moderately dry to dry, and in the hardiness zones indicated. Because conditions vary widely even within the zone, it is suggested that inquiries be made locally concerning the availability and advisability of planting the tree chosen. Check with the lists according to height for other notes as well as the scientific Latin name which should be used in ordering the tree in order to assure receipt of the proper species and variety.

COMMON NAME	HARDINESS ZONE	COMMON NAME	HARDINESS ZONE
Acacia, Gossamer Sydney	10	Mulberry, Common, also	
Angelica tree, Japanese	3	Paper-	6
Ash, Velvet and Modesto	5	Oak, Blackjack	6
Bauhinia, *see Orchid tree*		California black	7
Beefwood (Casuarina)	9–10	Interior live	7
Birch, Dahurian	4	Olive	9
Birch, Gray	3–4	Orange, Mexican	5
Bottle tree	9	Osage-orange	5
Box-elder	2	Orchid-tree (Bauhinia)	10
Cajeput	10	Pagoda tree, Japanese	4

197

COMMON NAME	HARDI-NESS ZONE	COMMON NAME	HARDI-NESS ZONE
Carob	10	Pepper tree, California	9
Chinaberry	7	Pine, Canary	8
Cottonwood	5–7	Jack	2
Cypress, Italian	7	Pitch	4
Monterey	7	Scrub or Virginia	4
Elm, Siberian	4	Torrey	8
Eucalyptus, species	9–10	Poplar, Plains (Cottonwood)	5–7
Fig, species	9–10	White	3
Golden-rain tree	5	Red-cedar, Eastern	
Hackberry, European	6	Sassafras	4
Honey locust, species	4	Silk-oak	10
Juniper, species	2–7	Silk-tree	6–7
Keteleeria, Fortune	7	Tea-tree, Australian	9
Locust, Black	3	Thorn, Jerusalem-	9
Mesquite, Honey	8	Tree of heaven	4

SMALL SHADE TREES

These are trees that may be used either to shade a terrace or to provide shade in other places. They are also useful to fill out and give height in places where shade is not really required, such as in a front yard. They are in scale with small and low houses. See also the Small Flowering Trees list, page 223. Some trees on this list may grow to higher proportions than is strictly within the limits of a small-tree category, but this will be dependent upon climate, soil, and other favorable conditions. Some may also grow to lesser heights for the same reasons. The heights are average for the country, according to the best research available at the present time.

COMMON NAME	SCIENTIFIC NAME	HEIGHT IN FEET	HARDI-NESS ZONE	COMMENTS
Ash, Flowering	*Fraxinus ornus*	to 60	5	
Green	*Fraxinus pensyl-vanica* 'Lanceolata'	45–60	2	produces seeds
Maries'	*Fraxinus mariesii*	25	7	
Marshall's seed-less green	*Fraxinus pensyl-vanica* 'Lanceo-lata' 'Marshall's Seedless'	45+	2	

COMMON NAME	SCIENTIFIC NAME	HEIGHT IN FEET	HARDI-NESS ZONE	COMMENTS
Ash, Flowering (*cont.*)				
Modesto (Arizona, Velvet)	*Fraxinus velutina* 'Glabra'	to 40	5–6	Arizona, South-west
Moraine Balkan	*Fraxinus holotricha* 'Moraine'	35	5	
Shamel	*Fraxinus uhdei*	30	9	California
Summit green	*Fraxinus pensyl-vanica* 'Lanceo-lata' 'Summit'	45+	2	produces seeds
Birch,* Cutleaf European	*Betula pendula*	30–50	2	
Gray	*Betula populifolia*	35	3–4	often used in multiple trunks
Slender European	*Betula pendula* 'Gra-cilis' (feathery) (sometimes listed *B. p.* 'Laciniata'	to 50	2	
White	*Betula alba*	35–50	2	
Citrus (*see Fruit trees*)				
Cork tree, Amur	*Phellodendron amu-rense*	35	4	Northeast, North-west
Crab apple, various	*Malus,* species and cultivars			fruit, flowers
Bechtel	*Malus ioensis* 'Plena'	to 30	2	
Dolgo	x*Malus* 'Dolgo'	40	3	
Iowa	*Malus ioensis*	30+	2	
Jack	x*Malus* 'Jackii'	40+	2	very hardy
Siberian	*Malus baccata* 'Gracilis', and cultivars	40+	2	may grow wide
Tea	*Malus hupehensis* (*theifera*)	to 25	4	wide

Key:
BLE = Broad-leaved evergreen
E = Needled evergreen
SE = Semi-evergreen (may be deciduous in northern reaches of hardiness zone)
x = Hybrid variety

* Birches are subject to attack by insects in several areas, and it may not be wise to plant them. Inquire locally about bronze birch borer, which is injurious to European birch, entering the trunk high up and killing the whole top. Birch-leaf miner defoliates gray birch, a tree that is in addition often bent and even broken by heavy ice and snows in the Northeast.

COMMON NAME	SCIENTIFIC NAME	HEIGHT IN FEET	HARDI- NESS ZONE	COMMENTS
Dogwood, Flowering (white)	*Cornus florida*	20–35+	4	white
Cultivars:	'Apple Blossom'	20–35+	4	apple-blossom pink
	'Cherokee Chief'	20–35+	4	deep red
	'Fastigiata'	20–35+	4	white, upright young, reverts
	'Gigantea'	20–35+	4	6-inch white bracts
	'New Hampshire'	20–35+	3	white, hardy in New Hampshire
	'Pendula'	20–35+	3	stiffly pendulous branches
	'Rubra'	20–35+	3	pink to reddish
	'Spring Song'	20–35+	3	rose red
	'Sweetwater Red'	20–35+	3	red flowers, red- dish foliage
	'Welchii'	20–35+	3	foliage variegated; cream, pink, green
	'White Cloud'	20–35+	3	profuse, creamy white
	'Xanthocarpa'	20–35+	3	yellow fruits
Pacific (Nuttall)	*Cornus nuttallii*	50–75	7	West Coast native
Fruit trees, various				Often doubling as shade and deco- rative trees: Apple, citrus, pear, peach, avo- cado, kumquat, loquat, and others. Some are tall enough to shade terraces and other spots. In the South, California, and Southwest, orange trees, loquats, and avocados are often worked into plantings.
Golden-rain tree	*Koelreuteria pani- culata*	25–30	4–5	
Hawthorn, Cock- spur thorn	*Crataegus crus-galli*	35	4	

COMMON NAME	SCIENTIFIC NAME	HEIGHT IN FEET	HARDI-NESS ZONE	COMMENTS
Hawthorn (*cont.*)				
English, Paul's scarlet	*Crataegus oxycantha* 'Paulii'	25–30	4	
Thornless	*Crataegus monogyna* 'Inermis'	30	4	
Washington	*Crataegus phaenopyrum*	30	4	
Holly, American (BLE)	*Ilex opaca*, and cultivars	to 45	5	
English	*Ilex aquifolium*	45+	6	especially in Northwest
Holly or Holm oak, *see Oak, Holly or Holm*				
Honey locust, Thornless	*Gleditsia triacanthos* 'Inermis'			
Cultivars:	'Moraine'	to 45+	4	light foliage, fast growing
	'Ruby Lace'	to 40+	4	reddish foliage
	'Shademaster'	to 40+	4	upright habit
	'Sunburst'	to 45+	4	green, yellow-tipped foliage
Hornbeam, Globe European	*Carpinus betulus* 'Globosa'	35+	5–6	
Japanese	*Carpinus japonica*	to 45+	4	slow growing
Pyramidal American	*Carpinus carolina* 'Pyramidalis'	45	2–3	
Hop-hornbeam	*Ostrya virginiana*	35–40	4	
Magnolia, Oyama	*Magnolia sieboldii*	20–30	6	
Saucer	*Magnolia soulangiana*	20–25	5	train to tree form
Veitch	*Magnolia veitchii*	40	7	fast growing
Yulan	*Magnolia denudata*	30–35	5	
Maple, Amur	*Acer ginnala*	20+	2	
Hedge	*Acer campestre*	25	5–6	
Hornbeam	*Acer carpinifolium*	30	5	
Manchurian	*Acer mandshuricum*	30	4	
Rocky Mountain	*Acer glabrum*	25	5	native in West
Tatarian	*Acer tataricum*	30	4	
Oak, Holly or Holm (BLE)	*Quercus ilex*	45+	9	can be clipped, restrained
Laurel (SE)	*Quercus laurifolia*	to 50+	7	
Willow	*Quercus phellos*	50	5–6	
Olive, Russian	*Eleagnus angustifolia*	25–40	2–4	

COMMON NAME	SCIENTIFIC NAME	HEIGHT IN FEET	HARDI- NESS ZONE	COMMENTS
Pagoda-tree, Japanese	*Sophora japonica*	to 50	4–5	
Pine, Eastern white (E)	*Pinus strobus*	to 100	3	keep low by pruning
Silk-tree	*Albizia julibrissin*	35	5–7	
Cultivars:	'Charlotte'	35	6–7	'fungus-, disease- resistant
	'Tryon'	35	6–7	fungus-, disease- resistant
Silverbell, Carolina	*Halesia carolina*	25–30	4–5	
Snowbell, Fragrant	*Styrax obassia*	20–30	6	
Japanese	*Styrax japonica*	20–30	5	
Storax, *see Snow- bell*				
Viburnum, Siebold	*Viburnum sieboldii*	30	4	

MEDIUM-HEIGHT TREES

These trees will go well with either one- or two-story houses, and if they are not too spreading, will fit into small- to medium-sized gardens. Smaller trees, especially the flowering ones, may be paired with them, providing a compositional counterpoint. Some of them are needled ever-greens, and these, for the most part, are not shade trees. They should be chosen with special care, therefore, and used for accent and for winter color, for windbreaks, and to provide a foil for the deciduous varieties.

The heights given are optimum—the maximum height they may eventually reach. Such heights usually indicate that the trees are grown under the best possible soil and moisture conditions and in favorable climates. In some cases the same species and variety of tree may vary from shorter and shrubby in the north to quite tall in the southern reaches of its hardiness zone. With these conditions stated, it seems that the best plan for the amateur is to inquire locally about the tree and to see one growing, if possible, finding out how fast or slow it grows before committing it to the plan. However, gardeners must also be optimistic and gamble a bit, so this caution is not really mandatory but is suggested only for gardeners with some particular problem.

The cultivars listed, as well as those in other lists, may vary from the maximum heights, even as children in the same human family may grow to different sizes and shapes, varying from those of both parents. Some trees do best in certain sections or conditions, and where such pertinent information is available, it will be found on our lists.

COMMON NAME	SCIENTIFIC NAME	HEIGHT IN FEET	HARDINESS ZONE	COMMENTS
Acacia, Bronze or Frosty (E)	*Acacia pruinosa*	60	10	southern California
Alder, Italian	*Alnus cordata*	45	5	
Red	*Alnus rubra*	60	4	West Coast
Arborvitae, American (E)	*Thuja occidentalis*	60	2	
Japanese (E)	*Thuja standishii*	40	6	
Oriental (E)	*Thuja orientalis*	50–60	3	
Ash, Black	*Fraxinus nigra*	40	3	
Green	*Fraxinus pensylvanica* 'Lanceolata'	40–60	2	seeds
Marshall's green	*F. p.* 'Marshall's Seedless'	30–50	5–7	
Moraine Balkan	*Fraxinus holotricha* 'Moraine'	35	5	
Velvet (Arizona, Modesto)	*Fraxinus velutina* 'Glabra'	to 45	5–7	Arizona, Southwest
Basswood, *see Linden, American*				
Beech, Blue, *see Hornbeam, American*				
Beefwood, Cunningham	*Casuarina cunninghamiana*	70	10	leafless; for alkaline and brackish soils
Horsetail-tree	*Casuarina equisetifolia*	70	9	Florida windbreak, takes salt spray
Scalybark	*Casuarina lepidophloia*	60	9	Florida, leafless
Bell flambeau (E)	*Spathodea campanulata*	to 75	10	

Key:
E = Needled evergreen
BLE = Broad-leaved evergreen
SE = Semi-evergreen (may be deciduous in northern reaches of hardiness zone)
var. = Variable
+ = Taller in some zones
x = Hybrid variety

COMMON NAME	SCIENTIFIC NAME	HEIGHT IN FEET	HARDI- NESS ZONE	COMMENTS
Birch, Canoe or Paper	*Betula papyrifera*	to 90	4	
Chinese paper	*Betula albo-sinensis*	to 90	5	
European	*Betula pendula,* and cultivars	30–60	2	
River (Black)	*Betula nigra*	to 90	4	
White	*Betula alba*	50	2	
Black gum, *see Tupelo*				
Bo tree (Sacred Bo) (SE)	*Ficus religiosa*	to 75	10	
Bottle tree, Flame	*Brachychiton aceri- folium*	60+	10	California, dry soil
Box-elder	*Acer negundo*	60	7	not a fine tree; use in Midwest for windbreak; dry soil
Bucida, Oxhorn	*Bucida buceras*	to 40	10	
Brush-cherry (BLE)	*Eugenia paniculata*	40	9	California
Australian (BLE)	*Eugenia australis*	75	8–9	California
Buckeye, Ohio	*Aesculus glabra*	50	4	eastern Midwest native
California-laurel (BLE)	*Umbellularia cali- fornica*	75	7	California coast
Camellia, Common (BLE)	*Camellia japonica*	to 45	7	
Camphor tree (E)	*Cinnamomum cam- phora*	40	9	slow growing, but better for larger gardens
Catalpa, Northern	*Catalpa speciosa*	to 75+	3–4	big leaves, too coarse for small gardens
Southern	*Catalpa bignonoides*	45–50	5	big leaves, too coarse for small gardens
Chestnut, Chinese	*Castanea mollissima*	60	4	
Cork tree, Amur	*Phellodendron amurense*	50	4	
Crab apple	*Malus,* species and cultivars	var.	var.	most are smaller, a few are tall enough for med- ium height, and only a few are not too spreading

COMMON NAME	SCIENTIFIC NAME	HEIGHT IN FEET	HARDI-NESS ZONE	COMMENTS
Cypress-pine, Sturdy (E)	*Callitris robusta*	15–70	9	California, Florida
Dogwood, Flower-ing	*Cornus florida*	to 40	4	
Nuttall (Pacific)	*Cornus nuttallii*	50–75	7	
Elm, Cedar	*Ulnus crassifolia*	50	5	
Chinese	*Ulmus parvifolia*	50	5	
Chinese ever-green (E)	*Ulmus parvifolia* 'Pendens'	50	8–9	drooping; ever-green in Cali-fornia
Siberian	*Ulmus pumila*	75	4	drought resistant on plains
Siberian	*Ulmus pumila*	to 75	4	cultivars are stronger and better
Cultivars:	'Coolshade'	40–75	4	strong wood
	'Dropmore'	to 60	2	hardy in Manitoba, Canada
	'Hamburg Hybrid'	to 75	4	fast-growing
	'Improved Cool-shade'	60–75	4	fast-growing
Eugenia, *see Brush-cherry*				
Eucalyptus, Redbox gum	*Eucalyptus poly-anthemos*	to 70	9	
Poplar gum	*Eucalyptus popu-lifolia*	40	10	
Red-flowering gum	*Eucalyptus ficifolia*	35–50	10	
False-cypress Hinoki (E)	*Chamaecyparis obtusa*	var.	3	compact forms
Fig, Benjamin (BLE)	*Ficus benjamina*	to 40+	10	Florida, rapid growing
Fiddleleaf (BLE)	*Ficus lyrata*	50–75	10	Florida, California
India laurel (BLE)	*Ficus retusa*	50–75	10	Florida, California
Lofty (BLE)	*Ficus altissima*	50–75	10	Florida
Moreton Bay (BLE)	*Ficus macrophylla*	50–75	10	California, moder-ately fast-grow-ing
Fir, Korean (E)	*Abies koreana*	50	5	
Flame tree, Pink	*Brachychiton dis-color*	40	9	Florida

COMMON NAME	SCIENTIFIC NAME	HEIGHT IN FEET	HARDI-NESS ZONE	COMMENTS
Flame tree, *see* *Poinciana*				
Golden-rain tree	*Koelreuteria pani-culata*	30	5	
Gordonia (Loblolly bay) (BLE)	*Gordonia lasianthus*	60	8	South
Gum, Black, *see* *Tupelo*				
Gum tree, *see* *Eucalyptus*				
Hackberry, Euro-pean	*Celtis australis*	75	6	Southwest, hot arid soil
Sugarberry or Western	*Celtis laevigata*	to 75	5	rapid grower
Hemlock, Carolina (E)	*Tsuga caroliniana*	75	4	
Holly, American (BLE)	*Ilex opaca,* and cultivars	to 45	5–6	
English (BLE)	*Ilex aquifolium,* and cultivars	to 70	6–7	for West Coast and South
Chinese (BLE)	*Ilex cornuta,* and taller cultivars	to 60	7	
Hop-hornbeam	*Ostrya virginiana*	60	4–5	
Hornbeam, Ameri-can (Blue beech, Iron-wood)	*Carpinus carolini-ana*	35	2	
European	*Carpinus betulus,* and cultivars	to 60	5	
Japanese	*Carpinus japonica*	45	4	slow grower, good shade
Horse-chestnut, Baumann	*Aesculus hippocas-tanum* 'Bau-mannii'	75	3	
Red	x*Aesculus carnea*	75	3	
Honey locust, Thornless	*Gleditsia triacan-thos* 'Inermis'	50+	4	
Thornless, cul-tivars:	'Moraine'	50+	4	light foliage, fast grower
	'Ruby Lace'	45+	4	reddish foliage
	'Shademaster'	45+	4	upright habit
	'Sunburst'	45+	4	light green, yellow-tipped foliage
Ironwood, *see* *Hornbeam,* *American*				

SCIENTIFIC NAME	COMMON NAME	HEIGHT IN FEET	HARDI-NESS ZONE	COMMENTS
Jacaranda, Sharp-leaf	*Jacaranda acutifolia*	50	10	
Judas-tree, *see Redbud, Eastern*				
Juniper, Chinese (E)	*Juniperus chinensis*	to 60	4	
Greek (E)	*Juniperus excelsa*	60	7	
Syrian (E)	*Juniperus drupacea*	to 60	7	
West Indies (E)	*Juniperus lucayana*	50	9	deep South
Katsura tree	*Cercidiphyllum japonicum*	60–75	4–5	
Larch, Eastern (Tamarack)	*Larix laricina*	to 60	1	
Siberian	*Larix sibirica*	60	3	tolerant of alkaline soil
Linden, American (Basswood)	*Tilia americana*			
Crimean	x*Tilia euchlora* 'Redmond'	60	4	good on prairie, in Midwest
Littleleaf	*Tilia cordata*	40–75	3	
Pendent Silver	*Tilia petiolaris*	to 75	5	narrow, drooping
Live oak, *see Oak, live*				
Loblolly bay, *see Gordonia*				
Locust, Black	*Robinia pseudo-acacia*	75	3	
Upright black	*Robinia pseudo-acacia* 'Fastigiata'	to 75	3	
Madrone, Pacific (BLE)	*Arbutus menziesii*	to 75	7	
Magnolia, Merrill	*Magnolia loebneri* 'Merrill'	to 50	4	
Sweet bay (SE)	*Magnolia virginiana* (*glauca*)	30–60	5–6	shrubby in North
Various	*Magnolia*, species	var.	var.	many within this height range are so coarse foliaged as to be unsuited to small gardens
Mahogany, West Indies	*Swietenia mahoganii*	to 75	10	fast growing
Maple, Florida	*Acer barbatum floridanum*	50	9	northern Florida

COMMON NAME	SCIENTIFIC NAME	HEIGHT IN FEET	HARDI-NESS ZONE	COMMENTS
Maple, Florida (*cont.*)				
Lobel	*Acer lobelii*	60	7	Norway type for South
Mesquite, Honey	*Prosopis glandulosa*	to 50	8–9	slow growing, resists drought
Mountain-ash, European (Rowan)	*Sorbus aucuparia*	25–45	3	narrow
Korean	*Sorbus alnifolia*	to 60	4	wider growing
Mulberry, Chinese paper-	*Broussonetia papyrifera*	50+	6	for poor soil, city
Russian	*Morus alba tatarica*	to 40	5	fruit may cause litter, but there are fruitless cultivars
Oak, Burr	*Quercus macrocarpa*	to 50	3	too large for small gardens, but tolerates dry, lightly alkaline soils
California (Coast) live (BLE)	*Quercus agrifolia*	75+	9	West Coast native; spreads widely
Interior live (BLE)	*Quercus wislizenii*	70	7	
Holly or Holm- (BLE)	*Quercus ilex*	to 60	9	especially near sea or in moist areas
Laurel (SE)	*Quercus laurifolia*	60	7	
Live (BLE)	*Quercus virginiana*	60–75	7–8	wide spreading, not for small gardens
Oregon white	*Quercus garryana*	75+	6	West Coast only
Pin	*Quercus palustris*	75	4	
Red	*Quercus borealis*	to 75	3	moderately fast growing
Scarlet	*Quercus coccinea*	75	5–6	
Shingle	*Quercus imbricaria*	75	5	rare; windbreak or sheared high hedge; native to central states
Shumard (Texas)	*Quercus shumardii*	to 75+	5	native to central states; use there as substitute for scarlet oak
Southern red	*Quercus falcata*	75	5–6	Southeast native

SCIENTIFIC NAME	COMMON NAME	HEIGHT IN FEET	HARDI-NESS ZONE	COMMENTS
Oak, Burr (*cont.*)				
Spanish	*Quercus texana*	40	8	Texas native
Texas, *see Oak,*				
Shumard				
Turkey, *see Oak,*				
Southern red				
Water	*Quercus nigra*	75+	6	Southeast native; moist soils
Willow	*Quercus phellos*	60+	5–6	Eastern seaboard, Gulf area
Olive, Russian	*Eleagnus angusti-folia*	25–50	5–7	
Osage-orange	*Maclura pomifera*	60	5	Southwest; endures drought, hot-cold climate; used as wind-break
Pagoda-tree, Japa-nese	*Sophora japonica*	75	4–5	
Paper-mulberry, *see Mulberry,*				
Parasol-tree, Chinese	*Firmiana simplex*	40	9	
Pear, Ussurian	*Pyrus ussuriensis*	50	4	hardy, not suscep-tible to blight
Pepperidge, *see Tupelo*				
Pepper-tree, Bra-zilian	*Schinus terebinthe-folius*	40+	9	Florida, sandy dry soil
California	*Schinus molle*	40	9	arid soil, not a shade tree
Pine, Aleppo	*Pinus halepensis*	to 60	9	sandy soil; sea-shore
Cypress-, *see Cypress-pine*				
Monterey (E)	*Pinus radiata*	60	7	seashore, especially West
Scotch (E)	*Pinus sylvestris,* and cultivars	50–75	2–3	
Swiss stone (E)	*Pinus cembra*	to 75	2	slow-growing
Pistache, Chinese	*Pistacia chinensis*	50	9	Florida, not a nut tree
Plane tree, London	*Platanus acerifolia*	to 75	6	especially in cities
Poinciana, Royal (Flame tree)	*Delonix regia*	40–50	9–10	
Poplar, Berlin	*Populus berolinensis*	75	2	hot-cold areas and prairies

SCIENTIFIC NAME	COMMON NAME	HEIGHT IN FEET	HARDI-NESS ZONE	COMMENTS
Poplar, Berlin (*cont.*)				
Simon	*Populus simonii*	50	2	substitute for the Lombardy Poplar and better
Red-bud, Chinese	*Cercis chinensis*	to 40	6	may be shrubby in North
Eastern (Judas-tree)	*Cercis canadensis*	35	5–6	slow grower
Rowan tree, *see Mountain-ash*				
Sapote, White	*Casimiroa edulis*	30–50	10	California patio tree
Sassafras	*Sassafras albidum*	60–75	4–5	
Silk-tree	*Albizia julibrissin*	25–40	7	
Sophora, New Zealand	*Sophora tetraptera*	40	9	sandy soils
Sorrel tree, *see Sourwood*				
Sour gum, *see Tupelo*				
Sour gum, Chinese	*Nyssa sinensis*	20–60	7	
Sourwood (Sorrel tree)	*Oxydendrum arboreum*	75	5	
Stewartia, Korean	*Stewartia koreana*	45	5	rare
Japanese	*Stewartia pseudo-camellia*	60	5	
Tamarack, *see Larch, Eastern*				
Tree of heaven (Ailanthus)	*Ailanthus altissima*	60–80	4–5	especially for city
Tulip tree, African, *see Bell Flambeau*				
Tupelo (Black gum, Sour gum)	*Nyssa sylvatica*	to 75+	4–5	
Walnut, Hinds black	*Juglans hindsii*	50	8	
Varnish tree, *see Parasol tree, Chinese*				
Wattle, Black	*Acacia decurrens mollis*	50	9–10	
Silver	*Acacia decurrens dealbata*	50	9	

COMMON NAME	SCIENTIFIC NAME	HEIGHT IN FEET	HARDI-NESS ZONE	COMMENTS
Willow, see Note				NOTE: most willows are not recommended except for wet-soil areas; elsewhere roots invade sewers and cause other damage.
Willow, Corkscrew or Contorted	*Salix matsudana* 'Tortuosa'	30–50	4	
Golden Curls	*Salix matsudana* 'Tortuosa Aurea'	30–45	4	
Wisconsin weeping	*Salix blanda* 'Niobe'	40+	4	for large gardens, wet soils
Yellow-wood, American	*Cladrastis lutea*	50	3	fast grower
Yew, English (E)	*Taxus baccata*, and cultivars	to 60	6	
Intermediate (E)	x*Taxus media*, and cultivars	30–40	4	
Japanese (E)	*Taxus cuspidata*, and cultivars	to 50	6	

TALL TREES

Forest trees, the tall ones that tower when mature, are in general too wide spreading and tall to fit into small gardens. We present them here for three categories of gardeners: (1) those whose properties are more extensive than the average suburban plot; (2) those beginning gardeners who have existing trees on their lot and wish to identify them in order to assay the prospects of future growth in order to decide which to retain and work into the garden scheme (it is a wise plan to keep some existing trees for the shade and beauty they give now, even if they will eventually be too big); and (3) those who have purchased an older house with established plantings. Some trees may have to be removed in order to let the sun into the garden. Formerly many plots were overplanted and they will now need thinning out for the good of other plants. Taking out some of the larger trees and replacing them with smaller ones or flowering ones will add to the beauty of the garden while allowing the sun into the house in wintertime.

211

In looking over this list, remember that the heights given are optimum mature heights. This is the recorded measurement of trees that have grown in favorable climates, good soil, with enough water and all the other conditions conducive to growth. In the various ranges of the hardiness zones they may do much less well and grow only to medium height, which is why the lists overlap here and there. Take into account, too, that many trees are slow growing and take a lifetime to achieve their maximum height, sometimes two hundred years. This information is included, where known.

COMMON NAME	SCIENTIFIC NAME	HEIGHT IN FEET	HARDI- NESS ZONE	COMMENTS
Arborvitae, Giant (E)	*Thuja plicata*	to 180	5	West Coast, northern Rockies
Ash, European	*Fraxinus excelsior*	75–120	3	
Oregon	*Fraxinus oregona*	80	6	Pacific Coast
White	*Fraxinus americana*	75–125	3	
Bald cypress, Common	*Taxodium distichum*	to 150	4	wet lands
Beech, American	*Fagus grandifolia*	90–100	3	slow growing
European	*Fagus sylvatica*	80–100	4	slow growing
Cultivars:	*Fagus sylvatica* cultivars			slow
Copper	'Cuprea'	to 90	4	coppery leaves
Cutleaf	'Laciniata'			leaves divided somewhat like oak
Fernleaf	'Asplenifolia'			deeply divided
Golden	'Zlatia'			leaves citron yellow

Key:
BLE = Broad-leaved evergreen
E = Needled evergreen
SE = Semi-evergreen (may be deciduous in northern reaches of hardiness zone)
var. = Variable
+ = Taller in some zones

NOTE: Many cultivars of these tall forest trees may be available. Some of them grow much shorter than the figures for the species, for there is an amazing number of dwarf and compact types in the plant world. Therefore, it is emphasized that the gardener should not lightly discard any cultivar offered by a good nursery until further checking determines that it is not a small- or medium-height variety of the taller species. A visit to your county agent or a telephone call will probably bring confirmation or guidance. If necessary, wait. A tree is a long-term investment and should not be chosen in haste.

COMMON NAME	SCIENTIFIC NAME	HEIGHT IN FEET	HARDI- NESS ZONE	COMMENTS
Beech, American (*cont.*)				
Green weeping	'Pendula'			branches drooping
Purple	'Atropunicea'			leaves purplish
Purple weeping	'Purpureo- pendula'			branches drooping
Pyramidal	'Fastigiata'			narrow
Rivers purple	'Riversii'			leaves purplish to blackish
Rohan purple	'Rohanii'			purplish leaves similar to 'Laciniata'
Tricolor	'Tricolor'			leaves copper, pink, white
Birch, Canoe (Paper)	*Betula papyrifera*	to 90	2	
River (Black)	*Betula nigra*	75–90	4	
Black gum, *see Tupelo*				
Blue gum, *see Eucalyptus*				
Buttonwood, *see Plane tree, American*				
Castor-aralia (Kalopanax)	*Kalopanax pictus*	to 90	4–5	
Catalpa, Northern	*Catalpa speciosa*	75–90	3–4	
Cedar, Atlas (E)	*Cedrus atlantica*	70–120	5–6	
Deodar (E)	*Cedrus deodara*	70–150	7	
Incense, *see Incense-cedar*				
Lebanon (E)	*Cedrus libani* 'Stenocoma'	90–120	5–6	
Red, *see Red- cedar*				
Cherry, Black	*Prunus serotina*	to 90	3	Northeast USA native
Sargent	*Prunus sargentii*	75+	4	
China-fir, Common (E)	*Cunninghamia lanceolata*	75	7	
Coffee-tree, Ken- tucky	*Gymnocladus dioicus*	80–90	4–5	
Cryptomeria, Japa- nese (E)	*Cryptomeria japonica*	100–150	5–5	
Plume (E)	*Cryptomeria japonica* 'Elegans'	to 100	5–6	

COMMON NAME	SCIENTIFIC NAME	HEIGHT IN FEET	HARDI- NESS ZONE	COMMENTS
Cucumber-tree	*Magnolia acuminata*	75–90	4–5	fast grower
Douglas fir, *see* Fir, Douglas				
Elm, American				not recommended because of Dutch elm disease
English	*Ulmus procera (campestris)*	to 120	5	city tree, grows slower, less tall in city
Scotch or Wych	*Ulmus glabra*	to 100+	4	
Smooth-leaved	*Ulmus carpinifolia*	to 90	4	suggested to replace American elm
Smooth-leaved, cultivars:	'Christine Buisman'			disease resistant
	'Bea Schwarz'			as disease resistant but slower growing than above, also hardier
Eucalyptus, Blue gum	*Eucalyptus globulus* 'Compacta'	to 100+	9	
White gum	*Eucalyptus viminalis*	to 100+	9	branches whitish
False-cypress Hinoki (E)	*Chamaecyparis obtusa*	to 120	4	slow growing
Lawson (E)	*Chamaecyparis lawsoniana,* and cultivars	to 120	5	
Sarawa (E)	*Chamaecyparis pisifera*	to 150	3	
Slender Hinoki (E)	*Chamaecyparis obtusa* 'Gracilis'	to 90	4	
Fir, Douglas (E)	*Pseudotsuga menziesii*	to 300	4–6	
Ginkgo, Maidenhair tree	*Ginkgo biloba,* and cultivars	to 120	4	good city tree, where it grows lower
Grevillea, Silk-oak (E)	*Grevillea robusta*	to 150	10	South and southern California
Hackberry, Eastern	*Celtis occidentalis*	90–100	3	
Sugar (Western)	*Celtis laevigata*	75–90	5	native
Hemlock, Canada (E)	*Tsuga canadensis*	90	3	native
Carolina (E)	*Tsuga caroliniana*	70–80	4	native

COMMON NAME	SCIENTIFIC NAME	HEIGHT IN FEET	HARDI-NESS ZONE	COMMENTS
Hemlock, Canada *(cont.)*				
Western (E)	*Tsuga heterophylla*	to 200	6	native west of Cascade Mountains higher altitudes
Hickory, Pignut	*Carya glabra*	90–120	4–5	
Shagbark	*Carya ovata*, and cultivars	100–120	4–5	
White, *see Mockernut*				
Honey locust, Common	*Gleditsia triacanthos*	100–125	4	native, thorny
Thornless	*Gleditsia triacanthos* 'Inermis' and cultivars	40–100	3–4	NOTE: see Small Shade Trees list for named varieties, some of which may grow taller in favorable places and climates
Incense-cedar, California (E)	*Libocedrus decurrens*	100–135	5–6	California and West Coast native
Indian rubbertree (BLE)	*Ficus elastica*	to 100	10	Florida
Juniper, Red-cedar, *see Red-cedar*				
Kalopanax, *see Castor-aralia*				
Katsura tree	*Cercidiphyllum japonicum*	60–100	4	
Larch, European	*Larix decidua*	75–100	2–3	does best in North
Japanese	*Larix leptolepis*	75–90	4	
Linden, Littleleaf	*Tilia cordata*, and cultivars	to 90	3	
Silver	*Tilia tomentosa*	to 90	4	
Live oak, *see Oak, Live*				
Maidenhair tree, *see Ginkgo*				
Magnolia, Campbell	*Magnolia campbellii*	to 150	8–9	
Southern (E)	*Magnolia grandiflora*, and cultivars	to 90	7	

COMMON NAME	SCIENTIFIC NAME	HEIGHT IN FEET	HARDI-NESS ZONE	COMMENTS
Maple, Bigleaf	*Acer macrophyllum*	90–100	6–8	Pacific Coast
Norway	*Acer platanoides*, and cultivars	75–90	3–4	red leaved
Norway, cultivars:	'Crimson King'	75+	3–4	
	'Erectum'	75+	3–4	narrower habit
	'Fassens Black'	75+	3–4	dark leaves
	'Green Lace'	75+	3–4	cutleaved
	'Summershade'	75+	3–4	upright, rapid grower
Red or Swamp	*Acer rubrum*	75–120	3	
Red or Swamp, cultivar:	'Red Sunset'	75+	3	
Sugar	*Acer saccharum*	90–120	3	
Sycamore	*Acer pseudoplatanus*, and cultivars	75–90	5–6	
Sycamore, cultivars:				
Purple-leaf	'Purpureum'	75+	5–6	
Upright	'Erectum'	75+	5–6	
Mockernut (White hickory)	*Carya tomentosa*	70–90	4–5	
Oak, Black	*Quercus velutina*	100+	5	native
California Black	*Quercus kelloggii*	to 90	7	West Coast native
California (Coast), Live (E)	*Quercus agrifolia*	to 90	9	West Coast native
Chestnut	*Quercus prinus*	to 90	4	tolerates dry rocky soil
English	*Quercus robur*, and cultivars	75–100	5	
Live (Southern) (SE)	*Quercus virginiana*	60+	7	Southeast native
Oregon white	*Quercus garryana*	to 90	6	West Coast native; dry, gravelly soil
Shumard	*Quercus shumardii*	to 100+	5	central and southern states native
Silk, *see Grevillea*				
White	*Quercus alba*	to 90	4	wide spreading
Pecan	*Carya illinoiensis*, and cultivars	to 150	5	
Pepperidge, *see Tupelo*				

COMMON NAME	SCIENTIFIC NAME	HEIGHT IN FEET	HARDI-NESS ZONE	COMMENTS
Pine, Austrian (E)	*Pinus nigra*	to 90	4	
Canary Island (E)	*Pinus canariensis*	to 80	8	fast grower in dry, rocky soil
Eastern white (E)	*Pinus strobus*, and cultivars	to 100+	3	
Jeffrey (E)	*Pinus jeffreyi*	120	5	Northwest coast only
Korean (E)	*Pinus koraiensis*	90	3	slow grower
Norfolk Island (E)	*Araucaria excelsa*	to 100	10	
Ponderosa (E)	*Pinus ponderosa*	to 150	5	western native
Western white (E)	*Pinus monticola*	to 90	5	western coast of British Columbia to California; narrow
Pittosporum, Dia-mond-leaf (BLE)	*Pittosporum rhom-bifolium*	to 80	10	
Plane tree, Ameri-can Sycamore	*Platanus occidentalis*	to 80	4	may be subject to blight
London	*Platanus acerifolia*	to 100	5	city tree, usually less tall
Oriental	*Platanus orientalis*	to 90	6	
Red-cedar, Eastern (E)	*Juniperus virginiana,* and cultivars	60–90	2	
Poplar, Tulip, *see Tulip tree*				
Silk-cotton tree (Kapok)	*Ceiba pentandra*	to 120	10	
Silk-oak, *see Grevillea*				
Silverbell, Mountain	*Halesia monticola*	50–90	5	
Spruce, Colorado (E)	*Picea pungens*	to 100	2	
Colorado blue (E)	*Picea pungens* 'Glauca', and cultivars	to 100	2	
Engelmann (E)	*Picea engelmannii*	to 150	2	
Norway (E)	*Picea abies*	to 150	2	
Serbian (E)	*Picea omorika*	to 90	4	
Sweet gum	*Liquidambar styra-ciflua*	75–100	5	
Formosa	*Liquidambar for-mosana*	to 120	7	West Coast

COMMON NAME	SCIENTIFIC NAME	HEIGHT IN FEET	HARDI- NESS ZONE	COMMENTS
Sycamore, *see Plane tree, American*				
Tulip tree (Yellow poplar)	*Liriodendron tulipifera*	100–125	4–5	fast grower
Tupelo (Black gum, Pepperidge)	*Nyssa sylvatica*	75–90	4	
Umbrella-pine, Japanese (E)	*Sciadopitys verticillata*	120+	5	slow grower
Walnut, Black or Eastern	*Juglans nigra*	to 150	4	best in Midwest
Carpathian	*Juglans regia* 'Carpathian'	to 90	3–4	very hardy
English or Persian	*Juglans regia*, and cultivars	to 90	5–6	nut bearing; West Coast has orchards
Yellow poplar, *see Tulip tree*				
Zelkova, Japanese	*Zelkova serrata*	90	5	substitute for American elm because of vase shape

COLUMNAR OR NARROW-GROWING TREES

For small areas the slender tree is an answer to the gardener's prayers. Some are columnar—narrow all the way up—others may taper to a shape more obelisk than pyramid, while some others may merely be less inclined to spread widely than the species or type, forming perhaps a tall oval rather than a circular or rounded shape. Wherever you see descriptive adjectives in a tree's name such as 'Erecta,' 'Fastigiata,' 'Columnaris,' 'Stricta,' or 'Pyramidalis' (or the other proper Latin endings of these words), you may be sure that these are narrow-growing trees. Not all have these designations, however, and that is why this list is offered.

COMMON NAME	SCIENTIFIC NAME	HEIGHT IN FEET	HARDI-NESS ZONE	COMMENTS
NEEDLED EVERGREENS:				
Arborvitae, American	*Thuja occidentalis* 'Fastigiata'	40	3	
Douglas	*Thuja occidentalis* 'Douglasii Pyramidalis'	40	3	
Giant	*Thuja plicata* 'Fasti-giata'	to 75	5	
Cryptomeria, Lobb's	*Cryptomeria japonica* 'Lobbii'	to 50	6–7	
Cypress, Common bald	*Taxodium distichum*	to 100+	4	moist, swampy
Italian	*Cupressus semper-virens* 'Stricta'	25+	7	
False-cypress, Column Hinoki	*Chamaecyparis obtusa* 'Erecta'	to 50+	4	moist
Nootka	*Chamaecyparis nootkaensis*	to 75	4	rare, moist
Scarab Lawson	*Chamaecyparis law-soniana* 'Allumii'	to 100	5	
Upright Lawson	*Chamaecyparis law-soniana* 'Erecta'	to 100	5	
Juniper, Columnar Chinese	*Juniperus chinensis* 'Columnaris'	to 45	4	
Hetz's columnar	*Juniperus chinensis* 'Hetz's Colum-naris'	to 50	4	
Irish	*Juniperus communis* 'Hibernica'	to 30	3–4	
'Mountbatten'	*Juniperus chinensis* 'Mountbatten'	50	4	Canada

Key:

x = Hybrid variety

+ = Taller in some places

* In the northern Pacific Coast area, Western red-cedar is a name also given to the Giant arborvitae (*Thuja plicata*). The two should not be confused for, while *Juniperus scopulorum* is a moderate-sized tree suited to the average garden, *Thuja plicata* is a towering forest giant, totally unsuited to any except a large natural garden on an estate. Any tree that grows more than 75 to 80 feet may be considered a forest tree, likely to be unsuited to small gardens.

COMMON NAME	SCIENTIFIC NAME	HEIGHT IN FEET	HARDI- NESS ZONE	COMMENTS
NEEDLED EVERGREENS (*cont.*)				
Narrow Greek	*Juniperus excelsa* 'Stricta'	to 15	6–7	
Pyramid	*Juniperus chinensis* 'Pyramidalis'	to 45	4	
Story	*Juniperus chinensis* 'Story'	to 40	4	
Syrian	*Juniperus drupacea*	to 60	7	
Pine, Austrian Pyramid	*Pinus nigra* 'Pyrami- dalis'	75	3	
Columnar Swiss stone	*Pinus cembra* 'Columnaris'	50	3	
Pyramidal East- ern white	*Pinus strobus* 'Fastigiata'	to 75	3	
Pyramidal Scotch	*Pinus sylvestris* 'Fastigiata'	to 75	2	
Sugar	*Pinus lambertiana*	100+	5	West Coast; not for home gar- dens; huge cones
Umbrella-	*Sciadopitys verti- cillata*	50+	5	slow growing
Red-cedar, Burk's Eastern	*Juniperus virginiana* 'Burkii'	30+	2–3	
Pyramidal	*Juniperus virginiana* 'Pyramidalis'	30+	2–3	
Schott	*Juniperus virginiana* 'Schottii'	25+	2–3	rare
—	*Juniperus virginiana* 'Venusta'	25+	2–3	
Western* (Rocky Mountain columnar)	*Juniperus scopulo- rum* 'Colum- naris'	35	4–5	
Spruce, Norway Columnar	*Picea abies* 'Columnaris'	to 85+	2	
Oriental 'Gowdy'	*Picea orientalis* 'Gowdy'	to 70	4	
Serbian	*Picea omorika*	to 75	4	
Sitka	*Picea sitchensis* 'Speciosa'	to 80+	6	slow
Dwarf white	*Picea glauca* 'Conica'	25+	2	narrowish dwarf
Yew, Intermediate	x*Taxus media*	to 40	4	
Irish	*Taxus baccata* 'Stricta'	to 50	6	

COMMON NAME	SCIENTIFIC NAME	HEIGHT IN FEET	HARDI-NESS ZONE	COMMENTS
DECIDUOUS TREES:				
Beech, Pyramidal European	*Fagus sylvatica* 'Fastigiata'	30+	2	
Birch, Pyramidal European	*Betula pendula* 'Fastigiata'	45–50	2	
Cherry, Columnar Sargent	*Prunus sargentii* 'Columnaris'	30+	4	
Fastigiate Oriental	*Prunus serrulata* 'Amanagawa'	20–25	5–6	
Chinaberry	*Melia azderach* 'Umbraculi-formis'	to 45	7	
Crab apple, Columnar Siberian	*Malus baccata* 'Columnaris'	to 50	2	
Scheidecker	x*Malus scheideckerii*	20	4	moderately narrow
Scheidecker cultivars:	x 'Guiding Star'	20+	4–5	narrow pyramid
	x 'Strathmore'	35+	3–4	dark red leaves
	x 'Van Eseltine'	20	4	narrow, upright
Upright cherry-crab	*Malus robusta* 'Erecta'	to 40	3	may spread later
Ginkgo	*Ginkgo biloba* 'Fastigiata'	to 70	4	
Cultivar	'Sentry'	to 70	4	
Golden-rain tree, Upright	*Koelreuteria paniculata* 'Fastigiata'	25–30	4	
Hawthorn, Pyramidal Washington	*Crataegus phaenopyrum* 'Fastigiata'	25–30	4	
Upright single-seed	*Crataegus monogyna* 'Stricta'	15–30	4	
Honey locust, Columnar	*Gleditsia tricanthos* 'Columnaris'	70+	4	
cultivar:	'Nana'	60+	4	narrow
Hornbeam, Columnar European	*Carpinus betulus* 'Columnaris'	40–60	5	narrow
Pyramidal European	*Carpinus betulus* 'Fastigiata'	to 45	5	wider
Linden, Pyramidal American	*Tilia americana* 'Fastigiata'	45	3	

COMMON NAME	SCIENTIFIC NAME	HEIGHT IN FEET	HARDI- NESS ZONE	COMMENTS
DECIDUOUS TREES (*cont.*)				
Pyramidal big-leaf	*Tilia platyphyllos* 'Fastigiata'	50–70	4	
Locust, Black 'Friesia'	*Robinia pseudoaca- cia fastigiata* 'Friesia'	30–50	4	
Magnolia, Upright anise	*Magnolia salicifolia* 'Elsie Frye'	30	5	West Coast
Maple, Black cultivar	*Acer nigrum ascen- dens* 'Slavin's Upright'	60	3	
Columnar Norway	*Acer platanoides* 'Columnare'	50+	3	
Columnar red	*Acer rubrum* 'Columnare'	to 90+	3	
Columnar sugar	*Acer saccharum* 'Newton Sentry'	75+	3	
Norway cultivar	*Acer platanoides* 'Cleveland'	75+	3	
Rocky Moun- tain	*Acer glabrum*	25	5	Western native; narrow
Upright Norway	*Acer platanoides* 'Erectum'	75+	3	
Upright syca- more	*Acer pseudoplatanus* 'Erectum'	60+	4–5	
Mountain-ash, Hybrid	x*Sorbus hybrida*	35	4	
Pyramidal European	*Sorbus aucuparia* 'Fastigiata'	up to 45	3	
Oak, Pyramidal English	*Quercus robur* 'Fastigiata'	up to 75	5	
Pagoda-tree, Japanese upright	*Sophora japonica* 'Fastigiata'	up to 75	4	
Poplar*, Bolleana	*Populus alba* 'Pyramidalis'	up to 80	3	
Berlin	*Populus bero- linensis*	up to 75	2	very hardy north
Pyramidal Simon	*Populus simonii* 'Fastigiata'	50	2	

* While poplars are commonly believed to be narrowly columnar, the genus is composed of many wide-spreading sorts, as well. Lombardy poplar (*Populus nigra* 'Italica') is subject to trunk canker and other ills and therefore is not recommended. Simon poplar (*P. simonii*) may be substituted, though it is wider growing, or the Bolleana poplar, which is narrow and has attractive silvery younger bark, may be grown where a narrow tree is desired. Berlin poplar is also very narrowly columnar, a good tree for the hot-cold climates of the northern prairie areas.

SMALL FLOWERING TREES

While this list tries to be comprehensive, it is by no means exhaustive. There are many regionally available cultivars or species that might be worthwhile pursuing. Regional preferences as well as climate limitations may determine availability. There are probably a number of small native trees in various sections that nurseries do not stock. If they are found in the wild, permission might be obtained to dig up a small plant and transplant it into the garden. This would be especially recommended for natural and informal gardens, though not necessarily for a more formal garden or for purposes of shade.

The use of the term *rare* in the list indicates that the tree is not widely available. Other limitations have also been inserted where they might guide the choice. Soil, moisture, and other factors as well as heat and cold may influence growth. Hence, where such things have been noted in research, they have been included.

COMMON NAME	SCIENTIFIC NAME	HEIGHT IN FEET	HARDI-NESS ZONE	COMMENTS
Acacia, Gossamer Sydney	*Acacia longifolia* 'Floribunda'	30	10	
Weeping boree	*Acacia pendula*	20	10	flowers minor
Acacia, *see also Wattle*				
Almond, Flowering	*Prunus amygdalus*	24	6	double, single
Apricot, Flowering	*Prunus armeniaca*, and cultivars	30	5	fruit
Japanese	*Prunus mume*, and cultivars	30	6	single, double
Ash, Maries' flowering	*Fraxinus mariesii*	24	7	
Bauhinia, *see also Orchid-tree*				
Bauhinia, Buddhist	*Bauhinia variegata*	20	10	
Buckeye, Ohio	*Aesculus glabra*	30	3	flowers medium
Black-haw	*Viburnum prunifolium*	15	3	
Southern	*Viburnum rufidulum*	30	5	

Key:
BLE = Broad-leaved evergreen
E = Evergreen
x = Hybrid variety
+ = Taller in some places

COMMON NAME	SCIENTIFIC NAME	HEIGHT IN FEET	HARDI- NESS ZONE	COMMENTS
Cajeput tree	*Melaleuca leucaden- dron*	35–40	10	
Camellia, Common (BLE)	*Camellia japonica,* and cultivars	10–40	7–8	
Cherry, Cornelian-	*Cornus mas*	20–25	4	
Weeping Higan	*Prunus subhirtella* 'Pendula'	20+	5	
Double weeping Higan	*Prunus subhirtella* 'Pendula plena'	20	5	
Flowering Orien- tal	*Prunus serrulata*	20–25	5–6	
Flowering Orien- tal, cultivars:	'Akebono' ('Day- break')	12–20	6	double pink
	'Amanagawa'	20+	5	narrow, upright
	'Kwanzan'	12–20	5–6	double deep pink, profuse
	'Hally Jolivette'	15	5	cultivar; double white
Higan	*Prunus subhirtella* 'Autumnalis'	15	5	blooms in the spring, some- times again in autumn
Nipponese	*Prunus nipponica*	18	5	
Pin (Wild red)	*Prunus pensylvanica*	35	2	native
	'Shubert'	30	2	cultivar; white flowers; foliage green, then turn- ing to reddish purple
Sour	*Prunus cerasus,* and cultivars	30	3	
Surinam, *see Suri- nam cherry*				
Cherry laurel (BLE)	*Prunus laurocerasus*	up to 30	6–7	
Chinaberry (Um- brella-tree)	*Melia azedarach*	25–50	7	
Clethra, Lily-of-the- valley	*Clethra arborea*	25	9–10	
Japanese	*Clethra barbinervis*	30	5	
Cornelian cherry, *see Cherry, Cornelian*				
Crab apple, Arnold	x*Malus arnoldiana*	20	4	
Bechtel	*Malus ioensis*	30	2	

COMMON NAME	SCIENTIFIC NAME	HEIGHT IN FEET	HARDI-NESS ZONE	COMMENTS
Crab apple (*cont.*)				
Carmine	x*Malus atrosanguinea*	20	4	
Japanese flowering	*Malus floribunda*	30	4	
Sargent	*Malus sargentii*	8	4	
Scheidecker	x*Malus scheideckerii*	20	4	
Crab apple, culti-vars:	'Crimson Harvest'	var.	var.	
	'Dolgo'			
	'Dorothea'			
	'Golden Harvest'			
	'Golden Wax'			
	'Hillieri'			
	'Hopa'			
	'Katherine'			
	'Patricia'			
	'Pink Weeper'			
	'Radiant'			
	'Royalty'			
	'Snowbank'			
	'Van Eseltine'			
	many others			
Crab apple, culti-vars, special:				
	'Guiding Star'			columnar
	'Red Jade'			semiweeping
Cucumber tree, Yellow, *see Magnolia, Yellow cucumber tree*				
Dogwood, Flowering	*Cornus florida,* cultivars	25	9	
Flowering, culti-vars:	'Apple Blossom'			pale pink
	'Cherokee Chief'			red
	'Rainbow'			variegated foliage
	'Rubra'			natural sport, flowers pink to reddish but not dependable
	'Spring Song'			rose-red
	'Sweetwater'			red with reddish foliage
	'White Cloud'			creamy white, pro-fuse flowering
	'Fastigiata'			upright habit while young

COMMON NAME	SCIENTIFIC NAME	HEIGHT IN FEET	HARDI-NESS ZONE	COMMENTS
Dogwood, Flowering (*cont.*)				
	'Gigantea'			huge 6-inch bracts, white
	'New Hampshire'			hardy in North beyond natural limits
	'Pendula'			pendulous branches
	'Welchii'			variegated leaves, cream, pink, and green; results not certain
	'Xanthocarpa'			yellow fruited
Kousa (Japanese or Chinese)	*Cornus kousa*, and cultivar	20–30	5	
	'Milky Way'			profuse, white
Nuttall (Pacific)	*Cornus Nuttallii*	30–75	7	West Coast native
Eucalyptus, Gum tree, several species				
Coral gum	*Eucalyptus torquata*	15–20	9	
Red gum (Yate tree)	*Eucalyptus cornuta*	35	9	
Evodia, Korean	*Evodia daniellii*	25	5	
Farkleberry (E)	*Vaccinium arboreum*	25–30	7–8	
Franklinia	*Franklinia alata-maha*	30	5	
French tamarisk, *see Salt-cedar*				
Fringe-tree	*Chionanthus virginicus*	30–35	4	
Geiger tree	*Cordia sebestena*	25	10	
Golden-chain tree, Scotch	*Laburnum alpinum*	25–30	4	
Waterer	*Laburnum watererii*	30	5	
Hardy-orange	*Poncirus trifoliata*	35	5–6	thorny
Hawthorn, English	*Crataegus oxycantha*, and cultivars	15+	4	
	'Paul's Scarlet'	15	4	
Glossy	*Crataegus nitida*	30	4	
Lavalle	*Crataegus lavallei*	20	4	
Cultivar:	x 'Winter King'	15	5	especially for Midwest
Huisache (Sweet acacia)	*Acacia farnesiana*	35	9	especially desert
Jacaranda	*Jacaranda acutifolia*	to 50	10	may grow less tall in some areas

COMMON NAME	SCIENTIFIC NAME	HEIGHT IN FEET	HARDI- NESS ZONE	COMMENTS
Jerusalem-thorn (Parkinsonia)	*Parkinsonia aculeata*	20–35	9–10	thorny
Judas-tree, *see Redbud, Judas-tree*				
Laburnum, *see Golden-chain tree*				
Loquat	*Eriobotria japonica*	20	7	
Macadamia, *see Queensland nut*				
Magnolia, Anise	*Magnolia salicifolia*	30	5	rare
Anise cultivar:	'Elsie Frye"	30	5	West Coast
Dawson	*Magnolia daw-soniana*	35	10	
'Merrill'	x*Magnolia loebneri* 'Merrill'	35+	4	
Saucer	x*Magnolia soulangi-ana,* and cultivars	25	5	
Star	*Magnolia stellata,* and cultivars	23	5	
Watson	*Magnolia watsonii*	20	5	
Yellow cucumber-tree	*Magnolia cordata*	30	5	
Mountain-ash, Dwarf showy	*Sorbus decora* 'Nana'	15–20	2	rare
Showy	*Sorbus decora*	30	2	
Snowberry	*Sorbus discolor*	30	5	white berries
Vilmorin	*Sorbus vilmorinii*	18	5	rare
Nannyberry	*Viburnum lentago*	30	2	
Olive, Russian	*Eleagnus angusti-folia*	20–50	2–5	
Orchid-tree, Hong-kong	*Bauhinia blakeana*	20	10	
Orchid-tree, *see also Bauhinia*				
Parkinsonia, *see Jerusalem-thorn*				
Paulownia, Royal	*Paulownia tomen-tosa*	to 45	5	
Peach, Flowering Cultivars:	*Prunus persica* 'Cardinal'	20–25	5	
	'Early Double Red'	20+	5	
	'Weeping Double Pink'	20	5	

227

COMMON NAME	SCIENTIFIC NAME	HEIGHT IN FEET	HARDI-NESS ZONE	COMMENTS
Pear, Callery	*Pyrus calleryana*	30	4	
Callery 'Bradford'	*Pyrus calleryana* 'Bradford'	35–50	4	
Willowleaf	*Pyrus salicifolia*	25	4	silvery young leaf
Photinia, Chinese	*Photinia serrulata*	35	7	large flowers
Poinciana, Royal	*Delonix regia*	to 50	9	may grow less tall in some areas
Privet, Glossy (E)	*Ligustrum lucidum*	to 30	7	
Queensland-nut (Macadamia)	*Macadamia tenui-folia*	35	10	
Red-bud, Chinese	*Cercis chinensis*	to 40	6	
Eastern (Judas-tree)	*Cercis canadensis*	35	4	
Judas-tree, European	*Cercis siliquastrum*	30	6	
Raceme	*Cercis racemosa*	30	7	
Red-Gum, *see Eucalyptus*,				
Retama, *see Jerusalem-thorn*				
Rhododendron, Rosebay	*Rhododendron maximum*	12–36	3	
Salt-cedar (French tamarisk)	*Tamarix gallica*	30	7–8	
Sea-buckthorn, Common	*Hippophae rhamnoides*	30	3	
Senna, Golden shower	*Cassia fistula*	30	10	
Serviceberry, Allegheny	*Amelanchier laevis*	35	4	
Apple	*Amelanchier grandiflora*	25	4	
Silk-tree	*Albizia julibrissin*	35	5–7	
Silverbell, Carolina	*Halesia carolina*	30–50	5	
Smoke-tree, American	*Cotinus americanus*	30	5	
Snowbell, Fragrant	*Styrax obassia*	30	6	
Japanese	*Styrax japonica*	30	5	
Southern Black-haw, *see Black-haw, Southern*				
Strawberry-tree	*Arbutus unedo*	10–30	8	
Surinam-cherry, *see Cherry, Surinam*				
Sweetshade	*Hymenosporum flavum*	50	10	

COMMON NAME	SCIENTIFIC NAME	HEIGHT IN FEET	HARDI- NESS ZONE	COMMENTS
Tea-tree, Australian	*Leptospermum laevigatum*	25	9	sandy soil
Tree-lilac, Japanese	*Syringa amurensis* 'Japonica'	30	4	
Tung-oil-tree	*Aleurites fordii*	25	9–10	
Umbrella-tree	*Melia azedarach* 'Umbraculi- formis'			
Viburnum, Siebold	*Viburnum sieboldii*	30	4	
Wattle, Cootamun- dra (Bailey's)	*Acacia baileyana*	30	10	
Sydney	*Acacia longifolia*	35	10	

TREES WITH DECORATIVE BERRIES OR FRUIT

Many trees produce fruits or berries, some edible and many not to be eaten. For instance, hollies, and among the needled evergreens yew, are often used as much with the bright colors of their fruits in mind as with their handsome foliage. Certain berries may stay on the branches well into the winter, making the off season less sad. Many of the berried plants are attractive to birds, bringing them into the garden where they also will find insect pests to add to their diet. Some berries are less conspicuous than others, but all add to the beauty and pleasure of plantings.

COMMON NAME	SCIENTIFIC NAME	FRUIT, COLOR	COMMENTS
Bayberry, Cali- fornia*	*Myrica californica*	berries, purple	(BLE)
Blackhaw	*Viburnum pruni- folium*	berries, blue-black	
Southern	*Viburnum rufidulum*	berries, dark blue	

Key:
E = Needled evergreen
BLE = Broad-leaved evergreen

* In order to produce fruit, certain plants are self-pollinating, that is, both male and female flowers are on the same plant. Others require a male plant to fertilize a female plant, one male being capable of fertilizing several adjacent females. Where the asterisk (*) appears on this list after the common name, both male and female plants will probably be required if fruiting is desired.

COMMON NAME	SCIENTIFIC NAME	FRUIT, COLOR	COMMENTS
Brush-cherry, *see Eugenia*			
Buckthorn, Dahurian	*Rhamnus davurica*	berries, shiny black	
Castor-aralia	*Kalopanax pictus*	seeds; small, black in clusters	
Cedar, Atlas	*Cedrus atlantica*	cones, upper side of branches; mature in two years	(E)
Deodar	*Cedrus deodara*	cones, same	(E)
Lebanon	*Cedrus libani steno-coma*	cones, same	(E)
Cherry, Black or Rum	*Prunus serotina*	cherries, red becoming black	
Wild red or Pin	*Prunus pensylvanica*	cherries, small red	
Chinaberry	*Melia azderach*	berries, yellow	
Cork tree, Amur*	*Phellodendron amurense*	berries, round, black	
Cornelian-Cherry, *see Dogwood,*			
Crab apple	*Malus*, species and cultivars	small apples, yellow to red, deep red	
Cypress, Arizona	*Cupressus arizonica*	cones, small	(E)
Italian	*Cupressus semper-virens*	cones, small	(E)
Monterey	*Cupressus macro-carpa*	cones, small	(E)
Dogwood, Cornelian-cherry	*Cornus mas*	red, not conspicuous	
Flowering	*Cornus florida*, species and cultivars	berries, bright red	
Japanese (Kousa)	*Cornus kousa*	raspberrylike, on long stems	
Nuttall (Pacific)	*Cornus nuttallii*	berries, bright red to orange	
Yellow cornelian-cherry	*Cornus mas* 'flava'	yellow, more conspicuous	
Yellow-fruited	*Cornus florida* 'Xanthocarpa'	berries, yellow	
Douglas fir, *see Fir, Douglas*			
Elder, Blueberry	*Sambucus coerulea*	berries, blue-black with whitish bloom	
Eugenia, Brush-cherry	*Eugenia paniculata*	berries, rosy purple	(E)

COMMON NAME	SCIENTIFIC NAME	FRUIT, COLOR	COMMENTS
Euonymus, Aldenham, *see Spindle-tree, Aldenham*			
Broadleaf	*Euonymus latifolius*	capsules, opening red to orange	
Evodia, Korean	*Evodia daniellii*	berries, red to glossy black	
Farkleberry	*Vaccinium arboreum*	berries, blue	
Fir, Douglas	*Pseudotsuga menziesii*	cones, pendulous	(E)
Fringe-tree*	*Chionanthus virginicus*	grapelike clusters, dark blue	
Hardy-orange	*Poncirus trifoliata*	yellow, orangelike, small	
Hawthorn	*Crataegus*, species and cultivars	berries, mostly red; orange and yellow cultivars	
Holly*	*Ilex*, species, particularly American, English, Chinese	berries, mostly red, some yellow, orange	(E)
Dahoon*	*Ilex cassine*	berries, red	(E)
Longstalk*	*Ilex pedunculosa*	berries, bright red, on stalks	(E)
Perny*	*Ilex pernyi*	berries, red, conspicuous	(E)
Yaupon*	*Ilex vomitoria*	berries, bright red	(E)
Juniper, Eastern red-cedar*	*Juniperus virginiana*	berries, bluish	(E)
Western red cedar*	*Juniperus scopulorum*, and cultivars	berries, bright bluish	(E)
others*	*Juniperus*, species and cultivars	berries bluish, greenish	(E)
Kalopanax, *see Castor-aralia*			
Larch	*Larix*, species	cones of various sizes	
Golden	*Pseudolarix amabilis*	cones, borne upright	
Loquat	*Eriobotrya japonica*	fruit, pear-shaped, orange-yellow; edible	(E)
Madrone, Pacific	*Arbutus menziesii*	berries, orange to red	(E)
Magnolia	*Magnolia*, species and cultivars	pods, colorful seeds show as pod splits	
Maple, Amur	*Acer ginnala*	winged keys, red	

231

COMMON NAME	SCIENTIFIC NAME	FRUIT, COLOR	COMMENTS
Mountain	*Acer spicatum*	winged keys, bright red	
Red or Swamp	*Acer rubrum*	winged keys, bright red	
Tatarian	*Acer tataricum*	winged keys, red	
Mountain-ash, European (Rowan)	*Sorbus aucuparia*	berries, bright red, in clusters	
Fastigiate	x*Sorbus hybrida* 'Fastigiata'	berries, red, in clusters	
Folgner	*Sorbus folgneri*	berries, red, in clusters	
Gibbs	x*Sorbus hybrida* 'Gibbsii'	berries, coral, in clusters	
Korean	*Sorbus alnifolia*	berries, scarlet to orange, in clusters	
Showy	*Sorbus decora*	berries, bright red, in clusters; hardy	
Snowberry	*Sorbus discolor*	berries, white, in clusters	
Vilmorin	*Sorbus vilmorinii*	berries, red, may turn to white later	
Nannyberry	*Viburnum lentago*	berries, black, in flat clusters	
Oak	*Quercus*, species	acorns	
Osage-orange*	*Maclura pomifera*	green, orangelike, large	
Paper-mulberry, Common*	*Broussonetia papyrifera*	berries, orange to red	
Pepper-tree, Brazilian	*Schinus terebinthifolius*	berries, small red	
California	*Schinus molle*	berries, red, profuse	
Photinia, Chinese	*Photinia serrulata*	berries, bright red	
Pine	*Pinus*, species	cones	many not for small gardens (E)
Sugar	*Pinus lambertiana*	cones to 20 inches long	not for small gardens (E)
Plane tree, London	*Platanus acerifolia*	ball clusters, two or three, on stems	
Possum-haw	*Ilex decidua*	berries, orange to scarlet	
Sourwood (Sorrel tree)	*Oxydendrum arboreum*	capsules, dried	
Sea-buckthorn, Common*	*Hippophae rhamnoides*	berries, bright orange	
Spindle-tree, Aldenham	*Euonymus europaea* 'Aldenhamensis'	capsules, opening pink	
Broadleaf, *see Euonymus,*			

COMMON NAME	SCIENTIFIC NAME	FRUIT, COLOR	COMMENTS
Spruce	*Picea*, species	cones, drooping	(E)
Strawberry-tree	*Arbutus unedo*	strawberrylike, brilliant orange-red	(BLE)
Surinam-cherry	*Eugenia uniflora*	berries, edible; changing color: green, yellow, orange, finally scarlet	(BLE)
Sweet gum	*Liquidambar styraciflua*	round horned balls, brownish	
Formosa	*Liquidambar formosana*	balls, bristly	
Sweetleaf, Asiatic	*Symplocos paniculata*	berries, bright blue	
Tulip tree (Yellow poplar)	*Liriodendron tulipifera*	dry pods, winter, yellow-whitish, in flower shape	
Viburnum, Siebold	*Viburnum sieboldii*	berries, red to black, on short red stalks	
Wax-myrtle, Southern*	*Myrica cerifera*	berries, small gray	(E)
Yew, English	*Taxus baccata*, and cultivars	fleshy berries, red	(E)
Intermediate	*Taxus media*, and cultivars	fleshy berries, red	(E)
Japanese	*Taxus cuspidata*, and cultivars	fleshy berries, red	(E)
Yew*	*Taxus*, species	fleshy pinkish to red	(E)

TREES WITH FRAGRANT FLOWERS, LEAVES, WOOD

Fragrance may be present in flower or leaf or in the twigs and wood, but it can be diminished or intensified according to the weather, soil, climate, or other influences.

This list has been prepared with what information was available. Probably other trees, particularly native ones or regional ones not widely available enough to meet requirements for this list, are also fragrant in flower, leaf, or twigs.

Needled evergreens are listed separately at the end. Some will be fragrant in themselves; others may need sunshine and heat to bring out the pungent, fresh odor of the needles. Balsam fir is well known as the Christmas tree that perfumes the entire house.

COMMON NAME	SCIENTIFIC NAME	HARDINESS ZONE	COMMENTS
Acacia, Bronze or Frosty (BLE)	*Acacia pruinosa*	10	
Ash, Flowering	*Fraxinus ornus*	5	
Bayberry, California (BLE)	*Myrica californica*	7	leaves, berries
Bay, Sweet, *see Laurel*			
California-laurel (BLE)	*Umbellularia californica*	7	leaves
Camphor tree (BLE)	*Cinnamomum camphora*	9	leaves, wood
Cherry, Black or Rum	*Prunus serotina*	3	little
Double Conradina	*Prunus conradina* 'Semiplena'	6	
European bird	*Prunus padus*, and cultivars	3	
Oriental	*Prunus serrulata*	5–6	some cultivars are fragrant
Yoshino	*Prunus yedoensis*	5	slight
Chinaberry	*Melia azedarach*	7	
Citrus (BLE-SE)	*Citrus*, species	9–10	flowers, leaves, fruit
Crab apple	*Malus*, species and cultivars	3–5	not all are fragrant
Eucalyptus	*Eucalyptus*, species	9–10	leaves, wood
Fringe tree	*Chionanthus virginicus*	4	
Hardy-orange	*Poncirus trifoliata*	5–6	very fragrant
Hawthorn, English	*Crataegus oxycantha*	4	
Katsura	*Cercidiphyllum japonicum*	4	leaves
Laurel, Sweet bay (BLE)	*Laurus nobilis*	6	leaves
Linden	*Tilia*, species	2–5	
Locust, Black	*Robinia pseudoacacia*	3	
cultivars	'Idaho'	3–4	
Loquat (BLE)	*Eriobotrya japonica*	7	
Madrone, Pacific (BLE)	*Arbutus menziesii*	7	
Magnolia,* Anise	*Magnolia salicifolia*	9	flowers fragrant; leaves lemon-scented
Fraser	*Magnolia fraseri*	5	

Key:

BLE = Broad-leaved evergreen

SE = Semi-evergreen (may be deciduous in northern reaches of hardiness zone)

* Not all magnolias are fragrant, though they are all worth growing for the flowers alone. Some are extremely fragrant, others moderately so.

COMMON NAME	SCIENTIFIC NAME	HARDINESS ZONE	COMMENTS
Magnolia (*cont.*)			
Oyama	*Magnolia sieboldii*	6	
Shinyleaf (BLE)	*Magnolia nitida*	8	
Southern (BLE)	*Magnolia grandiflora*	7	very fragrant
Sprenger	*Magnolia sprengeri*	7	
Star	*Magnolia stellata*, and cultivars	5	moderately fragrant
Sweet bay (SE)	*Magnolia virginiana*	5	very fragrant flowers
Watson	x*Magnolia watsonii*	5	
Yulan	*Magnolia denudata*, and cultivars	5	
Myrtle, Wax-, *see Wax-myrtle*			
Olive, Russian	*Eleagnus angustifolia*	2	
Pagoda-tree, Japanese	*Sophora japonica*	4	
Paulownia, Royal	*Paulownia tomentosa*	5	
Silk-tree (Mimosa)	*Albizia julibrissin*	6–7	
Snowbell, Fragrant	*Styrax obassia*	5	
Japanese	*Styrax japonica*	5	
Sourwood (Sorrel tree)	*Oxydendrum arboreum*	5	
Sweet bay, *see Laurel, also Magnolia, Sweet bay*			
Sweetleaf, Asiatic	*Symplocos paniculata*	5	fragrant flowers
Sweet-shade (BLE)	*Hymenosporum flavum*	10	
Wattle, Silver (BLE)	*Acacia decurrens* 'Dealbata'	9	
Wax-myrtle, Southern (BLE)	*Myrica cerifera*	6	leaves
Willow, Yellowstem	*Salix alba* 'Vitellina'	2	
Yellow-wood, American	*Cladrastis lutea*	3	

NEEDLED EVERGREENS:

COMMON NAME	SCIENTIFIC NAME	HARDINESS ZONE	COMMENTS
Arborvitae	*Thuja*, species	2–5	
Cedar	*Cedrus*, species, including:		
California incense-	*Libocedrus decurrens*	5	wood, leaves
Deodar	*Cedrus deodara*	7	
Lebanon	*Cedrus libani stenocoma*	5	
Fir, Balsam	*Abies balsamea*	3	
Hemlock	*Tsuga*, species	3–6	
Juniper	*Juniperus*, species	2–6	
Pine	*Pinus*, species	2–9	

235

TREES WITH COLORFUL AUTUMN FOLIAGE

COMMON NAME	SCIENTIFIC NAME	COLOR	COMMENTS
REDS AND ORANGES:			
Black gum, *see* *Tupelo*			
Black-haw	*Viburnum pruni- folium*	red, shining	
Southern	*Viburnum rufidulum*	red	
Cherry, Miyama	*Prunus maximowiczii*	scarlet	
Nipponese	*Prunus nipponica*	crimson to yellow	
Sargent	*Prunus sargentii*	red	
Wild red or Pin	*Prunus pensylvanica*	red	
Cornelian-cherry, *see Dogwood*			
Crab apple, Daw- son	*Malus dawsoniana*	red-yellow	rare; not very impressive
Dogwood, Cor- nelian-cherry	*Cornus mas*	red	
Flowering	*Cornus florida*	scarlet to purplish	
Kousa	*Cornus kousa*	scarlet	
Pacific (Nuttall)	*Cornus nuttallii*	scarlet and yellow	West Coast
Franklinia	*Franklinia alatamaha*	orange to red	
Hawthorn, Glossy	*Crataegus nitida*	red to orange	
Lavalle	*Crataegus lavallei*	bronzy red	
Washington	*Crataegus phaeno- pyrum*	scarlet to orange	
Hornbeam, Ameri- can	*Carpinus caroliniana*	orange to red	
Japanese	*Carpinus japonica*	red	
Oriental	*Carpinus orientalis*	red	
Katsura tree	*Cercidiphyllum japonicum*	scarlet to yellow	
Maple, Amur	*Acer ginnala*	scarlet	
Fullmoon	*Acer japonicum*	bright red	
Japanese	*Acer palmatum*, and cultivars	scarlet	cultivars red
Manchurian	*Acer mandshuricum*	red to scarlet	
Mountain	*Acer spicatum*	orange to scarlet	
Nikko	*Acer nikoense*	red to purple	
Norway	*Acer platanoides*, and cultivars	red	
Red or Swamp	*Acer rubrum*	brilliant red to orange	
Red Sunset	*Acer rubrum* 'Red Sunset'	bright red	holds leaves longer
Slavin's upright	*Acer nigrum ascen- dens* 'Slavin's Upright'	red to yellow	

COMMON NAME	SCIENTIFIC NAME	COLOR	COMMENTS
Maple, Amur *(cont.)*			
Sugar	*Acer saccharum*	red, orange, yellow	
Tatarian	*Acer tataricum*	red to yellow	
Vine	*Acer circinatum*	red to orange	
Mountain-ash, European	*Sorbus aucuparia*	reddish	
Folgner	*Sorbus folgneri*	russet red	
Korean	*Sorbus alnifolia*	orange to scarlet	
Snowberry	*Sorbus discolor*	red	
Oak, Black	*Quercus velutina*	red to dark red	
Pin	*Quercus palustris*	scarlet	
Red	*Quercus borealis*	red	
Scarlet	*Quercus coccinea*	scarlet	
Shingle	*Quercus imbricaria*	russet to yellow	
Shumard	*Quercus shumardii*	scarlet	
Pear, Bradford	*Pyrus calleryana* 'Bradford'	red to scarlet	glossy
Callery	*Pyrus calleryana*	scarlet	glossy
Pepperidge, *see* Tupelo			
Pistache, Chinese	*Pistacia chinensis*	red to orange	
Sassafras	*Sassafras albidum*	orange-scarlet	
Serviceberry, Allegheny	*Amelanchier laevis*	red to yellow	
Shadblow	*Amelanchier canadensis*	red to yellow	
Sourwood (Sorrel tree)	*Oxydendrum arboreum*	scarlet	
Stewartia, Japanese	*Stewartia pseudocamellia*	purplish red	
Korean	*Stewartia koreana*	orange-red	
Sweet gum	*Liquidambar styraciflua*	scarlet	
Formosan	*Liquidambar formosana*	red	West Coast
Tupelo (Black Gum, Pepperidge)	*Nyssa sylvatica*	scarlet-orange	
Viburnum, Siebold	*Virburnum sieboldii*	red	
Yellow-wood, American	*Cladrastis lutea*	orange to yellow	
YELLOW TO YELLOW-ORANGE:			
Ash, Green	*Fraxinus pensylvanica* 'Lanceolata'	yellow	
White	*Fraxinus americana*	yellow to purplish	
Beech, American	*Fagus grandifolia*	golden bronze	
European	*Fagus sylvatica*	bronzy yellow	
Birch	*Betula*, species	yellow	

237

COMMON NAME	SCIENTIFIC NAME	COLOR	COMMENTS
YELLOW TO YELLOW-ORANGE (*cont.*)			
Buckeye, Ohio	*Aesculus glabra*	brilliant orange	
Cherry, Nipponese	*Prunus nipponica*	yellow, orange to crimson	
Chestnut, Chinese	*Castanea mollissima*	yellow to bronze	
Japanese	*Castanea crenata*	yellow to bronze	
Fringe tree	*Chionanthus virginicus*	bright yellow	
Ginkgo (Maidenhair tree)	*Ginkgo biloba*	clear yellow	
Hickory	*Carya*, species	yellows	
Katsura	*Cericidiphyllum japonicum*	yellow to scarlet	
Larch	*Larix*, species	yellows	sometimes effective
Golden	*Pseudolarix amabilis*	golden yellow	
Magnolia, Star	*Magnolia stellata*	bronze to yellow	
Maple, Bigleaf	*Acer macrophyllum*	yellow	Pacific Coast
Norway	*Acer platanoides*	yellow	
Rocky Mountain	*Acer glabrum*	bright yellow	
Striped (Moose)	*Acer pensylvanicum*	yellow	
Mountain-ash, Korean	*Sorbus alnifolia*	yellow to yellow-orange	
Oak, Shingle	*Quercus imbricaria*	yellow to russet	
Pawpaw	*Asimina triloba*	yellow	
Poplar, Cottonwood (and others)	*Populus*, species	yellows	
Red-bud, Chinese	*Cercis chinensis*	yellow	
Eastern (Judas-tree)	*Cercis canadensis*	yellow	
Serviceberry, Allegheny	*Amalanchier laevis*	yellow to orange-red	
Apple	*Amalanchier grandiflora*	yellow to orange	
Sour gum, Chinese	*Nyssa sinensis*	yellow with some red	
Tulip tree (Yellow poplar)	*Liriodendron tulipifera*	clear yellow	
Zelkova, Japanese	*Zelkova serrata*	yellow to russet	

SMALL TREES FOR SHADY CONDITIONS

Some of the trees recommended are flowering and may bloom less well in shady conditions than where more light is available, though they will live and do reasonably well with high shade. Note also that among the tall treelike shrubs (see shrubs lists) there may be candidates for the home garden—shade-enduring shrubs, and many that bloom enough to make them worthwhile. Heights given are maximum under best conditions. In shade, plants may not equal or even come near these figures, depending upon soil, moisture, depth of shade, and climate. On the edges of woodlands or where light, even if not direct sun, can reach the trees they will probably grow taller and if flowering, bloom better.

COMMON NAME	SCIENTIFIC NAME	HEIGHT IN FEET	HARDI-NESS ZONE	COMMENTS
Arborvitae, American	*Thuja occidentalis*	to 60	2	(E)
Cherry, Wild red or Pin	*Prunus pennsylvanica*	35	2	
Dogwood, Flowering	*Cornus florida*, and cultivars	to 35–40	4	
Pacific (Nuttall)	*Cornus nuttallii*	to 70	7	
Hemlock, Canada	*Tsuga canadensis*	to 90	3	(E)
Carolina	*Tsuga caroliniana*	to 75	4	(E)
Holly, American	*Ilex opaca*	to 45	5	(BLE)
Various	*Ilex*, species	various	5–7	(BLE)
Maple, Mountain	*Acer spicatum*	25	2	
Striped (Moose)	*Acer pennsylvanium*	35	3	
Vine	*Acer circinatum*	25	5	West Coast
Red-bud, Eastern	*Cercis canadensis*	35	4	
Rosebay	*Rhododendron maximum*	15–35	3	(BLE) shrubby
Serviceberry, Allegheny	*Amelanchier laevis*	35	4	
Shadblow	*Amelanchier canadensis*	to 60	4	

Key:
BLE = Broad-leaved evergreen
E = Needled evergreen

TREES WITH INTERESTING BARK COLORS

To tree lovers, all bark is interesting in color, in texture, and in its general contribution to the total effect of the tree. However, some trees are more interesting than others in the color of their bark, and on the small-home property where all plants are seen at close quarters this becomes increasingly important to the gardener. Bark is ignored by the unobservant or the novice, or if it is thought of at all, it is assumed to be brown. Yet even among trees whose trunks are brownish, there are infinite shades and variations. Bear in mind that most trees at maturity may have changed bark color from somewhat bright to grayish, brownish, or some other shade. New wood on twigs and upward-growing trunks is often quite colorful, but as it matures it takes on more sober tones. Then there are those trees that all their lives provide interest with peeling or flaking bark— paper birches and sycamores, to name some well-known sorts. Bark is definitely a part of the picture and should be one of the considerations in choosing those most permanent of garden plants, the trees.

COMMON NAME	SCIENTIFIC NAME	BARK DESCRIPTION	COMMENTS
WHITE:			
Alder, White	*Alnus rhombifolia*	whitish to grayish	
Birch, European	*Betula pendula*	white, peeling	
Gray	*Betula populifolia*	white, black markings	
Paper or Canoe	*Betula papyrifera*	white, peeling	
Poplar, Bolleana	*Populus alba*	new wood silvery greenish white	
RED TO REDDISH BROWN:			
Birch, Chinese paper	*Betula albo-sinensis*	bright orange to orange-red, peeling	
Dahurian	*Betula davurica*	reddish-brown, peeling	
Manchurian	*Betula platyphylla* 'Szechuanica'	new twigs, glossy red-brown	
River	*Betula nigra*	reddish brown, peeling	
Sweet	*Betula lenta*	deep reddish brown, cherrylike	
Cherry, Japanese	*Prunus serrulata*	red-brown, especially when young	
Sargent	*Prunus sargentii*	dark mahogany red	
Wild red or Pin	*Prunus pensylvanicum*	red, shining	
Dogwood, Flowering	*Cornus florida*	young twigs reddish	
Maple, Mountain	*Acer spicatum*	red-brown, smooth	
Silver	*Acer saccharinum*	old trunks reddish brown	
Tree-lilac, Japanese	*Syringa amurensis* 'Japonica'	reddish, cherrylike	
REDDISH, ORANGE-RED:			
Pine, Japanese red	*Pinus densiflora*	orange-red	
Jeffrey	*Pinus jeffreyi*	cinnamon red to brownish	West Coast
Red or Norway	*Pinus resinosa*	reddish brown	
Scotch	*Pinus sylvestris*	trunk and old branches reddish	

COMMON NAME	SCIENTIFIC NAME	BARK DESCRIPTION	COMMENTS
GRAY TO GRAYISH:			
Beech, American	*Fagus grandifolia*	light gray, pinkish	
European	*Fagus sylvatica*	medium to dark gray	
Cucumber tree	*Magnolia acuminata*	gray when young	
Elm, Smooth-leaved	*Ulmus carpinifolia*	gray	
Hawthorn	*Crataegus*, species	gray to grayish	
Hornbeam, American	*Carpinus caroliniana*	gray, smooth	
Magnolia, Saucer	*Magnolia soulangiana*	warm gray	
Maple, Sugar	*Acer saccharum*	grayish to brownish gray	
Swamp or red	*Acer rubrum*	warm gray	
Mountain-ash	*Sorbus*, species	gray	
Oak, Basket	*Quercus prinus*	silvery gray	
Black	*Quercus velutina*	deep warm gray to sepia	
Red	*Quercus borealis*	young trunk branches gray	
Serviceberry, Shadblow	*Amelanchier arborea*	gray with sepia striping, later furrowed	
Sourwood (Sorrel tree)	*Oxydendrum arboreum*	gray, tinged red when young	
Tupelo (Black gum, Pepperidge)	*Nyssa sylvatica*	pale gray when young	
Yellow-wood	*Cladrastis lutea*	light gray, smooth	
GREEN:			
Hardy-orange	*Poncirus trifoliata*	trunk when young, new twigs, all branches	
Parasol-tree, Chinese	*Firmiana simplex*	multiple gray-green trunks	
YELLOW:			
London Plane	*Platanus acerifolia*	limbs, branches dull yellowish	
Willow, various, especially:	*Salix alba* 'Tristis'	upper branches, twigs	
	Salix alba 'Vitellina'	upper branches, twigs	
STRIPED:			
Madrone, Pacific	*Arbutus menziesii*	old bark cracks to show red or cinnamon	
Maple, David	*Acer davidii*	branches striped white in winter	
Striped (Moose)	*Acer pensylvanicum*	new and upper wood green and white	
Serviceberry, Shadblow	*Amelanchier arborea*	sepia striping on gray young wood	
Strawberry-tree	*Arbutus unedo*	dark, cracks to show bright red	

241

COMMON NAME	SCIENTIFIC NAME	BARK DESCRIPTION	COMMENTS
PEELING, SCALING:			
Birch, Chinese paper	*Betula albo-sinensis*	bright orange to orange-red, peels	
Dahurian	*Betula davurica*	reddish brown, curls, peels	
European	*Betula pendula*	white, peels somewhat	
Manchurian	*Betula platyphylla 'Szechuanica'*	white, peels paper-thin	
Paper or Canoe	*Betula papyrifera*	white, peels paper-thin in sheets	
River	*Betula nigra*	reddish brown, peels	
London plane	*Platanus acerifolium*	flakes, showing light greenish to yellowish new bark below	
Maple, Paperbark	*Acer griseum*	cinnamon brown, peels to reveal new red bark	
Sycamore (Button-wood)	*Platanus occidentalis*	brownish bark flakes, showing buff white, brownish gray, or pale tan new bark; old trees may have whitish upper limbs	

TREES FOR THE SEASHORE

Conditions near salt water are sometimes too much for trees to bear. Winds and sandy soil are not the only hazards, for windswept salt spray also comes inland, often for quite some distance during gales. Some trees are able to withstand such conditions, however, and may be able to grow reasonably well.

COMMON NAME	SCIENTIFIC NAME	HARDINESS ZONE	COMMENTS
Arborvitae, American	*Thuja occidentalis*	2	(E)
Oriental	*Thuja orientalis*	6	(E)
Ash, Velvet	*Fraxinus velutina*	5	
Beefwood, Coast	*Casuarina stricta*	10	(E)
Horsetail-tree	*Casuarina equisetifolia*	9	

Key:
E = Needled evergreen
BLE = Broad-leaved evergreen
SE = Semi-evergreen (may be deciduous in northern reaches of hardiness zone)

COMMON NAME	SCIENTIFIC NAME	HARDINESS ZONE	COMMENTS
Black gum, *see Tupelo*			
Bull bay, *see Magnolia*			
Cajeput tree	*Melaleuca leucadendron*	10	(BLE)
California-laurel, *see Laurel, California-*			
Cherry, Black or Rum	*Prunus serotina*	3	
Cryptomeria, Common	*Cryptomeria japonica,* and cultivars	5–6	(E)
Cypress, Monterey	*Cupressus macrocarpa*	7	(E)
Elm, Chinese	*Ulmus parvifolia*	5	
Siberian	*Ulmus pumila*	4	
Eucalyptus, Red gum	*Eucalyptus camaldulensis*	9	
White gum	*Eucalyptus viminalis*	9	
Yate tree	*Eucalyptus cornuta*	9	
Hawthorn, Cockspur thorn	*Crataegus crus-galli*	4	
Holly, American	*Ilex opaca,* and cultivars	5	
Holly oak or Holm oak, *see Oak, Holly*			
Horse-chestnut	*Aesculus hippocastaneum*	3	
Juniper, Eastern red-cedar	*Juniperus virginiana,* and cultivars	2	
Greek	*Juniperus excelsa* 'Stricta'	7	
West Indies	*Juniperus lucayana*	9	
Laurel, California-	*Umbellularia californica*	7	(BLE)
Linden, Crimean	*Tilia euchlora*	4	
Littleleaf	*Tilia cordata*	3	
Live oak, *see Oak, Live*			
Locust, Black	*Robinia pseudoacacia*	3	
Magnolia, Southern (Bull bay)	*Magnolia grandiflora*	7	(BLE)
Maple, Norway	*Acer platanoides*	3	
Sycamore	*Acer pseudoplatanus*	5	
Mulberry, Russian	*Morus alba* 'Tatarica'	4	
White	*Morus alba*	4	
Oak, Blackjack	*Quercus marilandica*	6	
California live	*Quercus agrifolia*	9	(BLE)
Holly or Holm	*Quercus ilex*	9	(BLE)
Live (Southern)	*Quercus virginiana*	7	(BLE)
White	*Quercus alba*	4	
Olive, Common	*Olea europaea*	9	(SE)
Olive, Russian	*Eleagnus angustifolia*	2	
Pepperidge, *see Tupelo*			
Pepper-tree, Brazilian	*Schinus terebinthifolius*	9–10	
California	*Schinus molle*	9	

243

COMMON NAME	SCIENTIFIC NAME	HARDINESS ZONE	COMMENTS
Pine, Aleppo	*Pinus halepensis*	9	(E)
Austrian	*Pinus nigra* 'Austriaca'	4	(E)
Cluster	*Pinus pinaster*	7	(E)
Japanese black	*Pinus thunbergii*	5	(E)
Monterey	*Pinus radiata*	7	(E)
Pitch	*Pinus rigida*	4	(E)
Scotch	*Pinus sylvestris*	2	(E)
Poplar, Bolleana	*Populus alba* 'Pyramidalis'	2	
White	*Populus alba*	2	
Red gum, *see Eucalyptus,*			
Sea-buckthorn	*Hippophae rhamnoides*	3	
Serviceberry, Shadblow	*Amelanchier canadensis*	4	
Spruce, Colorado blue	*Picea pungens* 'Glauca'	2	
Dragon	*Picea asperata*	5	
Tree of heaven (Ailanthus)	*Ailanthus altissima*	4	
Tupelo (Black gum, Pepperidge)	*Nyssa sylvatica*	4	
White gum, *see Eucalyptus,*			
Yate tree, *see Eucalyptus,*			

PALMS FOR SEASHORE GARDENS:

COMMON NAME	SCIENTIFIC NAME	HARDINESS ZONE	COMMENTS
Palm, Royal	*Roystonea regia*	10	
Palm, Mexican or Washington	*Washingtonia robusta*	10	
Palmetto	*Sabal palmatto*	8	

6

Special Places
Need Special Plants

SPECIAL CONDITIONS IN THE GARDEN

Even beginning gardeners soon feel that their gardens present them with a very special set of conditions with which they must cope. And many gardeners do have extra-special conditions due to climate, soil, and other things they had not bargained for. All gardeners are more or less right in assuming that every plot, every climate, every exposure entails certain problems. Unfortunately, the gardener may have a few ideas about what and how to grow things that are at variance with the realities of the situation. Nature tends to correct these false assumptions in time, but a gardener can save himself many difficulties and much labor if he faces squarely what he must deal with and plans accordingly within these limitations. This section will deal with those places where extraordinary conditions prevail— conditions that until they are understood, may prove to be serious deterrents to any kind of success in gardening.

Part of the trouble in such areas may be an overabundance of what all plants need in moderation, sunlight for instance. The desert, semidesert lands and some of the High Plains areas of the Southwest and Far West have more sunlight than they need, yet they lack some of the other vital elements for plant health: water, humus, and some of the other usual complements that provide a balanced environment. Yet in other places a superabundance of water may be the problem, making the soil soggy, even swampy for a good bit of the year. Houses are now being built on land with very high water tables, which, given the drainage problems inherent in development, may sooner or later become swampy land. The roots of most plants will sicken and rot if water is constantly present about them, for they need air in moderate quantities too. The soil in some other places may offer too much or too little of what certain plants require. Acidity, for instance, is required by some plants, while it may be slow poison for others. On the other hand, some soils are the opposite, quite alkaline or limy. They may prove fatal to plants that require a neutral to acid soil for their best growth and development. This latter is a condition found in much of the western plains country and in the Southwest, where salts in soil and water may also be a problem.

Cold, which is a problem in other parts of the country, is also a factor here, even in true desert lands. It is a condition to which some plants that are healthy in normally cold weather areas and some from warmer areas cannot adjust. The problem is hot days and cold nights. Fruit and flowering shrubs and trees, for instance, often require a period of cold in which to set their buds while dormant. Thus, they will bloom sparsely or not at all in this region, and where there is no bloom there can be no fruit. Others may survive but will be finicky and less inclined to flourish "like the green bay tree" of Biblical lore.

This may sound discouraging and complicated, even hopeless. But many thousands of gardeners have adjusted happily to gardening in the arduous climates mentioned and find satisfaction in their labors. The important thing to remember is that not every single one of the difficulties mentioned is encountered by all gardeners in their gardens. That immediately provides a ray of hope. Those who do have problems need not despair, for help is available. The main thing to remember is that a new set of gardening conditions requires a new way of looking at things. Learn what the problems are and then adjust your thinking toward solving them. You can zero in on success if you work with nature.

SPECIAL PLACES IN THE GARDEN

Among the other problems that gardeners face are those special places that need extra-careful planning and attention, privacy plantings for example. Although solid fences will mean instant privacy, they are frequently austere and unpleasant to a neighbor, and in some towns and cities ordinances regulate them as to height and placement. A hedge will, in time, achieve much the same desired result without insulting a neighbor or violating the law. Certain thorny kinds will also keep neighborhood children (or adults, for that matter) from using lawns and flowerbeds as freeways. Hedges fit into a number of other spots, too, as detailed in this section. There are all kinds to choose from—both deciduous and evergreen, tall, short, and in between—many sorts, all suited to the various climates and hardiness zones as well as to the purposes for which they will be utilized. For suggestions on planting hedges see pages 263–268.

Accent and individuality can be given to a garden by a special plant when it is sculptured and kept barbered into some distinctive form. This kind of work is called topiary, and it is an amusing, even absorbing garden hobby. Such a special plant will indeed lend distinction to a special place in the garden and is discussed on pages 269–272.

And then there is a problem common to a great many gardens—a place that is too small or too narrow for most plants, one in which ordinary plants simply will not perform the function of decoration or of practical use that is needed. This may be the place for an espaliered plant, one carefully trained to fill the space and produce fruit, let us say, on a property too small to allow for conventional-sized fruit trees, even the dwarfed types. Or it may be that a purely decorative function is desired, and a shrub or tree trained to grow flat against the wall would be the answer. Espaliering is coming into use more and more as our gardens grow smaller and land prices rise higher. Find out more about it on pages 273–279.

These are the major areas that call for further explanation and study, and one or more of them may be helpful to the reader attempting to deal with the vexations of such problems. Practical and basic methods are suggested together with the ways to obtain further information, should it be necessary.

DESERT GARDENING

Deserts are usually pictured as Saharas, wastelands of sand with but a few romantic palm-edged oases, but the American desert refuses to conform to this stereotype except in a few isolated places. It is much more interesting, if less romantic, than the desert of those Valentino sagas of yesteryear. Ask most people about our desert and they will immediately mention Arizona, and it is true that parts of it are arid and sandy. However, desert country spreads through parts of southwestern California, too, while at least semidesert conditions will be found in Utah, Nevada, and New Mexico.

In the popular view, a desert is an eternally hot, waterless, flat, and monotonous landscape, essentially plantless. Our desert country can be very hot, it is true, but it can be quite cold on occasion, also. It is certainly anything but plantless. The elevations run from lands below sea level to rather high, mountainous regions, and some moisture occurs at various times of the year, making it possible for certain kinds of plants to sustain

SOME CACTUS, according to genus, can be paired with big-leaved trees and evergreen shrubs to grace subtropical as well as tropical desert scenes. (*Paul E. Genereux*)

BREADFRUIT'S HUGE LEAVES, typical of lush subtropical growth, make a good contrast to complement the clean curving lines of palm tree trunks. (*George Taloumis*)

life and endure the severe conditions imposed on them. Because of over-grazing by cattle and sheep in the past, some regions are more bare than others, for once depleted, it takes plant life a long time to restore itself. Surviving in many areas are the cactus plants with built-in protection in their spines. Though man, rather than grazing beasts, has been the culprit in denuding the land of various sorts of cacti a great deal of cactus and other plant life persists. The same human willfulness that caused streams to silt up and floods to course down our great rivers when forests and other natural flood controls were removed has extended the natural desert considerably, as previous generations have cut timber, grazed the grasses to extinction, cleared land for little reason, and thereby gradually changed the climate to a degree. This is still going on, unfortunately, though recent years have brought more interest and research into the causes and effects of changing climates. It is possible that in a generation or two, if the process proves to be reversible, we may turn the tide and slowly restore our land.

Meanwhile, all we can do is to make sure we do not further compound past crimes against nature by trying to make moist-climate gardens in desert climates. Try basically to utilize natural and native material, adding some "camel" plants from other dry-land regions; save yourself much labor and also reduce water bills. Such a garden will fit more naturally into the landscape this way and, should a prolonged drought occur, and watering is taboo, it will outlive any abnormal garden. The same refrain is being sung here but with more urgency: work with nature and not against it; save labor and time and money. Moreover, this is especially applicable to special-problem gardens, though it's also valid in more usual climates and conditions.

California has a most unique set of climatic conditions. While its northern coastal region is cool and has considerable precipitation, the southern coastal areas are much warmer and have less rainfall. Inland, high mountains block off rains from reaching the southern and eastern desert areas and reduce rainfall even in other parts. Subclimates abound, created by altitudes as well as by the latitudes in which the areas fall. There are many modifications of the broad patterns of the region.

Although this is hot desert country in most spots, it can get much colder than one might assume, with drops of 30 to 50 degrees F. below the average winter minimum temperatures. This occurs in some parts of what is called in California Middle Elevations and in Arizona the High Altitude Desert and Cool Plateau Highlands. Arizona, of course, has also some Cold Mountainous Regions, with elevations of 6,000 to 8,000 feet. But in the lower areas, where desert conditions prevail, there is an arid, cool to subtropical climate, with surprisingly warm temperatures in winter on slopes and in valleys. Where daily average maximums run from 58 to 64 degrees F. and the lows are 31 to 38 degrees F., temperatures may fall to 11 to 14 degrees occasionally. Or they may run hotter than usual for winter—78 to 84 degrees at times and in various spots within the zone.

July average maximums are 115 to 117 degrees, with the minimums 70 to 75 degrees.

Thus it is apparent that a desert is a complicated and varied land. The gardener will do well to go from these generalizations to the specifics of his own particular part of the desert country, finding out what the conditions are that make this a special region and planting accordingly rather than trying to impose the wrong set of ideas on the land. The state agricultural colleges and their associated extension services (see the list in the Appendix) will be helpful in supplying information and can perhaps offer guidance. Also inquire of local gardeners and plantsmen what their experience has been, asking particularly about failures they may have heard of if not experienced themselves. What will not endure the conditions may be as valuable to know about as what will grow.

Because of the small amount of rainfall throughout this general area (many sections report as little as five inches annually, and only a small portion receives as much as ten inches) these Middle- and Low-Elevation deserts have very little humidity and that only in the brief rainy periods. Plants transpire—draw water from the soil and evaporate it through their leaves—and this process can result in the loss of a great deal of valuable water. An insufficient quantity of water will be immediately reflected in the plant by lack of growth and declining health. Whereas transpiration is noticed little, if at all, in more moist regions, in dry-land areas it is a vital point to be aware of.

Wind may also be a problem, not only in desert and semidesert regions but in all dry-land country, including the high plains. In the Southwest it may range from moderate ten- to twenty-mile-per-hour winds to as much as forty- to seventy-mile-per-hour blasts. And these may occur at any time of the year, with drying effects on plants and soil. From late autumn to midspring many sections can expect real wind storms, while in summertime, California desert dwellers may have dust storms and "tornillos," powerful whirlwinds that create small, violent dust storms but cause little local damage except the drying out of plants. Any wind, even a very mild one, will increase transpiration, so that it is imperative that measures be taken for protection of plants from winds.

In desert sections there is also a pleasant side to the story, for there is a great deal of sunshine and a long growing season, much longer than in most other regions. There may be an average of up to 275 days of sunshine, with only a small number of them cloudy to partly cloudy; the rest of the days are rainy, or, in a few isolated spots, some snow may fall. This long season means that, if the gardener can supply moisture needs, can protect the plants from excessive drying out and winds, and meet any other requirements of the plants, he will be able to garden and enjoy his efforts through most of the year. Diseases are in many cases nonexistent, particularly fungus-growth disease, which depends on humid conditions in order to thrive. Some pests and diseases are present, of course, but compared with some regions, this one is quite free of troubles. There are a few cautions one must observe, however, and these will be detailed further on.

One of the curious aspects observed in California and other areas is that gardens on slopes and higher ground may have a longer growing period than those in the valleys and lower-lying areas. The reason is that, as elsewhere, if there is frost and cold air, it will drain downhill to collect in lower places, nipping tender shoots and flower buds that, only a short way up the hill, are unscathed by frost-laden air. Therefore, if flowering plants or fruit are part of the scheme or if tender plants are included, locating a garden a bit up the hillside will lessen the possibility of cold damage in winter.

The best way to achieve success in this rigorous climate will be by choosing plants that are indigenous to the region, sturdy natives or relatives of them, plants that are strong and resist wind damage, and by protecting the garden from drying winds, protecting and anchoring the outer plants particularly until their roots tie them to the soil.

WINDBREAKS AND SHELTER BELTS

People encountering the windy country for the first time may not know what a windbreak or shelter belt is. These are plantings, usually, but might be any tall deflector of winds over a broad area. Trees, often evergreens, but also dense-branched deciduous trees of strong structure, are used in single, double, or multiple rows to break the force of the gales that sweep unobstructed over the land. In desert country and other areas in the West, larger plots are more usual than in the East, so that shelter belts can be recommended. Trees useful for such purposes in the actual desert are Arizona cypress, alligator juniper, and Rocky Mountain juniper among the evergreens, and eucalyptus is also sometimes employed. No material should be used that is not reasonably long lived and permanent. Any that is not, that must be removed and replaced, will offer a threat to the plants it is presumably protecting. Such plantings need not be as refined or beautiful as specimen or border plants, but they must be strong and tough, able to endure the often rapid fluctuations of temperature and the extremes of heat and cold they encounter. A good windbreak plant will have a somewhat open structure near the ground for penetration of air and maintenance of circulation to keep the air from stagnation inside the protected areas. Tops of windbreaks should be well branched and dense in order to give year-round protection.

Temporary fences to protect the small windbreak plants until they get sufficiently anchored with roots may be installed where winds are constant and severe. Where there is room, two or three rows of sheltering trees may be planted. Where only one row is possible in the space available, perhaps one of the evergreens mentioned would be the best choice, setting them three to five feet apart.

SOILS AND WATERING

There are many variations in the soils of this general region, ranging from pure sand in places to mixtures of loam and some clay, with deeper soils in valleys in a few places that will grow plants quite well. Composting garden wastes and kitchen garbage will give the gardener humus with which to improve the soil, or various kinds of humus can be purchased and mixed with it to help conserve moisture. Avoid excessive watering, for salts present in the soil or additional salts in the water itself may add to the troubles. Salts are brought near the surface by applied moisture, and because there is no rainfall as in other regions to leach them down again they remain there to the deteriment of plant growth. This is one of the main reasons why it would seem the best plan to purchase desert plants or those that require little water. To sum up, a desert garden is most successful when it is just that—a desert-plant garden.

WATER, WATER EVERYWHERE

At the other end of the scale is the land that is too wet, keeping it eternally moist around the roots of plants. The problems this condition presents are likely to increase in the future. As available land for development around the cities and their suburbs is built on or sold for businesses, swampy and bog lands are reluctantly bought by developers and laid out for building lots. A few places have strict zoning laws that govern what developers must do before building on such land, but many do not. Some will spend fortunes to drain the arcas, but many builders will pay only lip service to local laws, doing the minimum of what should be required. When the houses are sold, these developers clear out, to play the same game for fast profits elsewhere. The buyers are left with the drainage problems and periodic floods or constantly high water tables that are real problems in establishing gardens.

Even if the homeowner installs tiles and the usual drainage corrections that are expensive solutions, they do not always work, and tiles eventually clog up because the wetland conditions have not been basically changed. The high water table and occasional flooding may make it impossible to grow a good lawn. It certainly will reduce the choices of plant material if the condition verges on swampland. A great many plants cannot adjust to having waterlogged soil constantly around their roots and will sicken and die. Therefore, a prospective homeowner who wants a conventional garden will do well to think twice before purchasing. At the least, in order to understand the severity of the problem he should visit the plot to inspect conditions immediately after a rain and again a day or two later. Those who have already purchased such a plot will have one of two alternatives in making a garden.

POORLY DRAINED SOIL. Where soil is boggy and water table is high, it may still be possible to plant trees and shrubs that demand drainage. *Left,* by digging shallow holes, setting root balls higher than the surrounding level, and filling around the root balls to raise the grade, roots will establish and adjust to conditions in time. *Right,* where waterlogging is severe, a raised bed with masonry walls will lift the plants above boggy, sandy soil. Bed bottom should be filled with gravel.

254

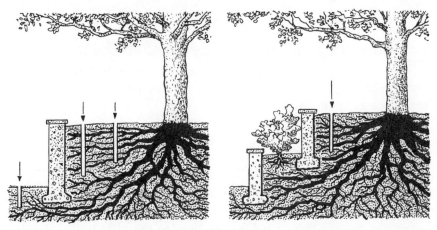

CHANGING GRADE AROUND EXISTING TREES to lower the soil level may endanger the tree if all the roots on one side are cut deeply. *Left,* single high wall cuts all roots, including important root ends where feeding roots grow. Tree recovers better if deep feeding holes or pipes are installed and foods in solution can be put where the roots will profit more than from surface feedings. On lower level, another hole encourages rooting and gives added nutrients for recovery. *Right,* sometimes a double wall will be better, and look better. A feeding hole aids surface roots cut by the upper wall. Low shrubs can be planted behind the lower wall, where surface feeding will leach down to foster growth around ends of the amputated roots. This double wall minimizes danger.

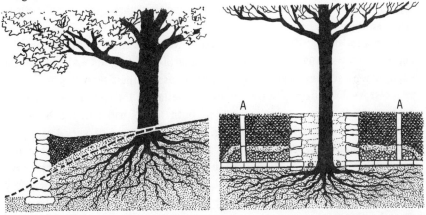

FILLING AROUND EXISTING TREES. Often trees are killed by soil fills that smother roots before they can readjust. *Left,* dotted line shows existing grade, an open stone wall containing the fill. *Right,* a well with open stone walls built 18 inches or more out from the trunk will let water percolate outward to roots. Deep fills require drainage tiles (*A*) set vertically to connect with tile lines radiating outward from the well on top of old ground level. Broken stone and gravel should be spread over tile lines outward to perimeter of limb spread before soil is filled on top. Do not use heavy or clay soil for fill, but keep soil open with humus and sand to permit air and water to pass through easily, reaching and encouraging root growth.

First, they can buy sufficient landfill to raise the level of the ground at least a foot, provided this does not channel water into the house or cause trouble by inundating a neighbor's lot. Second, they can accept the conditions and settle for a natural garden, using bog and swamp plants that will endure the excessive water. If the condition is severe, it may be well not to try to have a lawn but to keep to the natural woodland, swampland look and pave those areas that are raised a bit for whatever outdoor living is possible.

A third alternative to consider is one that lies between these two: bring in some soil fill, making small hillocks and an undulating landscape with paths between them. Establish plantings on this filled land as detailed in the sketch on page 255. In this way trees and shrubs not normally tolerant of moist soil can adapt and put down roots and grow into the environment. Even some normally wetland subjects can get established better this way and more quickly come into their own and embellish the garden.

While the list of trees and shrubs that will survive wetland life is not as extensive as we might wish, there are some really fine plants among it. And there are probably regional or local native plants that could also be adapted. Again, consult your extension service or state agricultural college for local advice and help.

The first trees to leap to mind when wetlands are mentioned are the weeping willows, of which there are several good kinds. Although not recommended for small plots elsewhere because of their tendency to search out moisture by entering sewer pipes, in wetlands they would be in their element. Bald cypress, which grows in both the North and the South in swampy land, is likewise a candidate, but it may grow to very large proportions at maturity so it should be cautiously handled. A much smaller tree, one that is even bushy when cut back often is the French pussy willow, which roots readily in moist soils and can be pruned yearly for pussy willows for the house. Red or swamp maple, as you would guess from its name, inhabits moist to wet areas in its natural habitat—from Florida northward to well into Canada. It grows well in most soils, even well drained ones, but there it might not have the spectacular red or orange foliage that it assumes in moist and cold areas.

Another brilliant-colored tree with star-shaped leaves is the sweet gum, an eastern North American native hardy to Zone 4 in wet soil, that usually grows to less than its hundred-foot-plus mature height. Buy container-grown plants if possible, and plant very early in spring, because this tree is not easy to transplant, though worth all of the effort involved.

In swampy lands as far north as western Maine and southern Michigan, and southward to parts of Texas, the native tree known variously as sour gum, tupelo, or pepperidge tree is found. Donald Culross Peattie called it "water nymph of the forest," and it is a graceful, beautiful tree. It is moderate in height, at maturity perhaps sixty feet, and its lustrous, leathery leaves are always beautiful, outstandingly so in their brilliant red autumn dress. This tree, too, is difficult to transplant but may be purchased in containers, and it should be planted in earliest spring.

Although most magnolias are thought to be tender, even Southern plants like sweet bay magnolia may be hardy. A small evergreen tree in its home areas, it becomes deciduous and more shrublike in the North, often producing multiple stems, and there its fragrant white blossoms may remain in bloom a long time in late spring to early summer. It is hardy into Zone 5.

Few evergreens are really at ease in constantly moist soils, but the American arborvitae grows naturally along brook banks in southern Canada and our northern states. Hardy to Zone 2, it may grow to fifty feet at maturity but probably would grow less tall, and it may be cut back to maintain a lower height. It is a narrow, columnar tree, especially handsome in some of its cultivated varieties, which may also be planted in wetlands. Nursery-grown plants should not be sunk into a hole in really wet ground but set very shallowly and have soil mounded about the root ball so that they can accustom themselves to the new environment and thrive.

There is also a choice, but somewhat limited, among the shrubs for wet soils. Many are less decorative than some other cultivated types but some are quite interesting in various ways, offering qualities appreciated in a natural garden or one with natural overtones. Several of these shrubs are likely to grow less tall and less vigorously in really wet soil than in better-drained rich soil, but this may be an asset in a small garden.

Always found in wet to swampy soil are some members of the dogwood family. Particularly prized in winter for their colorful bark are the red osier, the Siberian and the yellowtwig dogwoods, often planted together. Both are hardy into Zone 2 and spread by underground roots. Also growing in moist woods and on hummocks in swampy ground is the diminutive dogwood bunchberry (*Cornus canadensis*), which needs acid soil and will adapt to a wetland garden in the Northeast and perhaps in varying conditions southward. It makes a good ground cover less than a foot tall.

The buttonbush is very tolerant of wet soil, grows to moderate height, and is hardy into Zone 4. Its fragrant white flowers appear in July and August. The red chokeberry will grow less tall in wet soil, but its clusters of white flowers and in autumn its bright red berries gleaming through its red foliage make it desirable for gardens to Zone 4. Evergreen sheep laurel needs acid soil and does best in wet, peaty swamp soil. It is hardy to Zone 2, bearing clusters of deep-rose flowers in June on two-foot high bushes. Often found nearby in Zones 2 through 5 is the rhodora, growing in boggy acid soils to three feet, making low-mounded masses with handsome blue-green foliage and masses of rosy purple flowers in May. There is a white-flowered variety sometimes available.

The intensely fragrant white blooms of swamp azalea come in July, the latest of the native species to bloom and growing as far north as Zone 3 in New England and Canada wherever acid soil gives it proper conditions and around bogs or in moist soil. Plant it on mounds to enable it to adjust and put forth its glossy leaves and blossoms.

The inkberry, hardy to Zone 3, is unusual in the holly family. Its evergreen leaves may turn purple in winter, and they are handsome the rest of the year in their lustrous green guise. Shiny black berries on female plants (male plants are also needed to produce the berries) make it attractive to birds in winter. It may grow less than half its usual mature fifteen-foot height in wet and northern soils. Acid soil and moisture are needed, but it is recommended to be planted on mounded soil to do its best in very wet conditions. Cultivated varieties are shrubbier and more compact than the native genus.

The southern holly, dahoon, is also a wetland plant, evergreen and bearing profusely conspicuous but small red berries lasting into winter. Its foliage, too, may turn purplish in winter, although its large leaves are green in the summer. It grows northward only to Zone 7.

Hardy to Zone 3, the winterberry or black alder, a deciduous holly, is found native to swampy land but also grows in well-drained soil, bearing bright red berries in clusters that last into winter after its leaves fall. It may reach eight or nine feet in height, and for berry production both male and female plants should be planted. The female plants bear the fruit.

Shadblow is a small tree in well-drained fertile soil but becomes shrubby in bog soil. Its pure white flowers are familiar sights in April on the edges of swamps, and it shines again in autumn with red or orange leaves. From the southern part of Zone 4 to northern Florida it grows naturally, doing best in moist rather than wet soil.

Even roses will grow in wet soil. The native swamp rose is tough enough to survive where little else will grow. Fragrant bright pink flowers in June are succeeded by cherry red seed pods in autumn, and in winter its young red stems are conspicuous. From Zone 4 southward it will thrive in moist to wet conditions.

Both highbush blueberry and arrowwood are unspectacular but dependable plants for wet soil. Both have blue fruit, but that of arrowwood is not edible while blueberries are delectable if you can get them before the birds reach them. Cultivated varieties may not do as well in the wetter soils as the native genus. Both plants bear flowers in clusters in May to June, both have good autumn foliage coloring, and both are hardy to Zone 3, arrowwood perhaps hardy into Zone 2. Blueberries require an acid soil, but arrowwood is tolerant of many kinds of soils and either dampness or well-drained conditions. Plant both on mounds of soil to enable them to adjust more easily.

There are probably many other local native plants that will do reasonably well in wetlands and bog plantings, but these are the ones that are widespread enough to make them known to be dependable as well as available. Should you want more floral effects and smaller plants, look for perennial plants that will either demand wet soil or will be tolerant of it. And, of course, many ferns will do very well in damp soil and shady conditions.

Thus you can see that it is possible to garden, making a virtue of bald necessity, no matter what your conditions may be.

TROPICAL AND SUBTROPICAL GARDENING

In the extreme southern reaches of the country, both in Florida and the Gulf Coast area and in parts of coastal California, it is possible to grow plants from the subtropical regions. Occasionally even a tropical tree or shrub will also survive in this warm climate. Palms and other lush vegetation make this a fascinating place in which to garden. But, because it is so special and needs plant material not applicable to outdoor gardening in other parts of the land, we regret that we cannot cover it fully. Those who live in these regions will find exceptionally beautiful and unusual plants available in local nurseries. The state agricultural college offers booklets and advice on plantings for these regions.

There are some other problems, not associated with climate or soil, wetness or dryness that also need special attention, and many gardeners are turning their thoughts in this direction, utilizing plants in clever ways to fulfill beautifully the special place in which they are planted. These plants deserve their own section.

PLANT TRAINING, TRICKS AND TREATS

For special places, problem places, the answer may be to train plants to fit and fill the need. It takes a bit of skill, but nothing extraordinary, and for gardening devotees willing to put in some extra time and effort to solve a problem it offers rewards. There are countless ways to train plants, utilizing them to expand and embellish the delights of your garden. Plants shaped in this way can perform extraordinary decorative and practical functions. The ways are ancient, but modern applications and methods make the success of these operations almost foolproof.

There are three categories of training that we will discuss: hedges, both formal and informal; topiary (*toe'-pee-airy*) works, somewhat akin to sculpturing but employing living green material; and espaliering (*es-pal'-yer-ing*), the training of plants to grow in limited areas, usually flat against a wall but often freestanding. Hedges and espaliering have both practical and aesthetic applications, while topiary work is carried out for purely creative and aesthetic reasons, often with a most amusing result.

How do these three methods differ, or are they alike?

HEDGES are useful for defining property boundaries in a pleasant, friendly way, or for obtaining privacy from neighborhood eyes and protection from wandering animals and children through a means much less forbidding than a fence or masonry wall. A hedge can also be a living windbreak, and when properly placed and maintained, it allows ventilation while slowing or arresting the force of prevailing winds that might make outdoor living areas cold and unpleasant. A hedge may either be sheared so that it looks like a solid wall of green or it may be merely a row of similar plants allowed to grow more or less in their natural habit.

TOPIARY is an art of ancient origin, certainly dating back to Roman times, and possibly of even more ancient Greek origin, although little solid fact about its history can be obtained. It may suffice to say that the art has been practiced for well over two thousand years, that it is known in various forms throughout the civilized world, and it is still going on and giving pleasure and occupation to gardeners in many lands. Topiary is related to hedges in that it employs plants that may be clipped. Certain small-leaved or needled plants are most often used because they look smoother in the end result. It is most like sculpture in that it is three dimensional and rarely two dimensional. Unlike sculpturing, however, the shaping

ALEPPO PINES, clipped in an oriental version of topiary, contrast graceful curves with the crisp lines of the house and walk in this West Coast garden. (*George Taloumis*)

ESPALIERED PEARS, trained in Belgian Fence cordons top a low stone wall, flower in early spring and in late summer provide a harvest of fine fruit. (*Paul E. Genereux*)

must go on each year in order to keep the plant within the bounds of the sculptor's intentions. In Europe there are some amusing and amazing examples, some hundreds of years old—birds, animals, chessmen, even a hedge surmounted by a complete hunt that features huntsmen, hounds, and fox running the length of the hedge. Some subjects are rather grotesque, some are beautiful, and the ones most frequently seen and employed here and abroad are the architectural and abstract motifs. Balls, obelisks, arches, scalloped hedges, leafy grottoes and other such forms are all part of the art of topiary.

ESPALIERING is the ancient art of limiting growth, usually flat against a wall or fence, and of compelling plants to grow within a limited space and to perform definite functions, often practical ones. Fruiting plants— apples, pears, peaches, and bush fruits—are most frequently espaliered. By limiting the number of twigs and branches allowed to grow, all the nutrition taken up by the roots is channeled into the remaining wood. Fruits are usually larger and better, and because of their trained form they are easier to harvest. There may be fewer fruit in number than if there had been space enough for the tree to grow to its full size, but the fruit will be more choice, and the espalier can be fitted into spaces in which no normal-sized tree would possibly fit. The trees are more convenient to look after, too; tending them and spraying is simplified. The decorative effects are legion, whether fruiting or purely flowering and leafing plants are employed. The photographs and sketches will demonstrate some of the possibilities of this interesting and productive skill.

LOOKING AT HEDGES

What kinds of hedges are best to plant?

The best hedge is the one that most nearly fits the task assigned to it. Your choice is wide: evergreen or deciduous plants; dwarf or tall-growing shrubs; even trees can be kept to reasonable proportions if yearly cutbacks, pruning, shearing, and clipping is done. Tall, treelike shrubs may also be useful, provided they are the kind that retain their lowest branches and limbs. A list of trees and shrubs for hedges is given at the end of this section.

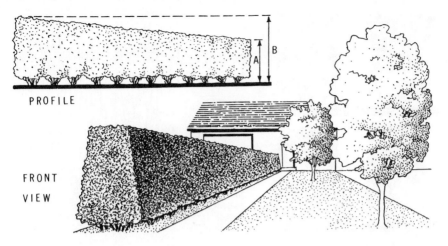

PROFILE

FRONT
VIEW

ENLARGEMENT PLANTING. Hedges can augment the visual length of a garden. Let the hedge grow higher nearest the point of usual observation (the house or terrace), then taper it gradually to the far end of the hedge. This will add several (visual) feet to a vista. Note the profile detail in which heights *A* and *B* can be related to the front view. Plant a taller tree close to the house, a lower-growing one at the far end of the lawn to heighten the distance effect.

If your property is small, are formal clipped hedges better than informal hedges?

So far as one can make a generalization, it may be best to have a sheared or clipped hedge, because it can be kept strictly limited to its narrow allotted area. A hedge, of course, can be of any size and kind of plant, provided the same kinds are planted in a row and maintained. The type of garden would also enter into the choice. If it were a natural garden, a tightly clipped hedge would be a false note, of course. But if the house and the garden design were traditional and formal, a hedge that followed straight lines and architectural effects would be quite in keeping with its surroundings. The height desired and the limits of width would naturally be the ultimate guiding and limiting factors.

Are informal hedges ever kept narrow?

Unsheared hedges can, of course, be kept narrower by selective pruning, but the more pruning that is done, the more formal will be the effect. Also, more work will be entailed, since selective pruning may be more time consuming than shearing if you are trying to keep the hedge to a very nar-

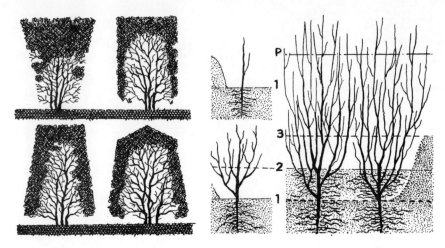

TRIMMING makes or breaks a hedge. Wedge-shaped, top left, gets lush growth on top but shades out lower branches which will die in time. Square-cut is better, although the bottom may also thin out and eventually die. Below, the Inverted-wedge gets light to all parts of its sloping sides and the Obelisk trim applies a double bevel to the top of the hedge.

QUICK AND THICK METHOD works well for California privet, to get a fine hedge quickly. *Right,* small plants are placed at wider than normal intervals in a deep furrow (1) and grown for a year until they branch. Furrow is then filled to (2) and grown a year to root and make good top growth. Fill the furrow to (3) and at the same time cut back the top to (P). By keeping it at this height another season a very thick hedge will result. In warm climates the process can be faster, two fillings a season.

row width. The best selling point for an informal hedge is usually that it can spread or sprawl, much as nature ordained, with only minimal cutting back needed to keep straggly shoots from spoiling the general effect or to thicken up the hedge in early years. Informal types may also employ a wider variety of plants than formal hedges—large or small, deciduous or evergreen, dull or shiny—and may or may not be flowering.

What kind of plants, then, are best for formal hedges?

In general, nonflowering plants are selected that are small leaved and with upright habits; thickly branched shrubs or small trees are best for this purpose. Upright growth immediately indicates that a narrower area is required for them, and small-leaved or needled plants give a more refined and smooth surface when clipped or sheared. Try to use a plant that at maturity is naturally somewhere near the height that you would like, for much less time will be spent in cutting back. Taller types can be kept to much less than normal height, but this will entail more work. While this

264

may seem rather limiting, there are really many choices, and climate and hardiness are actually the ultimate limiting factors. Think about whether an evergreen or a deciduous hedge will best fill your requirements. Evergreen hedges are presentable all year long, but deciduous hedges are also in many cases of some interest because of unusual twig structure or color. Deciduous hedges are sometimes faster growing than evergreens, but this need not be a major deciding point.

What are the major things to look for in plants for informal hedges?

Ordinarily, some of the same qualities that you look for in formal-hedge plants make good informal hedges. Upright growers and certainly ultimate height should govern your choices. Larger-leaved shrubs or trees, flowering kinds, and longer-needled evergreens may be utilized since the refined and smooth effects of sheared hedges need not be considered. However, a tighter structure than for specimen or border use is an asset, and the thorny kinds such as hawthorn and rugosa roses make an impenetrable hedge for most animals and all humans. Even low-growing barberries make good thorny barriers and in addition provide interesting berries and autumn color in the foliage. An informal hedge can be even more informal, if this is desired, by planting several kinds of plants but keeping those of the same sort grouped. Informal hedges need not be planted in a strict line but can bow in and belly out into wider growths or combine with shrub borders of informal character to achieve the privacy and barrier needs of the situation.

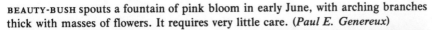

BEAUTY-BUSH spouts a fountain of pink bloom in early June, with arching branches thick with masses of flowers. It requires very little care. (*Paul E. Genereux*)

What other uses are there for formal hedges?

Oftimes formal hedges make architectural statements. Gateways, arches, and scalloped and crenelated patterns can be fashioned in the greenery by shearing and clipping. In a more subtle sense, a hedge can form a transition between the cold, hard materials of the house and other buildings and the warmer, living materials of the garden. Harmony between a formal house and a symmetrical garden is best maintained by the use of formal hedging. On the other hand, Japanese-inspired gardens, which are so often seen around modern homes, also have a certain formality, though of an asymmetrical balance. Moreover the very selectivity that is practiced in a true Oriental garden means that a kind of austerity and formality enters into the maintenance of the garden.

Are there any other uses for hedges?

First, let us review. Property boundaries are indicated by hedges, and privacy can be created and maintained by them. In addition, a hedge planting, even a low one, can act as a traffic guide or stopper where foot traffic across a lawn would produce wear and tear. Hedges can be used to screen trash and garbage containers from view of the house and from passersby. No gate will be needed if a baffle arrangement—a screening hedge plus a parallel hedge inside the area that is shorter in length, forming a kind of fence behind the access walk and gateway—is used. A low hedge, clipped or merely nipped back, can make shrubbery or flower-bed edges neat and emphatic. Hedges can be employed to enclose or partially enclose private or semi-private areas, while tall hedges can screen out unpleasant or unsightly vistas, acting also as windbreaks or as backgrounds for other plantings.

Are trees used as hedges?

Many trees readily lend themselves to this, and, amazing though it seems, even those that sometimes grow to considerable heights can be restricted to a moderate height by continual cutting back and shearing. One example is the Canadian hemlock, a native American evergreen tree that may reach a mature height of nearly a hundred feet, yet it can be kept down to six or eight, or possibly ten feet by keeping it cut back and sheared. Deciduous subjects include beech, certain elms and maples, Eastern white pine, and a number of other large evergreens, as you will note from the list at the end of this section. However, it should be pointed out here that constant yearly work, including two or more shearings are necessary to keep many of them cut back and within bounds. The large treelike shrubs may therefore be a better choice than tall trees mainly because they do not normally grow to more than twenty to twenty-five feet. Keeping them low would entail much less work.

Several of the yews are of shrubby habit or can be kept to moderate height by shearing. Japanese yew in some varieties, such as *Taxus cuspidata* 'Nana,' grows exceptionally slowly, reaching only a foot or less at maturity. Hick's yew (*Taxus media* 'Hicksii') or Tatfield yew (*Taxus media* 'Hatfieldi) are both upright in habit. Although Hatfield is by nature more pyramidal than the square-topped Hick's yew, it is in some ways more desirable and can be kept level and smooth by rigorous shearing of the top in its early years and by moderate clipping later. Japanese yew (*Taxus cuspidata*) normally grows to about fifty feet but can be kept much lower, of course. However, its 'Densa' form will grow only to four or five feet eventually, though usually spreading out to about twice that measure.

Depending upon climate and soil conditions, growth may be rapid or diminished, and various kinds of trees, evergreen and deciduous, may be considered for use within them. Perhaps local inquiries will turn up candidates that are so local that they are not on our list. Look under the list of trees, especially for columnar (pages 218–222) and dwarf types.

Are there many hedge plants that are thorny and make good barriers?

Many barberries have thorns and grow to various heights. Don't overlook warty and wintergreen barberries; both are evergreen and would make good informal hedges. Several others are semi-evergreen to evergreen in mild climates, and a number can be sheared. Dwarf Magellan barberry is notably low growing and would make a good low hedge. The hardy orange (*Poncirus trifoliata*) is often used in the South for its dense growth, long spines, and its leathery dark green leaves. It needs protection in areas north of Philadelphia. Hawthorns, of course, make good barriers when kept dense and low, and many varieties of the rose family with sparsely- to thickly-thorned stems are excellent. Firethorn also can be developed into a thorny barrier, particularly when espaliered or branches are interwoven. Buckthorn, some of the barbed-leaved hollies, and Oregon holly grape also might be considered.

Can hedges produce fruit or berries?

Pruning and shearing will, of course, remove a great many of the fruiting or berry-producing and flowering shoots. However, some shrubs and trees—hawthorns, buckthorn, English holly to name a few, and shrubs such as bayberry, some viburnums, and roses, if allowed to produce their red seed pods, may be colorful with fruit even though lightly trimmed.

How can you speed up thickening and branching of hedges? Should you plant more plants or is there another way?

With most, putting more plants to the linear foot of row will thicken the hedge temporarily, but as plants age, the competition by the roots for nutrition will make a weaker hedge and will thus work against what you are striving for. The best way is to keep plants cut back severely when young, forcing side growth that will thicken the lower part of the hedge. Periodic sharp cutbacks will do the same as the hedge grows upward. However, with quick growers and easy-rooting plants, such as common privet and others of the Privet family, the method shown in the sketch on page 264 will be a means of getting quick and thick growth, although it is a bit more work. Digging a trench and planting small hedge plants in it, then by degrees filling the trench and letting shoots root is the trick here. This method was used in the late nineteenth and early twentieth centuries, but has been rarely employed in the past fifty years.

PLANTS FOR HEDGES

There are several points to consider when selecting a hedge plant: climate and hardiness, soil—wet, average, or dry, purpose of hedge—privacy (tallness, thickness), decorative quality (texture of leaves), impenetrability (thick-branched and/or thorny), whether it is to be a formal sheared hedge or an informal natural one, the space available for it, and whether or not it should be evergreen. The final point is the height to which the hedge grows naturally, vital if it is to be informal, work-saving if it is to be sheared. Medium-height and low-growing categories follow. Further data about climate and height will be found in the complete small, medium-height and tall lists of shrubs.

SMALL HEDGE PLANTS—1 to 4 feet

Arborvitae, Dwarf cultivars
Barberry, Dwarf, low-growers
Box, low-growers
Coralberry, Chenault
Cranberry-bush, Dwarf (Dwarf snow-
    ball)

Euonymus, Dwarf cultivars
Euonymus, Japanese
Germander
Holly-grape, Oregon
Hydrangea, Hills of Snow
Lavender-cotton

Lavender, True
Pachistima
Pine, Dwarf Mugo
Skimmia, species
Snowball, Dwarf, *see Cranberry-bush*

Spirea, Dwarf and low species
St. Johnswort
Willow, Dwarf
Yew, Dwarf cultivars of species

MEDIUM HEIGHT—4 to 8 feet*
Abelia, Glossy
Andromeda, species
Arborvitae, Dwarf globe
Barberry, medium-height species
Bayberry (Eastern)
Black-alder (*Ilex*)
Box, medium-height cultivars
Buffalo-berry, Russet
Indian-currant
Deutzia, Lemoine and cultivars
   Pride of Rochester
   Slender
Euonymus, Dwarf winged
Firethorn, species and cultivars
Forsythia, Siebold
Holly, species and cultivars
   Chinese and cultivars
   Inkberry
Honeysuckle, species and cultivars

Jetbead
Juniper, medium-height species,
   cultivars
Mockorange, Lemoine and cultivars
   Virginal and cultivars
Pea-tree, Chinese
Pine, Mugo
Quince, Flowering and cultivars
Rose, native species and cultivars
   Rugosa and cultivars
Snowberry
Spirea, Billiard
   Garland
   Vanhoutte
Viburnum, medium-height species
Weigela, Early
   Flowering and cultivars
Yew, cultivars of medium-height

TAKING UP TOPIARY

Do any small-home gardeners still do topiary today?

It is surprising how many are interested in this ancient art and practice it. Lip-service gardeners, those who just want to get by, will not, of course, want to take on anything that requires a bit more time, a little skill, and creativity. But the same sort of person who will go to great lengths to create bonsai—dwarfed plants in containers—will also take to the creation of green sculpture, as some term topiary. Few will want to have more than one or two pieces in their garden, of course, though there are estates in this country that feature entire living museums of topiary pieces. One or two pieces accenting a garden are not much for a gardener to maintain, and anyone who wishes to pursue this hobby will find it an absorbing, enjoyable, and amusing occupation that gives distinction to any garden.

---

* Note that many of these plants are best used as natural, unsheared hedges.

Why not let the plant grow naturally?

There are numbers of gardeners who will take up the cudgels against "torturing" plants by making them into topiary pieces. Many times after lecturing on European and English gardens in which I showed slides of topiary work and suggested that anyone interested might introduce this into his garden, I have been bearded by audience members. These militant people, at least as blue-stockinged as they were green-thumbed, seemed to feel that I was some sort of plant vivisectionist. After talking reasonably with some of them, I found that they had no objections whatever to hedges. In fact, all of them pruned plants to shape and control them. I then made the point that topiary work was not essentially different, except that it required an aesthetic sense—as well as a sense of humor.

Nobody is going to be forced to do topiary work, but those who wish to try it may take heart and derive comfort from the argument above. All gardening is artificial to some extent, which is why we speak today of "natural" gardens rather than "wild" gardens. Natural gardens give the effect of nature, whereas wild gardens are exactly as nature formed them, with nothing added and nothing whatever taken away (even debris, I would presume).

What kind of plant is most suited to topiary shaping?

There are quite a number, although the best candidates are those with small leaves or tightly packed needles. These take to shearing and survive it with grace and beauty. The most often employed is yew, the heavily needled sort such as Hatfield yew being capable of quick recovery from shearing and making a very tight, smooth effect as time goes on. Boxwood and perhaps escallonia would also be interesting in their way, while Aleppo pine has been used on the West Coast for the kind of free-form topiary pieces that fit with Oriental-garden plans. Some of the small-leaved myrtles, the kind that do not grow to any great height and are used in Zones 8 to 9 for hedges, would be good subjects. In the North I have seen pot-grown topiaries formed of them that are taken indoors in winter and grace terraces in summer. In short, any dense-branching, small-leaved plants, particularly evergreens, might be candidates. Those recommended for low, tight hedges probably would also come in for scrutiny if the more usual types do not seem to suit your needs.

A TOPIARY ELEPHANT, sculptured from living green, performs the year round in its circle of neat low hedges in an American garden famous for its topiary. (*Paul E. Genereux*)

What kind of motifs are used for topiary?

The easier kinds are the geometrical types and architectural accents, such as balls, obelisks, finial shapes, discs of varying thickness succeeding each other with varying spaces between them and pointed or bullet-nosed tops to finish off the head. More ambitious and clever craftsmen fashion animals—elephants, pigs, dogs, cats, squirrels, foxes, and so on—or birds, some in flight, some sitting, peacocks displaying their tails, or swans serenely swimming atop a hedge. Chessmen and humans are also often used as subjects. Whatever strikes the fancy of the creator and whatever his talent or gift might allow him to complete seems to be the rule of the craft.

The classic way is to have a wire form made of the subject, fit it over the top of the growing plant, and induce the leader inside to form as many short spurs as possible. Then, as the growing top sends shoots out of the form, they are clipped back again and again until the shape is filled and

271

the wire form is no longer seen. However, a wire form is not necessary unless you are making an exceptionally fine, small topiary. I have seen freehand examples that rank high and have myself formed a topiary cat, working year by year with the idea of what I wanted to produce firmly implanted in my mind. This cat is seated on one side of a window watching a bird on the other side. The bird was started on a wire topiary form brought from England. Both, I think, will pass muster, though the methods of creating each were utterly different.

If the beginner is timid, perhaps a good way to start would be to shape a single plant, using the simple square, ball, or obelisk motif and watching how the plant grows and responds. Then when his confidence is greater, he might improvise and create more elaborate sculpture. If he decides against continuing, the plant will probably grow out and can be trimmed into a hedgelike form, so that nothing is really wasted.

How long does it take to shape a topiary piece?

This will depend somewhat on the subject and also on the size of the plant you start with. It will certainly not be an instant project. Sizable pieces begin to show their forms within four to six years after beginning for it takes time to fill out. Geometric pieces will reach their goal sooner than will more elaborate subjects, but again, it depends on the material used to form the topiary. Privet would be faster but will in the end require more frequent trimming back, so that quicker goals are perhaps a false economy of the time spent.

How often do topiaries have to be sheared or trimmed?

Two, three, or even four times a year, depending on the plant material and the climate. For shearing the soft new growth of my Hick's yew topiary I use a little cordless electric grass clipper, the rechargeable type. This can quickly go over quite sizable pieces and do more delicate work than an electric hedge shear. However, for large works and for the straight-line and solid areas, this latter is most useful and does the work quickly and efficiently. Watch your topiary, and when growth gets to an inch or a bit more, shear it back. This will induce thickening that in time gives a very solid-looking piece of green sculpture. Be sure to shear before winter dormancy, for fresh green growth hardens and is more difficult to remove in spring. Besides, a solid-topped mass will withstand snow better than one that catches it and bends twigs to open fissures that are unsightly.

ENGAGING IN ESPALIERING

Why do people distort plants into espaliers?

The original reason was probably to produce more fruit in a small available space. This is still a valid reason, as is the ease with which such plants can be sprayed, pruned, and the fruits harvested in the limited space. A small-home garden can produce quite a harvest if several espaliers are included in the plans, far more than if only one or possibly two plants were grown in the same total square footage. It is an excellent way to produce fruit or decorate blank walls without sacrificing valuable space that could be used for outdoor living or growing other plants. In cold areas, it may be a way to grow doubtfully hardy plants, especially fruiting ones—for example, by placing the espalier against an east wall that is protected from cold winds and frost; the morning sun, even in summer,

FLOWERING DOGWOOD, trained flat against a wall, is informally espaliered, as a delightful background for a terrace, whether bare-limbed or in full leaf. (*George Taloumis*)

will never make the wall too hot, and the warmth will linger throughout the day and into the evening.

Another reason for espaliering is for decorative effects. Where a too-narrow plot exists, between a walk or driveway and a building, for example, most plants would spread too much and interfere with human or vehicular traffic. An espalier will take the place of or will supplement the low upright plants that would seem to be the only answer, patterning the bare wall and making a feature of a problem space. Living greenery can frame windows and give diagonal or other patterns to a wall or fence that would be an eyesore or at best nondescript.

How is espaliering done?

You can create your own or you may purchase plants already started and formed into patterns of various sorts. These sell for prices that reflect the age of the plant and the necessary care that has been put into training it. However, the amateur who is patient and willing to work with plants can learn to make his own espaliers and will derive considerable creative satisfaction from engaging in this practical as well as aesthetic garden craft. Briefly, what is entailed is selecting a promising plant, tying a frame to it, and then, as new wood forms, carefully bending it into shape, thus encouraging it to grow in the direction intended. Excess growth and side branches are ruthlessly removed. With fruit trees, the preferred method is to buy a one- or two-year-old whip with buds opposite or nearly opposite at the approximate positions where "arms" are to branch out for training. Leaders, the top shoots, are left on for a time, or they may be shortened to force side arm growth. Branching should start low on the trunk. New and soft growth can be pinched out, with only selected spurs allowed to remain and fruit. The shoots that are allowed to remain and form the other branches of the espalier will be bent into place and fastened to the frame for training. Eventually, when growth is strong enough and well set the frame can be removed.

Are there any places aside from houses where you can grow espaliers?

In addition to fences, already mentioned, retaining walls or other garden walls are possibilities. Many gardeners also use them for living fences, to define the limits of the food garden, or to make a decorative side "wall" to a terrace. In the open, where light and air can reach all sides, they may be even more successful. Tending fruit espaliers is also more easily accomplished when access to both sides is provided.

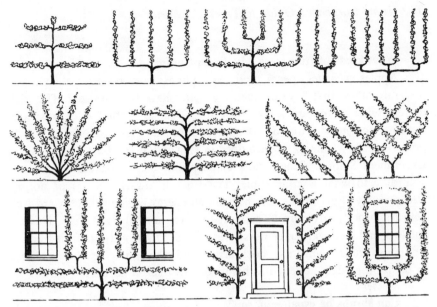

ESPALIERING of plants is a generic term, embracing a multitude of forms. Among them are the horizontal branching, with single, double, or multiple horizontal cordons and various U-shaped forms, as seen in the top row. Fan-shaped cordons, either spring from a single trunk or are made up of multiple shoots. Closely spaced horizontal cordons make beautiful "fences," and the crisscross Belgian Fence type that may be composed of single cordons (left), growing at an angle or Y-shaped ones that grow at opposite angles to form squares or diamonds. Sometimes, as in the bottom row, various forms combine to decorate a wall space and gracefully fill it, frame a doorway with spring blossoms and later fruit, or surround a window or merely make a triumph of a bare wall.

Can you do espaliering in every part of this country?

The extreme northern parts of the country might be fatal to some kinds of plants, and conditions are not conducive to growing many fruiting plants in this region. However, anything that is hardy in that area could be wall-trained, and hardy shrubs could be inveigled into making a fan or other shape against a wall. Southward, dogwood is a possible subject, and certain magnolias not ordinarily hardy very far north are good wall subjects. Magnolias are espaliered against walls in Princeton University in New Jersey. In the South and warm parts of the country subtropical plants could probably be espaliered, although if the climate is conducive to excessive growth, it may mean a good deal of work during most of the growing season to keep the plants in check.

275

What kinds of fruit trees take to espaliering?

Apples, peaches, pears, and even plums have been espaliered and probably others that have escaped my notice have been utilized. The trick to remember is to buy *dwarf* fruit trees—those grafted onto a special dwarfing rootstock. Most dwarf apples are on an East Malling rootstock, probably East Malling IX, developed in England at the East Malling Fruit Experiment Station. Other fruits employ different rootstocks, of course, according to what is compatible. The fruit on dwarf trees is of normal size, possibly larger than usual, because all energy is channeled toward fruit with less woody structure to support than on normal sized trees. Nursery catalogs and local garden centers offer several kinds of dwarf fruit trees.

Bush fruits—currants, gooseberries, and others, may also be espaliered in the food garden, attached to bamboo rods tied on horizontal wires.

Can shrubs be espaliered, too?

Many shrubs, especially the taller ones, can be espaliered or if not espaliered in the usual sense at least trained to grow fan-fashion against walls. Abroad, many shrubs, common and uncommon, are seen flat-trained against walls where space is constricted. In England's Kew Gardens there is a special brick-walled section where a great many specimen shrubs are trained against the walls.

An unobtrusive wire-fencing section may be fastened to any wall, about an inch out from it, if possible. Canes of shrubs are then bound loosely to this with twine or Twist'ems and kept in place until they are trained flat. All forward-growing shoots are cut back, which takes a bit of time and patience; lateral or side growth is kept, but thinned. Almost anything that will grow in your climate, particularly those shrubs with sturdy central trunks or canes, can be trained against walls to grow and bloom there.

What would be an easy plant for an amateur to start with on a wall?

In the shrub category, the vigorous forsythia that is hardy in Zone 5, is both inexpensive and widely available. One of the types that is upright in habit, such as Fortune forsythia, rather than those that arch or droop would be better suited to training on a wall, although several of the "droopers" are easily trained, according to reports in garden journals. Dogwood, with its horizontal branching habit, also lends itself to this treatment, the forward-growing twigs and other growth being merely trimmed off. While I have never seen sour gum or pepperidge trees actually espaliered, a volunteer seedling that was discovered in my own garden somewhat behind a tree lilac is now being denuded of back- and front-branching, while side shoots are allowed to extend horizontally in both directions. At about fifteen feet tall, it can be topped and the side branches will be allowed to grow until they reach the perimeters dictated by the space available. It has handsome leathery leaves of lustrous green that turn brilliant scarlet in autumn. Other plants easy to deal with include pyracantha or firethorn, yew, and the magnolias, where they are hardy.

How does an amateur go about espaliering fruit trees—apples, let us say?

The easiest type is the single cordon. This is one that is grown from a young whip (one-year or two-year tree) with all side branching excluded. It can grow vertically or it can be induced to grow obliquely. Both are best grown in multiple numbers. When single cordons cross (or sometimes when a single plant has opposite buds trained to grow at 45-degree angles) and intersections create diamond shapes or squares, this is called the Belgian Fence cordon method.

Purchase several one-year-old or older apples of the varieties you wish to grow, making sure they are on the same kind of dwarfing stock (East Malling IX or other) and the whips as straight trunked as possible. Prepare the soil as for any planting and set the trees, making sure that the grafting union or knob is about 4 inches above ground level (this will prevent the normal-sized upper part from rooting and nullifying the dwarfing of the rootstock) and that the trunk is vertical. If an angular planting is done, be sure to keep the knob on the upper side of the plant so that any pressures exerted will not later on force open the union.

For vertical training, a wire can be fastened at the top and bottom of the wall, with at least 6 inches space behind the tree and away from the wall. The whip is loosely secured to this wire. Or drive a stake or long pole into the soil beside the whip when it is being planted, making certain with a carpenter's level that it is truly vertical and the whip secured to it will be, too, as it grows upward.

For angle training, either build a wooden framework or set sturdy tall fence posts at either end of the area for planting. To these, attach securely clothesline or other heavy wire at 12-inch intervals. Then wire sturdy bamboo poles in place vertically on these horizontal wires at the intervals set for planting. Usually this is 2 to 3 feet depending on the variety or kind of tree being planted. Then dig holes and plant the trees, with the grafting union 4 inches above ground, and fasten the whips to the bamboo poles. As the cordons grow, there will be a need to extend the poles by either replacing them with longer ones or fastening others to them. Eventually, the fence posts and wires can be removed as the cordons reach the proper height and the tree gets stronger. For Belgian Fence training, two sets of poles are bound to the wires at opposite angles and on opposite sides of the wires.

How do you prune espaliered fruits?

The first summer after setting, particularly with one-year-old stock, do not cut back side growth (laterals) but prune it back to a promising bud, to about 4 to 6 inches, or to retain only three leaves. This can be done as leaves sprout or it can be done just before leaves fall in autumn. Every year thereafter *summer* pruning will be in order: About mid-July shorten all laterals from the main stem to about 4 inches, cutting just above a leaf. Other laterals arising from an existing spur (a lateral already pruned back in previous years) are shortened to just above one leaf of the new growth. In September any late growth is pruned as above, and any growth that has come from the July pruning is removed completely. Try to keep about 5 to 6 inches between laterals for spacing fruit and not overcrowding the cordons. When heavy fruiting occurs, it is a good plan to remove some of the small fruits before they sap strength that should go into producing larger and juicier mature fruit.

How are branching espaliers formed?

First decide on the form you wish the espalier to take, selecting one of the forms in the sketch on page 275. Wherever two buds occur on opposite or nearly opposite sides is a good place to start the branching. If double branching or triple branching is desired, then look for others above. If the central leader is not to be a part of the scheme, cut it back to the topmost promising buds to force the lateral growths into more vigorous production. Build your framework (for horizontal work a sturdy frame is more desirable than wires) and fasten the growth to it, bending down the fresh and pliable growth when it is young and easy to manage. Keep new growth bound to the frame until it reaches the limit of the space allotted and then bend it upward and fasten it to the vertical framework. If you wish to make another division, as in the U-shaped espaliers, again find two opposite buds and force side growth by cutting off the vertical leader. Repeat the horizontal and vertical training. In the meantime shorten the laterals to create fruiting spurs as detailed above, keeping them well spaced apart.

If growth is too vigorous as the tree begins to take hold, and long extra-soft growth results, root pruning may be in order. About 18 inches out from the trunk, thrust a sharp spade to about its full length into the soil in early spring. This will cut the roots and force new growth from them, while keeping aboveground growth and leaves down to a more normal rate. Removing some of the leafage during the summer will also slow growth, since it reduces the leaf area necessary for the photosynthesis process to take place. Espalier trees can be productive for many years if properly managed, and they will be decorative as well as useful.

How are the ornamental plants trained for espaliers?

The manner is similar to that for fruit trees in that some sort of support or framework is usually employed until growth hardens into the direction the gardener desires. Evergreens such as yew are usually trained in fan-fashion, while firethorn can be trained in a number of different ways. A framework can be set against a wall or out from it, or sometimes an espalier can be trained merely by fastening it to a wood or masonry wall, setting in the wall screw eyes or hooks to which the new wood can be fastened.

Do you prune and cut back on decorative espaliers like the fan shape?

Yes. Every spring as soon as growth starts, pruning should be done on fan shapes. Since many plants normally grow upright, cut back to an outward-facing bud (see illustration on page 292) to start the new growth in that section in the right direction. By bud selection you can ease the work of training somewhat. Keep the lateral growth cut back so that the lines of the plant will show cleanly. With yew, cut back the leader sharply each year in the young years so that new growth is forced along the stem or main growth. This will thicken up and make a handsome espalier. When it reaches its limit of growth, keep the lateral cut back, and shorten or remove excess growth along the stem to the length necessary for maintaining the pattern cleanly.

If the gardener is keenly interested in espaliering, it is suggested that he seek further advice and direction from his state agricultural college or extension service. There are also some books or pamphlets available through libraries that will provide further assistance. Should he wish to experiment with it on a small scale, trial pieces may be tried, using small shrubs such as creeping cotoneaster (*Cotoneaster adpressa*) as subjects. Tender small shrubs such as rosemary, not hardy in the North, may be espaliered growing in pots, taken indoors for the winter and serve as a decorative showpiece for the outdoor garden in summer.

INFORMAL TRAINING OF SHRUBS ON WALLS

As suggested earlier, many shrubs can be forced and trained to narrower than normal growth against a wall or fence. Plant the shrub, rigorously prune off any canes that try to come forward, and restrain others by fastening them to the wall or fence. Pruning back leaders on canes to an upward- or side-facing bud will keep growth headed in a compact direction. In a sense, it is somewhat like shearing a hedge, except that growth is kept headed back and definitely forward-growing shoots are pruned back to the main stem. Strive for an interesting pattern of growth with deciduous material, realizing that in winter only the pattern of the twig and stem growth will be seen. This can be very beautiful.

Choose, if possible, shrubs that are of the approximate height at maturity as the space allotted. While it may happen that growth will be more vigorous in the retained canes and stems and the shrub will eventually grow taller than normal if allowed to do so, still the work of pruning will be lessened if the gardener need not keep trying to restrain growth from a plant that is normally much taller.

In the lists that follow will be found many shrubs for many zones and for many uses. There are doubtless others that can be employed for the three purposes detailed here, depending upon local climate and plant material available, and there is always the chance that an enterprising amateur will develop new material. After all, nobody ever knows whether or not things will work until they are tried. But the rudiments are presented, and where you go from there is up to you.

POSSIBLE PLANTS
FOR ESPALIERING, WALL TRAINING

	HARDI-NESS ZONE		HARDI-NESS ZONE
TALL—6 TO 18 FEET:		Japanese	4
		Viburnum, various	3–5
Buckthorn	2		
Camellia, sasanqua	7		
Cotoneaster, Himalayan	7	MEDIUM HEIGHT—3 TO 8 FEET:	
Euonymus, Winged	3	˙Cotoneaster, Spreading	5
Filbert (Hazel), Purple-		Euonymus, Dwarf-winged	3
leaved	3–4	Holly, Japanese convex-	
Firethorn (*Pyracantha*)	5–6	leaved	5
Forsythia, various	5	Quince, Flowering	4
Holly, Chinese 'Burfordii'	6–7	Rosemary	6
Jasmine, Winter	5		
Magnolia, Star	5		
Mockorange	5	LOW-GROWING—1½ TO 4 FEET:	
Photinia, Smooth	4	Cotoneaster, Creeping	4
Chinese	7	Rock spray	4
Redbud, Chinese	6	Holly, Japanese 'Helleri'	6
Tamarix	4	Ivy, Baltic or English	4–5
Yaupon	6–7	Jessamine, Carolina (Con-	
Yew, English	6	federate)	6
Hatfield	4	Juniper, Sargent	4
Hicks	4	Yew, Dwarf Japanese	4

7

To Have and To Hold—
Maintenance

Once a garden is planted it must be maintained if it is to keep growing and blooming. This is easiest done when a program is set up to keep it neat and healthy. Some people prefer to make out a schedule and adhere to it come hell or excessive moisture. Others are in favor of a more relaxed method, doing the necessary chores at about the regular time they should take place, though not on the dot. There is nothing wrong with either plan, so long as the work gets done and trees and shrubs are given the care that is necessary.

The main concern, of course, is to see that they get enough food and water, that they are pruned when necessary, and that winter protection is provided where this is required. All plants need some pruning or they may grow straggly, may cease to bloom, or disease may enter when a storm snaps a branch or limb. Some plants grow too much in one area and not enough in others, so that the stragglers must be nipped back and the symmetry of the plant maintained. In order to know what is needed, this chapter will cover the general needs of plants.

WATER

As we have repeatedly stated, water is a prime requisite of all plants. Even desert plants need some moisture, for it is the lifeblood of the plant world. Foods present in the soil—the minerals and nutrients naturally occurring or applied by the gardener—can be taken up only when in solution, in liquid form. The feeding roots absorb this and send it along the production line to produce leaves and cell growth in the woody parts of the plants. It is astounding how many gallons of water even a moderate-sized tree can absorb and transpire in the course of a day, provided the moisture is there, of course. In wet springs, trees and shrubs make quick and vigorous growth of twig and leaf. If the summer proves to be dry and the roots cannot find enough water to sustain this lush growth, the tree will discard its leaves, and shrubs may also drop whatever cannot be fed and watered. Gardeners often become concerned over these summer drops of leaves when it is merely the lack of adequate rainfall or watering, unless it is an excessive leaf fall.

Leaf production, fruiting, and flowering depend upon adequate moisture, the amount varying with the nature of the plant. The type of soil also enters into the picture for this is important for good drainage. Plants need

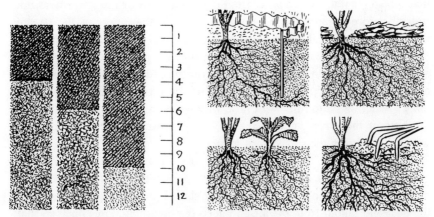

WATER ABSORPTION varies according to soil conditions. The same amount of water applied to three kinds of soil penetrates. *Left,* very little in clay soil; much is lost in runoff. *Center,* average soil with humus content absorbs more, retains it deeper and longer. *Right,* sandy soil lets water course through quickly and be lost, and is likely to allow evaporation, too.

to have air penetrate occasionally to the roots, as it does in well-drained soils. If the soil is too heavy and too continuously waterlogged, most plants will not profit from the water. A few, of course, like swamp and muck-soil plants, thrive best in an approximation of their natural habitat, but they are the exception.

Watch the weather carefully if you live in an area of regular rainfall. A light shower is not enough to give your plants the moisture they need, and you should then apply hose water. A shower may wet only the top half inch of soil, and a quick deluge may run off before it has penetrated more than a couple of inches. Use your judgment, and if you are in doubt, take a trowel and dig up a bit of soil to see how deep the moisture has penetrated. Remember, too, that leafage on trees and shrubs will deplete the amount of moisture that reaches the soil beneath, so that some irrigation under them may be in order. A drizzly rain that goes on for a day and a night is the most satisfactory natural watering, for the fine droplets will be absorbed, not run off and be lost to the plants and the soil.

In dry-land country, watering the garden is a way of life—every day and sometimes twice a day is the rule. Mulches are needed here even more than in places where it rains frequently, in order to conserve ground moisture and prevent evaporation. Mulches will also break the force of the driving showers that are often found in this part of the country. See pages 321–334.

Applying water with a hose must be done thoroughly but gently so that the soil is not washed away from the plant roots or the water does not run off before it can soak in. A way to restrain the power of the stream is to use a force-breaker—a metal contraption put on the end of the hose that has small holes in the receptacle so that no great force is exerted in any one place. An old woolen sock tied over the end of the hose will achieve much the same effect, but the faucet should be turned on only halfway. A longer watering period but with little wastage is the result. Apply water at the base of the shrubs, not on the leaves, to prevent mildew. In any case water is needed in the soil, not on leaves.

Water in early or late morning or midafternoon, not at night. This gives roots moisture at the time they are prepared to make the best use of it. Occasionally hose off the foliage of shrubs and evergreens to remove the dust and fallout from the air and keep the breathing pores open so that they can function. This will also make them look fresher.

Don't let plants, especially needled and broad-leaved evergreens, go into winter with dry soil. If the autumn is not normally rainy, water the shrubbery beds up to the time the ground freezes, for after that moisture cannot penetrate. In mild areas, water occasionally during the winter, whenever the ground gets dry. One exception might be the desert, where a special set of conditions prevails.

In spring start watering as soon as the ground thaws or as soon as buds begin to swell in mild areas. Don't overwater or overfeed, or the tender growth induced may get nipped by late frosts.

FOOD

Plants need occasionally feeding, but it is my conviction that in America we overfeed—force-feed—plants, giving them more than they can absorb. Double the amount of food recommended does not give double the growth. In fact, some of the food may be wasted, for plants can absorb only so much and the rest may be leached away into the soil. This may profit deep-rooted trees, but shallower-rooted plants will not be appreciably helped. Therefore, a good rule is to apply only moderate amounts at one time but make feedings relatively frequent. In traveling abroad I have found that gardeners use far less plant food than we do yet have better growth. I would conjecture that this is because they have more moisture, especially in England, and the foods are therefore in solution, ready to be taken up.

A good rule for trees is to use a pound of balanced plant food to an inch of diameter of the trunk, spreading it on the surface or placing it in holes (see sketch on page 160) around the tree. Start at least a foot out from the trunk. Shrubs should be fed in spring as growth begins or early in the season. Do not feed after mid-July in the North, in August to early September in the South, to avoid forcing tender growth that will be injured by the winter's cold.

Proper foods are important because different plants need different diets. Needled evergreens seem to thrive best on a high-nitrogen plant food. In cold and windy areas, a feeding late in the year after growth has ceased but before the ground is frozen will provide sustenance that will help to minimize the rigors of winter sun and wind. The formula suggested for evergreens is 10-6-4. Numerals on the bag symbolize the three major plant food components: Nitrogen (10), Phosphorus (6), and Potassium (4), as the ratio to each other. Numerals are always in this order on all commercial fertilizers. Some also provide trace minerals—elements that are needed but only in small quantities and that may be lacking in old farmed or gardened soils. The Big Three are used up regularly and need replacement accordingly.

Deciduous trees, especially the flowering ones, will probably do quite well on the 5-10-5 formula, which is a good general fertilizer. A high-nitrogen fertilizer might foster more leaf growth than flower production in many shrubs and small trees.

Most broad-leaved evergreens (except for boxwood, which will do well on a regular 10-6-4 fertilizer) should have a special acid-formula food. Cottonseed meal, an organic product, is also suggested for use with them as an occasional dressing on the soil.

What is the difference between organic and chemical fertilizers?

This is a question that is still being debated between exponents of natural gardening and those who take a scientific view. Where no food plants are being grown, both are acceptable, in my view, so that the question comes down to which is most convenient, least expensive, or best for the individual. I use both organic and chemical fertilizers in my own garden.

Organic Fertilizers: These are natural materials such as animal manures, generally lower in analysis of the elements and slower acting for the most part than are chemical fertilizers. One distinct advantage is that as they decompose and enter the soil, they will improve the soil structure as they slowly release their nutrients. Some fertilizers that are best placed under the chemical category are advertised to have an organic base. Any imbalance of the organics is presumably corrected by additives of chemicals to bring them up to strength as well as balance.

Chemical Fertilizers: These are the most widely available and are on the whole cheaper than the organic types. Often called "balanced plant foods", they are produced chemically and in strengths great enough to require considerable inert matter to be mixed with them in order to distribute the nutrients properly. They are likely to burn tender small roots on contact, and will also burn leaves if allowed to remain on them, because they are so quick acting. Since they are so rapidly used up, they are likely to need frequent applications. Some kinds are now billed as "slow release" because they are produced in ways that allow for slow breaking down over a longer period. In open and sandy soils these fertilizers are likely to leach away quickly, and roots cannot take full advantage of them. Here the organic types would be used to better advantage. In heavy soils, nutrients are held longer, especially in cool weather.

What fertilizer type is best?

In my view all are acceptable if used properly. Where organic materials, such as manure, are available, they may certainly be used. Where they are not—and increasingly this is so—other kinds must be used. Composting garden wastes is a good practice. All leaves that fall, all the small twigs, and discarded plants can be piled up to decompose, making a rich, humusy material that can be applied to the shrub beds. Some people use a high-nitrogen fertilizer to speed up decomposition, putting down a six-inch layer of plant material each time the wastes are available and scattering handfuls of fertilizer over it before applying a three-inch layer of soil. Keeping the pile moist will help to speed decomposition. Even large twigs can be kept in a compost pile and will eventually decompose to make a fibrous humus. Sifting the compost and, if desired, adding some chemical fertilizer to it before distributing it on the shrub beds, is a good way of adding fertility while improving soil structure.

PRUNING AND REPAIRS

Shrubs and trees almost always need pruning of some sort. The ones that need it least are the evergreens. Yearly pruning—occasional sharp cutbacks for renewal of the shrub—will result in healthy, lively growth with new shoots and bringing flowers and fruits. Plants need to be kept within bounds so that future troubles do not occur. Straggly shoots are cut back to preserve the symmetry of the shrubs, and new growth can be directed upward or outward, according to the cut. (See page 288.) Branches should not be allowed to encroach on walks or other traffic areas. Hedges, of course, need shearing if they are of the formal type, and sometimes two or more shearings are required each year. Informal hedges will need periodic examination to see that the hedge is kept somewhat restricted, neat, and not straggly, by heading back some branches. Depending upon the climate, such hedges will need attention each year.

Why is pruning back at planting done?

When a deciduous tree or shrub is planted, it is customary to do some pruning. Good nursery specimens will require little, but even they may profit from a little cutback. Evergreens are seldom pruned or only lightly. Thinning out the branches on a tree, cutting back the branches in general,

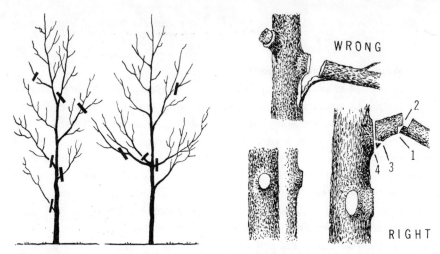

EARLY PRUNING removes future tree hazards. *Left,* removal of lower limbs as tree grows puts strength into upper growth for a high head. Double leader (twin top) will cause weak crotch and splitting if it is allowed to stay. Remove weaker leader near trunk. Cut back side branches that will soon be encroached on by lower limbs as they grow. *Right,* keep tree within bounds by removing some wide limbs, especially those that make a bad junction opposite a stronger one. Keep silhouette narrow.

Right, limb removal is a tricky task. A single cut (wrong) near trunk will let falling limb tear down bark and leave a bad wound. Correct method is to cut first (*1*) under limb a foot or so out, then (*2*) cut from top farther out. Falling limb cannot tear bark. Cut (*3*) from side allows for a very close cut (*4*) without danger of tearing bark. Always cut close to trunk, with no stump. Round end (*left*) means stump, while long oval (*right*) is correct. Treat all cuts over 1-inch diameter with tree-wound paint.

and cutting back shrubs will all compensate for the root loss that occurs when a plant is dug up. The cutback reduces the drain on the remaining roots and allows the plant to recover. Another reason is to make the shrub bushier than it would otherwise be by forcing side growths. A tree is also made bushier in this way, but an inflexible rule is never to cut the central topmost twig or leader. This is always left intact for upward growth. This is a good time also to look for weak joints and for double leaders that, if allowed to develop, might eventually cause the tree to split.

With roses, the cutback is especially necessary on the hybrid sort. Side branching and development of more bearing canes is the primary object of cutting back, as well as helping the plant to adjust to the shock of transplantation.

288

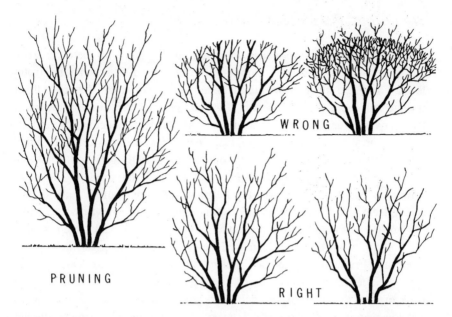

SHAPE, DON'T BUTCHER SHRUBS when they need pruning. *Left,* the shrub before pruning: overgrown in the center, twigs puny, not bearing many leaves or flowers, old trunks in need of renewal. *Above,* shearing in crew-cut fashion will only induce more short stubby twigs, spoiling the natural graceful habit of the shrubs. *Below,* selective thinning, with one old trunk amputated near the ground, gives chance for new shoots and will allow better side growth on the remaining wood.

Why are shrubs cut back later on, after planting?

Many shrubs will get leggy, that is, they will have few or no branchings low down but all growth concentrated at the top. This is not undesirable in shrubs at the back of the border, but for those exposed to view elsewhere it may be ugly and ungainly looking. Or in the back of the border the resulting growth may be thinner than is desirable. Early cutting back will ensure more cane growth and good side growth lower down so that branching is more profuse. Tops will be fuller and bear more flowers and fruit. Also, later cutting back is done to keep shrubs trim and to limit their height and width where this is desired. Occasional drastic renewal pruning is needed by most.

What is renewal pruning?

Some shrubs—lilac is a prime example—grow very tall and have thick trunks after eight or ten years, or in some cases sooner. New shoots that come up from the roots are not given much chance by the older wood, and it becomes necessary to amputate the old wood at or near the ground level. This need not be done all at once, which would cut down on flower production for a season or two. Instead, gradual removal of the oldest trunks over three or four years can keep the shrubs producing flowers fairly well as the new canes rise to replace the removed ones. On trees this is less necessary, although thinning out when growth gets too thick and branches interfere with each other will throw all the strength and flower power to the remaining growth, keeping the tree healthy and shapely. Shade trees need some renewal pruning, for as new growth comes, some old growth is shaded and will probably eventually die back. Such weakening and superseded growth can well be removed to keep the new growth vigorous. Fruit trees, such as apples, often get what are called "water sprouts" on the trunk and limbs, and these soft growths should be cut back even with the trunk or limb each winter before they get too big and sap the resources. Occasionally, one or two may be left to grow outward and improve the symmetry of the tree, if this is desired.

Is any other pruning needed on shrubs and trees?

The aim of good pruning is to keep a shrub as natural looking as possible. So often one sees a forsythia, for instance, cut back to a tight ball

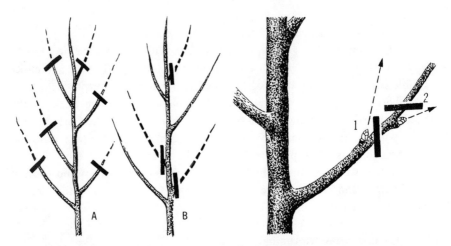

PRUNE TREES at planting time or soon after in one of two ways: (*A*) sides are cut back to shorten, or (*B*) thinned by removal. Thinning sometimes employs both methods to induce outward growth and extra branching. *Right,* choose buds when pruning; upward facing (*1*) means upward growth, while an outward-facing bud (*2*) will force branch to grow outward.

and, when in flower, looking like an elongated egg yolk rather than the golden fountain of a bush allowed to assume its natural graceful, arching spreading habit. Do not give shrubs a crew cut unless they are formal accents, geometric or hedgelike. Instead, cut back here and there, shortening straggly growths, letting the shrub have a natural in-and-out habit. In nature few plants grow to a rigid shape, and not only is it better to follow this example but it is also much less work for the gardener.

Can you prune at any time or is there a special time to do it?

The one rule about pruning at any time is to remove dead, diseased, or damaged wood as soon as possible. Otherwise, there are certain times when various kinds of trees and shrubs should be pruned. A few—maple, black walnut, and birch—should not be pruned in winter or the wounds will "bleed" (sap will run and the tree be weakened). Most trees can be pruned in summer and this is a good time, since the leaves are on the tree and the shape is most visible. The tree is growing and will recover from surgery more quickly. In winter the structure is most visible, of course, so that you can get at the limbs and remove them more easily if major removal is needed.

A number of evergreens are best pruned or nipped back in summer: arborvitae, cypress, hemlock, juniper, bull bay magnolia and sweet bay magnolia, spruce, and yew. (Sweet bay may be evergreen in the South though deciduous in the North.)

The deciduous ones that should be pruned in summer are: birch, catalpa, chestnut, chinaberry, cucumber magnolia, elm, ginkgo, hickory, jujube, golden-chain, golden-rain, kalopanax, Kentucky coffee tree, laburnum, maples, oaks of many kinds, paulownia, phellodendron (cork tree), podocarpus, poplar (including cottonwoods), sophora (pagoda tree), sourwood or sorrel, sweet gum, sweetleaf, walnut, and zelkova.

What about shrubs—should they be pruned in winter or summer?

The important thing to remember about shrubs is to prune them *after* they bloom. This means that spring-blooming shrubs, such as azaleas, spireas, lilacs, mock oranges, and the like, are best pruned in early summer, or as soon as they cease blooming. Late-summer bloomers, such as rose of Sharon, butterfly-bush, caryopteris, hydrangeas, crape-myrtle, franklinia, vitex, and other late-summer shrubs should be pruned in winter or early spring. The gardener who prunes shrubs out of season is, of course, cutting off next year's blossom buds and wood. Only for renewal or drastic cutbacks where a shrub had been neglected for a long time would it be a

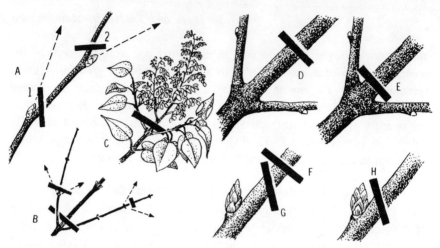

PRUNE SHRUBS with future growth in mind (*A*). Bud facing up (*1*) will produce upward-growing branch; bud facing outward will grow outward. Similarly, right and left growth can be forced according to position of the buds. Cutback (*B*) of central branch and shortening of side branches above opposite buds will produce four new shoots. Lilac (*C*) seed heads should be removed soon after bloom ceases to throw strength to lateral growths for next year's bloom. Cutting back (*D*) will leave long stump, inhibiting good growth, but short cut (*E*) puts all strength into side growth. *Below,* cut (*F*) is wrong, across the twig and also too far from bud. (*G*) is angled but still too far out. Cut at (*H*) is at a 45-degree angle, close to bud but not too close, and is correct.

good practice to sacrifice the next season's bloom, or if there had been extensive damage, so that reshaping was in order.

Can you train a shrub into a small tree?

Many large shrubs are treelike in height, and it is possible to train a good many into a "standard," or tree, by limiting growth to one trunk and by keeping lower branches removed, new shoots below the desired level being rubbed off or cut off as they appear. Lilacs may be so trained, and evergreens can also be trained to be treelike by clipping back and removing side branches. The aromatic-leaved sweet bay is often grown in large containers or in gardens here and abroad, shaped to a ball atop a trunk, or clipped into pyramidal shape. Training is a time-consuming but rewarding effort for those who wish to engage in it.

What about tree pruning, aside from the time element?

The amateur should limit pruning of trees to small ones or to the young trees newly set out, and hire professional help for any removal of limbs on large trees. This latter is dangerous work and is worth what it costs. In general, look for limbs and branches that are likely to rub each other, causing abrasions and wounds. Remove the limb or branch most likely to be least desirable from the standpoint of the structure and shape of the tree. Heavy foliage can make a tree impervious to light and limits ventilation, even in the winter time if the branches and limbs are too close. Thinning out the limbs will open it up to sun and air and keep the tree healthier and growing vigorously. Occasionally, as trees age, the lower branches have a tendency to droop, interfering with traffic or making it impossible to get under them for shade. Such lower branches and limbs can be removed from time to time, forcing the head of the tree upward and allowing light and ventilation under the tree as well as providing access. Opening up the structure will, as noted before, allow shrubs and other plants more chance to grow as light and sun get to them. In general, flowering trees are pruned only to thin out structure, to head back and make them thicker and bushier, or to keep them shorter. Many trees, such as the kousa or Chinese dogwood, tend to be rather shrubby; even the flowering dogwood is likely to let its lower branches sweep to the ground. These can be trimmed off or cut back and the tree given a higher head by judicious pruning.

How often should evergreens be pruned?

Needled evergreens are seldom pruned in the usual sense. It is usual to cut back growth on young trees only on the end in order to force thicker and more compact branching. Spruce and pine should have their new soft shoots clipped back by half in summer before growth hardens. Lateral growths will then fill out. Firs are never pruned except to remove dead or straggly growth, and that is done in winter. The tip bud on a branch and two or three tips on laterals just behind it can be removed to force thick side growth and retard outward growth. Douglas fir can be sheared to a cone shape when young, but older trees should be left unpruned. Arborvitae can be sheared if in a hedge or if you want to thicken growth, but never cut behind green shoots. If they grow too tall, they can be topped (cut back to the height desired); the top will green over again, and a leader will eventually start growing upward and will need pruning in future. In general, do not prune evergreens unless it becomes necessary, and do not cut back sharply on any except yew, which will put forth new growth, usually, from seemingly bare wood. Others will not put forth growth but will be bare forevermore.

Are broad-leaved evergreens like rhododendrons or holly ever pruned?

Again, these are not pruned in the usual sense. Hedges of box and holly may be pruned or sheared to keep them within bounds and perhaps should be kept cut back when young to induce thick growth. Rhododendrons may have the new shoots pinched back to two or three leaves in spring when new growth is established, about the time that spent flowers are removed. Occasionally, old rhododendrons need renewal pruning, but this should not be lightly embarked upon. It will take two years of heavy feeding, mulching, and watering to build up sturdy and vigorous new root systems before you should cut the trunks back to 6 inches above the soil. New shoots will soon spring from the stump from these later-winter cut-backs, and the strongest ones should be saved. Do not attempt to cut back all trunks at one time, but spread it over two or three years. Old azaleas should be well fed for a year or two and then the oldest canes may be removed near ground level. Cut back the new shoots or pinch back soft green growth for the first year or two to make them bushy and full-branched. On Kurume azaleas, hedge shears may be employed, but be sure not to clip them into tight balls or you will ruin the rugged and beautiful contour of the shrubs for some years to come. Follow the natural in-and-out contours of the shrubs and merely cut back. Mountain laurel can be shaped by pinching back new shoots that look as if they would become straggly. Also, when their great popcorn balls of blossoms are in season, cut some for indoor decoration, shaping the bush as you cut. The old woody trunks can be cut to the ground when they get leggy and lower bloom is sparse. New shoots will rise from the roots to replace them. Late spring to summer is the best time for shaping, summer for renewal, as soon as blooms have faded.

How can wind breakage and damage be dealt with?

Winter winds and summer squalls frequently cause breakage, damaging trees and shrubs, A limb may be blown from a tree, and as it falls, it will cause breakage in shrubbery below. Prompt attention is recommended. Carefully remove the fallen wood, taking care not to cause more breakage. On shrubs, cut back the branch to the nearest undamaged twig or bud, or if you have a choice of buds, choose one that will grow outward or upward, according to how you feel the new wood should be headed. See sketches on page 288 that indicate how to prune for directional guidance. If the wound is over one inch in diameter, treat the cut-off end with tree-wound paint. Do not leave a stub, but cut close to the bud or twig. Tree damage should also be promptly dealt with. Disease organisms may enter torn bark and other wounds or drying will occur that might cause nearby wood to die and further trouble might ensue. Remove the broken limb (see sketch page 288) being careful to undercut first so that no bark is torn down the trunk from the falling wood. Cut back stubs closely, and if there is roughness, smooth it with a sharp knife before painting the wound with tree-wound paint, which will seal the cut. Cutting the bark around the edge with a sharp knife will help to force new growth, and eventually the bark will grow over the wound and cover it, healing the cut completely. Large wounds should be painted yearly until the bark has grown over the scar. Keeping the wound sealed so that it will not dry out is important.

Can evergreens be repaired?

If the top of the evergreen is damaged, a new leader can be trained to take its place. See the sketch on page 288 for the method. Within a very short time the new leader will have taken over and eventually the damage will not be visible. Wind damage to evergreens with broken limbs cannot be repaired, unfortunately. However, when trees are blown over by strong gales or hurricanes, they can be set upright again, if they are not too large and old, and by careful watering and feeding, the roots can be reestablished if it is done quickly. Staking and guy wires will be needed for some years to hold them in place until the new roots become tenacious enough to anchor them.

What tools are needed for pruning?

As large an assemblage of tools can be purchased as you feel you need, but in general only a few simple tools are required. For big-branch and limb removal, two saws are needed. A heavy-duty saw with coarse teeth and a slight curve to the blade and a lighter saw, also curved for tight angles and small work, or a saw of this latter sort on the end of an extension-pole pruner with a pruning hook operated by a pull cord will suffice. A heavy pruning knife, one that folds if possible, for cutting back soft summer growth will do less damage to stems than most pruning shears.

Hand tools include: pruning shears of the anvil type—a blade that strikes against a flat piece on the opposite blade; "parrot beak" pruning shears, so called because of the shape of the blades; long-handled lopping shears for large and heavy branches or shoots, with strong steel arms and cushioned or wooden-handled ends. Besides these, only hedge shears will be needed if you have a hedge that is formal and needs shearing.

Electric hedge clippers are a boon to the gardener, either single- or double-edged types. Cordless electric clippers are also available. Other electric tools, saws, and chain saws are best forgotten unless you are clearing land, for they are so quick and destructive that they often cause more damage than good results.

One final caution: Do not purchase a double-edged pruning saw, for often you will have to saw in a constricted space, and the upper teeth will injure the bark or cut off another branch as you work. They may also snag clothing, while a smooth edge opposite teeth will not.

WINTER PROTECTION

Winter protection is generally assumed to refer only to the cold sections of the country, but in many other areas it may mean protection from hot bright sun and drying winds in the off season. Definitely in the coldest

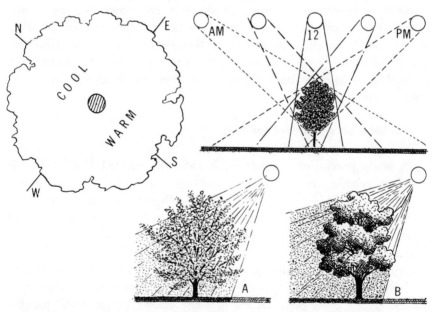

TREE SHADE VARIES with the time of day, also within the shady spot. On the sunny side, left, it is warmer than on the north or shady side. Sun casts a wide shadow in the morning, narrows gradually till the sun is nearly overhead at noon, then lengthens again in the opposite direction in the afternoon. Consider these factors when placing your tree. Also think of shade density when you are selecting a tree. Light-foliaged shade trees let more sun (and heat) penetrate than heavily-foliaged ones.

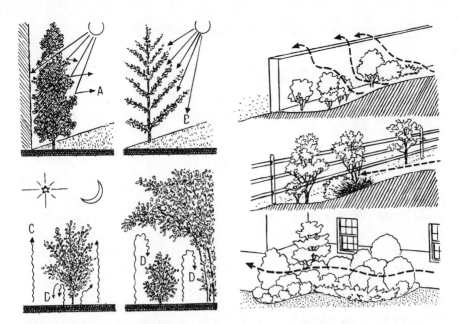

Left:

DEFLECTING THE ELEMENTS is a part of modern gardening. *Left,* the sun's rays are kept from a house wall by a thickly foliaged tree (A), making the house cooler than use of an open-branched type (B) that lets rays through. *Below,* heat rises at night from sun-warmed soil and escapes (C) unless it is impeded by overhanging branches and kept below them (D). It is possible to protect tender plants somewhat by providing such overhangs, either with plants or some man made shelter.

Right:

AIR FLOW DEFLECTION protects plants from frost and wind. *Top,* frosty air flows downhill to pool in bottom lands or pools behind a solid wall. *Center,* it can flow through an open fence, such as a rail fence. *Below,* plants in a corner formed by a structure are protected from a flow of air by the building, and also by the plantings the current first encounters.

parts, where temperatures go below zero and sometimes remain there for days at a time and where winds howling past plants may dry them out, some sort of protection is needed. Planting a windbreak of evergreens is one way (see page 252), erecting a fence to break the force is another, but for many plants protection means even more than that. Snow damage to evergreens is commonplace in the North. Newly planted trees are subject to sunscald, which causes bark damage, opening of a wound, and the letting in of decay and insects. Hence, the gardener will do well to reckon with his climate in advance of trouble and take such measures as will ward off or offset the ills that may occur.

What can you do to stop sunscald?

As outlined in the planting sections, newly planted trees should be wrapped with burlap or paper strips up to about the lowest limb. Keep this on for at least the first year, and two years is better.

Are all shrubs affected by the cold?

Frost damage to buds will deplete flowering and may affect leaves. Tender shrubs are often killed back part way or, if unprotected, may die at the roots. Hybrid roses are especially affected. Unless the shrubs are not hardy in your region, they should recover, and most should suffer no damage at all in an average winter. A few may be affected slightly in especially cold winters. Remember that frost flows downhill and remains pooled in low spots. This is where damage occurs or where frost is trapped behind an impediment, a wall, a building or a thick evergreen hedge (see sketch). If the garden is on a hillside, be sure that the downhill side is open enough for frost to flow past the plantings.

What can be done to protect shrubs in winter?

Roses should be hilled up and protected or cut back, and shrub roses tied together to prevent wind whipping. (See section on roses, page 123.) For other shrubs there are many methods, all of which are good, and whatever works for you is the proper method. Evergreens are likely to be bent out of shape by heavy snow and ice. Tie together the bottom branches, then run the heavy cord or rope spirally up the evergreen, knot it, and run it down in an opposite spiral. Fasten at the bottom. This will keep the branches close to the trunk and secure from damage. Spruces and other types that have downward-bending branches naturally should not, of course, be treated this way. They will spring back into place when the snow melts, or you can go out and lightly tap branches with a pole to release snow masses and let branches spring into place.

Other methods of protection are shown clearly in the sketches here, so they need only be enumerated. Burlap wrappings with a burlap top is one method. Use burlap, not plastic or other impervious fabric, so that heat and moisture can escape. Burlap screen on stakes will deflect wind and protect plants from the sun. A plywood A-frame houses an evergreen, protecting it from snowslides from the roof. Twiggy shrubs are best tied together to prevent wind whipping, with further protection, if desirable, provided by a wire-mesh cylinder filled with straw or leaves about the lower part of the plant. Burlap screens, either single or double, protect from the wind and sun and can be filled with straw or leaves if more protection is advisable. Grafted plants, such as trees, should have the graft union protected in coldest areas by hilling up soil. Wrapping the trunk with insulating cornstalks will also provide sunscald protection. A sun or wind shield for one side only is a slab of plywood held in place with stakes on the sunny or windy side.

Is there any other protection that can be given?

A commercial product called Wilt-pruf is an emulsion that can be sprayed on needled and broad-leaved evergreens. This forms a coating that effectively prevents excessive moisture loss. It will disappear in spring as growth begins and new foliage is put forth. It is effective against wind that causes evaporation at a time when roots are unable to supply replacement moisture due to frozen ground. It is claimed that the plant will be stronger and better able to grow because fewer winter demands are made on it.

In the southern and southwestern sections of the land, sun may be the most devastating problem. Too much sun can burn leaves if they are not properly protected by being given moisture. Hence, winter waterings may be in order in dry sections and even in other places if there is sandy soil that lets water pass through too quickly.

Maintenance, then, consists of watering, feeding, pruning for health and renewal, and giving winter protection where this is advisable. It sounds much more complicated than it is, once you establish the routine to follow and get into the swing of it.

PLANT DISEASES AND PESTS

Many of the formerly recommended chemicals for control of diseases and pests are being taken off the market for review or proscribed altogether, and because this area is very changeable at the moment these substances are not covered in this book. Many insect pests and certain diseases are limited to various regions in any case. Therefore, it is suggested that readers who may encounter troubles of this sort get in touch with their county agent or state college of agriculture for advice in dealing with the problem. These local authorities will be most likely to recognize the exact trouble from the symptoms and will have the new and approved controls to recommend as they are developed in the next few years.

One caution should be attached. It is no longer thought to be a good thing to broadcast pesticides that kill a broad spectrum of insects. Instead, the modern method is tending more toward spot control so that only the miscreants are eliminated, not a good many other insects as well, some of which may be helpful to the garden. Certain insects are actually predators that keep down the population of troublesome insects, but do no damage themselves to the garden.

THE ONLY WAY TO TRANSPLANT

Almost all gardeners complain that transplanting or even just planting trees and shrubs is a chore. Let's face it: it is.

Having courageously and honestly faced it, what do we do about it to make it no more of a chore than it need be? Possibly our best assistance will be found in the old maxim, "Do it right, do it once." That will bear thinking about before you ever put a spade in the ground. If you put the *proper* know-how and effort into planting when you set out a tree or plant a shrubbery bed, you are quite likely to ensure success. Therefore, you will not have to dig up the wrongly planted item and place it where it should have been placed in the beginning or, if it has expired in the interim, replace it with double the expense and more than twice the work involved. Perhaps worst of all, you will, in this latter case, have lost a year's growth from the plant.

Therefore, take time to find out what your plants need and give it to them as nearly as you can. Dig an adequate-sized hole, fill around the roots with the proper sort of soil, water well for the first summer and into the autumn, protect the roots with a mulch, and see that during the first years especially the plant gets as much attention and loving care as it needs—and deserves. Oh, yes. And complain bitterly about how much work it is to plant things properly. You will be surprised how this helps at first and how quickly you forget it as the tree grows and matures and as the shrubs put forth ever greater beauty of form and flower as the years speed by.

How can the job of planting be lightened?

By not doing it all at once. In most areas it is possible to plant early in spring, as soon as the ground can be worked. Then, if you have kept your early plantings to deciduous growth—or as much as makes good sense in the particular bed—you can go on planting evergreens into June in most places, provided you keep the soil moist and use balled and bur-lapped plants for anything larger than seedlings. Doubtfully hardy trees or any that may require extra care should be planted in spring, as early as possible so as to establish roots before hot weather. Birch, redbud, mag-nolias, certain hawthorns are also best planted in spring. Most other trees can be planted in autumn, and this is probably preferable for many kinds since they will go on working underground and growing good roots even when the tops are quite bare.

Can evergreens be planted in the autumn?

Yes, with some exceptions, they may be planted in September and a month or so later, depending on the climate. Note that they will need protection from drying winds, that they must go into the winter well wa-tered, and that balled and burlapped plants are needed. Mulches will pro-tect the soil from drying out in the warm days of autumn, when it is often dry for a week or more even in moist climates, and after the ground is frozen, a deep mulch will protect the roots from the thaws that lead them into false notions about spring being imminent.

When should shrubs be planted?

Deciduous shrubs as well as broad-leaved evergreens may be planted early in spring as soon as the ground can be worked or in holes dug the previous autumn. Most broad-leaved evergreens are more safely trans-planted in spring than in autumn, though in mild climates it is possible to succeed very well, with proper care. Deciduous shrubs may be planted in autumn, even good-sized ones, if they are balled and burlapped (B&B). Small ones may be planted and cut back as recommended in the directions for pruning at planting time (see pages 287–288.)

Is it better to plant young seedlings and small trees than to put in large ones that would give quicker results?

Some gardeners feel this is true, but actually, if you get good stock from a reputable nursery, particularly stock that is balled and burlapped, you will have quick recovery from transplanting shock and will soon have a mature-looking planting. However, mature stock or well-grown plants cost more. In some cases, with quick-growing stock it is possible to get fairly fast results from small stock, but since we do not recommend this (quick-growing usually means later replacement when such plants have run their course), it is beside the point.

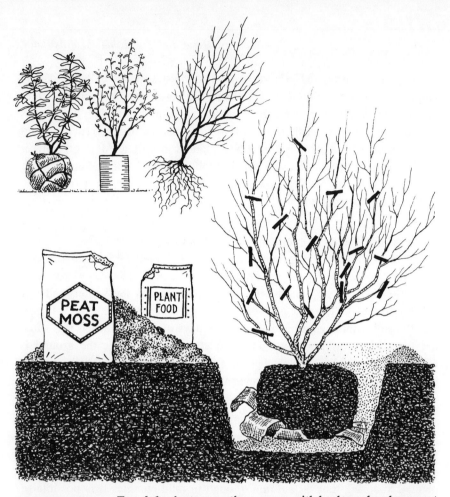

PLANTING SHRUBS. *Top, left,* plants come three ways—with burlapped and compact root and soil ball ("B&B" in catalogs); with roots in soil in a container (metal can, plastic or fiber pot); and bare rooted, with no soil. All are acceptable, although some, such as needled and broad-leaved evergreens, are best purchased with a soil ball, either B&B or in containers. Usually only deciduous seedlings and small shrubs or roses are sold bare rooted. Be sure soil and roots are in moist root balls when buying either of the first two categories.

PLANTING METHOD. For B&B and container-grown plants, dig holes 8 to 12 inches wider, 4 to 8 inches deeper than the root ball. Enrich soil with plant food, peat moss, and, if soil is clay or heavy, add sand to lighten it. Then put enough enriched soil on the bottom to bring top of rootball (former nursery ground level) even with the surrounding soil. Place root ball on it in center of hole; unfasten burlap and roll it down on the sides. Fill in hole, tamping down soil firmly, about halfway. Soak well, and when water has absorbed, refill to about two-thirds, then fill to top, repeating tamping and soaking each time. If soil sinks below ground level, refill. Build a low mound outside the hole to make a "saucer" to hold water. Keep soil moist, filling the saucer every day to two and filling in with soil if there are low spots. At planting, cut back (*black lines*) to thin out shrub, removing weak or dead wood, cutting back major shoots unevenly. Never give a shrub a "crew cut" unless it is a formal hedge.

302

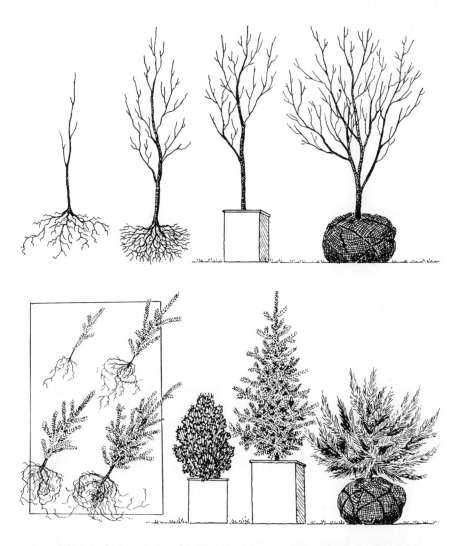

Top, left to right, bare-rooted seedling tree; bare-rooted older tree, root-pruned and transplanted several times in the nursery; young tree in container (can, plastic, or fiber) containing soil around compact root system; tree with roots in soil ball, covered with burlap sacking, listed in catalogs as "B&B" (balled and burlapped).

Lower, in box, bare-rooted seedling evergreens, sold in bundles of ten to twenty-five as follows: (1) two-year seedling, grown without transplanting for two years; (2) three-year seedlings, grown for three years without transplanting; (3) three-year seedlings, grown for two years, then transplanted to new bed for one year; (4) four-year plants, grown for two years, transplanted to new bed and grown two more years. Other plants, *left to right,* small evergreen in container (can, plastic, or fiber) is less expensive than plant in larger container, *right,* both with compact root systems in soil. *Far right,* evergreen with compact root system in soil ball, covered with burlap sacking, listed in catalogs as "B&B" (balled and burlapped).

303

What must one do to secure success in planting?

Give plants as nearly as you can what they need. Just as babies need a compatible formula, young shrubs and trees also need proper sustenance if they are to thrive, particularly as there is the added shock of transplanting to overcome, with the attendant change of environment, amputated roots, cut-back structure, and general upset of conditions.

What do plants need?

Good-quality soil, and of the sort they need. Some require acid soil, some neutral or alkaline; some thrive in sandy, light soil, some like a heavier soil; some not only tolerate but demand a moist, even wet soil; others will be happiest in a moderately dry soil, or at least somewhat dry between waterings and rains. Special requirements are noted in the lists throughout this book.

Is it possible to plant trees or shrubs in soil that is not really ideal for them?

Soil can be adjusted and improved, making it approach ideal tilth, and materials can be added to bring it into line with the needs of special plants. Where requirements are stated as "well-drained soil," for example, it is possible to loosen heavy clay soil, open it up with sand and gravel, peat moss, and other additives so that it will not stay too wet for the plant's needs. See text on soils, pages 319–321, for further information on adjusting soil content.

Why do gardeners say to dig an "adequate" hole? What is an adequate hole?

Old-time gardeners were fond of expressing it this way: "Don't try to put a dollar plant in a twenty-cent hole." Even today, when inflated prices of plants are many times the classic dollar, this holds true. An adequate-sized hole is one large enough to contain all the roots (or the soil ball of the B&B plant) without any bending, cramping, or crowding. A few inches on all sides is even better, though it means more digging. A shrubbery bed might be dug deeply throughout the entire length and breadth of it, although if the soil is moderately good and nearly right, holes can be dug within the perimeters of the bed, without overall spading.

What do you do with the dirt dug out of the holes?

If there is a lawn already established beside the bed or some other area that would be difficult to clean off later, put down a tarpaulin and

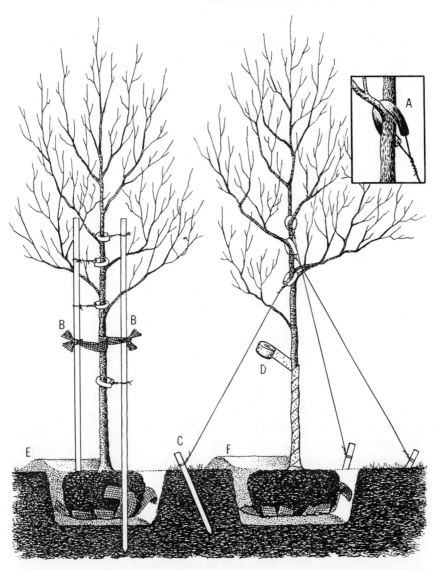

PLANTING TREES. Dig an adequate hole and enrich the dug-out soil (see text). Set root ball in place, even with surrounding soil on partial fill. Loosen burlap and fold down sides. Drive tall stakes (*B*) on either side, set well into the ground. Fill in soil, tamping and watering to settle, refill, and finish with a mound (*F*) to hold waterings later on. Fasten tree trunk to stakes with burlap strips wound once about trunk and tied or with guy wires passed through pieces of garden hose (*A*) above a branch, then wired to stake. Alternate method: Plant tree and fill in, omitting tall stakes. Use guy wires to low stakes driven well into the ground and attached as in (*A*). Wrap trunk with paper or burlap strips for first two winters to prevent winter injury from sunscald, which damages bark and impedes growth.

305

shovel the soil from the hole onto it. The additives can then be conveniently incorporated by mixing well into the natural soil before it is used to fill about the roots. Any excess can be taken up in the tarpaulin and transported to wherever it is needed.

How deep should the hole be?

Some gardeners say only as deep as the ball of soil in B&B plants. However, it will give plants a better start if the hole is dug out a few inches—up to 6 inches—deeper than the material seems to need. The trunk of the tree and the shoots or canes of the shrubs should be set at or just below the former ground level in the nursery. You can tell by the change of color and the texture of the bark on the trunk or shoots. Enrich the soil, then fill in the hole below the soil ball and pack it lightly to bring the former ground level even with the new one. With bare-rooted plants, put a rake handle or board across the hole, and test the ground level. Have someone hold the plant as you fill in around the roots. This way you can be sure of centering the plant in the hole.

Does this hold good for container-grown plants, too?

Those shrubs and trees purchased in a tin can or other container should be removed from it (see sketch) and carefully placed so as to avoid breaking up the soil ball from around the roots. Burlap-wrapped B&B plants may be set in place and the burlap unfastened, pushed down alongside the plant, and the soil packed in above it. The jute of the sacking will decompose in due time. In all cases be sure that the soil ball is moist before attempting to remove it or plant it. Moist soil will adhere and stay intact. Dry soil will disintegrate and expose roots to drying air and possibly cause air pockets about the roots.

Can the planting hole be just big enough for container-grown root balls? And how do you plant?

It is best to make all holes at least a foot wider than the soil ball, and 4 to 6 inches deeper. Then jab the spade into the bottom of the hole to loosen the soil, but do not dig it out. Fill as directed above, position the root ball, and fill in about the edges, holding the plant upright, lightly packing the soil with the flat of your hand until the hole is about half filled. Fill the hole with water and let it soak in, settling the soil. Poke a stick in here and there and work it about to make sure there are no air holes in the fill. Then check the position and uprightness of the plant, adjust it if necessary, and refill the hole to an inch or two from the top, and

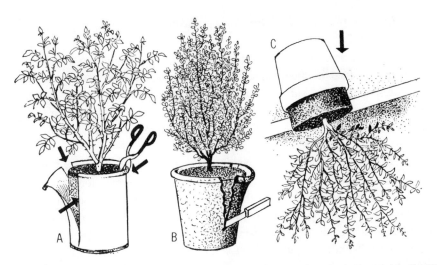

CONTAINER PLANTING. Soak the plant the day before so that the moistened ball will stay together when removed. For metal containers (A), use tinsnips to make at least three deep cuts down sides so that metal can be bent back and root ball lifted out. Similarly, fiber and pulp pots (B) are cut with a sharp knife. Break away or tear sides so that root ball can be removed. Heavy plastic or clay pots (C) should be upended, one hand atop the soil holding the plant while the pot is turned and its edge struck sharply on a bench or other solid surface until root ball detaches and slides out. Plant immediately after removing from pot.

again pat it down lightly, water, and let it soak in and settle. Finally fill the soil to a little above soil level, 1 or 2 inches, and mound up soil around the edge beyond the perimeter of the hole to make a sort of saucer to hold water. On sloping ground, only two-thirds to one-half a saucer will be needed or a piece of corrugated-metal lawn edging can be set into the soil to hold the soil and the water. Fill the saucer with water and let it settle, then refill if necessary to maintain ground level. Water daily for the first month or so, or as often as needed so that the soil does not dry out. Mulching will help to conserve moisture and will prevent the soil from cracking and admitting air to the root area. See section on mulches, page 321.

What's the procedure with bare-rooted plants?

If you purchase by mail order, as soon as plants arrive, unpack them and examine them to see if they are in good condition. If they are not, notify the sender immediately and explain what is wrong. If they are only a bit dry, or even if they are in good condition, take them out of the moist packing and plastic bags or wrappings, put them in a pail of water, immersing them to above the rootstock and roots, and if you have not yet dug the holes, begin to do so immediately. If you are unable to plant them immediately, heel in the plants. This means that you must dig a hole a foot or so deep, one side of which can be slanting, in which to put the plants until you can set them permanently. The best spot will be in a shady place, such as the north side of the house or where a tree will shade them at least during the middle of the day.

Take the plants out of the water and separate them, then lay them in the hole slantwise. If you find any broken roots or straggly long ones, cut back to sound wood or shorten them to the average length. Keep all plants in the pail until they are used, thus preventing drying out of roots that may weaken the plants. Heeled-in plants can be kept for a week or two before final planting. Seedlings are sometimes planted in rows in a home nursery to grow on for a year or so until they have developed a bit and can be dug up and planted where they are to stay permanently.

Planting bare-rooted material is similar in most respects to planting B&B. However, because there is no soil ball around the roots, it will be necessary to take greater care to keep the stems upright and centered in the hole, and roots should be spread outward evenly, trimmed back if they spread wider than the hole here and there so that they are not crammed in and twisted or broken. Filling and watering, allowing soil to settle and then filling and watering again until the hole is completely filled, and making a saucer, mulching, and all other procedures are the same as for B&B plants.

Should all plants be pruned back at planting, as some say?

Not all deciduous plants need it and evergreens almost never need pruning. Container-grown and B&B usually need none or only a minimum of pruning because there is no root loss and less transplanting shock involved. Bare-rooted plants, however, should be cut back to compensate for loss of roots and to prevent straining the plant's resources as it struggles to put forth leaf and flower with insufficient feeding resources. Some nursery plantsmen who plant for buyers ignore this precept because they fear ructions from the client, who may be angered at the visible loss of structure. But plants will stage a quicker recovery, be thicker, and come into full lush growth with strong structure and be healthier if they are cut back in the beginning.

Exceptions: Container-grown and B&B plants, as noted, and broad-leaved and needled evergreens need no pruning back except to remove dead, damaged, and broken wood; or, possibly, trimming to make them more symmetrical and shapely at the time of planting. Sizable plants in these categories are usually sold with the root ball or the container-grown roots intact in the soil. But bare-rooted deciduous shrubs and trees should be cut back. Roses grown in containers are also an exception, but it might make for a stronger, healthier bush to cut roses with long stems the first season, thus forcing shorter, sounder growth. One other exception in cutting back is trees. Only side growth of trees is cut back, never the leader or central top twig. This is the time to do corrective pruning to avoid weak crotches and growth. See sketch, page 288.

Newly planted material seems to be dead for weeks. Should such shrubs and trees be replaced if they do not start growth?

Growth is variable, even on well-established plants. Do not be impatient. It may take weeks for buds to break into leaf and longer for twig growth to begin.

If some twigs have leaves part way but not toward the top, does that mean the wood is dead?

When branches and twigs have not put forth leaves by mid- to late June, those portions that are leafless may be cut back to the first leaf beyond the dead portion. Always cut back to living green wood. See section on pruning, page 287.

Suppose you want to transplant a shrub from one place to another in the garden—what must you do to ensure success?

The main concern is to save as many roots as possible. If you can arrange ahead of time to do it, shove a sharp square-ended spade deeply into the soil all around the shrub not less than a foot out from the center, more if it is a big one. This should be done the fall before your intended spring transplanting. If you must do it with little notice, shove the spade into the soil as above, water well, and let the soil dry for a day or two. Then dig a trench around the outside of this cut-line as deeply as necessary to get a good, solid ball of earth around the roots. Cut under the ball with the spade, gently rocking the shrub to loosen it. It will help with large shrubs to put a tarpaulin or burlap bag around the trunks and shoots and tie it securely so that you can work more easily, and later on handle it well in shifting it to the new location. When it is loose, lift it out onto a tarpaulin or canvas alongside the hole. It can be slid across the lawn or ground to the new location, or the tarpaulin can be tied around it so that it can be lifted to whatever other transportation vehicle you may have. Don't forget to prune it back sharply, about one-third, and to thin out weak shoots from the ground to compensate for the root loss.

Should trees be staked after planting? How about shrubs?

In order to ensure upright growth and symmetrical development, trees should be staked when planted and stakes should remain for at least the first season, longer if the tree is in an exposed position. With shrubs, staking is less necessary, although certain shrubs that develop into more or less standard (trunk-type) growth will also profit by staking, particularly if there are strong winds on the site. Sometimes two stakes are needed, particularly on the larger trees (2½-inch caliper measurements) to prevent wind whipping or settling of soil that would make them develop at an angle. Never use wire alone to hold the trunk to the stake. Always run wire through a piece of rubber hose (see sketch on page 305) long enough to protect the tree from injury where the wire girdles it. Or use burlap strips, canvas, or heavy plastic ties (unless these latter have wire centers).

Suppose I must plant in a low spot where the soil is moist and I want to plant material that is not basically wet-soil tolerant?

You may be able to raise the soil level a bit (see page 305) and plant the root ball on it. Fill in around the root ball and make the usual saucer to contain water. Then, when the plant's roots begin to grow outward and down, they will find their own level. Such a raised planting lends variety and interest to the landscape, creating small hillocks and relieving the flatness of the general garden area. Many modern gardens here and abroad, where there is no wet-soil problem are using this device to give an informal natural look to the garden, and you may wish to follow suit if it appeals to you and seems right for your garden area.

How much fertilizer should be used in the planting hole?

This is a controversial matter. Some gardeners and nurserymen say to put no fertilizer whatever in it, yet other experts say to mix in plant foods with the soil being replaced. So far as chemical plant foods are concerned, I believe it would be better to abstain from adding any. Compost, organic fertilizers, and additives such as bone meal may be used, with the exception of fresh manure, if you happen to have access to it. Chemical fertilizers and fresh manure are likely to damage tender roots on contact, causing what is known as "root burn." In any case, I abstain, because transplanting is like a surgical operation in a sense and trying to feed and force a plant immediately into unwarranted growth is likely to cause trouble. Instead, wait until the following season and then scatter plant foods around the soil above the root area and water it in well, watering often so that nutrients may be taken up in diluted form as the plants need and can use them. Do not feed after midsummer in the North, late summer in the southern and southwestern states, or new growth may be formed that will die back in winter during a freeze.

SUMMING UP

• In transplanting trees, be sure that adequate root space is provided by digging widely and deeply and never cramping roots into a too-small hole.

• Cut back side growth by about one-third or more to compensate for root loss and transplanting shock. Never cut back the leader or top upright stem.

• Refill the hole, watering and letting settle, rewatering and letting settle again, and making a saucer to hold waterings around the trunk. Use adjusted soil, if there is need for it, for refilling.

• Stake the tree and be sure that bindings do not chafe or injure the bark.

• The time when trees should be transplanted will depend on type, but most can be transplanted in early spring or late autumn.

• Do not feed at first. Don't force growth that may be weak by fertilizing and trying to rush things.

• In transplanting shrubs, be sure to provide a big enough hole to give roots a chance to develop. Never cramp and twist roots to fit into the hole. It is better to cut them back if a large enough hole cannot be provided.

SOIL—IMPROVE IT, THEN MAINTAIN IT

Once a garden area has been cleared and planted it may seem to some that it is peculiar that soils must be maintained as well as the plants. Yet gardeners who ignore the necessary maintenance of soil quality run the risk of having gardens that flourish for a time and then begin to languish. Soil is basic to the needs and uses of all plants. It may be the most vital of the four elements that affect the growth and health of all growing plant life: soil, water, sun, and air.

That is why we assemble here a complete section on soil and its main-

311

tenance, although there have been many topical references here and there in other chapters. They were entered there to aid the reader directly to avoid the trouble of cross-referencing, which is always annoying. In this final summing up, therefore, you will find a complete and concise compendium of all pertinent information. The part on maintenance can be referred to by all gardeners when the soil seems to be at least part of a garden problem. There are many questions to be answered about this basic garden component.

What is soil? Is there a normal soil we should look for?

Garden soil is an agglomeration of various particles of different sizes and shapes, most of which have broken down from larger mineral or organic substances. These will vary in size from infinitesimal dust particles to quite large bits the size of gravel or larger. In clay and silt soils particles may be as fine as flour, so that they pack very closely together and exclude air and make it difficult for water to drain. Sandy and gravelly soils, on the other hand, are composed of such large pieces that water courses through them quickly because they are so loose and open. An average garden soil lies somewhere between these extremes, falling into what is termed a loam soil. This is composed of some clay particles, possibly some silt, some sand and gravel, and a good bit of organic matter in various sizes and stages of decomposition.

Strictly speaking, a "normal" soil is the one you find as you begin to garden, if the soil has never been turned before. All garden soils are disturbed once planting begins and no longer can be considered normal. However, there is an ideal soil toward which you can strive in adjusting your present soil.

How do you know what kind of soil you have?

If you dig up a shovelful of soil to a depth of a foot or more and examine it, you can decide quickly what rough division it falls into.

Sandy Soil. Completely sandy soils are found only on beaches and in the desert. We all know how sea water is rapidly absorbed as waves recede and how quickly beach sand dries as the tide turns. Desert dwellers are even more aware of how speedily a rain shower dissipates into the sandy soil, leaving the top dry in short order. Except for plants inured by nature and long residence in the desert, sand and sandy soils are not conducive to health and growth. The loose, open quality allows both water and nutrients to leach away before feeding roots can absorb and make use of

CLAY OR HEAVY SOILS are composed of infinite numbers of tiny, extremely fine particles but are deficient in (A) sand and (B) humus, though some larger particles may be mixed in with the clay. In the main, such soils are easily compacted and bake brick-hard in sun. Water may run off because it cannot penetrate easily or deeply, there being not enough space between particles for drainage or even air. Roots need a certain amount of air if plants are to flourish.

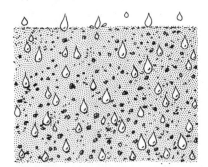

SANDY SOILS, at the other extreme, lacking both (A) clay and (B) humus, are so open that water courses through before questing roots can profit by it. Too much air penetrates, and fine feeding roots, even larger ones, may shrivel, dry out, or even die. Nutrients, too, may leach away before roots can utilize them, creating a need for more fertilizer than is the case with ideal or average soils. In desert sands, mineral salts surface because of watering and may cause trouble for plants.

them. Tender feeding roots shrivel and die, and the plant suffers. Sandy soils are sometimes referred to as light soils.

Silt Soil. Commonly found only in lake and pond beds or in eddies of rivers, silt may also be seen in mud puddles in the garden. Silt is powdery and ultrafine when dry. Silt makes a good contribution to other soils, however, whether it is broken down from sandy minerals or composed of fine particles of organic matter. It may be a mixture of the two. When constantly wet a silt soil is referred to as muck soil.

Clay Soil. Tiny particles closely packed together and with little or no organic matter, in general, make up clay soil. Typical of clay-soil qualities are its imperviousness to aeration and its being so tight that drainage is slowed almost to zero. Dry clay will allow water to run off rather than be absorbed. When it dries after a thorough wetting, it forms hard lumps. When wet from winter moisture or several days of rain, it is greasy and sticky, the particles adhering with gluelike tenacity. Although it may be rather light by weight, this is sometimes called "heavy" soil.

There is a soil that is composed of all or most of the foregoing components, and it is more likely to be encountered by the gardener:

Garden Loam. Because there is a mixture of all kinds of particles and many different sizes, with no predominance of clay or silt, a handful of this soil will crumble and break apart easily. Although it may be gritty, it is still not sandy enough to sift easily through your fingers. This means that it is open enough to admit air and water, yet has enough fine particles to retain some adherence to keep the moisture in it for a time. The structure may be composed of a half or more of particles of various sorts (and some organic matter) and up to a half of water and air.

What is the "ideal soil" previously mentioned?

While this will vary somewhat according to the natural preferences of the plants chosen, there is an ideal soil that will suit most shrubs and trees. Elsewhere we have spoken of muck-soil plants (those that grow in constantly moist silt soils). And also we have taken a look at desert plants that will survive arid to desert conditions, plants for which a good bit of water might sound the death knell. Between the two extremes that are presented in these two soils fall other kinds of soils—those that are arid most of the year with little rain, those that have quite a lot of moisture from rains and snows, and those that have moderate amounts of moisture. The compositions of the soils will vary widely, too, with some heavier because of a higher clay content and others lighter if there is more sand in their composition.

Ideal Soil is composed of a balanced mixture of sand, clay, silt, and organic matter. It is light enough and sufficiently open for hose water or rain to penetrate easily and to drain through slowly so that the roots can profit by the dissolving of nutrients, yet there is enough spongelike humus content so that it does not dry out easily even though there may be air

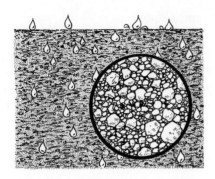
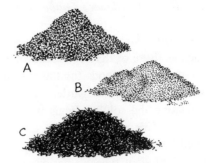

IDEAL SOILS are those that maintain a balance of all components, allowing roots to penetrate easily, water to drain but not too rapidly, moisture to be retained long enough to put foods into solution so that roots may absorb them. Although desert or swamp conditions are required for some plants, most others thrive in soils that approach the ideal balance: (*B*) some fine particles (clay), (*A*) some larger particles (sand), and (*C*) sufficient humus (natural fibers and materials).

HOW TO ADJUST SOILS TOWARD THE IDEAL

Clay soils should be dug deeply, clods broken up, and quantities of sand and humus should be added. The amounts needed will depend on the heaviness of the clay deposit, for not all soils have equal amounts of clay. Mix in the additives. Further drainage in the form of drainage tiles or other means may be required for low-lying clay soils. *Sandy soils,* on the other hand, need humus—either compost, leaf mold, or peat moss. Humusy wastes from the garden are best composted first, before being added. Mix in any combinations of humus and dig deeply. The circle detail in the IDEAL SOIL sketch gives some idea of how various-sized components fit together. It is greatly enlarged, but even so, fine particles are not emphasized, for they are so small and will fit between all the larger components. Roots can work their way through such soils easily and well.

penetrating toward the roots. Air is needed for healthy root action, a point sometimes overlooked by gardeners.

Isn't black soil the most fertile and rich?

It is not by color but by general structure that soil should be judged. Plant foods can be applied and will get to the roots if the soil is open enough for water to convey them. While compost is often dark and also rich, the color does not necessarily indicate fertility.

Does soil contain anything else that makes plants grow?

All soils possess tiny organisms not visible to the human eye but vital to plant health and life. Some are the friendly bacteria that act in the soil to trap and convey free nitrogen to the roots. Others are minute fungi that

315

act in other ways. For instance, some are found on roots of acid-soil plants, such as those of the rhododendron family. These fungi seem to function as pre-digesters of foods for the parent plants, making nutrients available for absorption. In good garden soils these bacteria and fungi are abundant, activating the soluble foods while also conserving and releasing them as needed. This will, of course, extend the usefulness of any fertilizers supplied by the gardener. These organisms are fewer in poorer soils, and they are of different types in various soils.

What is organic matter and how does it fit into the picture of soil improvement and maintenance?

Organic matter is composed of vegetable or animal matter. It is nature's own way of returning to the soil the elements used to grow the leaves, wood, or flesh of the organic material. Take leaf mold, for instance. The leaves of deciduous plants are discarded each year, while those of evergreens are periodically replaced and the old needles fall; broad-leaved evergreen leaves are also succeeded by new ones. Leaves act as a kind of factory while they live, converting raw materials sent to them by the roots and wood of the tree or shrub into structural cells by means of a process called photosynthesis. Sunlight is the vital element in this conversion process. So leaves contain many fertile ingredients, and when they fall, these are returned to the soil as they decompose into small particles of humusy material. Leaves of some plants, oak for one, are very tough and strong and take longer to break down than soft leaves, such as maple, those of garden flowers, vegetables, and grasses. Gradually leaves become part of the fertile topsoil in forests or on the prairies, where centuries of grasses dying down and decomposing have built some of the deepest topsoil known on the globe.

Why wouldn't shrubs and trees make their own humus in the garden, then?

If allowed to remain under the trees and shrubs, they would, of course, within a few years. But a garden is not nature. We are artificially creating an environment, using plants grown elsewhere, cutting back their roots and superstructure in order to persuade them to perform in the way we wish them to. This is anything but natural. Also, gardeners rake leaves off the lawn, and most gardeners clean up the garden to make it neat, something Mother Nature never does. Mother Nature may be a sloppy housekeeper, but she does not burn leaves, thereby robbing plants of their needed humus and fertilizer. Wise gardeners take their cue from natural processes and compost the leaves—that is, they pile them up in a corner, adding a layer of soil to every 6 to 10 inches of leaves, and adding weeds and any clean nondiseased plants or leaves from other plants in the garden, together with kitchen wastes. Vegetable parings, leftovers, tea leaves and coffee grounds, even clean bones may be utilized. Do not put greasy material in the pile. Pulverized limestone, wood ashes, and a few handfuls of a complete garden fertilizer with high nitrogen content may also be added. Keep the heap well moistened, especially in summer, but do not wet it in winter (except in warm climates). Turning it from top to bottom every two or three months will hasten decomposition. When it has mostly broken down, screen the residue and put the large bits left into a new pile to start the bacteria working with the next batch. The screened humus can be used to improve the soil and maintain its fertility.

How is this done?

When the compost has been screened, distribute it in a layer of 1 to 3 inches over the surface of the bed to be treated. Lightly dig it into the topmost layer. Be careful with shallow-rooted plants, such as those in the rhododendron family, for their feeding roots are near the surface. It might be better with them not to disturb the soil. Keep the soil moist, or water the compost well, being sure not to wash it out of place. Then put on a mulch. (See pages 321–334.) Mulches will eventually decompose and become humus themselves if they are organic, but a mulch will help to keep the soil moist and hasten integration of compost with the topsoil.

How can you change soils to improve them for the plants?

Let us examine the various kinds of soils and what is needed to improve them. Clay soil, since it is commonly encountered, is our first problem. This is closely packed, "heavy" soil, and to improve it we must open it up. Adding sand and humus will do the trick, but we should also add ground limestone as a kind of soil catalyst.

Sharp builder's sand of the sort that is used in making cement (not finish-coat cement) is coarse enough for our purpose. It should be clean. Never use sand from sea beaches. Salt is usually present in it and might sign the death warrant for many plants. Depending on the amount of clay present, mix in well a 2- to 5-inch layer of sand, incorporating it into the top 9 to 12 inches of soil. To open up the soil a bit more humus may be added, again using your judgment for how much to add—2 to 3 inches should be plenty for most soils. Peat moss is easily available and may be purchased almost anywhere, or compost and other kinds of humus may be utilized as available.

The last additive is ground limestone. Pulverized limestone is fine and quicker acting but more ephemeral, while other kinds of lime are, in my estimation, less desirable. Lime causes the tiny particles of clay to coagulate into larger units, opening up the soil and supplementing the work of the sand and humus. The limestone may be added together with the sand or humus, but be sure it is well distributed. Use 4 to 7 pounds per 100 square feet (10 feet by 10 feet) according to how much clay is in the soil. Lime will help to promote growth for most plants, since it assists the fertilizers and also allows moisture to penetrate to put them in solution. *Do not use lime in soil for acid-soil plants.* Lime has an alkalinizing effect that neutralizes soil somewhat which is against the best interests of rhododendrons, azaleas, holly, and other acid lovers. These three substances when added and mixed into clay soil will soon make it open, crumbly, and excellent for most other plants.

What can be done about sandy soils?

Soils with a large sand content need to be "tightened up," in contrast to the "loosening" effect described for clay soils. Addition of humus in quantities balanced according to the amount of sand will achieve this. Spread peat moss, leaf mold, compost, or other humus in a layer 2 inches thick or more if the soil is sandy to a great degree. Dig it into the top 9 to 12 inches of soil and mix it thoroughly. Mulching around the plants will conserve moisture, keeping the soil shaded and cooler in summer. Mulches will gradually decompose, and as they do, the humus thus created can be carefully worked into the topsoil. Be sure not to disturb or destroy shallow roots around the plants, especially close to the trunks.

Do garden-loam soils need improvement?

Few soils are ideal and even average to good garden-loam soils can pass muster on all counts. Soils in new gardens, particularly those near buildings, need cultivation and improvement on the whole. Debris may have been buried, and the fill around new foundations may be subsoil churned up in digging, often with a mixture of clay in it. Remove all debris—large stones (any up to the size of hen's eggs may be left), pieces of brick, wood scraps, metal scraps, asphalt shingles, and the like, and also old roots and logs. Then add humus, sand (if subsoil clay needs breaking up), and limestone (unless acid-soil plants are to be set in the beds). If removal of debris has lowered the ground level, add enough good soil to raise it to the proper depth. Even if the soil is good, it should be dug over at least once to break up clods and to open it up and make it easy for roots, moisture, and food to penetrate deeply.

Is there another kind of soil than acid?

At the other end of the scale is alkaline soil, and at the midway point is a soil neither acid nor alkaline called neutral soil. Few soils are either completely acid or alkaline, and most soils tend to be slightly neutral-acid or neutral-alkaline. It is important to know what kind of soil you have in order to select plants properly, or else to adjust the soil to their liking. Many plants prefer—even demand—a somewhat acid soil; others are more happily placed in a somewhat alkaline environment. However, most plants are rather tolerant, doing well in either slightly acid or slightly alkaline soil.

How can you tell whether your soil is acid, alkaline, or neutral?

There are soil-testing kits for the gardener available at garden centers or by mail-order, with complete directions for making a quick test. For a more exact (and professional) soil test, write to your state experiment station (see Appendix for list), and instructions will be sent for digging and sending a sample of soil. This is free in some states, or a nominal fee may be charged.

Can you change the reaction of soil to make it either more or less acid?

Soil can be adjusted to a degree, and if it is neutral, it can most certainly be made acid to accommodate such acid-loving plants as rhododendrons, azaleas, hollies, blueberries, and others. If it is more on the alkaline side, you may follow the advice of some gardeners in the Midwest—grow these plants in special raised beds, keeping the soil acid with additives. Acidity can be increased by using chemical fertilizers, such as ammonium sulfate, ammonium phosphate, and urea foods. There are also special-formula acidifying fertilizers sold as "Rhododendron and Azalea Foods," or "Holly Foods." Organic-minded gardeners can change soils more gradually by adding composted oak leaves or mulching with hardwood sawdust, both of which break down into a somewhat acid humus. See pages 287, 320.

Suppose you want to reduce acidity for growing other plants?

This can be done by applying 4 to 7 pounds per 100 square feet of ground limestone. Use the lesser amount for soils that are not very acid, more as acidity increases. Many plants may need a somewhat acid soil (even though they are not among those listed above); for these, do not reduce acidity, or else keep them in a separate bed. Ground limestone has larger particles than pulverized limestone, making it last longer and react more slowly. Occasional attention may be needed to keep acidity controlled. See page 321.

Should topsoil be bought and used for shrub beds?

In general the answer must be no. Topsoil is such an abused word that the gardener will do well to avoid buying from door-to-door salesmen or from other dubious sources. Good topsoil will be expensive, but poor topsoil is an even worse bargain. It will cost much more by the time you have finished improving it. Unscrupulous people often palm off mixtures of dubious quality, sometimes putting a layer of rich-looking soil on top of a load of poor soil. Cases are also noted of crooked operators who have sold oily black sawdust as topsoil, with dire results to gardens. At the very least you may also be buying a peck of weed seeds in most topsoil. You can make good soil out of your own soil, whatever its content, within a relatively short time. Invest in sand, humus, limestone, and fertilizer instead of spending money on dubious topsoil. This will ultimately be much more satisfactory.

These are the rudiments of preparing soil and adjusting it to suit the plants you choose. Planting operations are covered elsewhere and so is fertilizing. Once adjusted and improved, soil will be good for several years and perhaps forever. Moreover, certain soils need some yearly supervision and care and all soils will benefit by occasional renewal and cultivation.

MAINTAINING SOILS

Maintaining soils is generally thought of as meaning only the feeding of plants and occasional waterings, if it is considered at all. But if the soil has been adjusted and this has entailed opening up clay soil, making the content more acid or less acid, or making sandy soil more water retentive and heavier, then occasional attention will be warranted to ensure that these necessary conditions be maintained.

Clay Soil. For heavy clay soil, periodic applications of limestone are in order. Also, for acid soils that have been adjusted toward neutral, the addition of occasional limestone will keep this condition constant. The limestone had originally been incorporated by mixing into the soil. Later applications can be made on top of the soil, preferably in the autumn, so that winter moisture will convey it slowly downward into the soil where it can renew the binding together of clay particles, keeping the soil more open and crumbly in tilth. Light cultivation of the surface and removal of the mulch before application will enable the ground limestone to be placed where it can be easily assimilated. Do not cultivate deeply, for surface roots may be disturbed and destroyed.

Sandy Soil. Sandy soil may not need deep cultivation, but the renewal of humus lightly cultivated into the surface, whether placed on top as compost or as decomposed mulch, will keep the moisture-retentive qualities active. Fertilizing should be more frequent and lighter than for heavier soils, and watering more frequently will aid in the slow decomposition of humus into smaller particles that will filter down between the larger particles of sand.

Acidifying Soil. Neutral to slightly alkaline soil that has been adjusted toward acid will need periodic applications to keep this condition in the correct balance. While aluminum sulfate is often recommended, experts also warn that its prolonged use may cause some toxicity in certain soils. Therefore, it is safer to use dusting sulfur, the kind sold for use against fungus and leaf diseases. Spread it lightly but evenly over the soil in early June or late May, watering it in well before mulching the bed. Use up to ¼ pound per plant, but do not use more than this or you may injure the plant.

Reducing Acidity in Soil. A pound or two of ground limestone, spread as for Clay Soil, as noted in this section, will keep the soil sweet. Apply it in autumn or earliest spring, once a year where acid conditions are more severe, every other year in less acid conditions.

General Care. Fertilizing and watering are both of importance. Don't neglect either of them, for the best soil is useless if plants cannot assimilate foods and build structure.

MULCHES: FIRST AID FOR PLANTS

Perhaps we should first define this rather peculiar word so that all readers will understand its meaning and how it helps the garden. A mulch is a covering of some sort, placed atop the soil about the bases of plants

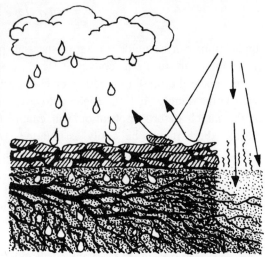

HOW A MULCH WORKS. A good mulch insulates the soil from drying effects of sun and wind but is open, allowing air as well as rain or hose water to penetrate to the soil. *Left,* sun's rays are deflected and cannot enter to heat and dry out soil and *right,* drying out new root growth and shriveling and inhibiting new growth on old roots.

to protect the roots and insulate them against the elements. A mulch can be any of a number of materials, as we shall demonstrate. By keeping soil temperatures relatively uniform it prevents damage to roots from violent fluctuations. For instance, in cold winters a mulch will keep soil from alternate freezing and thawing, which breaks tender roots as the ground heaves. In summer a mulch cuts down excessive drying out from evaporation, which may open up deep fissures that let air and heat penetrate to root areas. Moisture is conserved for root use, and hose watering is needed less even in dry climates.

A mulch will prevent soil from warming too quickly on "false spring" days, which foster soft new growth that will be injured when the mercury falls abruptly. As you can see, mulches serve a year-round purpose. For newly planted material, particularly during the first year or two, when plants are especially vulnerable to water starvation, to the freezing and thawing that plays havoc with tiny roots and uncertain plant structures aboveground, a mulch is a must to help get plants established.

CATEGORIES OF MULCHES

There are two broad categories with numerous choices in each for the ideal or nearly ideal mulching material—organic and inorganic. Natural materials, such as tree leaves, hay, and sawdust, to name a few, are on the organic list. They decompose at various rates, slow to fast, while inorganic materials either do not decompose at all or extremely slowly. Most lists of inorganic materials include gravel, stones, and crushed-rock mulches, but because they are natural materials we have put them with the organics, preferring to keep our inorganic list to those materials that are man made—metal foil, plastics, and the like. Some gardeners employ both categories in one mulch, and many use them where each does the best job for the garden.

Organic materials are preferred by most gardeners because they decompose and add humus and valuable nutrients to the soil, opening up the texture and giving plants a better root environment. Some will affect the character of the soil, adding acidity or neutralizing its acidity to a degree. Some materials might take nitrogen from the soil for the decomposition process, thus robbing roots of this vital element. Adding a bit of high-nitrogen plant food to the mulching material will overcome this drawback, however. Certain dry materials (as we point out in our descriptions) are especially flammable, and a mulch can be a fire hazard where, for instance, pine needles are used for a mulch and thoughtless people toss a lighted cigarette away. Fires can destroy plants or injure them irreparably, in addition to being dangerous to fences and structures. But if nobody in a family smokes, this may not be a factor to consider.

Mulches have fulfilled another function of late years, that of decoration. Shrubbery beds placed in a conspicuous place may be enhanced by bright brown bark, by stones or gravel, or some other pleasant material that provides a natural-looking foil for their leaves and flowers. It makes a bed look neat and attractive. A masonry or concrete mowing strip or a metal lawn edging around the bed will keep the material in place and define the edge of the bed, providing the line needed in the garden plan.

FACTORS TO CONSIDER

There are many considerations for the gardener to keep in mind when choosing the most practical mulch. Perhaps we should list them separately to make them easy to sum up as you decide which of the many possibilities will be best.

Appearance. Particularly in small gardens and on conspicuously placed beds this must be a prime consideration. Is it pleasant to look at and does it aid the garden picture?

Availability. Many mulches are excellent but may not be easily available or may be expensive because of transportation costs.

Durability. Where appearance is a factor, a durable mulch such as gravel, stones, or other long-lasting mulch should be considered. Some

323

mulches may be used in winter or for one season, then taken up and stored for reuse later on.

Nutritive Qualities, if any. Some mulches are relatively high in mineral and nutritional quality, while others are practically nil.

Soil-improvement Possibilities. A mulch can improve tilth of the soil, open up poor soil, or beef up sandy soil over the years. This will save labor and money that might be spent for fertilizer and other soil-improvement components.

Quantity Needed. The depth of the mulch will depend largely upon the character of the mulching material. Open, large-textured ones, such as those made of wood chips, may be used in deeper layers than peat moss and finer-textured types. Layers that are too thin may not give enough protection, while those that are too thick may smother the roots if the texture is fine and it is a material that packs down. Judgment is necessary, as is experimentation, since there can be no blanket rule except what has already been given.

Weather and Climate must also be considered. Lightweight mulches may be blown about by wind, piling up in corners and exposing soil to the drying sun and wind. Even the heavier mulches, such as evergreen boughs, may be displaced by a high wind and must be replaced. It may be wise to cover the mulch in windy places with rabbit wire or half-inch-mesh hardware cloth, staking it at the edges where wind is a problem.

When should a mulch be applied?

In placing the mulch for winter, it is usually a good practice to wait until after the first freeze, when the ground is frozen, and then place the mulch so that the plants go into the winter with cold soil that will be protected by the mulch from thawing until spring has finally arrived. Summer mulches are usually put on as soon as plants are in good growth to prevent the weeds from growing. Any weeds that do poke up through the mulch are easily pulled from the moist ground. If there has not been a heavy soaking rain within a few days, water the soil before positioning the summer mulch, and from time to time pull aside a bit of mulch and see if the soil seems dry. If so, water it, particularly in light and sandy soils.

What are the main benefits derived from mulching?

Aside from moisture-loss protection and winter aid, a mulch helps to keep down weeds, and to break the force of rain, splitting drops into small droplets that can penetrate the soil more easily, and they keep the soil from packing down by hard pelting rain, and sun baking. They prevent mud from splashing up on food plants and flowers during showers. Mulches provide safer weed control than chemical herbicides and are better than cultivation, which may break, injure or kill young surface roots.

How deep should the mulch be?

Mulches are usually 2 to 6 inches deep, depending on the coarseness of the material, and the coarser the material, the deeper will be the mulch. Deeper mulches are in order around trees and shrubs, evergreens as well as deciduous, than they are in flower beds and vegetable gardens. Such mulches may be kept on all year, more organic materials being added each year to keep them at the desired depth as the original mulches decompose. Moisture may be needed despite the water-saving character of the mulch, particularly in hot weather or in dry winters, and, of course, more often in dry climates than in moist ones.

What kinds of mulches are there?

Organic (natural) materials of all kinds are traditional, but man-made materials are also used, particularly in vegetable or cut-flower beds, and these may be placed beneath stone or gravel mulches. Usually they are best in small areas and, where appearance is a factor, covered with other materials. Natural but inorganic mulches include crushed rock, gravel, and coarse sand.

Why are organic mulches preferred by many gardeners?

Because as they decompose, they produce a somewhat gelatinous material that improves the physical structure of the soil by binding groups of soil particles together into granules. In heavy soil particularly, drainage and aeration is improved which in turn fosters root growth and activity.

Are there any mulches one should beware of?

If your plants are acid loving, an alkaline-reacting mulch may adversely affect plant growth and health. Plants such as azalea and rhododendron need acid soil, and a hard-leaf mulch is best. Oak leaves, pine needles, and certain peats are acid-reacting, but one should avoid soft leaves that pack and may prevent moisture from entering the soil or, if too wet, may produce a funguslike organism in the process of decomposing. Furthermore, it is possible that disease spores may "climb" the stems of the plants and seriously damage or kill them. Open mulches or hard leaves that decompose more slowly are best. For other kinds of plants, particularly those needing a neutral to more alkaline soil, leaves and all kinds of clean garden wastes may be used. If they can be shredded first, they will be more open and also decompose faster to make good soil.

Are there hazards involved in using mulches?

Aside from those just pointed out, the major hazard is fire. Most organic mulches dry out. Some, particularly evergreen needles, are quite flammable; if a cigarette end is tossed down carelessly, it can smoulder and the mulch may catch fire and injure or kill the plants, not to mention the hazard of setting fire to buildings and fences. Other qualities that are either transient or longer lasting are detailed in discussions of the individual mulches.

Should fertilizer or plant foods be put on before or after a mulch is applied?

Certain mulches—sawdust, wood, or bark, and a few others—may rob the soil of nitrogen. Therefore, it is wise to add a light feeding of high-nitrogen fertilizer in late autumn and again in early spring to compensate for such loss and to aid the decomposition process. Do not overfeed, however, for two light feedings are better than one heavy one. Nitrogen fertilizers may also be mixed in with the mulching material before application.

Nitrate of soda or a high-nitrogen general fertilizer (10-6-4, or other commercial plant food) or any of the organic materials such as dried blood, has somewhere near 12 percent nitrogen, 1 percent phosphoric acid, and less than 1 percent potash. Cottonseed meal, which may be more readily available, has about 7 percent nitrogen, 2½ percent phosphoric acid, and about 1½ percent potash. By adding a few handfuls of any of these (less of nitrate of soda) to the organic mulch material, enough nitrogen will be supplied so that the soil will not have to give it up and starve the roots of the plant. Any excess will enter the soil and leach down, becoming available to deeper roots as moisture carries it downward.

Are inorganic food sources better or worse than organic ones when applied to mulches?

Some authorities hold that although inorganic sources are quicker acting and more available, they can also cause a buildup of soluble salts in soils—especially heavy soils—and that therefore, organic nitrogen is safer. However, if a moderate amount is used and is well mixed with the mulch, there should be little trouble, particularly in moist regions, where the salts will dissolve fast and not be a problem.

Should mulches be replaced or can you use the same one year round?

As mulches decompose, more material should be added. It is a good plan to rake off all mulches occasionally and start fresh, particularly if there has been any fungus disease on the leaves or insect infestation on the plant. In that case, burn or otherwise dispose of the old mulch and do not compost it. Then put a good new clean mulch down for the winter.

Aren't mulches likely to harbor mice or insect pests?

It is true that a deep mulch may give shelter to mice, but this need give little trouble if the mulch is kept well away from the tree trunk or shrub shoots. Mice will gnaw bark in the dead of winter under the snow because food is scarce, girdling and even killing valuable small trees and shrubs. Keep mulches about a foot out from the plant in all directions.

To make doubly sure—mice can work their way under snow cover—take a piece of metal window screen or ¼-inch hardware cloth long enough to overlap when placed about the trunk and deep enough to cover it about a foot up. Set it a couple of inches into the soil and secure the covering with a loosely wrapped wire around it. In summer, when other sources of food are available to the mice, it can be removed for the sake of appearance. In any case it should not be left on after the trees are well established because the wires will constrict the growth and bark.

Mice and other rodents may be poisoned, too. Locate their runs and place poisoned seeds in a small tin can or bottle so that other animals and birds will not be able to get to them. Poison-seed bait is available at many hardware shops and most garden centers.

Particularly in moist regions, slugs and snails may be found in mulches. A snail bait that will destroy them will be found in the garden center or supplies dealer's shop. Follow directions on the package for its use. Other insects that overwinter can be dealt with by using the appropriate recommended controls.

What materials are used for mulches?

The following are the major materials for organic mulches. Availability will govern your choice, of course, as well as the cost of the mulching material. It should be pointed out that not all of those listed are available in all sections of the country. Some may be locally available but not found in the next state. There are probably other materials peculiar to your region if you inquire around.

Bagasse (sugar-cane pulp) is available in some parts of the South or in places to which it can be shipped inexpensively. Organic, lightweight, it needs protection from wind, and it may be expensive if a large quantity is needed. It gives moderate nutrition when decomposed.

Bark, Pine, Fir, and other kinds, has a pleasant color—brownish to red-brown—and is usually milled and sold in bags or other containers. Chunks of bark may range in size from fairly fine to two-inch pieces. For appearance choose bark that is uniform in color and size, for this looks best on conspicuously placed beds.

Bark, Redwood, is a durable, long-lasting mulch because of its peculiar cellular structure. Dark red in color, it is heavy enough to resist blowing by the wind.

Boughs, Evergreen, may be used alone or to cover more finely granulated mulching materials to prevent their blowing away over the winter. A good source is evergreen trees discarded after the Christmas season, or a tree dealer may sell leftover pine, spruce, or balsam trees for little or give them to you for hauling them away.

Buckwheat Hulls are sold in bags. They make a good small-textured mulch with a pleasant dark brown color. Light in weight, they may blow in high winds, piling up in corners and exposing the soil, but a summertime mulch of buckwheat hulls is most presentable. Cost may increase with transportation charges to some areas. They are lasting but provide little in the way of nutrients to the soil.

Cocoa-bean Hulls are relatively inexpensive where available (mostly near candymaking factories or where beans are roasted). They are fine textured and pleasantly colored, but they may pack down. A suggested solution to this is to mix them with sawdust—2 parts hulls to 1 part sawdust—before application.

Coconut Fiber, available in a few places, is a pleasant dark reddish brown, and makes a good cover.

Coffee Grounds may be available in quantity from restaurants or other sources. High in nitrogen but not long lasting, they quickly decompose into a gluey mass. Best used with sawdust mixed in half and half to give more texture. Nitrogen will aid in sawdust decomposition. Grounds alone or with sawdust from oak and some evergreens may add some acidity to soil.

Compost may be used. Partially decomposed compost or what is left over after screening for use in improving flower beds will add fertility, is a pleasant earth color, but will need periodic renewal.

Corn Cobs (ground) are widely available in the Middle West and in some other spots. Not very attractive because of the light color, not very durable, but cheap and available. May blow away in windy spots.

Cottonseed Hulls. Long lasting, neat, and unobtrusive for use on conspicuous beds. Brownish black color with gray cotton fibers often still attached. Available in the South, but may have disease spores of wilt disease or be contaminated with defoliant herbicides.

Cranberry Vines. Usually available baled in cranberry-growing regions of the Northeast. An easy-to-spread and reasonably attractive mulch that is open and lasting. Some nutritive value as it decomposes.

Excelsior, though a fire hazard because it is made of shredded wood, should be further shredded or chopped. Not attractive because of its light color, but when weathered or dyed with a spray, it can make a lasting, unobtrusive mulch that is open and may be used anywhere. Little or no nutrition, but durable.

Grass Clippings are not durable, but decompose rapidly. The nutritive value will vary with the type of grass and other content in the clippings. They are a fire hazard when dry and are not particularly attractive, but make a good hillside mulch to hold soil. They may provide a haven for various pests. Do not use them fresh or wet, but dry them before using, and

329

for best effect, mix half and half with peat moss and spread lightly to about 3-inch depth. Fresh grass clippings will heat up the soil and may also mildew before drying. Do not use clippings with grass seeds set, or weed grasses in the mulched bed may be a problem.

Gravel and Stones offer many desirable qualities. Widely available, often in selected colors—reds, yellows, pinkish, etc.—a very attractive open mulching material for shrubs and around trees. Nonnutritive but very stable in windy areas, naturally durable and no fire hazard, these make a fine foil for evergreens and most shrubs. Stones may be small to large— 1-inch to 3- or 4-inch diameters are available, often called "water-washed stones". They may also be collected from river beds or creek and lake bottoms by a diligent gardener. All stone and gravel mulches insulate the soil and, if applied three inches or more deep, will keep the soil moist and allow waterings and rains to penetrate easily. *Note:* White or very light stone and marble chips are not a good foil for shrubs and cause an unpleasant glare in bright sunlight.

Hay, Salt. A product of seashore meadows, salt-marsh hay is a tough, durable-fibered material. It makes a very good winter mulch because it is wiry, does not pack down and is likely to stay put except in high winds. Because it is coarse and not very sightly, it is mostly used as a winter mulch in cold areas, raked off and stored over the summer, to be replaced for the season with an attractive summer mulching material. Because it is coarse, however, it allows winter moisture to penetrate, and as it slowly decomposes it will add some nutrition to the soil.

Hay, Various. All sorts of hay or forage such as that fed to horses (including alfalfa) is moderately durable though not particularly attractive. It does not pack down excessively, allows water to penetrate and will add organic content and nutrition to the soil as it decomposes. However, it is a fire hazard when dry and also may contain seeds of weeds as well as those of hay or alfalfa.

Hops. Spent hops are available from breweries and are acceptable except for the odor. They are not, therefore, recommended for use near a house or outdoor living space.

Leaf Mold. Either collected from the forest or composted from home leaf-gathering, leaf mold usually contributes minerals and other nutrients to the soil. Mixed with chopped leaves and spread four inches or more deep, leaf mold will aid in decomposing the leaves. A little high-nitrogen fertilizer may also be added to aid in the breaking down process, when making a mulch for shrubs. Each year the mulch should be renewed, and the leaf mold can either be scratched into the soil or it can be removed to the compost pile.

Leaves, Various. Not all leaves make universally good mulches, despite their known qualities of mineral content and nutritive value, plus the fact that they decompose to add humus content to the soil. Soft leaves such as maple, birch and the like are subject to flattening and packing down, and, as they decompose, form a slimy, unpleasant mass. Oak and other hard leaves will stand up and are more durable. It is best to shred and chop soft leaves and partially compost them before use as a mulch or to mix them with compost when preparing the mulch. Hard leaves may be used as they are or coarsely shredded to aid in breaking down, which also gives them a more uniform, pleasant appearance as a mulch. Note that oak leaves add a bit of acidity to the soil and are thus recommended for use around azaleas, rhododendrons, camellias and other acid-soil plants. Soft leaves should *never* be used around such plants because of the danger of disease resulting from the slime. The diseases may mount the stems to injure or kill the plant. If leaves are collected from the street (town road departments often will deliver a truckload if asked) beware of trash in the leaves, also where mixed sand and salt are distributed on streets to melt ice and snow, some salty sand may be present in the leaves which may injure plants.

Manure, Fresh. Animal manures should never be used when fresh, for nutrients are too strong and may burn roots. Furthermore, the odor is repulsive. However, old manure that has been weathered and partially composted may be used where available. Fresh manure mixed with leaves and other vegetable wastes will decompose rapidly, for the heat and strong nutrients will aid quick composting and the odor is also minimized.

Mushroom Compost is sometimes available from mushroom growers when they finish using it. It is highly satisfactory, for it is easily spread, has a pleasant dark color, and has some nutrition in it.

Peanut Hulls, other nut shells. Available in peanut-growing and -packing areas, and from nut processors elsewhere, hulls and shells are satisfactory except for their color, which may be too light and draw attention to itself. Also, sometimes shells have been treated to control pests and may be chemically contaminated to a degree.

Peat, Granulated. Peat that is packaged and sold as "granulated" is a good mulch and is particularly recommended for use with camellias.

Peat Moss, Sedge Peat. Sphagnum peat moss is brown, fine textured, and moisture absorbent. Attractive, though expensive in quantity, it should be spread thinly and cultivated frequently for it has a tendency to cake and dry out, shedding water rather than absorbing it. Finely ground and shredded peat may also blow away when dry. Mixed with other materials, it is satisfactory. *Sedge Peat* is humusy and fine, has more nutrition (nitrogen) than sphagnum peat, but both have minor nuitritional value. As a winter mulch to be cultivated into the soil in spring, sphagnum peat has a place, but it is less recommended for summer use than sedge peat.

Pine and Other Needles. Many kinds of evergreens shed their needles yearly, and in undisturbed forests old needles may be several inches deep. Where the owner's permission is granted, the needles may be bagged and transported for use as a mulch for acid-soil plants (azaleas, rhododendrons, etc.), for which their pleasant-colored reddish to gray carpeting is satisfactory. They decompose slowly, have a good supply of nutrients, but are a fire hazard when dry. A 3- to 4-inch mulch may be used, renewing it as it decomposes.

Sawdust is a satisfactory mulch, although it has some drawbacks. When fresh, its color is distracting; also, it will draw nitrogen from the soil in its decomposition process, while redwood sawdust may contain tannic acid, which is detrimental to young seedlings. However, as noted previously, other materials may be mixed with sawdust (see *Cocoa-bean Hulls, Grass Clippings*) to their mutual benefit, and many gardeners add some high-nitrogen fertilizer to sawdust mulches. It can be weathered before use, of course, achieving a pleasant gray color and minimizing the amount of nitrogen it will pull from the soil, or it may be sprayed with or soaked in a bath of green or brown dye. Use 2 to 4 inches deep, and add a bit more each year, being sure to apply some high-nitrogen fertilizer at the same time.

Seaweed is available for the taking along the shores of the ocean and adds mineral elements to the soil as it decomposes. It is not ornamental or particularly attractive, but when shredded would make an acceptable mulch.

Stones. See *Gravel and Stones.*

Straw. Not generally recommended because of the probable presence of seeds, weeds, and other elements, and because of its obtrusive color. It is not long lasting and is a fire hazard, but in the vegetable garden and around strawberries it would be satisfactory.

Tobacco Stems, available in tobacco-growing and -processing areas, make a coarse, not unattractive mulch that often discourages insect infestations. However, it may also introduce mosaic disease to the soil, which is bad for tomatoes, if they are planted nearby.

Wood Chips, either obtained from a supplier, from town road-work departments, or from chipping pruned branches and hedge clippings on the home property, are excellent natural mulches for shrubs and trees. Excellent lasting quality, soon weathering to an unobtrusive grayish color and open so that air and moisture can penetrate. Good for hillside or flat plantings. Only moderately hazardous from fire, they do not blow easily and are less likely to draw on available soil nitrogen. Chip mulches should be renewed as they decompose.

Wood Shavings. Longer lasting than sawdust and more open, but they will blow away in high winds. May be mixed with wood chips.

Man-made, inorganic mulches include:

Aluminum Foil. Too conspicuous for permanent mulches but can be used to reflect sun and keep soil moisture in new plantings. The heavy-duty grade seals in soil moisture, smothers weeds, and keeps soil up to 20 degrees cooler than unmulched soil nearby. Can be rolled up and reused.

Newspapers. Either shredded or whole, a thin layer (three or four sheets thick) of newspapers under a gravel mulch will soon decompose. Or, put on in winter under salt hay, the papers will have decomposed by spring and can be cultivated into the soil as humus content.

Plastic Film. May be used for temporary mulch to seal in moisture, similar to aluminum foil. Also used under gravel or stone mulches but not practical for sharp crushed stone unless insulated with an inch or two of sand. In moist areas particularly, puncturing film with a pitchfork here and there will allow moisture to drain into the soil and keep it moist.

333

Tar Paper of the sort used under roofing on houses can also be used for a temporary mulch or under stone. It is awkward to handle, however.

Another kind of "mulch" to be recommended is the living mulch or ground-cover planting. In beds where they fit the need, these low-growing plants soften the effect, provide a green or other-colored carpet, shade the soil, and allow moisture and air to enter.

8

Rejuvenating Old Gardens

An old garden can be brought back to vigorous new life and made over to conform to today's standards of gardens and gardening. Sometimes it is necessary to perform major surgery, whereas sometimes merely a light face-lifting operation will suffice; this depends on the garden and the care it received both in conception and in maintenance. The latter may be more difficult in some ways than starting from scratch. On the other hand, providing that the plant material is good and the trees and shrubs are in good health, even though a bit overgrown, you may have a distinct advantage: your garden will be mature looking, and the feeling of belonging that comes with maturity will be achieved faster than with newly planted gardens that take a bit of time to reach this stage.

The first step is to evaluate what you have in terms of seeing what the general effect is. Does the garden layout please you in general or does it not lend itself to being moderately revamped and brought into line? If it does not, are there parts possible to renovate and salvage? If either of these questions is answered in the affirmative, you can begin from there. Today's gardens are much more geared to outdoor living than those designed and planted thirty to forty years ago. We sit out, entertain, and eat outdoors now with family and friends wherever the climate permits it. Since this is primarily a book on plants, not garden layout and design, this subject will not be pursued here, but it is one of the things to be taken into account if you are the inheritor of or purchaser of an older home and garden.

Walk around your garden and study it from all angles. See if the plantings are in good condition, if they are overgrown, if the shrubs obscure the view from the windows, the evergreens impede progress through the doors, the trees block off air and light from windows. These are the common failings of older gardens, the evergreens in particular presenting a problem because they may have been wrongly selected and allowed to sprawl. A house may be pleasantly shady and cool in summer because it is topped by thick leafage, but it can be equally gloomy and depressing in winter, because the excessive amount of branches and twigs also shut out sunlight that would brighten the drab months. Many older homes have foundation plantings that probably will need replacement. These evergreens and shrubs were not suited to the purpose when they were selected and now have grown up in front of windows, arch out over walks and doorways, and in general have become straggly and unkempt. There are many dwarf and low-growing evergreens and shrubs that will serve very well as replacements and never grow out of proportion to their space or can be kept inside it with a minimum of attention.

Another failing of older gardens is that many of them have been neglected for years through lack of knowledge of how to prune and renew the plants. Judicious surgery can bring many a plant back to vigorous beautiful growth. Make notes of the drawbacks as you go about the garden. Then go indoors and look out again at the garden, noting carefully what the assets and liabilities are, what you think you might like to keep, and what you feel must go or may be borderline cases for future reference. The best thing to do is to observe the garden carefully for the first year and not make immediate moves except for what is absolutely necessary. Living with a garden will prove to you better than anything else what its true qualities are, in addition to showing you the plant material in all seasons—in flower, in leaf, in fruit, and the bare bones of the plants in winter—and then you will be in a better position to judge what is needed.

This means that identification will be easier and you will be better able to assess the contributions or lack of them. Identify as many of the shrubs as you can, seeking help from neighbors and other gardeners if necessary, so that you can see by the lists in this book what the qualities are. Observe whether the borders are a dull conglomeration of shrubs that

WEEPING CHERRY is an appealing small tree with cascades of pink blossoms before the leaves appear, but needs space to develop and spread widely. (*Paul E. Genereux*)

have grown out of line, shade the lawn or encroach on traffic or living areas. If tall bare trunks of shrubs show prominently without medium or low plantings to obscure them, they are candidates either for cutting back and renewal—if their constitution will permit it—or for replacement if it does not. Perhaps they are taking up valuable space that might better grow more interesting shrubs. If the border is thickly overgrown, monotonous because the textures are too similar, the heights of too many shrubs are the same, or because one of this and one of that was planted it is "spotty"— making a kind of restless confetti mixture rather than a serene though contrasting appearance—then you will want to take steps to remedy this shortcoming also.

Rejuvenation and thinning may be all that is needed if the shrubs are worthwhile. (See Chapter 7 for pruning and renewal methods.) But first look at the surroundings. Are there any buildings, utility poles, and other unsightly things that are blocked out by these thick plantings? In that case you may want to proceed carefully and thin and renew them over a longer time.

This brings us to another aspect of the older garden. Probably new buildings or new ugly things have been added since the house was built and the garden laid out. You will want to plan to mask these or block them out, just as you would in a new garden. Are there any new and good views that have been opened up by adjacent clearing out of woods or other features? You may be able to use these new openings to have a vista of a distant hill, a nearby pond, or some other pleasant view.

Make a list of all of these items and add it to your other lists so that your garden picture is complete. You should now be ready to give your attention to the garden, area by area, deciding on what projects to launch for renewal or replacement, and making a kind of master plan.

PROCEED WITH CAUTION

Doubtless you will want to review your feelings about gardening, and it might be well to reread the portions of this book where trees and shrubs and their contributions are covered. As you read, make notes of any of the trees and shrubs mentioned that you already possess; also start a checklist of possible successors to the ones you may remove. Perhaps you will begin to get an idea of how to develop some particular area and you can make a rough sketch. Think of where you want to put your outdoor terraces for your outdoor living and entertaining and try to visualize how plants will dress up the edges, make it private, contribute fragrance, blossoms and/or fruit, year-round greenery, and all the other desirable things such places should include. The winter is a good time for this when there are fewer outdoor chores to perform and you can see the skeletons of the plants, deciding now also what needs some winter color.

When you have your plans ready and you have chosen the shrubs and any new trees you mean to plant, think about the construction that may be necessary for your outdoor life—paving, built-up terraces with part of them covered, privacy fences, walls and walks to be added or relocated. Decide right then to postpone planting these areas until the construction is completed, for workmen, even the better ones, sometimes ruin new plantings or it might cost you more if they have to be especially careful in doing their work. If you are going to preserve some of the plants, make it part of the contract for the work that trunks of trees and worthwhile evergreens and shrubs are to be boxed in and protected until the work is completed. Also make sure that workmen do not bury and dispose of debris and trash in the beds where you will have to cope with it later when you plant your new shrubs and trees.

There are other good reasons for not doing the whole job at once. If you are doing the work yourself, pruning, thinning, removal, and replanting, you may find it wise to budget your time and energy so that it is not expended all in one season. Too much strain can be dangerous to your health, and at the least it is a road to quick disenchantment. Decide on what is of most immediate concern and then realistically decide what can be accomplished. It may be the street side of the house that needs your attention first: trees may need to be thinned out and maybe some that are too overgrown and gloom producing should be cut down and replaced with lower growers, possibly flowering trees, some with lighter foliage or more open growth. If large trees must be removed, this is a job for professionals, not the amateur who does not have proper equipment and often falls prey to dangers inherent in lack of knowledge. Large limb removal is also best handled by tree men with tall ladders and the knowledge of how to do this with the least danger to the trees. Other pruning, even major cutbacks on shrubs, can be handled by intelligent gardeners who proceed with caution to enhance the beauty of the plant, never blundering in and butchering it through haste.

If you feel that some of your shrubs, particularly evergreen ones, should be transplanted elsewhere in the garden, this also is a place where the professional plantsman should be called in. A good one with the proper machinery and help can do a job in a few hours that would take the amateur many days of hand digging and backbreaking labor if, in the end, he could actually manage to move the large root ball. A mature shrub, perhaps cut back a bit to compensate for loss of roots in the transplanting, will come back quickly and give an air of maturity in its new location very quickly. Many times the original planting was put in with too little spacing between plants. By taking some out, good plants that remain can be given an opportunity to spread and take their true form. On the other hand, it may be that the original plants were inferior and not up to the standard you wish your garden to maintain. In this case you must think in terms of complete replacement.

It takes courage to look at big evergreens and mature shrubs and decide that they must go. Yet the only course is to be ruthless and remove them entirely if they are below par. There is nothing to be gained but dissatisfaction from living with another person's past mistakes. Do not be sentimental, but steel yourself and get rid of whatever does not fit; do it quickly so that the successors will get started on their way to mature beauty as soon as possible. Get rid of them, roots and all. And note, "*roots* and *all*." Anything cut off merely at soil level will not be much of an improvement, for the roots may sprout again or at the very least will be in the way of the new plantings. Get rid of as much as you can, dig the beds, enrich and open up the soil, making it acid or more alkaline if the new material demands it. Add humus and/or sand if the soil requires it, for any new planting.

STUDY THE SURVIVORS

Sum up the plants you have decided to keep in terms of foliage, flowers, fruit, the time of bloom, the color of blossoms, and check the mature height. (It may be the present height, depending on when they were planted.) Now think of what would best complement them, contrast with them, bloom simultaneously with them or later or earlier, just as you would for an entirely new border. Would some evergreen shrubs or broad-leaved evergreens enhance and give a lift to the composition? If you decide to make it all evergreen, how about some of those with silvery needles, yellowish green, or blue-green? If it is to be a deciduous border, think in terms of foliage texture and color, the winter color of twigs, or any other out-of-season aspects that might enhance the shrubbery bed. Consider incorporating a small tree as a foil for the shrubs and thus cutting down on maintenance, because the tree will not be situated on the lawn with the necessity for trimming around it. It might support the blossoming bed, contrast with it or coincide with its time of bloom, give added height well away from the house and help to block out views and maintain privacy. Soon you will have put together an exciting and pleasant new border, using the older shrubs as the nucleus. When the old shrubs are removed, you can see what is needed in the way of pruning, cutting back, and restoring shape and health to the remaining ones. Review the section on renewal pruning, pages 289–290, to refresh your memory before you do this.

As indicated above, this is also the time to refresh the soil and get it in shape for replanting. The same instructions apply now as for making a new bed (see Chapter 7), except that you are only partially planting it. But be sure that adequate holes for replanting are made, the soil opened up for good drainage or whatever is needed. Once planted and established, all that will be needed is maintenance by feeding and watering, and the same care will produce results with the renewed older plants.

CARE AND FEEDING OF OLD PLANTS

If your shrubbery borders are satisfactory, perhaps only thinning out and some pruning will be needed. In that case maintenance from then on will be concerned mainly with watering and feeding the plants until further pruning is needed. If the plants have not been fed properly, they may have become straggly, leggy, and not very well proportioned, with sparse leafage and fewer blossoms. Watering in plant food will help to bring them back quickly. Do not overfeed them, for plants cannot take in more than they need and too much feeding can result in more leaves and fewer flowers until nature adjusts the balance. For most plants, the soil will need cultivation, stirring up the surface before feeding. The exceptions are the shallow-rooted kinds, such as dogwoods, rhododendrons, and azaleas, and some of the needled evergreens. For these, use a rake or a hand cultivator to stir the surface only, raking off debris and opening up the soil a little bit. Then lightly scatter the dry plant food over the surface and again rake it in before watering. Put a mulch on top of the soil and keep it moist through the growing season so that the plants can take up the food in solution and utilize it.

For other plants, cultivate the soil more deeply, mixing in the plant food and then watering it, mulching the bed and again keeping it moist. A good feeding in early spring and another in June if it is needed should suffice. Do not feed plants after midsummer (July 15) in colder regions where temperatures go below freezing or, in the milder regions, a month or so later. All plants need a period of rest, and winter gives it to them. New soft growth in late summer will be frozen back in the cold areas so that nothing is gained, and dead wood will merely mean more work in cutting it off in the spring. One exception to this late feeding rule is the needled evergreens. A moderate feeding shortly before the ground freezes will give them nitrogen in the needles and help them to resist browning and winter burn of needles. November is a good time for this, too late to cause growth, yet early enough to allow absorption.

341

A WORD ABOUT TREES

Although we have advocated the use of medium to small trees for shade, if your garden has larger old trees that are in good condition, there is no reason to dispose of them. Often, however, the plot has been over-planted and the trees have grown into a canopy that shades out most other plants, with branching that makes the interior of the house gloomy in winter, with perhaps some dead or storm-broken limbs appearing here and there. Take to heart the thoughts expressed in this chapter: thin out limbs or have the work done by professionals with proper equipment. And if there is so much shade that you cannot grow flowers or shrubs or have a hard time flowering them well, then you certainly should consider having some of the trees removed. Study the shade cast at various times of day, seeing which trees—if kept—will give you the most shade where you need it in the hot parts of the day and which—if removed—will let in the life-giving sun and air, opening up views and allowing the expansion of others in order to maintain privacy and enhance composition. On the street side, perhaps one or more trees can be removed and the whole area profit thereby. New and smaller flowering trees that may be in better scale can be put in, this time where they will mean the most to the house and the street and not just placed arbitrarily and bisymmetrically in the front yard as so often was done in the past—and is still done by the unknowing amateur.

If the trees are thinned out, it is probable that stronger limbs will result, because with fewer limbs to maintain, all the building materials will be channeled into the remaining limbs. If the shade is too thick by the house but the branches are needed to maintain privacy from upstairs windows or streets and walks, uphill from the house, consider having some of the limbs removed and the remainder thinned on the side of the tree nearest the house. From the windows and outdoor sitting areas the limbs and structure of the tree will be seen, yet because of the thinning out, more light and more air circulation will come into the house area without any loss of privacy.

Many times we see evergreens towering above little houses, forest trees that should never have been planted in the first place and that are now becoming shaggy or sparse in the lower limbs, and are a menace in windstorms and gales because they are shallow-rooted. Spruces, hemlocks, and other trees that may grow to over 100 feet in the forest are shallow rooted and do not belong in the yard close to houses. They are beautiful when young and in age have a majesty, yet they give little shade and are likely to be too big to be seen and appreciated from nearby. They are better removed before a windstorm brings them down and damage to the house or property occurs. If a replacement evergreen is desired, choose a moderate-height one that will not get out of hand within the time you expect to live in your home and enjoy your garden.

To sum up, if you possess an older garden, don't feel that it must be endured as it is. A garden is a living thing, and like all living things it goes from youth to maturity to extinction. That is nature's way. And as history shows us, the human way is to change our lives, develop new wants and needs, evolve socially, constantly revealing new aspects as we progress. We are now returning to the enjoyment of nature and an appreciation of the outdoors after many centuries of trying to become city dwellers. We are now realizing that we are a part of nature and that when we ignore it or counter the ancient urgings to ally ourselves with the living world, we are less than whole people.

All through history the great gardens have changed and evolved, sometimes being completely remade as life and fashion demanded changes, sometimes only subtly changing. The plants matured and sometimes died so that they had to be replaced. Sometimes new ones were substituted, even before the plants expired, and this kept the gardens fluid as new ideas entered into their composition. No garden can ever be a true museum. Even the great ones at Versailles are constantly being renewed, though they now keep to the original plan and are not redesigned as they were in earlier days.

Therefore, any gardener can take heart when changes should be made and make them with good conscience. When new plants are added, the gardener can make sure that they are at least as good as the old ones. Probably they will be better in certain ways as knowledge advances and as choices widen to give us plants that fit the space, stay within bounds, offer more flowers and color, are hardier, more disease resistant, and capable of bringing new beauty in our gardens.

Appendix

AGRICULTURAL COLLEGES
AGRICULTURAL EXPERIMENT STATIONS

(From U. S. D. A. Agriculture Handbook No. 116.)

STATE	CITY	NAME
ALABAMA	Auburn 36830	School of Agriculture, Auburn University
	Auburn	Agricultural Experiment Station
ALASKA	College 99701	Department of Agriculture, University of Alaska
	Palmer 99645	Agricultural Experiment Station
ARIZONA	Tucson 85721	College of Agriculture, University of Arizona
	Tucson 85721	Agricultural Experiment Station
ARKANSAS	Fayetteville 72701	College of Agriculture, University of Arkansas
	Fayetteville 72701	Agricultural Experiment Station
CALIFORNIA	Davis 95616	Agricultural Experiment Station
	Los Angeles 90024	Agricultural Experiment Station
	Riverside 92502	Agricultural Experiment Station
COLORADO	Fort Collins	College of Agriculture, Colorado State University
	Fort Collins 80521	Agricultural Experiment Station
CONNECTICUT	Storrs 06268	College of Agriculture, University of Connecticut
	Storrs 06268	Storrs Agricultural Experiment Station
	New Haven 06504	The Connecticut Agricultural Experiment Station
DELAWARE	Newark 19711	School of Agriculture, University of Delaware
	Newark 19711	Agricultural Experiment Station
FLORIDA	Gainesville 32601	College of Agriculture, University of Florida
	Gainesville 32601	Agricultural Experiment Station
GEORGIA	Athens 30601	College of Agriculture, University of Georgia
	Tifton 31794	Georgia Coastal Plain Experiment Station

STATE	CITY	NAME
HAWAII	Honolulu 96822	College of Tropical Agriculture, University of Hawaii
	Honolulu 96822	Agricultural Experiment Station
IDAHO	Moscow 83843	College of Agriculture, University of Idaho
	Moscow 83843	Agricultural Experiment Station
ILLINOIS	Urbana 61801	College of Agriculture, University of Illinois
	Urbana 61801	Agricultural Experiment Station
INDIANA	Lafayette 47907	School of Agriculture, Purdue University
	Lafayette 47907	Agricultural Experiment Station
IOWA	Ames 50010	College of Agriculture, Iowa State University of Science and Technology
	Ames 50010	Agricultural Experiment Station
KANSAS	Manhattan 66502	Kansas State University of Agriculture and Applied Science
	Manhattan 66502	Agricultural Experiment Station
KENTUCKY	Lexington 40506	College of Agriculture, University of Kentucky
	Lexington 40506	Agricultural Experiment Station
LOUISIANA	Baton Rouge 70803	Louisiana State University and Agricultural and Mechanical College, University Station
	Baton Rouge 70803	Agricultural Experiment Station, University Station
MAINE	Orono 04473	College of Agriculture, University of Maine
	Orono 04473	Agricultural Experiment Station, University of Maine
MARYLAND	College Park 20742	College of Agriculture, University of Maryland
	College Park 20742	Agricultural Experiment Station
MASSACHUSETTS	Amherst 01002	College of Agriculture, University of Massachusetts
	Amherst 01002	Agricultural Experiment Station
MICHIGAN	East Lansing 48823	Michigan State University of Agriculture and Applied Science
	East Lansing 48823	Agricultural Experiment Station
MINNESOTA	St. Paul 55101	Institute of Agriculture, University of Minnesota, St. Paul Campus
	St. Paul 55101	Agricultural Experiment Station, St. Paul Campus
MISSISSIPPI	State College 39762	School of Agriculture and Forestry, Mississippi State University of Applied Arts and Sciences
	State College 39762	Agricultural Experiment Station
MISSOURI	Columbia 65201	College of Agriculture, University of Missouri
	Columbia 65201	Agricultural Experiment Station

STATE	CITY	NAME
MONTANA	Bozeman 59715	Montana State College
	Bozeman 59715	Agricultural Experiment Station
NEBRASKA	Lincoln 68503	College of Agriculture, University of Nebraska
	Lincoln 68503	Agricultural Experiment Station
NEVADA	Reno 89107	Max C. Fleischmann College of Agriculture, University of Nevada
	Reno 89107	Agricultural Experiment Station
NEW HAMPSHIRE	Durham 03824	College of Agriculture, University of New Hampshire
	Durham 03824	Agricultural Experiment Station
NEW JERSEY	New Brunswick 08903	State College of Agriculture and Mechanic Arts, State University
	New Brunswick 08903	Agricultural Experiment Station of Rutgers
NEW MEXICO	University Park 88001	College of Agriculture, New Mexico State University
	Las Cruces 88001	Agricultural Experiment Station
NEW YORK	Ithaca 14850	New York State College of Agriculture, Cornell University
	Ithaca 14850	Agricultural Experiment Station
	Geneva 14456	New York State Agricultural Experiment Station
NORTH CAROLINA	Raleigh 27607	North Carolina State College of Agriculture and Engineering, University of North Carolina
	Raleigh 27607	Agricultural Experiment Station
NORTH DAKOTA	Fargo 58102	College of Agriculture, North Dakota State University of Agriculture and Applied Science, State University Station
	Fargo 58102	Agricultural Experiment Station
OHIO	Columbus 43210	College of Agriculture, Ohio State University
	Wooster 44691	Ohio Agricultural Experiment Station
OKLAHOMA	Stillwater 74074	Oklahoma State University of Agriculture and Applied Science
	Stillwater 74074	Agricultural Experiment Station
OREGON	Corvallis 97331	School of Agriculture, Oregon State University
	Corvallis 97331	Agricultural Experiment Station
PENNSYLVANIA	University Park 16802	College of Agriculture, Pennsylvania State University
	University Park 16802	Agricultural Experiment Station
RHODE ISLAND	Kingston 02881	College of Agriculture, University of Rhode Island
	Kingston 02881	Agricultural Experiment Station
SOUTH CAROLINA	Clemson 29631	Clemson Agricultural College of South Carolina, School of Agriculture
	Clemson 29631	Agricultural Experiment Station

STATE	CITY	NAME
SOUTH DAKOTA	College Station	South Dakota State College of Agriculture
	Brookings 57006	Agricultural Experiment Station
TENNESSEE	Knoxville 37901	College of Agriculture, University of Tennessee
	Knoxville 37901	Agricultural Experiment Station
	Martin 38237	Martin Branch, University of Tennessee
TEXAS	College Station 77843	Agricultural and Mechanical College of Texas
	College Station 77843	Agricultural Experiment Station
UTAH	Logan 84321	Utah State University of Agriculture and Applied Science
	Logan 84321	Agricultural Experiment Station
VERMONT	Burlington 05401	College of Agriculture, University of Vermont
	Burlington 05401	Agricultural Experiment Station
VIRGINIA	Blacksburg 24061	School of Agriculture, Virginia Polytechnic Institute
	Blacksburg 24061	Agricultural Experiment Station
WASHINGTON	Pullman 99163	College of Agriculture, Washington State University, Institute of Agricultural Sciences
	Pullman 99163	Agricultural Experiment Station
WEST VIRGINIA	Morgantown 26506	College of Agriculture, West Virginia University
	Morgantown 26506	Agricultural Experiment Station
WISCONSIN	Madison 53813	College of Agriculture, University of Wisconsin
	Madison 53813	Agricultural Experiment Station
WYOMING	Laramie 82070	College of Agriculture, University of Wyoming
	Laramie 82070	Agricultural Experiment Station

Glossary

Terms used in plant descriptions, often encountered in catalogues, in botanical references, in books and encyclopedias.

ALTERNATE-LEAVED: Growing from opposite sides alternately

ASYMMETRICAL: Unbalanced, unequal

AXIL: Inside angle between leaf and branch

BISEXUAL: Containing both sexes; a flower with both stamens and pistils

BRACT: A leaflike growth surrounding flowers that may be small and inconspicuous. Dogwood "flowers" are conspicuous bracts; the true flowers are in the center.

CANE: A term applied to shoots of shrubs such as roses

CONE: Fruit of coniferous trees

CONIFEROUS: Trees bearing cones, such as pine, larch, etc.

CULTIVAR: A word of recent origin (coined from "cultivated" and "variety"); including cultivated varieties, hybrids or selections, with the first letter capitalized, the word enclosed in single quotation marks. Since 1959 no new cultivars may be in Latin or have a Latin ending.

DECIDUOUS: Falling off, as autumn leaves

DIGITATE: Several parts radiating from one point or nearly one point

DIOECIOUS: Having stamens and pistils in separate flowers on different individuals.

DRUPE: A single-seeded fleshy fruit, as yew

EVERGREEN: A term usually applied to narrow-leaved or needle-leaved plants. Broad-leaved evergreens are plants with broader leaves and is a term sometimes narrowly applied to only a few genera. Evergreen plants hold leaves all year, discarding old ones occasionally but never shedding all leaves.

FOLIAGE: Leaves

GENUS: A group of species within a plant family or order

HERMAPHRODITE: See PERFECT

HIP: The fruit of the rose

INFLORESCENCE: A flower cluster of any kind. Also, the arrangement of flowers on the stem.

LATERAL: Belonging to the side; side branch

LEAFLET: A small leaf, usually one of the divisions or blades of a compound leaf—one that has several leaflets on a common stem

MARGINS: Outer edges of leaves

MONOECIOUS: Having stamens and pistils in separate flowers on the same plant

OPPOSITE: Growing directly across from each other on a common stem or branch.

PALMATE: Shaped like a hand with fingers spread

PENDENT: Hanging down

PENDULOUS: Somewhat hanging; drooping

PERENNIAL: Any plant living more than two years, some woody

PERFECT: Having flowers with both male and female attributes

PETIOLE: A slender stem that supports the blade of a foliage leaf.

PINNATE: Having leaflets borne on a common petiole

PISTIL: The central seed-bearing organ of a flower. Some plants have more than one.

POLYGAMOUS: Having both perfect flowers and those of one sex

SAMARA: A winged fruit. A maple has a double samara

SELECTION: A plant differing from the genus and having desirable characteristics; sometimes a sport, which can be propagated. See CULTIVAR.

SERRATE: Toothed. On some plants leaves are sawtoothed on margins

SPECIES: A specific kind of plant, reproducing itself with little or no variation; a division of its genus

SPORT: A plant differing from species or variety, occurring naturally

STAMEN: The pollen-bearing organ of a flower

STANDARD: A plant trained to a single stem in tree form; or, a plant grafted on an upright stem some distance above ground

SUCKER: A sprouting shoot, especially one from low on trunk or plant. Sometimes applied to sprouts from below ground on roots.

TERMINAL: The topmost end of a branch or tree trunk

VARIETY: A species or group subordinate to the species; now usually called "cultivar"

WHIP: A first- or second-year tree plant; usually applied to fruit.

Index

Note: Trees listed in tables throughout the text have not been indexed.

fragrant, 233–238
listed according to region, 179–229
medium-height trees, 202–211
for seashore areas, 242–244
shade trees, 198–202
small trees for shady conditions, 238–239
tall trees, 211–218
mature height, 161
placement around house, 150–153
planting methods, 305
recommended for specific regions, 177–229
for seashore areas, 167, 242–244
selecting, 150–167
growth rate, 154–159
hardiness, 164
height of trees, 153, 156, 161
for small houses, 161–162, 169
street-side planting, 161–163
shade trees, 152–153
medium-height, 202–211
small, 198–202
tall, 211–218
for shady conditions, 238–239
shapes for special purposes, 175–177
columnar, 175, 218–222
weeping form, 175–176
shedding leaves, 165
soil preferences, 164
water requirements, 164–165
for wet soils, 168, 256–257
wind breakage and damage, 294–295
for windbreaks and shelter belts, 152, 252--253, 298–299
See also names of trees.
Tropical and subtropical areas, 259
Tupelo. See Sour gum.

Viburnum
Arrow-wood (*Viburnum dentatum*), 168
Burkwood (*Viburnum burkwoodii*), 64
Cranberry-bush, American (*Viburnum trilobum*), 168

Hobblebush (*Viburnum altifolium*), 168

Watering, 21, 283–285
applying with a hose, 284
leaf production, fruiting, and flowering, 283–284
mulches and, 284
old gardens, 341
roses, 131–132
soil condition and, 283
winter, 24, 299
Weed killers, trees damaged by, 165–166
Wet and moist areas, 253–259
changing grade around trees, 255
drainage problems, 254–255
shrubs for, 74–75, 257–258
trees for, 168, 256–257
Wetlands and bog plantings, 256–259
Willow
Corkscrew (*Salix matsudana*), 72
French pussy (*Salix discolor*), 256
Weeping (*Salix babylonica*), 256
Wind, protection from, 22–23, 45–46, 252–253
hedges and fences, 22, 45–46
repairing damage, 294–295
Windbreaks and shelter belts, 45–46, 54, 252–253, 297
Winter protection, 22–24, 296–299
burlap wrappings or screens, 22–23, 298–299
deflecting elements, 297
frost damage, 298
placement of trees, 296–297
sunscald, 297–298
use of Wilt-pruf, 299
windbreaks, 45–46, 54, 252–253, 297
Woody perennials, 57
Wyman, Donald, 12

Yew (*Taxus* species), 279
Hatfield (*Taxus media*), 267, 270
Hicks (*Taxus media*), 267
Intermediate (*Taxus media*), 267
Taxus media, 267, 270, 279